BEIJING RULES

BEIJING RULES

HOW CHINA WEAPONIZED ITS ECONOMY
TO CONFRONT THE WORLD

Bethany Allen

HARPER

An Imprint of HarperCollinsPublishers

HarperCollins books may be purchased for educational, business, or sales promotional use. For information, please email the Special Markets Department at SPsales@harpercollins.com.

FIRST EDITION

Library of Congress Cataloging-in-Publication Data has been applied for.

ISBN 978-0-06-305741-8

23 24 25 26 27 LBC 5 4 3 2 1

For Mom, Dad, and the boy who lived

It was a game and we lost, because we didn't do several simple things: we didn't create our own class of capitalists, we didn't give the capitalist predators on our side a chance to develop and devour the capitalist predators on theirs.

—Gleb Pavlovsky, longtime confidant of Vladimir Putin,
on why the Soviet Union lost the Cold War

CONTENTS

INTRODUCTION

A virus is the smallest unit of life. Or it would be if scientists agreed that viruses are actually alive. Viruses are more like rogue strands of genetic code. They can't make their own proteins, they lack a cellular structure, and they can't reproduce without hijacking and then destroying a host cell's metabolic infrastructure.

There are more viruses on earth than there are stars in the universe. At a particular moment in late 2019, one of these viruses—measuring around one hundred nanometers in diameter and crowned with a halo of spikes—infected its first human being. At the time, no one noticed.

This tiny, unmarked moment sparked a chain reaction that would give the world its first taste of the People's Republic of China as a true superpower. The most populous country in the history of humanity would make its conclusive global debut through the auspices of the tiniest unit of existence known to man.

At first, Wei Guixian thought she was coming down with a cold. Her symptoms began on December 10 and were mild at first. The Wuhan seafood seller first sought treatment at a local clinic, returning each day for an IV drip of antibiotics, she later told the *Wall Street Journal*. But, within days, her condition worsened, and she struggled to breathe. Her daughter got her an appointment with a specialist, and by December 18, she was in a hospital, fighting for air. She soon lapsed into unconsciousness. Her daughter worried she would die.

Wei wasn't *patient zero*, a term referring to the first person to be infected with a new disease. But hers was among the earliest suspected cases of the novel coronavirus. We would soon learn of others. On December 16, a sixty-five-year-old man was admitted to Wuhan Central Hospital with an infection in both lungs. Doctors treated him with antibiotics and anti-flu medication, but his condition didn't improve. He, like Wei, had worked at the Hua'nan Seafood Market. By the next week, according to a study released the following month by the Chinese Center for Disease Control and Prevention, about three dozen people were showing similar symptoms. Doctors began to see connections among patients with the mysterious new illness.

Toward the end of December, health officials in Wuhan learned that the new illness was caused by a coronavirus, much like the pathogen responsible for SARS. Doctors and scientists sought to understand the new virus and spread the word, but they were repeatedly stymied by local government and security officials—a delay that would ultimately have immense consequences.

On December 30, Ai Fen, a top doctor at Wuhan Central Hospital, read a lab report that included the words "SARS coronavirus." Alarmed, she posted information about the illness on WeChat. But after she was reprimanded by superiors at the hospital, Ai started to keep her views to herself. Weeks later, as the death toll from Covid-19 in China mounted, she expressed regret for not speaking out more forcefully. "If I had known what was to happen, I would not have cared about the reprimand," she said in an interview with a Chinese magazine. "I would have fucking talked about it with whomever, wherever I could." The interview was eventually removed from the web.

Ai wasn't the only person to face consequences for speaking out. On December 30, eight doctors were called in for questioning after sharing scientific information about the virus on WeChat. On January 1, Chinese state media outlets reported that police in Wuhan had arrested eight people for "spreading fake news online" about the proliferation of "viral pneumonia" in Wuhan.

The following day, the World Health Organization's China office was alerted about this unknown illness that had infected twenty-seven patients with viral pneumonia in the city of Wuhan. Chinese scientists mapped the virus's full genome by January 5 and posted it on a public website less than a week later. Officials in Hong Kong and Taiwan—still mindful of the risks associated with the SARS scare of two decades earlier—began to screen passengers arriving from Wuhan.

But a simultaneous cover-up was already well under way. On January 1, an official at the Hubei Provincial Health Commission ordered laboratories to stop testing and destroy samples. Chinese president Xi Jinping began directly managing China's Covid-19 outbreak on January 7; this fact was kept from the public for several more weeks. The World Health Organization announced on January 14 that Chinese officials had found "no clear evidence" of human-to-human transmission of the virus.

While Chinese Communist Party officials held an important meeting from January 11 to 17 in Wuhan, the city's health commission asserted that there were no known cases—announcing fresh ones only minutes after midnight on the eighteenth. The Spring Festival holiday loomed just days ahead, a weeklong holiday in which hundreds of millions of people travel back to their hometowns across the country. It was the worst possible timing for a new viral outbreak to occur, but life carried on as normal. Local officials in Wuhan permitted forty thousand families to gather for a celebratory banquet on January 18, driving a further spike in cases.

"Everything was down to not collecting cases, not letting the public know," Dali Yang, a prominent scholar of China's governance system at the University of Chicago, told the *Washington Post*. "They were still pushing ahead, wanting to keep up appearances."

But soon, the virus ceased to be solely a Chinese concern. On January 13, a patient in Thailand tested positive for the virus, becoming the first known person outside China to have contracted Covid-19. Two days later, a person infected with the virus traveled to the United States, thus spreading the disease there.

China's central government decided it could no longer keep Wuhan's virus under wraps. On January 19, Beijing dispatched epidemiologists to the provincial capital. On January 20, Zhong Nanshan, a leading pulmonologist assigned to coordinate the virus response, reversed WHO's earlier declaration by stating that human-to-human transmission was indeed occurring. On January 23, Chinese authorities announced lockdowns in Wuhan and three other cities, and by the following day, more than 36 million people were ordered to remain largely in place—unprecedented restrictions that would be implemented repeatedly for the rest of the pandemic throughout the country.

But it was too late. More than five million residents had already fled the city out of fear of the mysterious new disease—many of them likely carrying it back to their hometowns for the upcoming holiday. The damage had already been done. "I think we have passed the golden period of control and prevention," Guan Yi, an expert on viruses at Hong Kong University, said on January 24.

In a study published in March 2020, researchers at the University of Southampton found that if Chinese authorities had acted three weeks earlier than they did, Covid cases could have been reduced by 95 percent and the virus's geographic spread limited. The Chinese government cover-up had lasted, as fate would have it, precisely three weeks.

In retrospect, we can all remember where we were and what we were doing at the end of January 2020, when the die foretelling the end of the world as we knew it had already been cast. We were, most of us, oblivious.

I was in Switzerland. The World Economic Forum at Davos that year kicked off on January 21, and I was among the small contingent of reporters Axios had sent to cover the annual gathering of the global elite.

Davos is always a monstrosity, known by the factual cliché as a conference where rich people fly in on their private jets to discuss climate change over expensive wine and hors d'oeuvres. The small Alpine ski resort town, temporarily overrun with summit attendees, was plastered with mindless slogans like "Liquid democracy has arrived" and "The view from the top should be more than the bottom line." We had rented an actual Swiss chalet, and my bedroom had furs on the floors, a bathroom with black pebbles and artistically placed granite stepping-stones for flooring, and—I kid you not—a custom-built sauna. I bumped elbows with Facebook's chief operating officer, Sheryl Sandberg, at the coat check and snapped photos from a distance of Prince William descending an elegant flight of stairs.

But, looking back, I see the 2020 forum as an almost-intentional exercise in the grotesque. On January 21—the same day the United States announced its first case of Covid-19—Davos attendees piled into crowded rooms to hear World Health Organization director general Tedros Adhanom Ghebreyesus, soon to become a controversial household name, to speak not about pandemics but about mental health stigma. On January 22—the day CNN started featuring live coronavirus updates—Richard Hatchett of the Coalition for Epidemic Preparedness Innovations mentioned the novel coronavirus in passing on a panel called "The Next Super Bug," only to then warn of "social reactions that are probably going to be disproportionate to the current threat." Another panel hailed the successes of Gavi, a major global vaccine alliance. China's senior vice premier, Han Zheng, gave a speech defending globalization and vowing that China would work closely with multilateral institutions, saying, "Openness is a trademark of today's China." Of course, he did not mention the new virus already ravaging Wuhan. On Friday, January 24, the forum's final day, the Chinese government implemented the strictest lockdown in history, freezing 36 million people in place.

At Davos, the conference rooms and the lobbies beyond were cramped, humid, and stifling as we all breathed the same recirculated air. The wine flowed freely. No one wore masks. We boarded planes, trains, and buses, inhaling and exhaling all the way back to the dozens of countries from whence we had come.

The 2020 summit now reminds me, rather horribly, of Edgar Allan Poe's short story "The Masque of the Red Death," in which a prince sequesters himself and a thousand of his peers inside a castle to drink, dance, and make merry while contagion rages outside the walls. Eventually, the pestilence comes for the guests as well.

Davos would be canceled the next year, and the next.

No individual represented the tragedy and transgression of China's early pandemic response better than Dr. Li Wenliang, a young ophthalmologist in Wuhan. In December, he had noticed several patients exhibiting SARS-like symptoms. He decided he needed to warn colleagues, and on December 31, he posted about the illness in a WeChat group.

Not only did local authorities avoid acting on these early reports of a mysterious new illness, but they punished the doctors who were reporting it. Li thus became one of the eight doctors who were called to the local police bureau, where officials berated them. He was made to sign a letter accusing him of "making false comments" that "severely disturbed the social order."

"The police believed this virus was not confirmed to be SARS. They believed I was spreading rumors," Li later said in an interview. "They asked me to acknowledge that I was at fault. I felt I was being wronged, but I had to accept it. Obviously I had been acting out of good will."

Li began coughing on January 10 and soon contracted a fever. He was hospitalized just days later, and on January 30, he was diagnosed with the disease later to be known as Covid-19. From his hospital bed, he posted information about his case and of the other patients he had seen. He continued to give media interviews and posted a now-famous selfie as he lay in a hospital bed with an oxygen mask strapped to his nose and mouth.

Facing intense domestic and international criticism for its early cover-up, the Chinese government knew that it had to act fast. So, in late January, officials decided to bring daily life to a screeching halt. In Wuhan, authorities completely closed off transportation into and out of the city, even for emergencies. The school holiday for the Spring Festival was extended indefinitely. All shops in the city, except for those selling food and medicine, were shut. Only one member of each household was permitted outside every other day; in some places, residents were required to have any food and supplies delivered. Security guards at apartment complexes took the temperature of anyone entering, while officials went door-to-door to enforce compliance with quarantine rules.

Citizen journalists in Wuhan, such as Zhang Zhao and Wuhan native Fang Fang, who kept an online diary, chronicled daily life under the unprecedented lockdowns. Soon, all other major cities in Hubei Province were locked down as well, extending the mass quarantine to a historically unprecedented 60 million people. The entire country was transfixed. Soon cities in other provinces around China began to implement varying degrees of restrictions on travel, schools, and businesses.

But Li's condition worsened. On February 7, 2020, the young doctor died. He was thirty-three years old.

At the news of Li's death, China's heavily censored social media platform Weibo exploded with anger. To Chinese people, Li felt like a martyr. He had embodied the courage, heroism, and selflessness the Chinese government lacked in what felt all too much like SARS 2.0.

The grief and rage were irrepressible. With hundreds of millions already under some form of lockdown, people took to the virtual streets to lodge their protest. The hashtag #LiWenliangDies was viewed more than 670 million times. Despite the Chinese government's expert social media censorship, #IWantFreedomOfSpeech almost instantly became the most-viewed hashtag on Weibo. Some people quoted Soviet dissident Aleksandr Solzhenitsyn: "We know they are lying, they also know they are lying, they know we know they are lying, we also know they know we know they are lying, yet they continue to lie." When censors managed to remove the viral hashtag after a few hours, a second hashtag, #WeWantFreedomOfSpeech, rocketed to the top of the list. It had been years since I'd seen this kind of national outpouring surpass the ability of Weibo censors to repress it. It was as if the entire country had taken to the internet all at once to register their anger.

The death of Dr. Li Wenliang marked one of the Chinese Communist Party's most vulnerable moments in years, perhaps even decades. It was a moment of profound crisis for the party. Its governing philosophy of social stability and top-down control had backfired spectacularly. Local officials, striving perhaps to keep their own personal governance records clean and to avoid dealing with any troublesome social disturbances, had silenced medical personnel and prevented an effective response in the crucial first several weeks. Hospitals were full, and people who couldn't get beds were dying in their homes and even in the streets.

Internationally, the crisis was dragging the CCP's reputation through the mud. Within a few weeks of Dr. Li's death, outbreaks in South Korea and Iran transfixed the world. On March 11, the World Health Organization declared a pandemic. Case counts soared in Europe and the United States. Economies around the world ground to a halt. Deaths began to rise.

"The delay of China to act is probably responsible for this world event," Howard Markel, a professor at the school of public health at the University of Michigan at Ann Arbor, told *Nature* magazine in March 2020. Some commentators speculated that it might be the party's "Chernobyl moment," revealing its inner weakness and foretelling its downfall.

It was first and foremost a crisis of public health, but to the party, so much more was at stake: its domestic legitimacy, its global reputation, the governance model it was offering to the world as an alternative to liberal democracy. With the party's egregious failure to stop the virus, all this was poised to crumble.

The party's response to this moment is where this book really begins. A less confident and less effective regime might have spiraled further into disaster. But the Chinese Communist Party doubled down. Domestically, it determined to wage a total "people's war" on Covid-19, implementing measures seen nowhere else in the world to bring the case count down to zero and keep it there. Globally, the party reached for a toolkit of influence and coercion it had honed over the past three decades to change the global narrative—by force if necessary—about where the pandemic had started and China's role in it.

In the first goal, the Chinese government was wildly successful. The measures it had pioneered in Wuhan (mass lockdown, strict contact tracing, mass testing) were repeated around the rest of China. Chinese construction companies were ordered to build massive new centralized quarantine facilities. The government developed smartphone apps to monitor citizens' health and assist with contact tracing, a testament to the power of China's surveillance state. Neighborhood party committees proved to be a fast and effective conduit for communicating and implementing quarantine rules and other vital health measures to all residents. When new cases were detected, authorities would immediately seal off apartment buildings, neighborhoods, or whole cities until testing and quarantine ensured that the virus was gone. At their peak, the extreme lockdowns saw some 760 million Chinese people confined to their homes or neighborhoods.

The measures worked. Though official reporting of the country's true number of Covid-19 cases was somewhat questionable, it's clear that by the end of February 2020, cases had dropped dramatically. A delegation from the World Health Organization that toured China in February expressed astonishment at the virus's virtual disappearance from the country. "China has rolled out perhaps the most ambitious, agile, and aggressive disease containment effort in history," the WHO report read. Government actions set the stage for the effective response, but the report also gave credit to the dedication and sacrifice made by Chinese people themselves. "Achieving China's exceptional coverage with and adherence to these containment measures has only been possible due to the deep commitment of the Chinese people to collective action in the face of this common threat," the report stated.

Winning the public health war wasn't enough, though. The party also wanted to stamp out the memory of its initial failures, both domestically and around the world. Zhang Zhao and other citizen journalists who had documented the early weeks of the Wuhan outbreak were arrested. After Dr. Li's death, China's army of censors went into overdrive, scrubbing

social media comments, deleting articles chronicling the Wuhan outbreak, and paying internet users to post pro-party content. Media outlets
were directed to tell positive stories about the struggles of Chinese people
to fight the virus. The effort involved an extraordinary mobilization of
the systems and bureaucracies China had established over the previous
decade as Xi Jinping waged his war for information control.

What stood out as even more extraordinary, however, was the party's
attempts to rewrite the global narrative—attempts that soon began to
unfold in real time through economic coercion, overt propaganda, and
disinformation. It all began with the CCP's ability to mobilize the country's economy for geopolitical influence abroad.

As China's star rose, Beijing determined that it faced a short window
of strategic opportunity to pull ahead of a distracted West—putting it on
a collision course with a dysfunctional but belligerent United States and
showing the world, definitively, the kind of superpower China was set to
become.

———————

By late March 2020, the party was back on its feet, projecting an image
of confidence and success that at first felt forced but soon gained momentum as the country's Covid-19 case count plummeted, lockdowns were
lifted, and the economy came roaring back—just as the United States
and much of Europe descended into a sort of pandemic hell, with botched
government responses, hundreds of thousands of bodies piling up, and
growing domestic turmoil.

The United States, meanwhile, had never looked so dysfunctional. By
the end of March, it would have the highest case count in the world and,
by mid-April, it was reporting more than 2,200 deaths daily, with more
than 2,700 deaths on April 15 alone.

The rest of the world looked on in horror throughout 2020 as the U.S.
president refused to wear a face mask and ridiculed people who did, made
bizarre and misleading claims about Covid-19 treatments, withdrew the
United States from the World Health Organization, and repeatedly disparaged his own top adviser leading the U.S. pandemic response, Dr. Anthony Fauci of the National Institutes of Health, calling him a "disaster"
and an idiot.

"We used to look to the U.S. for democratic governance inspiration," said Eduardo Bohórquez, the director of Transparency International Mexico, summing up the perspective from abroad. "Sadly, this is not the case anymore."

The United States' absence left an opening for China to exploit. The 2008 financial crisis was a "decisive moment emboldening Beijing and altering global perceptions of relative power between U.S. and China," Ely Ratner, a former deputy national security advisor under Vice President Joe Biden who would later be tapped to lead a new China task force at the Pentagon after Biden became president, wrote on Twitter at the time. "I worry now we're at risk of another decisive moment for the U.S.-China competition as the Trump administration badly mishandles coronavirus."

Back in Beijing, it was clear by late spring that the immediate danger to the regime had passed. In late May, the party more or less declared victory over the domestic epidemic, and its efforts received international praise as well, including from unlikely sources such as the American rapper Cardi B, who said with admiration that "when they quarantined people, they were spraying shit in the streets," a reference to disinfectant.

It was a success the Communist Party didn't hesitate to tout. "Daring to fight and daring to win is the Chinese Communist Party's distinct political character, and our distinct political advantage," President Xi Jinping exulted in March 2020. Even if the reports of minuscule case numbers strained credulity, it was clear that China's decision to impose rigid controls during the initial weeks of the crisis had paid off, particularly in saving lives. By year's end, more than three hundred thousand Americans and a roughly equal number of Europeans had lost their lives. China, by contrast, had reported fewer than five thousand fatalities in spite of its much larger population. Although this number is likely somewhat too low, casualty counts in the hundreds of thousands would have been impossible to hide. It's clear that many fewer people in China died of Covid in 2020 than in many other countries.

The rage and fear so many Chinese people felt in February and March began to turn to pride. Inspired by the country's genuine successes in getting the domestic outbreak under control and by the mile-high wall of propaganda and censorship presenting China's efforts as superior to those of the rest of the world, many Chinese people began to feel a strong sense of superiority in their nation's response to Covid-19 and pity for the residents of Western nations whose government failures had led to so many deaths. One poster on Weibo, China's Twitter, lamented foreigners' being "unable to copy the homework that China has already done for them."

When top CCP leaders met in Beijing in October 2020 for the Fifth Plenum, the country's most important planning meeting that sets policy for the next five years, they declared that the world was undergoing a "profound adjustment in the international balance of power." Though Xi had previously spoken of trends working in China's favor, this appeared to be the first time a top-level party document had declared that a "profound adjustment" was under way.

China was the only major economy in the world to expand in 2020. Amid the unprecedented lockdowns, travel bans, and business closings, the global economy contracted 4.3 percent, with the U.S. economy shrinking by 3.6 percent and the EU economy by 7.4 percent. But China's economy grew—and not just by a hair, but by a relatively robust 2.3 percent. There is perhaps no better modern example of a nation's leaders snatching victory from the jaws of defeat.

A widely shared WeChat post captured this sentiment well: "The Western media said that the coronavirus would be China's Chernobyl, and at that time it really felt that way. But in the end, it was not China's Chernobyl, but the West's."

———

Against this backdrop, it's small wonder Xi seems to have determined that China's time had come. With the West flailing, he saw a window of opportunity to go on the offensive. The Chinese Communist Party used the conditions of the pandemic to push its national interests, often in a manner incompatible with open democratic values. Its long-term ambitions and strategies, sometimes veiled or hard to read in the past, now became explicit.

Beijing took bold, even brazen measures to block scientific inquiry into the origins of the pandemic. In May 2020, China slapped tariffs on a swath of Australian goods after the Australian prime minister called for an independent inquiry into the origins of the novel coronavirus. This wasn't the first time that the party had used economic tools to pursue illiberal geopolitical interests. But it was the first time it had deployed its economic toolkit on an issue directly related to the health and well-being of quite literally every person in the world. It marked the global debut of the cornerstone of the Chinese Communist Party's power in the twenty-first century—what, in this book, I refer to as authoritarian economic statecraft.

China's authoritarian economic statecraft comes in the form of a clearly communicated set of rewards and punishments based on gatekeeping access to China's huge markets, capital, and investments—access that companies and countries around the world increasingly see as vital to their prosperity. In short, China is shaping global markets to incentivize adherence to its most fundamental geopolitical objectives. It's a system that the CCP is continuing to hone, codify, and, in some cases, enshrine into law whose extraterritorial reach grows along with the reach of China's economy. Beijing uses this leverage not just to stifle global dissent but also to shape the behavior of companies and governments, legitimize its political model as a superior alternative to liberal democracy, support its expanding military and defense objectives, weaken U.S. alliances, expand its surveillance state, and gain sway over international institutions.

Observers have termed China's growing ability to shape behavior that occurs beyond its borders as "influence," "interference," and "sharp power," among other terms. These terms are useful in describing the visible effects of Beijing's actions, but they don't identify the primary foundation of this type of power: China's economy. A more precise frame through which to understand the pressure China puts on foreign organizations and governments to avoid certain behavior is that of economic statecraft, a concept that American political scientist William Norris defines broadly as "state manipulation of international economic activities for strategic purposes."

Over the past two decades, CCP leaders have tested and honed remarkably innovative forms of economic statecraft and are using these methods not simply to pursue neutral national interests but also to achieve illiberal political goals. It's the international extension of what some scholars now call China's "party-state capitalism," referring to the leading role that the party now takes in directing vital sectors of the economy at key political moments.

China's leaders used their gatekeeping control over the economy and their rapidly expanding security state to bolster Beijing's influence in other ways during the pandemic. The Chinese government took advantage of the skyrocketing number of Zoom users during the pandemic—and the company's dependence on China, where its research and development team was located—to spy on global users and even to shut down U.S.-based meetings that Beijing determined to be against its national interests, without the company's knowledge.

Chinese authorities directed the country's enormous manufacturing base to mass-produce personal protective equipment, which Chinese authorities then sold to other countries struggling with outbreaks, an important global contribution that Beijing also used for maximal propaganda value. Government leaders all over the world woke up to discover that their countries did not have the manufacturing capacity to produce face masks and were thus largely dependent on China. This sudden collective realization brought to center stage the previously fringe debate over industrial policy and the national security risks of supply chain dependence on China. Later on in the pandemic, the Chinese government sometimes used its vaccines as leverage, at times handing over vaccines to other countries when certain political conditions were met and withholding them when they weren't.

Beijing also took advantage of the West's total preoccupation with Covid-19 to impose authoritarianism in Hong Kong, breaking a treaty China had signed with Britain in 1984 and attempting to weaponize Hong Kong's status as a global financial hub in an attempt to repress dissent anywhere in the world, a worrying trend toward extraterritoriality.

The CCP flexed other channels of influence during the pandemic as well. Chinese state–backed online disinformation operations conducted on foreign social media platforms, which first drew attention during the 2019 pro-democracy protests in Hong Kong, really took off during the pandemic, as the Chinese government sought to deflect blame for the spread of the virus onto the United States, or Italy, or cold chain storage, or supposed U.S. biolabs in Ukraine—anyone or anything at all besides itself.

It's not all bad news, of course. The Chinese government's extremely effective Covid-19 response, after its initial failures, unquestionably saved the lives of millions of Chinese people by preventing Covid from sweeping the population until most were vaccinated. Chinese-made vaccines, a product of the dedication of Chinese scientists and of the government's massive investments in science and technology, also saved millions of lives in developing countries that weren't able to buy up doses of Western-made vaccines.

But in the end, the party's lack of political restraint brought things full circle, hobbling its soft power and reversing its stunning mid-pandemic triumph to make China once again the object of global pity. Xi Jinping insisted on maintaining a strict zero-Covid policy far longer than other countries like Taiwan and Australia did, even as the lockdowns became more and more extreme to stop the spread of the highly transmissible Omicron Covid variant. At the same time, Xi also refused to green-light the import of Western-made mRNA vaccines, even after China's domestic vaccines proved less effective at combating infection. This left 1.4 billion people less protected against a deadly virus—a decision almost certainly made out of the party's perceived need to preserve face by not relying on Western-made vaccines. Pandemic restrictions battered the economy, separated families, disrupted educations, and prevented people from accessing lifesaving medical care. Some people, trapped for too long in buildings chained shut from the outside, reportedly jumped from windows or even starved.

By wedding the reputation of China's government model, and even his own political legitimacy, to the zero-Covid policy, Xi Jinping boxed himself in. It became politically impossible to scrap the harsh policy until the Chinese people themselves had had enough, and rose up in the largest nationwide protests since Tiananmen to demand an end to lockdowns, quarantines, and even the reign of Xi himself.

By the end of the pandemic, Beijing had shown itself clearly to the world, in both the height of its power and the depth of its weakness.

The rise of an authoritarian style of state capitalism seems to have caught many Americans off guard. But it shouldn't have. It is not difficult to understand that money, like any form of power, is morally neutral; it projects the values of those who have it. Similarly, a market economy, without a regulatory framework in place to guide it in one direction or another, is also morally neutral; it projects the values of those who command its resources.

Milton Friedman didn't envision a world in which an authoritarian foreign government could hold sway over a U.S. company's profits and, thus, its decisions. He honed many of his ideas in the late 1960s and early 1970s, when China's gross domestic product was a mere $92 billion, compared with the United States' $1 trillion. While the Soviet Union during that era enjoyed considerable economic heft, its economy and that of its satellite states were largely separate from that of the United States, due to a sweeping economic embargo between the Eastern and Western blocs that lasted until the end of the Cold War. What antidote might Friedman have recommended for a situation in which U.S. companies took action in support of a Communist Party's social and political goals in order to maximize profits for their shareholders?

The rise of neoliberalism in the West over the past four decades has equated democracy—a political system focused on protecting fundamental human rights—with privatization, deregulation, and minimal government intervention in markets.

President Bill Clinton's speech in March 2000 upon China's accession to the World Trade Organization made this clear. China hadn't become any more democratic since Clinton delinked human rights and trade back in 1994, but that didn't seem to discourage his faith in the power of open markets to bring liberal change. "By joining the WTO, China is not simply agreeing to import more of our products; it is agreeing to import one of democracy's most cherished values: economic freedom," Clinton said. "The more China liberalizes its economy, the more fully it will liberate the potential of the people . . . And when individuals have the power not just to dream, but to realize their dreams, they will demand a greater say."

But when global wealth became concentrated in the hands of an expansive Communist Party, the fallacy of equating open markets with political freedom became painfully clear. The U.S.-led global embrace of a too-lightly regulated capitalism allowed the party to develop and deploy its toolkit of economic coercion.

While Beijing's ambition to shape the world in its own image arose from the party's logic, the United States is deeply complicit in creating the conditions that have allowed China's authoritarian economic statecraft to flourish. In the United States, a systematic dismantling of the state, years of deregulation, free trade without democratic guardrails, and less corporate accountability, combined with a political culture that eschews government involvement in business decision making, means there are fewer tools available to counterbalance the pressure the Chinese Communist Party is placing on U.S. organizations. And it means more opportunity for that pressure to shape not just the decisions of individual businesses but also our political system, and even the individual freedoms of speech and assembly that we so cherish. It's an economic system that has granted vastly disproportionate power to the wealthy, whose interests have little to do with protecting human rights.

Our collective belief in a diminished role of government in the economy has also blunted our national imagination, shutting off entire lines of inquiry as to how to respond to the weaponization of China's economy, with a self-imposed inner dialogue replaying the constant refrain *That's not something the government can do.* As a result, we have floundered in our attempts even to envision, much less carry out, adequate responses. "Today, people often speak in the language of markets, not the language of politics or morality. We talk more about consumers or taxpayers than about citizens," Ganesh Sitaraman, a legal scholar at Vanderbilt University and a longtime adviser to Senator Elizabeth Warren, observed in his 2019 book *The Great Democracy.*

China's economic statecraft thrives in this environment and, indeed, has been crafted to take advantage of these conditions. If China's markets are the largest in the world, and if China has both weaponized access to those markets and successfully conveyed its rules to all who would profit from that access, then China is simply playing by the rules established by neoliberalism. If we speak in the language of markets, to channel Sitaraman, then China hasn't just learned that language. It has learned to speak it louder than anyone else.

Both Democrats and Republicans have contributed to this state of affairs. Since Reagan, Republicans have promoted the idea that government should have as little involvement in the economy as possible and have systematically dismantled mechanisms of corporate accountability. Democrats, too, were ineluctably drawn in, with Bill Clinton declaring in 1996 that the "era of big government is over." American society has largely come to believe that there is simply nothing the government can or should do about a phenomenon like China's authoritarian economic statecraft. If U.S. companies self-censor to please China, the thinking goes, only consumers—not governments—can respond, with hashtags, personal decisions to avoid purchasing affected products or services, or organizing a coordinated boycott. And if a U.S. company chooses to defy Beijing and suffers market losses as a result, the thinking remains the same—only consumers can respond, by choosing to reward that company with personal purchases or social media campaigns.

This is a losing strategy. If the United States and other major economies continue to pursue the same policies, both domestically and abroad, that they have for the past fifty years, China's authoritarian state capitalism could push the world toward an era of "embedded illiberalism"—an international trade system dominated by enforced political loyalties and international institutions severed from their liberal democratic roots, beholden to China's support and to de facto economic sanctions levied without rule of law, transparency, or a means of appeal.

But three trends have now emerged that suggest that the era of morality-free trade in the international sphere and the blind veneration of corporate profits in the domestic sphere may not continue indefinitely.

The first trend resulted from the economic and political shock of the novel coronavirus pandemic. Americans experienced firsthand the real-world consequences of a hollowed-out government's inability to provide basic health protections readily adopted elsewhere in the world, and every single U.S. household also personally experienced what it was like to be completely dependent on China for a scarce but absolute necessity: face masks. The concept of industrial policy—long a near-taboo term more recently come to be seen as the domain of far-right Trumpian nationalists—suddenly took on mainstream urgency as people in countries around the world faced a shortage of personal protective equipment, manufactured largely in China.

The Trump administration began to overturn decades-long assumptions about what kinds of actions the U.S. government could take, repurposing existing mechanisms such as the Commerce Department's federal Entity List for the first time to blacklist companies for human rights violations. As the Biden administration continued these policies and even built on them after Biden took office, some progressives who had viewed the previous administration's China-related actions as yet another rogue Trumpian endeavor began to change their minds. As a senior Biden administration official said in early February 2021, "We looked at what the Trump administration did over the last four years and found merit in the basic proposition of an intense strategic competition with China."

The second trend is China's own overreach. Like sanctions, China's economic statecraft worked best when it was deployed only occasionally.

Used too often, and it gives companies and governments sufficient motivation to diversify their supply chains to less politically risky markets—as the United States, Europe, and other nations are now beginning to do. Growing awareness of the political demands of China's party-state capitalism has also fostered suspicion among foreign government officials toward any economic dependence on China at all. The party's failure to guide the country safely out of the pandemic also made Beijing's audacity look more like hubris than wisdom.

The third trend, meanwhile, is the growing movement to take on U.S. tech monopolies and, more broadly, the growing belief since the Great Recession that the economy as currently structured is siphoning more and more resources into the hands of those who already wield great economic and political power, hollowing out the promises of democracy and leaving more and more Americans struggling to get by. Overall, American society seems to have stopped believing that an economic structure without democratic guardrails, either domestically or internationally, is worth perpetuating.

This offers a glimmer of hope that U.S. society and liberal democratic societies elsewhere might be able to formulate a set of responses to China's authoritarian economic statecraft that neither carve the world into mutually exclusive economic blocs nor scapegoat people of Chinese heritage, but that, instead, embrace the solution: the belief that markets and economic structures need democratic intervention, both domestically and internationally.

Building a democratic economic statecraft is the most effective response to the challenge of China's authoritarian economic statecraft. It is neoliberalism's resistance to democratic intervention in economies that continues to stymie robust action to counter Beijing. The actions of the Chinese Communist Party are only one side of the coin. For the United States to challenge China's capitalism-powered authoritarianism, Americans will have to come to terms with the chameleon that is capitalism—and, in doing so, come to terms with ourselves.

There are now numerous books on the threat posed by a rising China led by the Communist Party. But that literature is largely theoretical, examining how Beijing is covertly moving chess pieces to position itself for a future triumph. This book shows how those chess pieces, put into place years or even decades ago, were actually deployed during a major global crisis to serve the CCP's narrow interests and in ways that affected just about every person in the world.

Throughout this book, I aim to bring a perspective that steers clear of partisanship and simplistic China bashing. Many, though certainly not all, right-wing politicians in the United States have relied on careful research by respected analysts to sound the alarm about the Chinese Communist Party's activities and goals. They had to face down the pro-business interests within their own party to do so, and that took courage. But conservative leaders have also used inflated threat language and dismissed the legitimate concerns of Chinese Americans that some U.S. policies and rhetoric could victimize their communities. The deadly danger of such rhetoric became tragically clear as anti-Asian violence in the United States spiked during the Covid-19 pandemic, including the March 2021 mass shooting in Atlanta in which a white man killed six women of Asian heritage.

Conservatives also tend to cast the U.S.–China rivalry too strongly in black-and-white terms, in which the United States can do no wrong and China can do no right. That is a distortion. The Chinese government has accomplished many positive things; that's a simple fact. And the United States has made many grave mistakes, both domestically and on the world stage. Any effective, predictive foreign policy paradigm must take both these realities into account.

But I also aim to avoid the simplistic America bashing and "what-aboutism" that sometimes masquerades as nuance among progressives. During the Trump administration, and persisting to a lesser extent into the Biden era, there was a persistent belief in left-of-center circles that the Chinese Communist Party couldn't *really* be trying to supplant the United States or overturn the liberal rules-based world order; that nothing Beijing did could possibly be as bad as Western imperialism; and that concerns over China's covert political influence in democracies around the world were simply racism by another name. These beliefs do not hold up to fact-based scrutiny.

U.S. progressives are often motivated by a desire to avoid repeating the previous excesses of U.S. foreign policy and to make the United States look at itself in the mirror before going on the offensive against perceived foes. Both these characteristics are admirable. But when taken too far, such an obsession with self-criticism can result in dangerous policy paralysis, or even absolving autocratic regimes of their crimes. The Chinese Communist Party also preys on confusion and racism to discredit fact-based arguments, complicating U.S. domestic narratives further. But there is a true north by which to orient oneself: At the end of the day, Beijing has agency and is responsible for its own behavior. No U.S. action has forced the CCP to make the choices it has made.

The pandemic gave the world a clear look at how the People's Republic of China acts in a moment of global crisis. From this, we can draw five conclusions about China's behavior as a superpower. First and most important, the Chinese government is willing to expand, at least implicitly, its conception of "core interests" to include major global issues that affect people far beyond China's borders. This means that the party is willing to draw on its full arsenal of leverage, influence, charm, deception, and coercion to achieve narrow geopolitical goals that intersect with and may be detrimental to the national security and interests of many other nations, and to liberal democratic values at large. This point is the subject of much of this book's inquiry.

Second, this extension of power comes with reputational costs that the party so far seems to have underestimated. In 2020, negative views of China and its leaders reached historic levels. Sixty-one percent of respondents in fourteen advanced economies, including Australia, Canada, Japan, and Spain, a Pew survey published in October 2020 found, said that China had done a poor job at handling the coronavirus. Only the United States fared worse, with 84 percent of respondents saying the U.S. government mishandled the pandemic. This sense of disapproval also extended directly to the person of Xi Jinping. The same survey found that 78 percent of survey respondents across the same fourteen countries had little or no confidence in Xi to act correctly in world affairs, a dramatic rise in negative sentiment from previous years. The fact that China also saw a rise in xenophobia against foreigners living in the country didn't help. Negative views of China have only continued to intensify. In a survey published in September 2022, the Pew Research Center found that unfavorable sentiment toward China under

Xi Jinping had risen "precipitously" in advanced economies around the world.

Third, the Chinese Communist Party has created a model of domestic governance that can effectively achieve meaningful goals, sometimes in ways that outperform the United States' own ailing political system. In order to fully understand both China and the direction the world may be heading, Western political leaders must preserve space within domestic debates for this fact to be discussed openly without accusing one another of being Communist sympathizers on the one hand or Cold War–mongers on the other.

Fourth, the United States and Europe cannot meet the public health needs of the entire globe. China's recent advances in medicine, science, and technology and the country's resulting ability to swiftly manufacture and export vaccines in large quantities saved many lives. But these invaluable contributions were undermined by the Chinese Communist Party's worst impulses—to withhold information and deny facts about the relative ineffectiveness of Chinese-made vaccines and, occasionally, to use the vaccines as a form of geopolitical leverage, not just as passive and well-earned soft power. Xi Jinping's zealotry in enforcing the zero-Covid policy long past the period of its public health necessity also underscores how political logic can easily trump science in a dictatorship, with little recourse if the strongman cannot be convinced to change course.

Finally, all these conclusions offer lessons for future cooperation on major global issues such as climate change. If our species is to survive the catastrophic effects of global warming, the world needs all of China's best qualities—its emerging leadership in science and technology, its unparalleled ability to mobilize its population to overcome a crisis, and its ability to swiftly mass-manufacture essential supplies. But the Chinese Communist Party's worst impulses—hiding failures, rebuffing inquiry, punishing loyal critics, and putting politics before science—could also be our undoing. Only the Chinese people themselves can determine if the better angels of their government's nature will shine through.

THE RISE OF CHINA'S AUTHORITARIAN ECONOMIC STATECRAFT

Chester Osborn doesn't exactly fit the profile of a prosperous winemaker. He has a long mop of unruly curls, a penchant for wearing outrageously multicolored shirts, and a boyish playfulness that belies his sixty-one years; he once dressed for a photo shoot as a very convincing Willie Wonka.

But winemaking is in Osborn's blood. He is the chief winemaker at d'Arenberg, a storied winemaker in McLaren Vale, one of Australia's premier wine regions. The company was founded by his great-grandfather Joseph Osborn in 1912 and has been run by four generations of the Osborn family. Osborn's mother carried him around the winery at age two, and he knew from a young age that he would continue the family business. In 1984, he became its chief winemaker.

Known in the Australian wine world for his ebullient personality, Osborn tends to project a preternatural confidence about his professional endeavors. In 2016, as he was building a five-story restaurant in the shape of a giant Rubik's Cube on the d'Arenberg estate, he told *The Drinks Business* that it would become "the best restaurant in Australia." The restaurant, opened in 2017 and known simply as "the Cube," has certainly achieved national prominence, if not exactly universal admiration, and has even hosted a multimillion-dollar Salvador Dalí art exhibition.

Osborn felt a similar optimism about d'Arenberg's prospects in China. "China was our biggest market. We got up to about thirty importers, growing fast, with more wanting to come on board," he said in a phone interview.

His confidence seemed well placed. Imported wine had first started to become popular in China in the late 1990s, as newly affluent urban Chinese saw it as a more sophisticated choice than the traditional *baijiu*, made from fermented sorghum. That's when d'Arenberg first started selling in China, occupying the premium end of the market. By 2019, China's wine market had become the fifth largest in the world, even though just 3 percent of the population consumed wine—meaning the already huge market had enormous growth potential.

Australia's wine exports to China had exploded following the signing of a free trade agreement between the two countries in 2015, which kicked off a gradual elimination of wine tariffs on both sides. According to data from the Australian Bureau of Statistics, wine exports increased from approximately 70 million liters that year to more than 160 million liters in 2018. By 2020, the Australian Bureau of Agricultural and Resource Economics and Sciences reported that the China market comprised 40 percent of the total value of Australian wine exports that year, easily surpassing the U.S. market, which comprised just 16 percent.

The possibilities offered by China's huge wine market seemed limitless for d'Arenberg. In 2020, according to Osborn, the company made 11 percent of its sales, 20 percent of its revenue, and 30 percent of its profit in China. "There are a lot of thirsty people there," Osborn said.

But in November 2020, Australia's wine exports to China collapsed almost overnight, shaking even Osborn's effusive confidence. It wasn't because Chinese winemakers had started outcompeting foreign brands or because a change in people's disposable incomes meant fewer people were buying wine that year. It wasn't the pandemic-related lockdowns or supply chain backlogs that did it, either. It wasn't even a genuine trade dispute.

Rather, hundreds of Australian wine exporters like Osborn suddenly found themselves gazing into a revenue abyss because the Chinese government was trying to prevent independent scientific inquiry into the origins of the coronavirus pandemic—and Australia's wine industry was caught in the middle.

———————————

In mid-February 2020, after the initial government cover-up in the earliest stages of the pandemic, the Chinese government permitted a team of

WHO scientists to enter China. The earliest moments were still obscure. Typically, in the case of a zoonotic spillover event—meaning a virus that jumped from animal to human—epidemiologists search for "patient zero" because that person can provide invaluable information about the virus and, crucially, how to prevent the next outbreak. The world had yet to learn how the virus that causes Covid-19 had infected humans.

"If we don't know the source then we're equally vulnerable in future to a similar outbreak, and understanding that source is a very important next step in the strategy," Michael Ryan, an Irish epidemiologist serving as the World Health Organization's emergencies director, said that month.

But, at every turn, the team was blocked from doing independent research. In the following months, the Chinese government continued to stymie researchers, hoard samples, and refuse to share complete data with the global scientific community.

By April 2020, the pandemic had already spread to dozens of countries, with 2.5 million infections and 177,500 deaths. It was then that Australian prime minister Scott Morrison decided to put his foot down. On April 23, he publicly called for an investigation into the origins of the coronavirus and recommended that WHO be given "weapons inspector" powers so that, in the case of future pandemics, it could enter countries forcibly without having to wait for an invitation. "We will need an independent inquiry that looks at what has occurred here," he said at a press conference in Canberra. "We'd like the world to be safer when it comes to viruses . . . I would hope that any other nation, be it China or anyone else, would share that objective." Australia sits on the World Health Organization's executive board, and Morrison vowed to push for the investigation at the organization's assembly meeting the next month.

It shouldn't have been a controversial suggestion, but his announcement went off like a bomb in Beijing. "The so-called independent inquiry proposed by Australia is in reality political manipulation," Chinese foreign ministry spokesman Geng Shuang retorted the very same day. "We advise Australia to give up its ideological prejudices."

Chen Jingye, China's ambassador to Australia, implied a few days later that a boycott of Australian goods might be forthcoming. "Maybe the ordinary people will say 'Why should we drink Australian wine? Eat Australian beef?'" he said in an interview published in the *Australian*

Financial Review on April 26. Australian foreign minister Marisa Payne immediately denounced the statement as "economic coercion."

Two weeks later, that coercion materialized: China banned meat from Australia's four largest slaughterhouses. Then it placed 80 percent tariffs on Australian barley, effectively banning that import. Soon, more import barriers followed, targeting sugar, lobster, coal, copper ore, and cotton, with wine listed as another possible target. In November, China's Ministry of Commerce announced preliminary anti-dumping tariffs ranging from 107 percent to 212 percent on Australian wine. The tariffs were later confirmed by Chinese authorities in a final decision in March 2021.

These moves were widely understood to be retribution for Australia's calls for an independent inquiry. China justified the tariffs by saying that Australian exporters were dumping products at below-market prices and that the Australian government was subsidizing them. But there's no evidence for this. In any case, Ambassador Chen had already telegraphed the real reason for the actions. They were in essence a form of authoritarian sanction, aimed not at upholding multilateral interests or the integrity of international institutions but, rather, intended to shut down scientific inquiry and legitimate criticism related to global public health.

On November 3, three days before the wine tariffs were announced, Beijing made that connection even clearer. The Chinese foreign ministry listed Morrison's call for an independent international inquiry into the pandemic origins as one of China's "Fourteen Grievances" against Australia, alongside Canberra's criticism of China's repression in Xinjiang and the ban on Huawei and ZTE from Australia's 5G networks.

The tariffs decimated Australia's wine exports to China, its biggest market. By December 2020, Australia exported just $9 million worth of wine to China, down from around $240 million year-on-year. By the end of 2020, China's tariffs were estimated to have cost Australia $19 billion. And that was just the start. The value of wine exports to China remained at nearly zero throughout 2021.

Beijing responded to Morrison's push for a coronavirus inquiry with such economic force because that push had collided with the Chinese Communist Party's new core interest: to ensure that the party could not be blamed for the pandemic and to deter other countries from making that claim. China's leaders had seemingly decided that the best way to counteract blame was to attempt to control the global narrative about the virus's origins and to establish political control over the public health processes used to uncover basic scientific facts.

———————————

For more than two decades, as China's economy has become increasingly intertwined with the international system, the Chinese Communist Party has studied how to leverage its rapidly expanding domestic market for geopolitical gain. In what could be viewed as a kind of de facto sanction, Chinese authorities at first started blocking market access to companies and organizations that promoted speech the party viewed as harmful to its core interests. One early visible result of China's economic statecraft, thus, was pervasive censorship and self-censorship among those who desired access to China's markets—leading some Western analysts to overlook or dismiss the trend as one merely affecting speech rather than other, more tangible forms of behavior. But as Beijing's power and confidence have grown along with its economic and financial heft, China's leaders have increasingly used market access and denial to shape state behavior, security outcomes, legal regimes, multilateral institutions, and performative allegiances on the global stage.

This strategy wouldn't work for almost any other country. Deploying sanctions on a global scale to enforce a wide-reaching set of norms requires an economy large enough that companies and governments around the world determine they have little choice but to pay the price of entry. Only the United States and now China currently gatekeep enough of the world's riches to weaponize their economies in this way. But it's a power that runs the risk, at least in theory, of becoming weaker if used too much. If the price of entry becomes too exorbitant for too long for too many parties, those parties may eventually band together to create alternatives.

To be sure, critics of Western sanctions abound. Some view Western sanctions as a violation of national sovereignty and have pointed especially to how the United States approached the "war on terror" by drawing on its international financial and economic dominance to enforce its domestic laws abroad, extending its extraterritorial reach. A total sanctions regime, such as that targeted at Iran, can harm innocent civilians without resulting in the desired change in government behavior. The U.S.

government has sometimes even been guilty of the very same behavior for which it has sanctioned others—the U.S. military invasion of Iraq without the United Nations' approval comes to mind.

It may seem counterintuitive to claim, then, that U.S. economic statecraft has been characterized by a degree of political restraint. Nonetheless, this is the case. Generally speaking, the United States has used sanctions extensively but only for a limited number of reasons: to combat abuses of the international financial system such as terrorism funding, money laundering, and corruption; to combat weapons proliferation; to punish those who commit violent regime change or aggression against other countries that is illegal under international law; and to punish those who perpetrate gross human rights violations.

U.S. sanctions, in theory and largely in practice, are intended to uphold the integrity of the international financial system and certain multilateral red lines, not the raw "realpolitik" national interests of the United States. Generally speaking, the United States does not levy sanctions on foreign people or groups for criticizing U.S. policies in nonviolent ways, for organizing anti-U.S. protests, or even for diplomatic efforts to reduce U.S. influence abroad. There have been exceptions, such as during the U.S. war on terror, when the definition of what comprised harboring terrorist sympathies became at times fuzzy and overly expansive. This is also not to say that the United States has never sought to push back against nonviolent anti-Americanism abroad; the CIA's history of political interventions proves otherwise. Rather, the point made here is that the United States has largely avoided direct economic coercion for basic acts of nonviolent political speech or organizing abroad.

The U.S. Treasury Department, in other words, does not freeze the assets of foreign citizens because of a tweet comparing the U.S. president to a cartoon character. The U.S. Commerce Department does not put a foreign pharmaceutical company on the federal Entity List because company executives comply with European sanctions prohibiting the export of drugs used for lethal injection in U.S. state executions, which in Europe is considered a human rights violation. The U.S. State Department does not systematically deny visas to foreign academics due to the ideological content of their research. The Committee on Foreign Investment in the United States does not make a habit of blocking foreign investment deals by companies whose executive leadership has criticized systemic racism in U.S. society. All these are examples of political restraint.

Under Trump, some of these norms did experience a degree of erosion. In September 2020, the U.S. Treasury Department levied sanctions against International Criminal Court chief prosecutor Fatou Bensouda and head of jurisdiction Phakiso Mochochoko, who were leading an investigation into potential war crimes committed by U.S. troops in Afghanistan. The two were added to Treasury's "Specially Designated Nationals" list, which means that any of their assets in the United States or subject to U.S. law would be frozen. (In April 2021, the Biden administration ended these sanctions, calling them "inappropriate and ineffective" and reaffirming U.S. support for rule of law and accountability for mass atrocities.) But, largely, the exception proves the rule—this kind of sanction is rare.

In contrast, China's authoritarian economic statecraft is overtly and intentionally "politics first." It is the opposite of political restraint. The primary purpose of its growing state control over both domestic and international economic activity is not to achieve purely economic goals but, rather, to promote the political bottom lines of the Chinese Communist Party, as narrowly defined by the party's self-interest rather than by a set of universal principles it believes will make the world a more decent place.

But China does not enjoy dominance of the international financial system, and the renminbi (RMB) is not the world's reserve currency, as is the dollar. Instead, what China has is its markets, its companies, and its capital. The party is using China's markets to create what is, in essence, its own heavily political sanctions regime.

Beijing views the dominance of the U.S. dollar, as well as the international banking system, as a key source of U.S. power and hegemony. But leaders in Beijing know that China won't be able to overtake the U.S. dollar anytime soon. And, indeed, they don't necessarily want to. For the RMB to become one of the world's great reserve currencies, they would have to relinquish their control of it, and they don't want to.

Without massive influence over the international banking system or control of the world's most important currency, China can't use the international financial system to enforce its own laws abroad, as the United States has done to fight terrorism and, especially under Trump, to enforce its sanctions on Iran. So China's leaders have instead used gatekeeping power over the country's economy to accomplish a similar end.

Beijing typically reserves the sharpest tools of its economic statecraft for what it defines as its "core interests," a once-static list that included the basic legitimacy of the Communist Party and the three taboo *T*s: Taiwan, Tibet, and the Tiananmen Square Massacre. But in recent years, the concept of core interests expanded to include any issue of territorial sovereignty, including Hong Kong, Xinjiang, at times the South China Sea, and now, at least informally, the narrative surrounding the origins of the novel coronavirus pandemic—the first time the party has appeared to treat as a core interest an issue with direct implications for everyone in the world. Though there are many examples in human history of rulers using economic coercion to force their political will on others, such a project has never been attempted in such a systematic and global way and to explicitly subvert existing liberal democratic counter-norms.

The party's turn toward economic statecraft as a global strategy did not occur in a vacuum. It was carefully calibrated to take advantage of the vulnerabilities resulting from the U.S.-led global advent of neoliberal policies—and, more broadly, to make use of China's full membership in an ever-developing global order not originally intended to accommodate a powerful illiberal peer. A system in which the "primary regulator of social interests is the marketplace," as Sitaraman has described neoliberalism, has few defenses when the marketplace itself has become a mechanism for direct political influence by an authoritarian superpower.

When did China first grasp how effectively it could flex its economic power against the West? As early as the late 1990s, even before China's entry into the World Trade Organization dramatically amplified its global economic engagement, the party had already used the promise of its market to tame Hollywood, one of America's preeminent instruments of soft power projection.

The last time major Hollywood studios made movies that presented a vulnerable group as the victim of Chinese government aggression was in 1997, with two films about Tibet. With the first, *Seven Years in Tibet*, starring Brad Pitt, the Chinese government responded by imposing a five-year ban on Columbia TriStar, the production company that made the film. The second film, Disney's *Kundun*, directed by Martin Scorsese and portraying the life of the Dalai Lama, resulted in a ban on Disney films until CEO Michael Eisner traveled to Beijing to apologize for the film, telling party officials that it had been a "stupid mistake." There have been no further motion pictures from major studios featuring Tibet or its exiled spiritual leader. These responses from Chinese authorities broadcast a clear message that cast a chill over the U.S. movie industry.

The allure of the Chinese box office has only grown since. The number of Chinese cinemagoers grew rapidly in the 2010s and was projected to soon surpass the U.S. market. That moment arrived in October 2020, as American movie theaters were shuttered due to Covid-19 restrictions while China's effective coronavirus response saw Chinese cinemas packed with moviegoers.

Beijing has wielded this power skillfully, rejecting all films that don't portray China as the party wishes. The result has been silence from Hollywood on the realities of Chinese Communist Party rule and, increasingly, a requirement that China's government, military, and territorial claims be featured in a proactively positive way.

"For 10 years, you haven't seen any bad Chinese guys" in films from major U.S. studios, Schuyler Moore, a partner at Los Angeles–based law firm Greenberg Glusker, which focuses on the entertainment industry, observed. "If I saw a script with an anti-Chinese theme, I would advise my client that that film would never be released in China."

In an eerily prescient precursor to the events of 2020, the makers of the 2013 zombie flick *World War Z* changed the location of the origin of the zombie epidemic from China, as portrayed in the original book, to North Korea. The book's author, Max Brooks, who had long been interested in infection and disease, had written the book in part as a warning about the dangers of China's Communist Party; in the novel, the CCP covers up the early zombie outbreak, enabling it to spread globally. "When I was thinking up an origin story for my fictional pandemic, it wasn't enough to choose a country with a massive population or a rapidly modernizing transportation network," Brooks wrote in February 2020, after the Covid-19 pandemic had begun. "I needed an authoritarian regime with strong control over the press. Smothering public awareness would give my plague time to spread, first among the local population, then into other nations. By the time the rest of the world figured out what was going on, it would be too late."

"Sound familiar?" Brooks added.

This isn't all bad news. Hollywood's frequent portrayals of Russians, Muslims, and others as antagonists have resulted in harmful stereotypes and contributed to pervasive Islamophobia. "From my perspective, the fact that we don't have Chinese villains in Hollywood films is a good thing," noted Aynne Kokas, assistant professor of media studies at the University of Virginia and author of the book *Hollywood Made in China*. "It's deeply dehumanizing when certain groups become the target of villainy." The Soviet Union, modern-day Russia, and Middle Eastern nations have lacked the ability to prevent U.S. film studios from associating their citizens with evil. In that sense, China's economic statecraft, when exercised in this manner, provides a tangible example of how government power can be wielded to protect its citizens.

Hollywood is a particularly prominent case study of how the party has used denial of market access to control the speech of private corporations in democratic countries, but there are many others. In the past twenty years, company after company has succumbed as Beijing has dangled in front of them the glittering riches of a market size of 1.4 billion. Google, LinkedIn, Apple, Marriott, Mercedes-Benz, Zara, United Airlines, and the National Basketball Association—all have acceded to censorship demands or apologized with great contrition after the release of a tweet or a survey or a map that didn't fully align with the Chinese Communist Party's priorities, swearing to avoid such "mistakes" in the future.

China's messaging on this has been so clear and so consistent, and the punishments so harsh—the NBA is estimated to have lost two hundred million dollars in revenue after Houston Rockets manager Daryl Morey tweeted in support of the 2019 Hong Kong protests—and the financial rewards of access to the Chinese market so great that acquiescence to Beijing's red lines is now automatic for many corporations with business interests there.

But it's a misunderstanding to view the taming of Hollywood and other corporate speech as simply extraterritorial censorship. A more predictive framework is to see censorship and self-censorship as an early manifestation of China's growing ability to use market access to change behavior of many kinds—a process that is gradually coalescing to form a comprehensive and codified foundation of China's international power.

For more than a decade, Beijing has used tariffs, de facto bans, and other economic measures to punish foreign governments for political actions that displeased China's leaders. After the Norwegian Nobel Committee awarded Liu Xiaobo the Nobel Peace Prize in 2010, salmon exports to China, an important market for a key Norwegian industry, fell dramatically as fish shipments rotted at Chinese ports for weeks, denied entry due to sudden and unexplained bureaucratic red tape. Chinese authorities never formally acknowledged this block, but Norwegian salmon exports did not return to pre–Nobel Prize levels until the two countries resumed diplomatic ties in 2016, when Norway stated that it "attaches high importance to China's core interests and major concerns" and "will not support actions that undermine them." An article in the *Global Times* published at the time wrote explicitly about the Chinese government's behavior, even referring to the block on salmon exports as "sanctions," writing, "The sanctions on Norway that lasted for six years have demonstrated China's firm determination against any external intervention into China's internal affairs."

The Chinese government has used economic measures to punish governments for defending their territorial claims against incursions by Chinese-flagged vessels in the South China Sea. In 2012, China blocked banana imports from the Philippines and limited Chinese tourism there amid a standoff between Chinese fishing vessels and the Philippine Navy over the contested Scarborough Shoal, a resource-rich reef located within the Philippines' exclusive economic zone, where international law gives the Philippines the right to exploit maritime resources. China claims the Scarborough Shoal and most of the expansive South China Sea in which it is located. Chinese authorities said the bananas had an insect infestation, though the customs authorities in Japan and South Korea reported no such issue with banana shipments from the Philippines.

The lesson that Philippine government officials learned from this experience was to avoid becoming overly reliant on economic ties with China. "We need to intensify our efforts to diversify our trade with other countries," Arsenio Balisacan, the country's economic planning secretary, told reporters at the time. "Whether or not this event with China occurred, we should have been diversifying our exports."

Beijing used a panoply of similar measures to punish numerous sectors of the South Korean economy for the country's deployment of THAAD (Terminal High-Altitude Area Defense), a U.S. missile defense system first announced in 2016. Both the United States and South Korea said the advanced missile system was intended to deter North Korea, but its technical capabilities could be used against China as well—a fact that led Beijing to vehemently oppose the system's deployment. For much of 2017, Chinese authorities shuttered most of South Korean retail conglomerate Lotte Mart's 112 retail stores in China due to what they claimed were fire safety concerns after a U.S. missile defense system was installed on what had been Lotte-owned land. Retaliations against Lotte weren't the only economic measure Beijing implicitly used to punish South Korea for installing the missile defense system. K-pop bands were denied entry to China to perform at their own concerts, streaming platforms blocked the popular music, and Chinese tourist companies froze group travel to South Korea.

The South Korean government provided some tax relief for companies that sustained financial losses due to economic pressure from Chinese authorities and state-fanned boycotts, but no other assistance, leaving companies to deal with the Chinese market largely alone. This failure suggests that, in the future, South Korean firms may assess an even higher level of political risk for engaging in any action that might be perceived to challenge China's core interests—and possibly lobby their government to avoid taking future actions that could engender a similar response from Beijing.

The CCP has also pushed international corporations to continue buying and selling products made through Uyghur forced labor, an attempt to bestow international legitimacy to the Chinese government's colonial and genocidal aims in Xinjiang and to erode the power of existing human rights laws and conventions. But after H&M, Nike, and other companies began to issue public statements disavowing their use of Xinjiang cotton—an industry especially tainted by coerced labor—China's heavily censored internet erupted in outrage. H&M products disappeared from e-commerce platforms, and H&M stores were removed from navigation apps. Chinese celebrities cut ties with H&M; one stated that "the country's interests are above all." In the following months, H&M's sales in China dropped 23 percent from the previous year. The boycotts of Nike,

Boss, H&M, and other international clothing retailers in 2021 further demonstrate that Beijing increasingly demands actions, not just speech, that are in line with its core interests.

China's coercive policies even extend to the skies. The Chinese government has threatened to physically close off its airspace to airlines if they don't comply with certain demands. In August 2019, the Civil Aviation Administration of China, the country's airlines regulator, warned Hong Kong–based carrier Cathay Pacific that any employees who "support or take part in illegal protests, violent actions, or overly radical behaviour" would not be permitted to enter China's airspace—resulting in a spate of terminations. By October 1, 2019, according to one tally, at least twenty-six Cathay Pacific employees were fired for support of the protests.

Taiwan, as one of the party's longtime core interests, remains a top target of China's evolving economic statecraft. Beijing has sought to use economic tools to stave off international political engagement with Taiwan, including visits by politicians to the self-governing democracy. Klavir Petrof, a Czech piano company founded in 1864, found itself facing de facto Chinese sanctions for this reason. In a diplomatic letter dated January 10, 2020, China threatened retaliation against Czech companies if a senior Czech politician carried out his stated plans to travel to Taiwan. After a second Czech official visited Taiwan in August, China made good on that threat. A Chinese company suspended a $23.8 million order of the Czech-made pianos, which was reported in the *Global Times* as a "natural business response" to the "provocation of the Czech senate speaker's visit to China's Taiwan in August." This was potentially devastating for the company, which relies heavily on the Chinese market; in 2020, Klavir Petrof sold around five thousand pianos in China, producing revenue that comprised 38 percent of its annual profit. A Czech billionaire intervened and bought the pianos himself.

China is also using its economic heft to construct a sphere of influence through its Belt and Road Initiative, in which it offers infrastructure loans and investment to numerous countries in tacit exchange for their support of Beijing's geopolitical objectives. A good example of this is how, in a set of opposing letters sent to the UN Human Rights Council regarding China's imposition of a draconian national security law on Hong Kong, forty-three of the fifty-three countries that had expressed support for Beijing were included in the Belt and Road Initiative, while the twenty-seven countries that had criticized China's repression in Hong Kong were almost without exception not involved. This initiative is global, complex, and sweeping, though less innovative than the party's weaponization of market access; trading aid for influence or local resource rights is hardly new.

These examples of China's economic statecraft all share one key feature: They were deployed to defend what the CCP sees as its core interests, which traditionally included issues of national or territorial sovereignty— anything relating to Tibet, Taiwan, the South China Sea, or Xinjiang, for example—or very nearby issues of obvious military security, such as the deployment of THAAD systems in South Korea.

For years, people whose work intersects with China's core interests have observed this phenomenon and sounded the alarm. In 2016, Mongolia hosted the Dalai Lama but publicly distanced itself from the Tibetan spiritual leader shortly thereafter when China closed a key border crossing and halted loan negotiations with its capital, Ulan Bator. Tibet historian Robert J. Barnett called the incident "part of a near-global collapse in diplomatic capacity to handle certain kinds of pressure from China"—a warning that predated by several years Washington's recognition of this type of pressure.

But warnings about China's growing ability to translate economic power into political and diplomatic heft went largely unheeded by the international community because it was believed that the party's core interests, while obnoxiously defended, would remain narrowly defined. It was certainly unfortunate for the small number of Tibetans, or Uyghurs, or Taiwanese, or Hong Kongers, or Chinese pro-democracy activists in the world, the thinking went, but it simply wasn't an issue of global concern.

Western ethnocentrism may have played a part in our collective blindness as well. To many people in Washington, London, Brussels, and elsewhere, it simply felt impossible to believe that any non-Western government could actually succeed at imposing its geopolitical interests through such means, and thus, there was little cause for concern. Who would have believed, twenty years ago, that Hollywood could no longer make movies that China's party censors nixed? Or that Hugo Boss, facing a nationalist backlash in China, would hastily reassure its Chinese customers that it would absolutely continue using Xinjiang cotton despite European laws against forced labor in supply chains?

The Covid-19 pandemic, and the party's sensitivity over the origins of the coronavirus becoming what effectively amounted to a new core interest, shattered these illusions, shaking the world into a belated awareness that China's economic statecraft could pose a direct threat to anyone, anywhere. During a truly global emergency, with millions of lives hanging in the balance, the Chinese government deployed the same channels of leverage previously reserved only for issues like Taiwanese sovereignty and the Dalai Lama. The Chinese government punished people, organizations, and countries for repeating the basic scientific fact that the pandemic had originated in China.

Winemaker Osborn experienced this directly. China's wine tariffs in November 2020 immediately choked off d'Arenberg's largest export market at a time when the winery was already seeing reduced foot traffic due to the ongoing pandemic. These dual threats left Osborn unnerved. "With Covid, we didn't know how it would turn out, we were pretty worried, so we went to the bank to increase our facility," he said in an October 2021 interview.

Even so, he had it relatively easy. D'Arenberg had increased the prices of its wines in early 2020, and the pandemic-driven shift of wine consumption from restaurants to stores played to the winery's strengths as an established label. D'Arenberg also benefited from Australian government stimulus during the pandemic. In March 2020, the Australian government announced its JobKeeper program, which paid wage subsidies to Australian employers for each employee they continued to employ during the pandemic.

Major Australian wineries with footprints in multiple countries have also been able to diversify their exports into other countries. In particular, there has been renewed interest in the historically large U.S. and UK markets. Tony Battaglene, the chief executive of industry group Australian Grape and Wine, told Australia's ABC News that the UK market grew by 30 percent between April and June 2021. Australian wineries have also explored expansion into markets as diverse as Canada, South Korea, and Sweden. According to Tyrrell's Wines managing director Bruce Tyrrell, in the twelve months prior to the end of June 2021, the winery, based in New South Wales's Hunter Valley wine region, made up 80 percent of its former revenue from China through diversification.

For some Australian wine producers, however, the tariffs proved fatal.

Battaglene stated that approximately a thousand producers—primarily wine traders with Chinese cultural ties—shut down in 2022 after they were unable to shift to other markets. "We will never rely as much on an individual market as in the past . . . we need to be diversified for when these shocks come," he said. According to Tyrrell, "China turned the whole thing political" by backing Chinese domestic winemakers' claims of Australian dumping, despite the high prices for Australian wine in China.

Even for producers who have been able to diversify, the China market is so large that diversification can't fully replace it. The Australian Bureau of Agricultural and Resource Economics and Sciences expects that by 2025, the Australian industry will make up 60 percent of its previous exports to China through diversification to other markets, but that still leaves a 40 percent shortfall. While the tariffs have awakened the Australian wine industry to the dangers of over-reliance on a single market, this reality still gives China enormous leverage in its relationship with Australia.

Osborn can see the challenges on the horizon for d'Arenberg. China lifted numerous tariffs on Australia in early 2023, after the new prime minister Anthony Albanese—the head of the first Labor government the country has had in almost a decade—met with Xi Jinping on the sidelines of the G20 summit in Indonesia the previous November. But as of March 2023, the tariffs on Australian wine remained. "Now there's a lot of uncertainty," he said.

"We were victims of a bigger game," said Battaglene. To China, that game means advancing its agenda from simply batting away human rights criticisms to a much bolder and proactive use of its power.

2

THE GLOBAL RUSH FOR MASKS

A global pandemic creates a set of collective memories that transcends borders, languages, and culture. This was true, albeit in slow motion, during the 1918 Spanish influenza pandemic, as cases were first reported among soldiers in Kansas, then in Germany and France, and gradually around the world. The common memories from that pandemic, in which up to a third of the world's population eventually contracted the virus, were rather more dire in an age before modern medicine: Bodies piled up on city streets. People fell dead off their horses. Families were afraid to leave their houses. Almost everyone lost someone.

Collective memories are even more common in the era of the internet and globalized supply chains. No matter where you are in the world, you know what it's like to first hear rumors of the virus; then to see it dominate headlines; then to see news of the first cases in your country; and, finally, to live through unprecedented lockdowns and border closings.

By February 2020, this shared experience generally entailed trying and failing to locate a surgical mask. Medical workers in Wuhan were the first to beg for more personal protective equipment (PPE). Mask shortages meant that doctors and nurses had to use tape to repair disposable face masks for reuse. It was a matter of life and death; by February, hundreds of medical staff in Wuhan had contracted the virus, and six had died, according to official Chinese government figures.

But everyone would soon be clamoring for a mask. As cities around the world descended into lockdown, pharmacies were sold out. In the United States, Amazon offerings were out of stock. *Wear a mask!* government health offices urged. *Don't buy masks!* the same government health offices also urged, in order to preserve the limited supply of masks for frontline health workers, who needed them more. Confusion reigned, but one thing was clear: there simply weren't enough masks.

Randomly select any group of humans from almost any location on earth, and you could probably swap stories with them about the inability to find masks during this time and of having to fashion them from pieces of fabric lying around. We all graduated at the same time from the same global crash course in scarcity, supply chains, and industrial policy. Given the sudden skyrocketing global demand, the scarcity of masks was inevitable. What wasn't inevitable, government officials and policymakers around the world soon realized in a terrible collective aha moment, was that few countries in the world had the capacity to mass-produce masks—and that most of the world's masks, and the factories that made them, were located in China.

The realization that the populations of countries with advanced economies were heavily dependent on China for basic lifesaving medical supplies was a shock to the system. The global rush for PPE revived the debate over industrial policy, bringing what had for decades felt like a fringe idea to the mainstream in both the United States and Europe. It was a realization that very quickly spread to other critical industries. For the first time in decades, Americans from all walks of life had a tangible example of what it meant to lose control over a vital industry—an experience that made concerns over China's growing dominance in telecommunications, solar panels, and artificial intelligence no longer seem like right-wing paranoia but, rather, common sense.

———————

As demand for masks, medical goggles, and protective garments spiked in Wuhan and surrounding localities, the Chinese government acted quickly to meet that demand. On January 30, 2020, the State Council ordered governments at every level to quickly bring local manufacturing facilities up to full capacity following the Chinese New Year holiday lull and orient them toward producing PPE.

The government also required some state-owned enterprises to shift to producing PPE. Xinxing Cathay International Group, an offshoot of the People's Liberation Army that had primarily manufactured pipes and textiles for military use, began manufacturing protective garments for healthcare workers for the first time. Government ministries aided them in this by expediting the provision of equipment and raw materials and the required certifications so they could begin production.

As a result of these state-led efforts, PPE production increased dramatically. In the early stages of the pandemic, Chinese factories were producing 20,000 protective garments and 200,000 N95 masks per day. By early March 2020, the country's arsenal of factories was putting out 500,000 protective garments and 1.6 million N95 masks per day.

But something else was going on, too. While China's domestic production of PPE increased in the first quarter of 2020, its exports of PPE to the rest of the world fell noticeably. According to Chinese customs data, exports of masks and respirators declined by 12.5 percent during this period, while exports of protective garments fell by 22.1 percent.

This matters because China had long been a major source of PPE for other countries. In 2018, it provided more than 50 percent of world imports of many types of PPE, including masks, medical goggles, and protective garments. Many developing countries were almost totally reliant on China for certain types of PPE.

China's outsize role in the global PPE supply chain, combined with the Chinese government's tight control over the country's domestic economy, meant that when it came to getting PPE, other countries were at Beijing's mercy. Medical suppliers based in the United States and Canada said that the Chinese government had instituted a de facto export ban on PPE. "Overnight it was 80 percent of the world supply [of masks] which was cut," Guillaume Laverdure, the COO of Canadian medical supplier Medicom, told CNN in early March; according to Laverdure, the Chinese government had requisitioned all production from the company's three factories in China.

It makes sense that the country at the epicenter of an outbreak would want to do everything it could to reduce infections, including by ensuring a supply of PPE for its population. But the lack of transparency around PPE supply, combined with the Chinese authorities' early cover-up of the pandemic, contributed to an overall sense that Beijing was engaging in deception. The Chinese government denied reports of an export ban and insisted that the decline in exports was due solely to market forces. In some cases, that decline appears to have been closely linked to the pandemic; Hubei Province, the epicenter of the pandemic in China, had been the largest producer of protective garments prior to the outbreak. But PPE exports declined even in areas that were relatively unaffected by the pandemic, such as Shanghai, Guangdong Province, Jiangsu Province, and Zhejiang Province. This suggests that the Chinese government played an active role in keeping PPE in China.

In a May 1 intelligence report, the U.S. Department of Homeland Security assessed that there was a 95 percent probability that the Chinese government had intentionally reduced the export of PPE and increased its import during January while simultaneously publicly denying the severity of the epidemic. The report also proposed a link between these behaviors: that Beijing dismissed concerns over the virus in order to buy the country more time to obtain protective gear from abroad. This is an unlikely scenario, as it would have involved perfect synchronization of many moving parts and because it assumes a greater plan for what was more likely panicked behavior by myriad government bureaucrats.

But this particular assertion in the report was part of a larger phenomenon that would quickly become apparent in the earliest months of the pandemic: Very few people really trusted the Chinese government. As a result, behavior that was innocuous or even bumbling often came under suspicion as being part of a nefarious grand plan. During this time, this suspicion would taint the activities of overseas Chinese diaspora groups, who responded with remarkable speed and efficacy to the Chinese government's calls for PPE donations.

On January 27, 2020, Wei Chengbing landed in Nagoya, Japan, after spending some time in his hometown of Fuqing, Fujian Province, prior to the Chinese Lunar New Year holiday. Wei was fifty-two years old with thinning hair parted down the middle. Like many Fujianese families, members of the Wei clan had immigrated to a range of countries over the years and established successful businesses, including a chain of supermarkets in Toronto and a food manufacturing company in Hong Kong. Wei's cousin Wei Chenghui (Sam Goi Seng Hui) had built a business empire selling spring roll skins in Singapore, becoming the country's fourteenth richest person and its ambassador to Brazil.

Wei Chengbing was well established in Japan. In 2003, he had established J & C Corporation, an import-export company that leveraged connections to Wei family business ventures around the globe.

But Wei had never forgotten his roots. Born in October 1967, at the height of the Cultural Revolution, he had witnessed his country transform from isolationist and poverty-stricken to cosmopolitan, globe-trotting, and prosperous. He had played his own small role in his motherland's rise to prosperity. The *J* and *C* in his company's name stood for "Japan" and "China," chosen to emphasize his connection to his home country. "Let's become a bridge between Japan and China," Wei states on the company's website. In Japan, Wei was the honorary vice president of the Fuqing Huaqiao High School Alumni Association and president of the Fujian Economic and Cultural Exchange Association. These organizations bring together Fujianese people living in Japan for social and cultural activities and promote Chinese patriotism based on their shared heritage.

During his visit home, Wei had originally planned to make a stop in Ningbo, on China's eastern coast, but he rushed back to Japan after hearing about the mysterious new virus now raging in the Chinese city of Wuhan.

The epidemic had already caused a massive nationwide PPE shortage. In addition to increased demand, the *People's Daily* attributed the shortage to manufacturing slowdowns following the Lunar New Year holiday and a lack of necessary raw materials. The shortage was particularly severe in Wuhan; Voice of America reported that medical personnel there were being asked to wear diapers over their faces instead of protective suits.

Wei and the Fujian Economic and Cultural Exchange Association enjoyed a positive relationship with the Chinese government and were part of a constellation of party-affiliated groups with ties to Fujian. China's consul general in Nagoya had attended the Fujian Economic and Cultural Exchange Association's founding ceremony in November 2019 and would later attend the organization's annual meeting in July 2021. On January 18, during his visit to Fuqing, Wei had met with members of the Ōbaku Cultural Promotion Association, ostensibly a nonprofit organization dedicated to promoting Japan-China ties with a focus on the Ōbaku school of Zen Buddhism, brought to Japan from Fuqing in the seventeenth century. But it also has close ties to local offices for Overseas Chinese Affairs and for the All-China Federation of Returned Overseas

Chinese (ACFROC), both of which are overseen by the United Front Work Department (UFWD).

On January 25, the Overseas Chinese Affairs and ACFROC offices in Fuzhou, the municipality in which Fuqing is located, issued a call for all overseas Chinese to donate funds and medical supplies to combat the pandemic. The Fujian Economic and Cultural Exchange Association responded to the call, and on the same day that Wei landed in Japan, the Fuzhou ACFROC office issued a statement noting that the Fujian association was raising funds to purchase two hundred thousand masks to send back to Fuzhou, one of many such donation drives carried out "under the joint efforts of the municipal Overseas Chinese Affairs and ACFROC offices."

Upon arriving in Nagoya, Wei immediately organized a group of thirty-six Fujian association members to gather the masks. The small group soon swelled to more than four hundred overseas Chinese from Fujian, who set aside their day jobs to scour pharmacies in Nagoya for any available masks. When pharmacies attempted to enforce limits on mask purchases arising from Japan's own Covid-19 outbreak—the first known Covid-19 case in Japan had been documented on January 16, 2020, in Kanagawa Prefecture, south of Tokyo—the Chinese mask hunters begged them to sell more. According to China News Service, some association members even visited twenty-four-hour convenience stores in the dead of night in the hope of finding more masks.

Their efforts were successful. Between January 28 and February 2, Fujian Economic and Cultural Exchange Association members gathered a total of seven hundred thousand masks, which they sent in three shipments to Wuhan, Fuzhou, and the rest of Fujian Province. According to a local news report, Wei credited branches of the United Front Work Department, Overseas Chinese Affairs, and ACFROC in Fujian with facilitating the shipments. The Fujian association also donated about $73,000 to fight the pandemic in China, and Wei himself donated about $14,500.

During February, the scene in Nagoya was replayed in cities across the globe as United Front–linked groups abroad heeded the call to gather PPE and send it back home. Chinese state media provided glowing coverage of similar efforts by overseas Chinese organizations in countries around the world, including Argentina, Australia, Canada, and the United States. By the end of the month, according to an estimate by Bloomberg, overseas Chinese individuals and organizations had sent to China 2.5 billion items of PPE valued at $1.2 billion. The global rush for PPE had begun.

As the novel coronavirus pandemic spread abroad and PPE became scarce, however, these efforts by overseas Chinese to send aid back home became highly controversial. In January and February, Australian media outlets reported that local branches of multiple Chinese state–owned companies sent hundreds of thousands of masks and other PPE back to China even as they were desperately needed by residents caught in bushfires raging in eastern Australia. The *Sydney Morning Herald* reported on internal communications showing that the Australian headquarters of Polygroup, a Chinese state–owned arms trading and real estate conglomerate, organized employees to search local pharmacies and stores for masks to send back to China. These incidents led the Australian Medical Association to warn that the country needed to protect its stocks of PPE from being exported.

Jorge Guajardo, a former Mexican ambassador to Beijing, called these PPE shipments back to China a "surreptitious" effort that left "the world naked with no supply of PPE." An article in Canada's *Global News* described it as a successful attempt by Beijing to "quietly corner the world's supply of PPE in a state-level operation" while maintaining that China's domestic outbreak was nothing to worry about.

Diaspora communities have long pooled resources and raised money to send aid back home in times of famine, natural disaster, or conflict. After the devastating Tangshan earthquake of 1976, which killed more than 240,000 people, Chinese restaurants in the United States served as hubs for collecting community donations, which were sent to China. In 2008, Chinese community groups in the United States raised money to help with relief efforts after an earthquake in Sichuan killed around seventy thousand people, including many schoolchildren. In 2021, Indian student groups in the United States raised hundreds of thousands of dollars for Covid-19 relief in India. None of these efforts was controversial.

The global rush for PPE was perhaps the first time the full impact of highly motivated Chinese diaspora communities could be felt in such a tangible way—both to the grateful recipients of lifesaving masks back in Hubei and to people in cities in Japan, Canada, Australia, the United States, and elsewhere who could not find masks in their local pharmacies.

In January and early February, it was difficult for anyone to foresee that the entire world would soon be starving for PPE and that the individual efforts of people in overseas Chinese communities, when spurred by the top-down guidance of globe-spanning party organizations, would result in $1.2 billion worth of PPE sent back to China within a period of less than two months.

Usually, this kind of organizing doesn't attract suspicion. The many overseas Chinese who participated in the PPE drive during the early months of the pandemic saw their activities as perfectly legitimate. But in this case, it was the United Front's involvement that drew outside scrutiny, making this a perfect case study of how China's dual-function strategy could backfire, casting suspicion on genuine humanitarian activities and breeding resentment toward and feelings of alienation among diaspora communities—a topic I will explore further in the next chapter.

The backlash also likely involved an element of scapegoating. While it is a fact that large quantities of PPE were shipped back to China, increased domestic purchasing of masks was certainly under way as people who had previously never bought face masks began to stock up just in case. Usual supply couldn't accommodate this spike in demand. The enormous rise in anti-Asian attacks that would soon begin as the pandemic spread around the world demonstrates that many people had the capacity to blame their fear and uncertainty on anyone around them who happened to look Chinese.

Before Covid-19, face masks were not considered a particularly strategic industry. Certainly, the Chinese government hadn't thought of them in that way; it would be outrageously conspiratorial to suggest that Beijing had purposely sought to dominate global PPE manufacturing to prepare for the day when a global pandemic would give them an opportunity to shut off exports and bring Western governments to their knees. But what is most certainly true is that, in the span of a few months, the Chinese party-state had used its influence over its domestic economy and international supply chains and its established links with overseas Chinese groups to reshape the global PPE landscape. Regardless of intentions, the results point to an exercise of power that shook the world.

On January 29, as Wei and his team were scouring Nagoya for PPE and the Chinese government was ramping up domestic production, White House trade adviser Peter Navarro sent a memo to the U.S. National Security Council warning about the potential human and economic costs of the pandemic. He would follow this with a second memo on February 23, which forecast urgent needs for PPE as the pandemic spread.

Despite warnings from the World Health Organization; intelligence agencies; his acting chief of staff, Mick Mulvaney; the secretary of health and human services, Alex Azar; and economic adviser Peter Navarro, President Trump failed to take action. The consequences would be fatal. One investigation found that, in the first year of the pandemic, 3,607 healthcare workers died across the United States from Covid-19, including many who lacked adequate PPE.

The seventy-year-old Navarro had had a long career in academia, where he had written about a range of economic subjects since the 1980s. His first book, published in 1984, criticized the influence of special interest groups over the American political process. In the 2000s, Navarro turned his attention to China, writing three books that were strongly critical of Chinese economic policy. His stance led *The Economist* to describe him as a "China-bashing eccentric," and he was widely considered one of the Trump administration's leading anti-China hard-liners.

As a result, it was easy for some of Navarro's colleagues in the administration to dismiss his two memos as agenda-driven posturing; Axios quoted a senior administration official describing the January memo as "an alarmist attempt to bring attention to Peter's anti-China agenda." President Trump's subsequent behavior seemed to reinforce this idea. Navarro's January 29 memo also recommended cutting off travel from China, and the president immediately did so, issuing his first pandemic travel ban—a move that drew criticism from abroad and from Anthony Fauci, the top U.S. health official overseeing the pandemic response. Trump critics tended to view the move as part of the president's anti-immigrant agenda rather than as a legitimate public health measure, even though such travel bans quickly became standard measures enforced by many countries over the course of the pandemic. Trump's subsequent refusal to take public health warnings seriously and his active undermining of basic measures such as the wearing of masks only served to reinforce this interpretation of the China travel ban. The day after Navarro sent his first memo, Trump said in a speech that the pandemic would have "a very good ending for us."

PPE distributors in the United States saw a different picture. The nation's healthcare system had not been fortified with additional beds, staff, or—most shockingly—medical devices like ventilators and face masks, gloves, and gowns. While the United States had domestic manufacturing capacity for certain types of PPE, it was woefully insufficient to meet the challenge of the pandemic. Rear Adm. John Polowczyk, the head of the Trump administration's Covid-19 Supply Chain Stabilization Task Force, in place from March to November 2020, later said that "we made about 500 million nitrile gloves [a year] in America, pre-pandemic. [During the pandemic] we were using 1.8 billion a week." These gaps in production were too large to fill simply by expanding production at existing facilities.

The trade war between the United States and China had also imperiled PPE supplies in the United States. The Trump administration had imposed tariffs on multiple categories of PPE in September 2019. As a result, U.S. imports of PPE from China declined in the months before the pandemic, and U.S. distributors may have ended business relationships with Chinese suppliers.

Another reason for the United States' dire shortage of PPE was that the federal government under both the Obama and Trump administrations had allowed its national supply of important equipment like highly protective N95 respirators to remain depleted—according to some reports, since the swine flu outbreaks in the early 2010s. Ernest Grant, president of the American Nurses Association, told PBS's *Frontline*, "When you stop and think that we send soldiers into battle with the equipment that they need, yet we were asking nurses to do the exact same thing, but without the equipment that they needed. There's a failure in the system. I think those who are in position to ensure that the supply chain was being maintained, they failed us big-time."

Alarmed at the prospect of PPE shortages, distributors pushed for meetings with the administration. The Health Industry Distributors Association organized at least four calls between private PPE distribution companies and Trump administration officials. In discussions with the House Committee on Oversight and Reform, company representatives described these meetings as largely informational, with administration officials declining to provide specific policy guidance on meeting anticipated PPE demand. AdvaMed, another industry group, sent a letter to the Trump administration in late January urging it to remove the trade war tariffs; the administration did not act to grant temporary tariff exceptions for PPE until mid-March 2020.

The distributors made clear that their preferred approach was for the federal government to directly procure PPE, which would then be distributed by the private sector. But the administration opted not to pursue this course, believing that procurement was the responsibility of the states and the private sector rather than the federal government. "We're not a shipping clerk," President Trump said at a daily press conference on March 19. This decision forced state and local governments and hospitals to compete to acquire PPE through Chinese brokers, creating opportunities for fraud and price gouging. In mid-March, instead of directly procuring PPE, the Trump administration launched Project Airbridge. This effort, managed by the Federal Emergency Management Agency, was intended to expedite PPE shipments by providing free air freight to private PPE importers. Project Airbridge was also highly dependent on China: the majority of PPE transported through the initiative came from China, and U.S. diplomats coordinated with Chinese officials to secure the shipments. At the same time, the Trump administration sent out feelers in search of more PPE. On March 22, Undersecretary of State David Hale sent an urgent email to embassies in Europe and Asia requesting that they appeal to host governments to sell PPE to the United States.

By mid-June, when the administration phased out Project Airbridge, the program had facilitated 249 shipments of PPE, including nearly 1.5 million N95 respirators, more than 2.5 million face shields, and 937 million gloves. However, this was a fraction of the country's need; the state of Michigan alone requested 20 million N95 respirators in late March. The United States found itself in a race against time to secure the PPE it needed.

Like their U.S. counterparts, EU officials initially viewed the pandemic as a Chinese problem. As a result, EU member states, aside from restricting flights to and from China, would take little concrete action in January and February to address the risk of a pandemic in Europe.

The European Union's domestic stockpile of PPE was woefully insufficient. In early March, member states began restricting the export of medical equipment and supplies, choking off the distribution of PPE in Europe. On March 15, the European Commission instituted a ban on PPE exports to outside the bloc, in part to encourage PPE circulation within the European Union. At the same time, European countries began individually contacting Chinese PPE manufacturers. Like their U.S. counterparts, EU officials were forced to turn to China for needed PPE.

As Raphaël Glucksmann, a French member of the European Parliament, would later tell me, "In France, we discovered that we could no longer make masks ourselves."

The shortage of lifesaving medical equipment, the resulting scrutiny of supply chains, and debate over invoking war powers that would soon follow brought the concept of industrial policy into the limelight. In late February, U.S. health secretary Alex Azar told reporters that if the government was unable to procure sufficient stores of N95 masks and other protective gear, he would consider invoking the Defense Production Act, a Korean War–era law that gives the federal government the power to direct private companies to produce materials vital for the national interest. At a congressional hearing, Azar said that China has control over "a lot of the raw materials as well as the manufacturing capacity" for masks, making it difficult for the United States to ramp up production.

But to invoke the Defense Production Act to produce millions upon millions of masks for use by the general U.S. public would represent a more dramatic use of the act than in any recent decades. On March 27, Trump finally did, ordering General Motors to produce ventilators. The next week, he issued another directive, requiring additional companies to produce ventilators and directing the procurement of N95 masks from U.S. multinational 3M.

Meanwhile, calls for the United States to adopt an industrial strategy to counter more broadly China were getting louder. "The COVID-19 pandemic, with its disruptions of supply chains, has put U.S. dependency on China in the news on an almost daily basis," wrote Rob Atkinson, a Canadian American economist and founder of the DC-based Information Technology and Innovation Foundation, in an April 2020 report. "It is time for the federal government to put in place a national industrial strategy that focuses on supporting key industries critical to America's economic vitality, public health, and national security: in other words, industries that are 'too critical to fail.'"

The United States had previously directed critical industries to great effect during the Civil War, when Northern factories were able to outfit Union Army troops with a great quantity of weapons and supplies; during the rapid wartime mobilization for World War II; and, famously, during the technology and arms races of the Cold War. But the difference between those eras and the current challenge, Atkinson wrote, was that "neoclassical economics now dominates U.S. policymaking." Across society, politics, and the government, it was widely believed that markets on their own could buoy the United States to continued economic dominance, that government intervention in economic structures would only result in corruption and inefficiency, and that only companies could drive sustainable innovation and economic leadership. It was as if the United States were using the "neoliberal shock therapy we proposed for former communist states on ourselves," Atkinson wrote. As a result, there was enormous resistance to the idea that the U.S. government should take action to boost the nation's competitive edge in the growing technology rivalry with China.

In May, the Semiconductor Industry Association, a U.S. trade group, proposed $37 billion in subsidies, billing this as a vital step toward preserving the United States' competitive edge against China, which provides extensive state support for its own growing semiconductor sector. Commerce secretary Wilbur Ross expressed support for the general idea behind the proposal, and a State Department spokesperson told the *Wall Street Journal* that the department was "working closely with Congress and industry to ensure that the future of the semiconductor industry remains in the United States."

"Debates like this weren't happening two years ago," said Eric Sayers, who had served as a special assistant to Adm. Harry Harris at Indo-Pacific Command headquarters in Hawaii, in May 2020. He described the shift under way as a "generational alignment of political interest on investing more federal dollars into critical industries to compete with China."

In June 2020, U.S. senators Marco Rubio and Elizabeth Warren, ideological opposites in many ways, co-sponsored a bill that would require the Committee on Foreign Investment in the United States to conduct a study examining the "overreliance" of the U.S. pharmaceutical and DNA analysis industries on "foreign countries" and the impact of foreign direct investment on those industries. "To defeat the current COVID-19 crisis and better equip the United States against future pandemics, we must take control of our supply chain and rely less on foreign countries for our critical drugs," Senator Warren said at the time.

A more interventionist industrial policy has traditionally faced opposition from both the right and the left in the United States. Those who lean right of center have opposed industrial policy out of the belief that open international markets free from government intervention are most efficient and produce the best economic outcomes. For those left of center, who may not be ideologically opposed to government action to reshape economic structures, opposition has arisen from the view that industrial policy aimed at securing supply chains and critical industries represents a counterproductive overreach by national security analysts fearful of foreign adversaries.

———————

Debates over U.S. industrial policy at large are nothing new. It's long been easy for right-of-center opponents to dismiss industrial policy as "central planning," a term that conjures up the inefficiencies and shortages of Soviet-era planned economies. It's an example of the unfortunate U.S. tendency to conflate a greater role for government in the economy, as has long been practiced in democratic capitalist societies in Europe and Japan, with "socialism" or "communism" as implemented in the Soviet Union, North Korea, and China.

"Industrial policy has been the Lord Voldemort of terms. You can't say it," said legal scholar Ganesh Sitaraman during an October 2020 virtual talk he gave at the DC-based German Marshall Fund of the United States. "But every country has an industrial policy. When you give tax breaks to sectors like oil, that is an industrial policy."

Government guidance in strategic investment is, of course, a far cry from a group of technocrats sitting down and deciding how many clothes hangers, cars, widgets, and tubes of lipstick should be produced for the next five years. In reality, the United States has often employed industrial policy, both explicitly during wartime mobilizations and less explicitly through defense procurements, subsidies, and tax policy. For the United States, World War I was a sobering lesson in the realities of military mobilization. When the United States entered the conflict in April 1917, unclear lines of authority and conflicts between industrial advisory committees with overlapping jurisdictions delayed the effective mobilization of wartime production. One study noted that the U.S. government ordered 50,000 artillery pieces from domestic manufacturers in 2017, but only 143 were completed in time to be used before the armistice in November 1918.

On the eve of World War II, as the specter of war was clearly visible over Europe, the United States sought to avoid the mistakes of two decades earlier. On September 8, 1939, President Franklin Delano Roosevelt proclaimed a limited national emergency and called for national defense mobilization. In December 1941, less than two weeks after the Japanese bombed Pearl Harbor, the United States passed the First War Powers Act, which was followed in March 1942 with the Second War Powers Act, which built on the first. These acts made it possible to quickly ramp up wartime production and allowed for seizures of land for military purposes, among other measures. The War Powers Acts formed the foundation for the 1950 Defense Production Act, which the United States rather belatedly invoked in its Covid-19 response.

Following World War II, U.S. economic policy generally followed the macroeconomic theories of John Maynard Keynes. Keynesian economics, with its focus on government investment to increase demand, went hand in hand with active government planning. In February 1960, President Dwight Eisenhower organized the President's Commission on National Goals. The commission's final report, issued in November 1960, proposed national goals in fifteen areas of domestic and foreign policy.

U.S. industrial policy during the 1950s and '60s was predominantly Keynesian, with some tariffs protecting certain industries that lessened over time. During the 1970s, the United States experienced economic turmoil in the form of rising inflation and an energy crisis. At the same time, Japan rose as a new economic competitor. These twin pressures led to renewed calls for a U.S. industrial policy.

Lester Thurow, an MIT economist, was emblematic of the new promoters of a U.S. industrial policy. Tall and blond, Thurow was a prolific writer who became a fixture on television and the lecture circuit in the late 1970s. He believed that inflation and unemployment would not resolve automatically and that, to keep up with a rising Japan, the U.S. government needed a hand in the coordination of major investment decisions. "Japan Inc. needs to be met with U.S.A. Inc.," he wrote in *The Zero-Sum Society* in 1980.

Industrial policy proposals also became the subject of discussion in Congress. In May 1975, Democratic senator Hubert H. Humphrey and Republican senator Jacob Javits introduced the Balanced Growth and Economic Planning Act, which would have created an economic planning board within the Executive Office of the President with the responsibility to create a balanced economic growth plan and assure adequate national supplies of raw materials and energy. Humphrey cast economic planning as a necessity for avoiding economic catastrophe.

While the bill had support from academics and union leaders, it was opposed by the incoming Carter administration and did not receive a vote. Congress ultimately passed the Full Employment and Balanced Growth Act of 1978, also known as the Humphrey-Hawkins Act, which required presidential administrations to set employment and inflation goals, but created no new institutions to achieve them.

In a 1982 article, Robert Reich, an economist who later served as secretary of labor under Bill Clinton, made an impassioned call for an industrial policy to restructure the U.S. economy to fit the era of globalization. The piece could easily have been written in the United States during the 2016 presidential election season or the years following:

> *Today, in the public mind at least, unemployment lines in Detroit have replaced the traditional belching smokestack as the symbol of the nation's economy. Fueled by this grimness of mood, discussions of industrial policy in America have finally lost their innocence. Or perhaps it is fairer to say that the nation itself has lost its economic innocence—the genial assurance that American industry would, without government intervention, provide an unfailing engine for bettering the American standard of living.*

*Under these changed circumstances, we can no longer afford the lux-
ury of easy or painless answers to the problems of industry . . . Instead,
we must face the fact that wrenching structural changes will have to be
made in the economy if America's industrial base is to regain its full
international competitiveness. And these changes will, in turn, require
a carefully drawn industrial policy both to encourage the flow of capital
where it is needed and to ease the inevitable dislocations of the labor
force.*

Reich offered a vision for how the United States could adapt to globalization and technology. He suggested that the emphasis on strategic
investment, rather than stimulating demand, was the key to structural
economic change. He compared industrial policy to a more large-scale
version of how companies plan their futures: by strategically choosing
where to invest their resources for maximal growth.

But Reich's plan was never adopted. The election of Ronald Reagan
in 1980 had presaged a hard turn toward supply-side economics and the
end of the abortive moves toward industrial policy that characterized the
1970s. In a sense, the United States has not had an intentional industrial
policy since the beginning of the Reagan era. It has continued to push
free trade through agreements like NAFTA, under the assumption that
the free market is the best way to ensure prosperity.

In 1992, Bill Clinton promised to convert military resources to fund
civilian infrastructure and research projects. To this end, he selected
Laura Tyson, an industrial policy advocate at the University of California
at Berkeley, as the chair of the Council of Economic Advisors. However,
it was not Tyson but conventional free-market economists Robert Rubin
and Lawrence Summers who ended up driving economic policy during
the Clinton administration. Clinton abandoned the conversion policy
and pursued an economic policy focused on liquidity, limited spending,
and free trade. That basic policy continued during the Bush and Obama
administrations.

––––––––––

It took three powerful new forces to make U.S. policymakers rethink
these assumptions. First was the rise of China, second was the rise of

Trump, and third, as just outlined, was the novel coronavirus, which served as a catalyst.

Since the 1990s, China has pursued a strategy of civil-military fusion designed to remove barriers between the country's civilian and military sectors so that technological advances can strengthen both China's economy and its military. President Xi has particularly emphasized this strategy, which, since 2010, has led to major increases in the capabilities of the People's Liberation Army.

Civil-military fusion has effectively blurred the line between the commercial behavior of Chinese companies and the goals of the Chinese state. The Chinese telecommunications company Huawei is one of the most prominent examples of this phenomenon; although Huawei is nominally owned by its employees, its CEO, Ren Zhengfei, was a member of the PLA prior to founding the company in 1987. The United States and other Western countries have implicated Huawei in multiple instances of espionage and intellectual property theft.

The newfound acceptance, at least in theory, that industrial policy might not be merely a relic of the United States' wartime past had immediate implications for several other areas of U.S.-Chinese competition, from investment in critical industries such as telecommunications and artificial intelligence to shutting China out of the semiconductor industry and even to pharmaceuticals.

Huawei again provides a good example. National security analysts had sounded the alarm for years about the risk the Chinese telecommunications giant would pose if it were allowed to dominate global 5G network rollouts—potentially gaining access to information highways the world over. That's a lot of power for any company to have, but it's especially concerning given Huawei's close ties to the Chinese government and to Beijing's explicit and increasingly strict policy of requiring total political loyalty from private companies. Though Huawei has claimed it would rebuff any requests by Chinese government officials to hand over data, it doesn't seem to have any legal standing to do so. China's 2017 National Intelligence Law requires that "any organization or citizen shall support, assist, and cooperate with state intelligence work according to law."

Huawei didn't rise to global prominence purely out of the sheer brilliance and hard work of its executives. Since 2008, as a December 2019 investigation by the *Wall Street Journal* revealed, the company had received up to $75 billion in government support in the form of favorable loan terms, tax breaks, grants, and other discounts. This sum dwarfs any state support received by Nokia and Ericsson, its primary competitors. The massive financial support had allowed Huawei to grow into a global behemoth that could undersell competitors by up to 30 percent, making it nearly impossible for firms from other countries to compete.

As early as 2012, the U.S. House Intelligence Committee had pushed to block Chinese telecommunications firms from expanding in the United States and winning major infrastructure contracts. That block was put in place, but in subsequent years, no efforts were made to address the market failures that had prevented U.S. telecommunications firms from becoming 5G competitors or that were allowing Huawei to undersell competition and achieve global dominance.

These measures were defensive at best. They didn't address the underlying problem because it was a problem that neoliberal leanings in the United States had predetermined could not exist: market forces alone were unable to resolve the challenges that China's economic and political rise was creating.

That's because there were at least three kinds of market failures under way: the Chinese government's own intervention in international markets through state support provided for Chinese companies; the distortion of markets through the addition of often illiberal political incentives; and the overwhelming tendency of private firms to pursue profit over any other, larger social objective unless forced by law to do so.

Thus, debate over Huawei stalled for years. Politicians and business leaders in the United States and Europe suffered from an ideological handicap. It was impossible to believe that Chinese government industrial policy had buoyed Huawei to global success, because that would imply that massive government intervention worked. It was easier to believe that either Huawei posed no real risk and that any warnings were simply a result of the national security complex's overactive imagination; or that Chinese state support for Huawei would ultimately backfire, as state intervention always must, and thus there was nothing to worry about.

Huawei was, in some ways, a case of extremes. The company was the clear global champion of 5G—Nokia and Ericsson are too expensive to be able to compete in almost any developing market—and the risk it poses is extremely high. Imagine a world powered by 5G that is more or less directly accessible by the Chinese government.

———————

Enter President Trump. His presidential campaign and election had already turned the traditional left-right divide over free trade on its head. Republicans had long opposed government intervention in the economy or overly cumbersome regulations on free trade. Democrats, for their part, had supported trade regulations that protected labor rights, making them less supportive of free trade agreements. But Trump drew the Republican Party in a heavily protectionist direction and spent much of his campaign railing against Chinese trade policies that he said harmed U.S. workers. Though he was widely scorned on the left, mainstream U.S. news outlets still sent scores of reporters to cover the difficulties of life in hollowed-out former industrial towns. Trump consistently framed China as an existential threat that required breaking old norms. In May 2016, in response to concerns over his proposed tariffs on Chinese imports, he said, "We're losing $500 billion in trade with China. Who the hell cares if there's a trade war?"

Almost through sheer force of personality, Trump succeeded in convincing most of the United States that China's trade policies were in fact harmful to Americans and that the U.S. government needed to take action, even if what actions those should be remained highly controversial.

After more than a year of China policy doldrums, Trump finally launched a trade war on Beijing in the summer of 2018 by levying tens of billions of dollars in tariffs on Chinese-made goods. Beijing soon reciprocated, prompting a downward spiral of mutual tariffs.

Trump's trade war with China was a watershed moment that scrambled traditional political coalitions. Some Democrats in Congress praised the president's actions, while some Republicans were more apt to warn about the potential economic impacts of the tariffs. At its core, the trade war was the first expression of a new bipartisan consensus that policymakers could no longer rely on free markets alone to curb China's policies.

The trade war more or less ended in a stalemate in early 2020 with the signing of the Phase One Trade Agreement, which removed some but not all of the tariffs without accomplishing the significant structural change Trump had promised. There was never a Phase Two. The Phase One Trade Agreement is not viewed as a success, and few are interested in reviving it. But Biden maintained many of the tariffs Trump first levied, and the vast controversy this created resulted in extensive public debate over the U.S. economic relationship with China and close scrutiny of whom the status quo was actually benefiting.

While Trump's actions initially focused on the economic impact of China's policies, policymakers and U.S. officials soon began to see the protection of U.S. industries as a national security imperative as well. The transformation was relatively swift. In January 2018, U.S. Air Force Brig. Gen. Rob Spalding was removed from a detail at the National Security Council for pushing a plan under which the U.S. government would partner with private industry to construct a 5G network. Axios has reported that the draft plan cited China's "dominant position in the manufacture and operation of network infrastructure" as a rationale for its creation. At the time, Gary Cohn, director of the National Economic Council and Trump's chief economic adviser from 2017 to 2018, thought the plan was, simply put, nuts.

But in February 2018, the Trump administration approved a U.S. Strategic Framework for the Indo-Pacific region as part of its National Security Strategy. The framework, which was declassified in January 2021, laid out some elements of a China-focused industrial strategy, though these were often couched in language that made them less off-putting to those concerned about government intervention in market forces. Four objectives in particular called for a government role in reshaping America's economic ties with China and with other countries in the region. These objectives included: to "incentivize the U.S. private sector to reignite an expeditionary spirit so that it expands two-way trade and investment in the Indo-Pacific"; to "assign strategic purpose to the combined financial resources and economic power of the United States"; to "create a task force on how best to use public-private partnerships"; and to "promote the U.S., ally, and partner-led development of energy, telecommunications, and logistics standards and infrastructure."

"The pandemic has certainly highlighted the prescience of this strategy," a senior White House official whose work focused on China told me in early January 2021, on the day the administration declassified the Strategic Framework. "A lot of countries are talking about 'How do we diversify from overdependence on the Chinese market?' The pandemic revealed things that accelerated that trend."

Throughout 2018 and 2019, U.S. officials began pushing allies and partners to give 5G contracts to Norway's Nokia or South Korea's Samsung, to cancel contracts with Huawei and ZTE, and even to remove existing Huawei equipment already in their telecommunications infrastructure. In 2020, U.S. secretary of state Mike Pompeo launched "the Clean Network," an initiative aimed at garnering international commitments to avoid China's 5G makers and, more broadly, to support data privacy and cybersecurity. By the time the Trump administration ended, a public-private partnership to ensure that China stayed out of U.S. 5G networks would seem like a moderate proposal.

———

Global mask scarcity in the early days of the Covid-19 pandemic landed right amid this transformation, turning a problem largely within the purview of economists and national security wonks into one right in front of the noses of every American.

The supply chain shock had a powerful and lasting impact on industrial strategies in both the United States and Europe. Policymakers concluded that they could no longer trust that the free market would speed needed supplies to them in times of need. As a result, there has been growing support for stockpiling medical equipment, reshoring production domestically, and diversifying supply chains.

The European Commission endorsed the concept of a medical stockpile in March 2020, and since then, the European Union has established six separate stockpiles—in Denmark, Germany, Greece, Hungary, Romania, and Sweden. These "rescEU" stockpiles have delivered more than one million masks to EU member states since their creation. The European Union has also considered policy measures to reshore production. In a March 2021 study, the policy department of the European Parliament's Directorate-General for External Policies of the Union recommended that the bloc establish minimum domestic manufacturing capacities for critical products like PPE.

In the United States, policymakers showed a new willingness to use the levers of government to encourage domestic PPE production. Between

April 2020 and June 2021, the U.S. Department of Defense provided $1.2 billion in subsidies to domestic manufacturers of PPE and to domestic suppliers of key raw materials used in PPE production. In a July 2020 letter to White House chief of staff Mark Meadows, Senator Lindsey Graham—previously an opponent of protectionist industrial policy—proposed requiring that PPE for the U.S. national stockpile be supplied by U.S. producers, describing it as "an issue of national security."

However, the long-term sustainability of these policies remains an open question. The March 2021 European Parliament study found that global supply chains for PPE are centered on lower-income countries and that high-income countries cost producers more and lack the necessary economies of scale and regional supplier networks. In addition, domestic stockpiles of PPE can be neglected and not replenished, just as they were in Europe prior to the Covid-19 pandemic. Nonetheless, the pandemic was a wake-up call for policymakers, exposing China's ability and willingness to manipulate global supply chains in its favor.

3

DUAL-FUNCTION STRATEGY AND CHINA'S CORE INTERESTS

There are now around 60 million people of Chinese heritage living around the world—a figure roughly equivalent to the entire population of Italy. Concerted actions of overseas Chinese communities can have far greater impact than ever before.

The diaspora's efforts to buy up face masks at the start of the Covid-19 pandemic didn't just see billions of items of PPE sent back to China. Their efforts also ended up bringing unprecedented international scrutiny to United Front work. Researchers soon noticed that many of the groups helping to organize the shipments had links to the Chinese government's Overseas Chinese Affairs Office and to the party's United Front Work Department and that these offices—both tasked with political guidance of overseas Chinese groups—had issued calls for PPE shipments back to China.

The United Front Work Department, after spending decades virtually unknown outside China and Chinese-speaking communities, has recently achieved a degree of international notoriety. It's a party bureau and, really, an entire way of thinking, one that played an instrumental role in the party's eventual triumph over the Nationalists during the Chinese Civil War that ended in 1949. The department is tasked with reaching out to all levels of Chinese society that aren't already incorporated into the party bureaucracy in some other way and ensuring that everyone is working toward the party's goals or, at the very least, not actively working against them—hence, a "united front."

United Front work, on a grassroots level, harnesses the organizing power of what would otherwise be an independent civil society. By no means is this all sticks; there are plenty of carrots. In contemporary society in China, United Front work often involves party cadres identifying up-and-coming members of society—youth activists, prominent members of ethnic minority groups, successful entrepreneurs, rising journalists—and offering them positions in related party-affiliated organizations such as the All-China Women's Federation, the All-China Journalists Association, and local and provincial bodies of the Chinese People's Political Consultative Conference. This gives the emerging leader a platform, recognized social status, and a clear upward trajectory through the ranks of that organization's bureaucracy; in return, the emerging leader brings their activities in line with the organization's goals, representing their community upward and representing the party's goals and interests downward and back to the community from which they came.

Party-affiliated organizations in China can offer a meaningful outlet for community building and social organizing. They can facilitate business development and international exchange. You could call United Front work a kind of consensus building with Leninist characteristics, offering party outsiders a path to representation, success, and prosperity—as long as they agree to conduct their activities within party parameters and to participate when needed in various party initiatives. A less flattering way to put it would be that United Front work co-opts true civil society and independent community leaders in China by giving them a position that carries prestige and opportunity, but that also places their work under the direct oversight of the party, commandeering their successes and making their continued prestige dependent upon their obedience to the party. This is precisely the kind of relationship that the Chinese Communist Party wants to have with overseas Chinese groups.

The Qing dynasty, which fell in 1911, did not establish this oversight—and that was its downfall. Chinese reformist and revolutionary groups were crushed inside imperial China but flourished beyond its borders, with communities of like-minded intellectuals and activists networking everywhere from Japan to the United States to Britain. Chinese revolutionary leader Sun Yat-sen, later to become the father of modern China, founded the Tongmenghui, or the United League, in 1905, to unite far-flung Chinese secret revolutionary societies. The United League expanded quickly, with three dozen offices in Southeast Asia alone and chapters in Boston, Chicago, Havana, Honolulu, Montreal, New Orleans, New York,

San Francisco, Vancouver, and Wellington, New Zealand. From abroad, the United League masterminded a series of rebellions inside China, with one final rebellion, the Wuchang Uprising, eventually leading to the fall of the Qing dynasty and the creation of the Republic of China in 1912.

The Chinese Communist Party is often quite good at learning from history, and the danger of Chinese dissidents abroad is one lesson it learned very well. The party's United Front Work Department and those who do its work regardless of their official title have long operated beyond China's borders. In the early decades of the People's Republic of China, the department's primary overseas target was Taiwan's Nationalist Party (also known as the Kuomintang), which hadn't been exterminated after its defeat in 1949; it simply fled to Taiwan, where it continued its rule as a government with embassies and supporters around the world enabling its continued existence, supplanting the diplomatic recognition and international power the CCP viewed as its own. The party wouldn't view its civil war triumph as complete until it had replaced the Kuomintang—and, later, the government of Taiwan—as the sole recognized ruler of a complete and unified greater China.

The United Front Work Department's "work" abroad began, then, as a struggle against Kuomintang supporters in Taiwan itself and within diaspora communities in leading cities around the world. From the 1950s until the '80s, United Front work abroad was limited primarily to tiny turf wars within Chinatowns, as people aligned with Beijing sought to supplant local opportunities for pro-Taiwan groups.

After the 1989 Tiananmen pro-democracy movement was decimated by the party's military crackdown, pro-democracy Chinese fled abroad in droves. The fear of overseas pro-democracy organizing set off the party's most urgent internal alarms. So leaders in Beijing made a huge new push, pouring resources into United Front work abroad to co-opt overseas Chinese community organizations; keep tabs on dissidents; co-opt or shutter independent Chinese-language community newspapers; and establish new, well-funded pro-Beijing organizations to drown out independent groups.

The effort has been incredibly successful. There are now thousands of chapters of various Beijing-aligned organizations in cities all around the world—from party fronts such as "peaceful reunification" societies, now located in more than seventy countries, to Chinese business associations and other community groups founded with the party's blessing. Chinese students abroad have been a particular target; foreign universities once served as fertile ground for Qing dynasty–era Chinese reformers and even, ironically, for China's earliest Communists.

Under President Xi Jinping, United Front work has increasingly become a critical component of China's foreign policy, a type of shadow diplomacy that operates outside official channels. In October 2018, the United Front Work Department was reorganized to place greater emphasis on targeting overseas Chinese, and the Overseas Chinese Affairs Office, a government office, was put under the direct supervision of the department, a party bureau, suggesting that greater political control would be exerted over Beijing's relations with the Chinese diaspora. In other words, the party ate the state.

The Chinese government has downplayed the importance of the United Front Work Department, but the way it allocates resources to the department suggests otherwise. The Ministry of Finance doesn't publish the budget of the central UFWD, though it does for many other government and party departments. But one clever American researcher, Ryan Fedasiuk, compiled budget documents for key organizations affiliated with the central UFWD and found that its combined annual budget circa 2019 amounted to at least $1.4 billion and perhaps as much as $1.8 billion. "There is a universal truth known to government bureaucrats in every country: budgets speak louder than words," Fedasiuk wrote.

On an organizational and strategic level, the United Front Work Department sometimes acts more like an intelligence agency. This is particularly true in its operations abroad, where, as a party bureau, it can't operate aboveground. The UFWD sometimes works directly alongside, or even competes with, the Ministry of State Security and the PLA's political intelligence arm. Party cadres who hold an official position in the United Front Work Department may "double-hat" as government bureaucrats, such as diplomats posted to Chinese embassies abroad who also hold publicly undisclosed positions in the department.

To be clear—by no means is every ethnic Chinese person or group around the world linked to the Chinese Communist Party, and to perpetuate this idea would result in harmful profiling and discrimination. "This isn't necessarily representative of Chinese diaspora communities," Alex Joske, a researcher at the Australian Strategic Policy Institute, said in a September 2020 interview with Bloomberg. "Only a small number of overseas ethnic Chinese might be tied to United Front groups, but the groups can be highly effective at mobilizing and getting their message out there."

The key to understanding groups that do at times throw their lot in with the Chinese embassy or the party's United Front is that they are, the vast majority of the time, real community organizations that also engage in meaningful and genuine community activities, such as children's educational events, Chinese New Year celebrations, elderly support, and local political engagement. At the same time, they are careful never to cross any of the party's red lines and may also respond to the party's calls for assistance from time to time. It is thus very difficult to parse from the outside which overseas Chinese community groups are truly independent and which fall somewhere along the spectrum of alignment with Beijing.

———

This explains why researchers raised alarms when organizations as benign-sounding as the Fujian Economic and Cultural Exchange Association started shipping masks back to China. Researchers who focused on Chinese Communist Party–linked organizations abroad had never seen so much activity all at once, in so many places around the world, to accomplish the same goal. Because the United Front Work Department's efforts in Chinese diaspora communities have so often focused on pushing the party's political goals and silencing dissent, a global humanitarian campaign involving these groups attracted scrutiny and suspicion.

This is the essence of what I call the party's "dual-function strategy." Party leaders choose to use—abuse, in fact—legitimate organizations for their own political purposes. Dual-function strategy goes hand in hand with United Front work, both inside China and beyond its borders, and stems from the party's fundamental belief that its power belongs everywhere. The strategy has obvious ill effects. It casts suspicion on community organizations and fans fears of a "fifth column," the idea that a significant number of members of a society are secret sleeper agents loyal to a foreign power.

Organizations that are either formally part of the party bureaucracy (such as government-run organizations and party committees) or informally guided by the party (such as some overseas Chinese organizations, "sister city" relationships, and, increasingly, private enterprises) frequently work toward goals that could universally be considered good. Neighborhood party committees in cities across China served as pandemic response teams in the early days of the Covid-19 pandemic, informing local residents about swiftly evolving government policies, delivering food and medicine to people in lockdown, and helping identify which residents needed to be hospitalized. In January and February 2020, while Hubei Province was still buried in unprecedented lockdowns, overseas Chinese groups under the United Front umbrella collected masks and other PPE to ship to Wuhan and other Covid-19 hot spots. By April and May, as China began to get control of its domestic epidemic, masks began to flow in the other direction; Chinese cities began facilitating donations and sales of PPE to their sister cities around the world, including numerous cities across the United States.

But these same structures can and have been used as levers of coercive party power. Party committees can relay political directives downward to local residents and report on any potentially subversive political activities just as effectively as they can deal with public health–related directives. United Front–linked overseas organizations often work to suppress dissent in Chinese diaspora communities. Sister city relationships have been used to block, or attempt to block, U.S. municipal-level engagement with Taiwan. In one example from Rockville, Maryland, pro-Beijing members of the board overseeing Rockville's "friendship city" relationship with a Chinese city tried, unsuccessfully, in 2018 to prevent Rockville from also forming a sister city relationship with Yilan, Taiwan—a story I will explore further in the next chapter. As Xi Jinping has extended party guidance to private enterprise, business ties too have become a means of Chinese party-state political coercion abroad.

Dual function is one important manifestation of the party's lack of political restraint in its diplomatic, economic, and people-to-people exchanges with other countries. As a strategy, dual function was highly effective as long as Beijing was able to implement it quietly and without being noticed. It allowed China's leaders to claim they were engaging openly with the democratic world while simultaneously maximizing their access to political, economic, and social targets around the globe. But as democratic societies have become more aware of the party's actions, the dual-function strategy has begun to backfire, bringing greater, not less, attention to party activities.

The dual-function strategy is incredibly divisive within host societies. People who focus on defending the rights of Chinese immigrant communities often believe that suspicion targeting them is racist and McCarthyist fearmongering, while those who focus on uncovering the party's influence abroad often deride pro-immigrant, anti-racist work as naive at best and complicit at worst.

Overseas Chinese communities are the first and the last victims of this dynamic. They are caught in the middle, between a powerful Leninist state with expansive global aims on the one hand and the legitimate fears and illegitimate fearmongering and racism that simmer in host countries on the other. If the Chinese government truly cared about the well-being of ethnic Chinese abroad, as it claims to, it would immediately cease its decades-long efforts to control, harass, surveil, and influence them. It would prioritize their freedom and well-being over its own geopolitical ambitions.

Without a change of heart in Beijing, however, its dual-function strategy is unlikely to cease anytime soon. The best approach for democratic societies to blunt Beijing's strategy while preserving the civil rights of Chinese diaspora communities is three-tiered: to increase public awareness of the dual-function strategy; to ask Chinese communities what they need in order to feel safe and welcome in their homes; and to offer extra attention and support to members of the Chinese diaspora who are the primary targets of United Front pressure—namely, activists, political and religious refugees, Uyghurs, Tibetans, Hong Kongers, and Taiwanese.

4

SPIES AND SISTER CITIES

One of the most egregious examples of the Chinese Communist Party's abuse of otherwise legitimate organizations is the case of Christine Fang, a suspected Chinese intelligence operative who used a friendship city relationship as a launching pad for a yearslong operation targeting U.S. politicians and government officials from coast to coast. She initiated sexual relationships with between ten and fifteen mayors in states across the country and had other sexual encounters with California officials—including an up-and-coming young Democrat named Eric Swalwell. And she did this, U.S. intelligence officials believe, while under the direction of the Ministry of State Security, China's intelligence agency.

Fang's operation was part of a twofold strategy, U.S. intelligence officials believe. The first was a long game of cultivating close ties with up-and-coming U.S. politicians and officials, knowing that today's mayors and city councilors are tomorrow's governors and members of Congress. If Fang could build trusting relationships with even just a few officials who ended up in the upper echelons of power a few years down the line, that would be espionage gold. She very nearly succeeded; Swalwell did not learn of her true motives until the eve of his appointment to the House Intelligence Committee, whose members are privy to some of the United States' top state secrets.[*]

The second element of her strategy was what is known as subnational

---

[*] This chapter includes extensive reporting contributed by Zach Dorfman, who coauthored the Axios investigation on Christine Fang and Eric Swalwell.

engagement, which refers to direct outreach to state and local governments instead of to the federal government—or, as the Chinese Communist Party calls it, "using the local to surround the center" (以地方包围中央). The party views subnational engagement as a backdoor channel of influence with interlocutors who often lack the knowledge and leverage to deal with the party in a fully informed way. These ties can be used for purely economic reasons, such as to help Chinese companies win local U.S. contracts. But, more important, by building up close relations with local and state governments and shaping their views of China, the party can rely on them to support policies that are friendly to Beijing—an especially important lever of influence when the national government itself is hostile.

In Christine Fang's aggressive pursuit of both strategies, her case was among the most sensational that U.S. intelligence officials had ever seen. Rodney Faraon, a former CIA analyst who had helped lead a major investigation into a covert Chinese state–backed attempt to influence the 1996 presidential election, described the Fang case as a new classic in the canon of espionage cases. "It's got everything. It's got politics of the highest stakes. It's got the Chinese government, the U.S. government, it's got sex," Faraon said. "Usually things are much more mundane. There are times when truth is far more interesting and exciting than fiction."

———————

Christine Fang is almost a mirage, both prominent and elusive. Next to nothing is known about her life before she set foot on U.S. soil or what she has done since she left. Despite the wide circle of high-powered acquaintances she accumulated during her years in California, no one really seemed to know her well. She never spoke of her family. No one knew what city in China she was from, though one person referred to her on social media as "Beijing Christine." There is no known video footage of her; there are no publicly available court documents or government indictments laying out her alleged actions.

There's certainly one part of her background that Fang's Bay Area friends could never have guessed. Fang met on multiple occasions with a man named Zhang Weiwei, a diplomat at the Chinese consulate in San Francisco who, U.S. intelligence officials believe, was a Ministry of

State Security official under diplomatic cover. (Placing intelligence agents under diplomatic cover in embassies abroad is a common practice among many governments, including the United States.) Later, FBI counterintelligence officials would come to suspect that Fang's parents worked for the Ministry of State Security, China's main civilian spy agency. In China, working for the Ministry of State Security is often a family affair.

My colleague Zach Dorfman and I spent more than a year tracking Fang down, interviewing twenty-two people who knew her personally and diving deep into archived corners of the internet to retrieve long-deleted photographs and social media posts. Despite all the unknowns that remain with regard to Fang's background and her life in China, we were able to uncover a wealth of information about what she did, both openly and secretly, while in the United States.

Fang is beautiful. Photos of her show a confident young woman with a cascade of hair and a sweet smile. She looks very young in photos, but most people we spoke to said she was in her late twenties or early thirties and that she seemed mature. Bay Area acquaintances said she dressed well, carried designer bags, and drove a white Mercedes. Several acquaintances said she seemed to come from money; there is no evidence that she held any paid positions during the years she lived in the United States. Fang told one acquaintance that she had previously worked as a flight attendant, but that is scarcely more than a working-class job in China and seems inconsistent with her expensive, job-free lifestyle in California.

(The crews of some Chinese airlines have a history of alleged involvement in espionage-related activities. Most recently, in November 2021, the U.S. Department of Homeland Security noted in an internal memo that it had "observed instances of possible assistance with foreign intelligence collection being conducted by Air China airline employees" at Los Angeles International Airport.)

Fang enrolled as a student at California State University, East Bay, as early as fall 2011. CSU East Bay is a commuter school. Much of its undergraduate and graduate population comprises nontraditional students who hold full-time jobs while going to school or who have enrolled in college at a later age, meaning that students ranging in age from eighteen to forty and above may be in classes together. The university declined to confirm Fang's enrollment or what degree she was pursuing, but several

acquaintances said that she spoke of wanting to work in the hotel industry. CSU East Bay offers both a bachelor's and a master's in hospitality.

It's unclear how Christine Fang chose CSU East Bay. There are numerous major universities in the Bay Area—Stanford, Berkeley, San
Francisco State University, and UC San Francisco, to name a few—and
dozens of smaller schools and community colleges. Though the prestige
that a major university would have conferred could have given Fang easier
access to the halls of power, it would also have come with a greater degree
of scrutiny—from the university itself, from world-wise classmates, and
from well-placed alumni. She would have had to compete for leadership
positions on campus and gradually work her way up. In 2020, for example, the Chinese Students and Scholars Association at Berkeley had
almost five thousand registered members.

But at CSU East Bay, Fang was the unopposed queen. Within weeks
of enrolling, she was already the president of the school's Chinese Student
Association. The group didn't seem to exist before her arrival; it's likely
she founded the organization herself as soon as she arrived, with the blessing of the Chinese consulate in San Francisco.

Politically speaking, the 2011/12 academic year was Fang's quiet year.
Very few people we spoke to in Bay Area politics knew her back then. Her
Facebook profile includes hundreds of photos showing her at local political events, but few of these date as far back as 2011. Rather, she seems
to have spent that year getting her bearings and building up the Chinese
Student Association (CSSA). Under her leadership, the CSSA organized
basketball tournaments, Chinese New Year celebrations, and other student events. Participants in these events described Fang as busy and enthusiastic. In 2013, the university awarded her a campus pride award for
her work with the CSSA.

Fang also began making some initial connections in the local Asian
American community. One of those early connections was C. C. Yin, the
Chinese American founder of Asian American Pacific Islander American
Public Affairs (APAPA), a Bay Area–based civic organization dedicated
to helping Asian Americans, a traditionally underrepresented group, get
involved in politics. Yin, who was in his mid-seventies when Fang arrived
in the United States, owned more than two dozen McDonald's restaurants in the Bay Area and used his considerable wealth to support Asian
American political candidates.

Fang soon became president of the campus chapter of APAPA, which she used, alongside the CSSA, as a platform for attracting local politicians and government officials to campus events. In October 2012, the APAPA national organization sponsored the Chinese Student Association's annual member gala, which Fang organized. Yin was a featured speaker at the event, as was Mark Green, the mayor of Union City. Another was Eric Swalwell, then still a Dublin city council member. This event would mark the first documented meeting between Swalwell and Fang—perhaps, for both of them, a fateful meeting. The next month, Swalwell would win his campaign to serve as U.S. representative from California's Fifteenth Congressional District, unseating a longtime progressive Democrat.

Fang's political activity began to take off during this period. As her star rose, she left behind an ever-widening set of footprints in Bay Area society, and it became easier for Zach and me to fill in the details of her life. In 2012, she organized a town hall with Representative Judy Chu, the first Chinese American woman to serve in the U.S. Congress; in a group photo taken at the time, Fang stands next to Chu. In 2013, Fang co-hosted a fund-raiser for Representative Tulsi Gabbard, posing for a photo with her and then-U.S. House congressional candidate Ro Khanna and Raj Salwan, a Fremont city council member. In 2014, she volunteered at an on-campus activity supporting Khanna's campaign for Congress. (The campaign failed in 2014 but succeeded in 2016.) Fang attended fund-raisers and other political events in support of then-San Francisco mayor Ed Lee, according to an acquaintance present at the gatherings. Lee passed away in 2017.

Throughout 2014, Fang interacted frequently with Swalwell's office. That year, she bundled donations for Swalwell's reelection campaign. She often sent the résumés of young Chinese students to be considered as interns in his office; at least one of these students was given an internship in his office in Washington. In May 2014, Fang organized a "Miss China University" student beauty pageant and invited local politicians to attend; Swalwell did not attend, but he sent the Chinese Student Association a signed "certificate of special congressional recognition" for the event. One local elected official told us that, during this period, they had seen Swalwell and Fang arrive at political events together on at least three occasions.

Fang's bundling activities caught the attention of one local political operative, who made some quiet inquiries to ensure that the donations were legitimate and weren't "straw donations," a form of illegal donation in which a person is compensated for their contribution. The political operative told us that the Katrina Leung case in the early 2000s had had a chilling effect on the involvement of Asian Americans in California politics. Leung, a prominent California-based socialite and Republican activist, had served as an FBI informant—until the U.S. government charged her with serving as a double agent for China. Leung had championed the participation of Asian Americans in U.S. politics; her fall had compounded the reservations that many Asian Americans in California had about getting politically involved. The political operative wanted to ensure that no such scandal again damaged the ability of Asian Americans to participate in politics without suspicion. The person found no evidence that the donations Fang brought to Swalwell's campaign were illegal, easing their concerns.

By 2015, Fang's list of acquaintances was a veritable who's who of prominent Bay Area figures, including current and former mayors, city commissioners, state representatives, and many staffers and local donors. "She was everywhere," Raj Salwan told my colleague Zach. "She was an active student. I was surprised at how active she was and how she knew so many politicos."

During this time, Fang also expanded her network across the United States, first through a position as an intern in the office of Fremont mayor Bill Harrison. She then led the creation in September 2013 of a friendship city relationship between Fremont and Yiyang, a city in China's Hunan Province. In a photo taken at the signing ceremony, Fang is standing behind Harrison and the Chinese official from Yiyang, with the U.S. and Chinese flags on either side.

Harrison told me in a phone call that he first met Fang through events hosted by the Chinese Student Association. "She was interested in learning more about politics," he said. As she became more involved with the mayor's office, and with the Fremont-Yiyang city relationship, she began to travel with Harrison and other colleagues when they attended meetings of the U.S Conference of Mayors, held twice each year, once in Washington, DC, and once elsewhere in the United States.

Mark Stodola, who served as the mayor of Little Rock, Arkansas, from 2007 through 2018, told me in a phone call that he saw Fang on at least two different occasions at the U.S. Conference of Mayors. He did not recall what years or in what cities he saw her. Little Rock has a sister city relationship with the northeastern Chinese city of Changchun. Stodola told me that Fang was "very personable" and that she was "greeting lots of different people." He said he has no other recollection of her and that they had no further contact.

Fang's affiliation with sister cities and a mayor's office was all the access she needed. It was during this time that she began to initiate sexual relationships with mayors from around the United States—as many as fifteen. On one occasion, she met a mayor in a parked car, where they had a sexual encounter. Unbeknownst to them both, however, the car was under FBI electronic surveillance. The elected official seemed to understand that it was almost unbelievable that such a beautiful young woman would be interested in him. When he asked her why, she told him she wanted to spend time with him in order to improve her English. On another occasion, according to one former U.S. intelligence official, the FBI intercepted a phone call between Fang and a local official that started out as a coded conversation and then turned into sexually explicit banter.

In March 2014, Fang flew to Washington, DC, to attend the U.S.-China Sister Cities Conference. The event was hosted by the Chinese embassy and jointly held by Sister Cities International and the Chinese People's Association for Friendship with Foreign Countries (CPAFFC). It brought together mayors from across the United States and China, including the mayor of Shenzhen and the mayor of Cupertino, and other U.S. elected officials, including U.S. Representative Mike Honda. That weekend, the Chinese embassy also hosted a celebration of the thirty-fifth anniversary of the establishment of diplomatic relations with the United States. Fang posed for photos with various dignitaries, including Judy Chu, and also snapped a photo of Swalwell, Judy Chu, and the Chinese ambassador to the United States, Cui Tiankai, as they posed together for a group photo. (Fang would later send two other photos taken at this event to a student journalist in California, who captioned them as Fang together with Nancy Pelosi and Fang together with Swalwell and Ambassador Cui; while the captions remained in an archived version of the article, the images themselves were not saved.)

Gilbert Wong, at the time the mayor of Cupertino, told us that he saw Fang at the Sister Cities Conference and also at a hotel, where she was accompanied by an older white mayor from the Midwest. The mayor told Wong that Fang was his girlfriend, emphasizing that their relationship was genuine despite the large age difference between them.

Wong had met Fang at several events in California but was stunned to see her at the Chinese embassy in Washington, DC. "I saw her as a young, attractive Chinese lady who is an international student," he said. He had noted her very forward behavior but thought that she was perhaps trying to secure a husband and a green card to have a better life in the United States. It "never crossed my mind that she was involved in any espionage," he said.

———————

To understand how profound an abuse of sister city relationships Fang's behavior represents, it's helpful to jump back in time seventy years, to the early days of rivalry between the democratic West and the Communist East.

The Cold War often brought out the United States' worst impulses. But the creation of sister cities represents a time when it brought out our best. In 1956, the Iron Curtain seemed vulnerable. A series of popular uprisings in Poland and then Hungary made international headlines as people protested their Soviet-led governments. The protests renewed discussion in Western democracies of pushback against Soviet dominance.

In September of that year, U.S. president Dwight D. Eisenhower offered a new proposal to "widen every possible chink in the Iron Curtain"—an international people-to-people program that would bring together students, professors, business executives, tourists, doctors, and labor unions from different countries.

This new program, Eisenhower said in a speech at the White House, would be "based upon the assumption that no people, as such, wants war—that all people want peace." Lack of understanding of other peoples and societies was a major barrier to peace, he said, because ignorance made it easy to believe the worst of one another. And governments were making it difficult for people from different countries to have the chance to get to know each other. The solution, then, was to find a way to "evade governments, to work out, not one method, but thousands of methods by which people can gradually learn a little bit more of each other." Eisenhower hailed the "great promise of people-to-people and sister city affiliations in helping build the solid structure of world peace."

That's how the U.S. nonprofit Sister Cities International, which facilitates international local-to-local partnerships, was established. U.S. cities first began partnering with cities in Germany and Japan, aiming to strengthen ties between these former enemies. The program gradually expanded to include many other countries. As of 2019, Sister Cities International counted more than 1,800 partnerships across 138 countries.

If you speak to people involved on both sides of sister city relationships and who attend local meetings, you'll find that they are usually far more motivated by ideals than by politics. The original goal of sister cities as laid out in the postwar period remains a driving principle: to form grassroots friendships between people of two different cities without the strain of politics getting in the way. Typical activities coordinated between sister cities include high school student exchanges, cultural celebrations, music festivals, community lecture series, and reciprocal delegations between local officials.

The people-to-people exchanges that sister relationships foster are local, genuine, beneficial, and, generally speaking, free of the international political tensions that might inhibit higher-profile exchanges. Many sister cities have student programs that bring high school students from the partner city for short-term homestays. These programs are part of a healthy multilayered fabric of civil society organizations that help expand international opportunities to students who may not have access to elite programs such as the National Security Language Initiative for Youth, which is funded by the State Department, or to private student exchange programs that may charge thousands of dollars in fees.

China also has sister cities. Since the normalization of Sino-American relations in 1978, it has established hundreds of sister city and provincial-level relationships with U.S. states and municipalities. The first relationship was created in 1979, when Nanjing and St. Louis became sister cities, followed soon after by Shanghai and San Francisco. By 2005, China maintained friendship relationships with 1,247 cities and 405 provinces in 129 countries. The lion's share of these friendship cities and states were in the United States, followed by Europe, then East Asia and Southeast Asia. Africa and South America had relatively few.

A sister state relationship played an important role in Xi Jinping's early ties to the United States and, later, as part of his debut as China's top leader. In 1980, Xi's father, Xi Zhongxun, led a group of Chinese provincial governors to Iowa, where they met with the state's governor. Three years later, Iowa governor Terry Branstad and the governor of China's Hebei Province formed an official sister state relationship between Iowa and Hebei.

In April 1985, a young Xi Jinping led an agricultural delegation to Muscatine, Iowa, among the earliest delegations from Hebei Province to Iowa after the sister state relationship was established. It was the future CCP general secretary's first visit to the United States. As Sarah Lande, who served on the Iowa Sister State Friendship Committee board at the time and, later, as the executive director, recalled, "I was eager for them to come to Muscatine. Muscatine industries and friends gave a warm welcome with potluck meals, home stays, industry visits, and a Kent Feeds boat ride on the Mississippi River."

On February 12, 2012, Xi—now vice president and soon to become China's top leader—paid another visit to Muscatine. Lande hosted Xi at her home, before a big fire kindled in the family's hearth, along with Branstad and other "old friends," as Xi referred to the people he had known years ago. "Coming here is really like coming back home," Lande recalls Xi Jinping saying during the visit. "You cannot even imagine the deep impression I had from my visit twenty-seven years ago, because you were the first Americans I came in contact with. My impression of America came from you. For me, you are America."

But as much as we would like to believe otherwise, the U.S. and Chinese governments have always approached sister city relationships differently. U.S. cities and states typically decide for themselves whether to engage in diplomacy with their counterparts in foreign countries, without any direction by the State Department; Sister Cities International is a nongovernmental organization that provides support and structure. Chinese sister city relations, however, are directly managed by the Chinese People's Association for Friendship with Foreign Countries (CPAFFC), a government organization directed by the party's United Front Work Department.

CPAFFC is a direct extension of the Chinese party-state. It is tasked with "implement[ing] China's independent foreign policy of peace." Its leaders are typically taken from among China's political elites. From 2011 to 2020, the CPAFFC chair was a woman named Li Xiaolin, the daughter of former Chinese president Li Xiannian, who held that position under Deng Xiaoping and then later served as the chair of the Chinese People's Political Consultative Conference. Li herself spent most of her career holding various positions within CPAFFC, except for two years during which she was a political secretary at the Chinese embassy in Washington, DC. She was also deputy director of the foreign affairs committee of the Twelfth Chinese People's Political Consultative Conference National Committee.

Since Xi came to power in 2012, CPAFFC has become more aggressively ideological and has itself, at times, pushed Xi's policies and principles into international partnerships. The efforts to bring sister city relationships in line with Chinese foreign policy goals are evident in the way that Chinese government officials have touted the role of sister cities in the Belt and Road Initiative and that China-based sister cities have themselves frequently promoted the initiative. According to the Guangzhou Foreign Affairs Office, city-to-city relationships should "serve the overall diplomacy of a country." At a November 2019 conference commemorating forty years of sister city relationships with Guangzhou, the capital of Guangdong Province, CPAFFC vice president Xie Yuan gave a keynote speech hailing the Belt and Road Initiative as a key to "reform and improve the global governance system."

The 2018 Sister Cities International annual conference, held in Aurora, Colorado, even included an entire parallel track of events on a Silk Road theme, a reference both to the historic network of trade routes across Central Asia and to Xi Jinping's signature foreign policy initiative, which aims to put China at the center of global diplomacy through extensive infrastructure and investment deals. Now known as the Belt and Road Initiative, China's "New Silk Road" initiative has been accompanied by years of wall-to-wall propaganda. Countries that sign on to the Belt and Road, either formally through a memorandum of understanding or informally by cooperating on projects and investment, have shown a strong tendency to back China on the international stage.

People who participated in the conference's Silk Road track confirmed that the Chinese government initiative was a big focus. As one attendee from Albuquerque described it, the first day of the track "focused on how much of China, Central Asia, India, and Africa—all part of the ancient Silk Road and Water-Ways—is being revitalized. China's 'One Belt–One Road' policy, set into motion by Chinese President Xi Jinping in 2013, is investing over a trillion dollars in building up the infrastructure with its neighbors reached from 'land and sea.'"

Kathleen Roche-Tansey, a state representative with Sister Cities International in California, has worked with the organization for decades. She has a clear-eyed view of Beijing, describing Sister Cities International's relationship with China as "fruitful but challenging." "I can tell you that China is the interesting component in everything we do in Sister Cities," she told me. "China is very competitive. China wants to surpass Japan and become *the* premier international program. They have done so much outreach. It's been a goal for a very long time."

How a country manages its sister city relationships is very telling, Roche-Tansey explained. The United States has Sister Cities International, but not every country has its own organization. The fact that China has the CFAPPC, directly managed by the government, is indicative of the importance that the central government places on sister city relationships—and its management approach and goals, she said. "They are looking at building opportunities for China. They're not leaving a stone unturned."

A decade ago, when Roche-Tansey learned that a U.S.-Chinese sister state relationship had been formative for China's incoming president, she "was very hopeful about the potential kind of relationship we might have. That maybe it would be more cooperative and collegial rather than competitive," she told me.

But she had also witnessed firsthand how the Chinese government could view sister city exchanges as a ground for geopolitical competition. In the late 1980s, she served as the chairperson for the International Affairs Board for the City of San Diego. Each year, the board would host an event for incoming university students to introduce them to San Diego's sister city programs, putting up flags from each of the countries represented by the sister cities. The key detail: San Diego had a sister city relationship both with Yantai, in mainland China, and with a city in Taiwan.

"Lo and behold, the first time we did this—and we had the flags of both Taiwan and the PRC—the PRC sent a whole team down to San Diego from the consulate in Los Angeles and raised such a ruckus that they forced us to take down the flag from Taiwan and the People's Republic," Roche-Tansey told me. The delegation from the Chinese consulate, between four and six people, told the event's organizers that Taiwan was a part of China and, thus, could not have its own flag.

"We were hosting students. And we did not want to engage in some kind of long, drawn-out confrontation with the People's Republic. Our obligation was to our students. When they complained, we took down just those two flags," Roche-Tansey said. The conflict was unfortunate; she had previously visited Yantai and loved the people she met there. "Subsequently, to avoid that, in future events we only put up city flags from the cities where we had relationships," instead of country flags.

During Roche-Tansey's decades working with the Sister Cities International network, she's heard of other, similar episodes. "The conflict has been between Taiwan; any kind of visible attention to Taiwan" from U.S. sister cities tends to attract attention from Beijing in some way, she said. "We have quite a few sister city relationships in Taiwan; they are very good relationships." Roche-Tansey said that, overall, she is concerned that Beijing might distort opportunities with sister cities and use them for an agenda of power rather than for cooperation and exchange, their true intended purpose.

Unfortunately, the Chinese government seems to have only doubled down on its view of sister city relationships as a tool of its geopolitics. "Friendship city relations have become one of the important channels to implement the BRI," CPAFCC president Li Xiaolin said in April 2019. "Sister city relations play an important role in boosting cooperation and exchanges among Chinese and foreign cities under the framework of the BRI." In January 2020, the city of Shanghai canceled its sister city relationship with Prague when Prague's mayor signed a sister city relationship with Taipei.

In April 2020, a new head of CPAFFC was announced: Lin Songtian, the former Chinese ambassador to South Africa. To anyone following the early months of China's wolf warrior diplomacy, Lin was an obvious figure. His Twitter account was one of the earliest Chinese diplomatic accounts to be opened in the new wave of Chinese diplomatic Twitter accounts. He quickly drew global attention for his aggressively critical posts attacking the United States, suggesting the coronavirus might not have originated in China, and defending China's repressive policies in Xinjiang and Hong Kong. When the Twitter account he used as China's ambassador to South Africa briefly went silent and all prior tweets were scrubbed in early 2020, observers wondered if this was meant to signal a crackdown from Beijing on the new wolf warrior diplomats. It did not. Lin shortly reappeared as CPAFFC president—by no means a demotion.

In a statement posted to the CPAFFC website, Lin said the organization seeks to "contribute to the fostering of a new type of international relations and the building of a community with a shared future for mankind by doing our part in people-to-people diplomacy" in accordance with "Xi Jinping's Thought on Socialism with Chinese Characteristics in The New Era and his Thought on Diplomatic Work [*sic*]."

Sister city relationships are yet another example of how China's dual-function strategy casts suspicion across a wide swath of activities that are very often valuable and beneficial. By putting a wolf warrior diplomat in charge of China's sister cities, by using city ties to promote Xi Jinping's global order building, by using the relationships as leverage to crowd out Taiwan, and by using a friendship city relationship as a key platform for an intelligence operation, the Chinese government is putting these hard-won relationships at risk.

———

It wasn't Christine Fang's participation in sister city exchanges or even her many liaisons with U.S. mayors that first got her on the FBI's radar, however. It was her regular meetings with a Chinese consular official named Zhang Weiwei.

Fang maintained close ties to the Chinese consulate in San Francisco throughout the years she was in California. There are dozens of Chinese student associations at campuses around the United States, and many of them maintain close contact with their regional Chinese consulate or embassy. But Fang's relationship to the San Francisco consulate was especially close. She attended several student leadership events held at the consulate for students from universities around the Bay Area. In 2012, the San Francisco consulate presented Fang with a certificate recognizing her "enthusiastic public service on behalf of Chinese students and the local community" and "excellent organizational and leadership skills" during the 2011/12 academic school year as chairperson of the Chinese Student Association. In an April 2015 interview with a student journalist, Fang described herself as a "communication bridge between students and the Chinese consulate."

It's common for Chinese students to meet with Chinese officials posted to the education section of their consulate or embassy. Indeed, it is the job of Chinese consular education officials to meet with Chinese students abroad; in the past, these officials were often invited to U.S. campuses to attend Chinese student events and provide information and safety sessions.

But Zhang was no education official. On paper, he was a diplomat posted to the San Francisco consulate and officially registered under the State Department's registry for foreign diplomats on U.S. soil. But U.S. intelligence officials believe that he was, in fact, a Ministry of State Security official—in short, a true spy. U.S. intelligence officials believe that Zhang's remit for the Ministry of State Security was subnational engagement and local influence operations, targeting local U.S. officials and prominent community members for hidden purposes beneficial to the Chinese state.

The United States was conducting covert surveillance on Zhang. In the course of that surveillance, around 2014, U.S. officials noticed his repeated meetings with a young Chinese woman and decided to look into her background. What they found raised major red flags. The year 2014 marked the height of Fang's closest ties to Representative Eric Swalwell and his office. She was bundling donations for his campaign and had access to countless local elected and government officials; everyone knew her. Fang's activities themselves were soon recorded through covert surveillance authorized through a Foreign Intelligence Surveillance Act warrant over the course of a sweeping U.S. counterintelligence operation.

The FBI's findings became a matter of urgent national security when it became clear that Representative Swalwell would be appointed to the House Intelligence Committee in early 2015. Members of that committee have access to some of the United States' most sensitive secrets and have oversight of the Central Intelligence Agency and other U.S. intelligence agencies. This turn of events would be the Ministry of State Security's dream, the culmination of a yearslong operation—a covert operative with close ties to and a history of sexual contact with a congressman sitting on the House Intelligence Committee.

On the eve of Swalwell's appointment, U.S. intelligence officials gave the congressman a defensive briefing in which they shared their knowledge of Fang's activities and her suspected ties to the Ministry of State Security. Swalwell was shocked. He immediately severed all ties with Fang. When we offered Swalwell the opportunity to comment, his office sent us this statement: "Rep. Swalwell, long ago, provided information about this person—whom he met more than eight years ago, and whom he hasn't seen in nearly six years—to the FBI. To protect information that might be classified, he will not participate in your story." Swalwell has never publicly denied having a sexual relationship with Fang.

Over the next few months, FBI officials fanned out across California to trace Fang's steps. By the end of May 2015, she knew something was up. She was supposed to attend the opening ceremony for the new APAPA chapter in Washington, scheduled for early June. But just days before her flight to DC, she told a fellow APAPA member that a problem had arisen at home and that she would have to make an unexpected trip back to China.

And with that, Christine Fang vanished. She did not return to California. She stopped replying to emails and Facebook messages. No one knew what had happened to her. "She disappeared off the face of everything," remembered Gilbert Wong, the former mayor of Cupertino. "When she left kind of abruptly, we all kind of scratched our heads," former Fremont mayor Bill Harrison told me.

The FBI-led probe didn't stop, though. U.S. investigators obtained Fang's extensive collection of business cards from her abandoned California apartment and began reaching out to her contacts one by one. Agents asked about her activities and background. They asked about her ties to Swalwell and other elected officials. FBI officials spoke with so many of Fang's former contacts that rumors began to swirl on the CSU East Bay campus and in Bay Area political circles that the FBI was after her.

"There were always people talking about this person who had just disappeared," Steven Tavares, a local reporter in the East Bay Area, told me. Tavares would spend the next several years collecting bits of information about Fang from people who had known her. He estimates that about two hundred people in the Bay Area knew that the FBI was after Fang and that it was somehow connected to Swalwell.

Harrison told me that FBI agents had briefed him about Fang's activities in August 2015. The agents told him that Fang's activities were part of a "long game play" targeting local politicians and that the Chinese government's strategy was "to strike up a relationship with you and see if you move up the line."

Fang's case is especially sensational, but it's just one of numerous known Chinese state–backed attempts to use covert methods and hidden motives to influence the U.S. political system. U.S. intelligence agencies have been tracking and fending off such attempts for decades.

Rodney Faraon worked on China at the Central Intelligence Agency for more than fifteen years before leaving government to work as Disney's director of global intelligence and threat analysis. The son of Filipino immigrants, Faraon first became interested in China when, one day in the early 1980s, his mother brought in the new issue of *Time* magazine that had Deng Xiaoping on the cover and told young Faraon, "You know what? I don't think Russia is going to be our enemy. It's going to be China in the future."

Faraon never forgot that. He became fascinated with China, and with spy thrillers, and decided he wanted to join the CIA. He attended Georgetown University in order to be as close to the Agency as possible, and as his graduation date approached, he cold-called the Agency to try to secure a job. He sent in an application and eventually ended up with a position, starting out looking at China's missile sales around the world, analyzing China's industrial espionage, and spending several years overseas.

In 1996, Faraon was tapped to serve as the deputy director of a task force set up to investigate an alleged Chinese government attempt to influence the congressional and presidential elections that year. Chinagate, as the scandal became known, involved Chinese government efforts to buy influence in elections and in Clinton's reelection campaign. The subsequent Department of Justice investigation found that Chinese government officials had tried to get campaign donations sent to the Democratic National Committee in advance of the 1996 presidential campaign. Through the use of electronic surveillance, U.S. investigators also found that Chinese government officials had used the Chinese embassy in Washington, DC, as a headquarters for planning the donations scheme, the *Washington Post*'s Bob Woodward and Brian Duffy reported in 1997.

In 1996, one DNC fund-raiser, Yah Lin "Charlie" Trie, had leveraged his political connections to secure a White House meeting between President Clinton and Wang Jun, who ran a Chinese military–owned weapons trading company, the *Washington Post* reported. In 1999, former DNC fund-raiser Johnny Chung admitted before a House committee that he had received $300,000 from Gen. Ji Shengde, the chief of China's military intelligence, who intended the money to be used to influence the 1996 presidential election. Chung denied acting as an agent of the Chinese government. He pleaded guilty to tax evasion and campaign finance violations, charges that could have led to up to forty years in prison, but Chung agreed to cooperate with the investigation and, in exchange, received five years' probation.

Faraon was long gone from the CIA by the time U.S. counterintelligence officials were investigating Christine Fang. When I first told him about what we had found out in California, he was openly shocked. *Holy fuck. They did it* was his first thought when I told him about Fang, he later told me. He described the operation as "aggressive." "The use of honeypots and kompromat"—techniques used particularly by the Russians and Chinese, who learned a lot of their intelligence techniques from the Russians during the Cold War—"that's pretty classic," Faraon said. "The fortunate thing in this case is that it was discovered. Now what I worry about are the cases that haven't been discovered."

Chinagate helps explain why the FBI took a strong interest in Chinese American donors to Swalwell's 2012 and 2014 campaigns. As part of a different investigation, one that began in 2014, the FBI interviewed dozens of Chinese Americans who gave money to Swalwell's campaigns from those two election cycles, according to court filings from this separate investigation.

In October 2019, James Tong, a well-known East Bay real estate developer and prominent early supporter of Swalwell's, was found guilty in a Northern California federal court of engaging in an illegal straw donor scheme. According to U.S. prosecutors, Tong bundled donations but reimbursed the donors (at least one of whom was not a U.S. citizen), whose checks he collected in order to evade the limits placed on individual donations, providing tens of thousands of dollars to Swalwell's 2012 and 2014 political campaigns.

Filings by Tong's lawyer, based on documents provided to the defense during the discovery process, indicate the investigation into him was one part of a wider probe by federal investigators into donations to Swalwell's campaign. "The investigation that precipitated the current case appears to be just a smaller part of a larger investigation into improper campaign contributions," Tong's lawyer wrote in a court filing, adding there was an "earlier and much more sweeping investigation into the campaign contributions solicited and received by a certain Bay Area congressman."

Swalwell, who was not accused of any wrongdoing in the Tong case, testified during the trial. Tong died in March 2020, aged sixty-five.

Christine Fang's activities, suspicions about whom she was really working for, her ties to Swalwell and other local politicians, and the FBI investigation into her have long been an open secret in Bay Area political circles. At least five people I spoke with in California who knew Fang personally told me that they had heard rumors back in 2015 that she was "probably a spy" or that the FBI was after her. Swalwell's relationship with Fang was another widely shared rumor; three people told me he was believed to have a "thing" for Asian women.

I did not mention the existence of these rumors in the Axios article. But two days after we published our story, a local Bay Area news outlet, East Bay Citizen, did. "The undercurrent of local buzz about Fang over the past five years almost always suggested romantic dalliances with Swalwell, and perhaps other elected officials," the December 9 article stated. "Almost every Fremont and Tri-Valley elected official and political insider seems to hold the same vivid memories of Fang. Many remarked that she appeared to have come out of nowhere and was suddenly meeting every local official and seemingly showing up at every event. Others also described holding deep-seated suspicions about her intentions."

When I came across this article, I was immediately intrigued. I had heard these exact sentiments from numerous people I had interviewed in the Bay Area. Whoever wrote the article had clearly spent a significant amount of time looking into Christine Fang's background, which means they became aware of her activities long before Axios published the story.

I contacted the reporter who wrote the article, Steven Tavares, who at the time ran *East Bay Citizen*, essentially, as a one-man local reporting shop. He told me he had been working on the story bit by bit for years. "At least two hundred people know this story in Swalwell's district," Tavares told me. "That's a conservative estimate."

There were also rumors swirling of Fang's romantic rendezvous with numerous local politicos. Each circle of people seemed to suspect that at least someone they knew was involved with her. One person I spoke with said that, even in 2014, people would say, only half-jokingly, that Fang was "probably a spy." But that person and others said they just shrugged it off and continued to associate with her.

Fang was able to parachute into these upper echelons of Northern California local politics by establishing herself within several organizations or even founding some herself, which she then used as a platform. This highlights an uncomfortable and even dangerous paradox: that the Chinese government has at times supported the creation of legitimate organizations and institutions it occasionally used for illegitimate purposes. It's the most extreme example I know of the party's dual-function strategy at work.

The organizations that Fang, Katrina Leung, and other prominent Chinese agents in the United States often worked through were founded by and for Asian communities in the country. By its very nature, this strategy recklessly endangers Chinese diaspora communities. The U.S. Central Intelligence Agency, for example, does not permit its officers operating abroad to pose as journalists or missionaries without explicit case-by-case authorization by the president, because U.S. intelligence officials know that doing so would cast real journalists and missionaries under a cloud of suspicion and thus endanger the well-being of groups of people who are already vulnerable.

Chinese American fears about racial profiling by the U.S. Department of Justice have a long history, and some of the Trump administration's actions and rhetoric caused deep alarm in Chinese communities, which were targeted in a spate of hate crimes during the pandemic. But the Chinese government's own choice to abuse these communities by embedding intelligence operatives within them, without their knowledge or permission, is a key source of U.S. government suspicion. If Beijing truly cared about the well-being of overseas Chinese communities, it would scrap its dual-function strategy once and for all.

———————

As cases of Covid-19 fell in China within a few months of the outbreak in Wuhan, freeing up China's huge supplies of PPE, Chinese sister cities began to send donations of face masks to their partner cities in the United States and around the world. In many cases, this local-to-local assistance demonstrated the enormous potential for Chinese society, when it is less encumbered by the political strictures of a one-party state, to make positive contributions during global crises. It also demonstrates the best of what United States–China engagement was envisioned to be.

As many U.S. cities grappled with a mask shortage in March and April 2020, their sister cities in China sprang into action. The sister city relationship between Norfolk, Virginia, and Ningbo, in China's Zhejiang Province, is a representative example. The relationship between the two cities was formally established in April 2013, at a signing ceremony in Ningbo. The two cities held several joint activities over the next few years, and in early March 2020, before U.S. lockdowns began but after Chinese high schools were already transitioning to virtual classrooms, high school students in Norfolk video-chatted with students in Ningbo about their experiences during lockdown.

Just a few days later, however, Virginia, too, shut down its schools, and people scrambled for personal protective equipment. Chinese officials in Ningbo offered to help. "They read news stories about how serious the situation has gotten in the United States, so they reached out and asked whether we needed masks," said Harry Zhang, chairman of the Ningbo-Beilun Committee of the Norfolk Sister City Association. The Ningbo-Beilun municipal government donated two thousand masks, five hundred gowns, and five hundred goggles.

These donations occurred across the United States. "We have read stories of sister cities in China and the US helping each other during this time. My own city is an example," Sister Cities International chairman and mayor of San Antonio Ron Nirenberg said in April 2022. San Antonio has been sister cities with Wuxi, a city in China's southern Jiangsu Province, since 2012. At the height of China's outbreak, San Antonio residents raised money to help support Wuxi. Then, just a few months later, Wuxi pledged to provide thirty thousand masks to San Antonio. "These acts of compassionate exchange have been important symbols reinforcing the reality of our common experience," Nirenberg said.

A few months later, as the pandemic raged across the United States, China conducted mask diplomacy with dozens of local governments there. Using publicly available press releases advertising PPE donations in the first half of 2020, public records requests to dozens of states and local governments that received PPE donations or purchased equipment from China, and hundreds of pages of emails and other internal records, we examined twenty-nine cases where a branch of the Chinese government or an affiliate such as a state-owned enterprise donated or facilitated sales to U.S. state and local governments, although there are almost certainly many more examples. The scope of the donations is remarkable: together, they amounted to more than a million individual pieces of PPE, including hospital gowns, surgical masks, N95 respirators, gloves, and other crucial equipment, sent to individual hospitals and governments in every region of the United States, from New York to San Antonio.

Yet, because of the growing suspicion surrounding the Chinese government's true intentions in its relationships with U.S. cities, and because of the simultaneous top-down "face mask diplomacy" push, some local-to-local shipments of PPE during the pandemic were received with suspicion in the American public eye.

The Chinese government, in a number of cases, used its mask diplomacy to coerce foreign politicians into publicly praising China on the world stage and to garner support for closer economic ties with the People's Republic. In March 2020, China sent six doctors on an Airbus A330 plane to Serbia filled with masks, gowns, and respirators to help the country fight the Covid pandemic. In a lavish ceremony at Belgrade's Nikola Tesla Airport, Serbian president Aleksandar Vučić kissed the Chinese flag. China's relationship with Vučić and Serbia has remained ironclad ever since; Vučić repeatedly visited Belgrade's airport in 2020 and 2021 to welcome donations of PPE and, eventually, deliveries of the Chinese-made Sinopharm vaccines. Later, he would become something of an evangelist for Chinese-made vaccines in the Balkans, personally delivering thousands of doses to neighboring Bosnia and North Macedonia and sending vaccines to ethnic Serbian enclaves within Bosnia and Kosovo.

In May 2020, during a party-to-party summit between the Chinese Communist Party and Bangladesh's ruling party, Bangladesh Awami League, party officials offered a proposal: establish six sister city partnerships with Chinese cities, and China will offer pandemic assistance to Bangladesh. "If the sister city proposal is approved, China will give all kinds of technical and financial support to combat the Covid-19 epidemic, dengue outbreak, and similar problems in those areas," the *Dhaka Tribune* reported one official as saying.

"The Chinese proposal, considered a friendly gesture, is widely appreciated in Bangladesh. Nevertheless, the Chinese offer of sister-city alliances in the time of Covid-19 attracted international attention leading to concerns about China's intention behind the proposal made," Joyeeta Bhattacharjee, an analyst of Bangladesh's domestic politics and foreign policy, wrote at the time. "The Chinese motivation exceeds the promotion of cultural ties and it has a larger geostrategic objective."

Around that same period, three Swedish cities terminated their relationships with three Chinese cities amid swiftly deteriorating Sweden-China ties. In 2019, after the Swedish government awarded a human rights prize to Swedish citizen Gui Minhai, long detained in China, Chinese ambassador to Sweden Gui Congyou warned Sweden in an interview on Swedish public radio, "For our friends, we produce fine wine. Jackals, we welcome with shotguns." The implication was that Sweden would get the shotguns.

The PPE donations in the United States had raised the profile of Chinese sister cities at a time when the Trump administration was actively pushing back against activity linked to the Chinese Communist Party. The United States had signed a memorandum of understanding in January 2011 that would establish the U.S-China Governors Forum to Promote Sub-National Cooperation. In October 2020, the United States revoked its participation in that agreement. "Following the signing of the MOU, however, Chinese Peoples' Association for Friendship with Foreign Countries (CPAFFC) a Beijing-based organization tasked with co-opting sub-national governments, has sought to directly and malignly influence state and local leaders to promote the PRC's global agenda. CPAFFC's actions have undermined the Governors Forum's original well-intentioned purpose," Secretary of State Mike Pompeo said in a statement. "Authentic people-to-people exchanges are crucial for establishing understanding between cultures, but the [United Front Work Department] is not a vehicle for people-to-people exchange."

With this same action, the United States also designated the peaceful reunification associations a foreign agent. The foreign agent designation does not prohibit an organization from operating in the United States but, rather, institutes mandatory disclosures that it must file with the Department of Justice about its funding and activities.

CPAFFC condemned the United States' action in no uncertain terms. "Pompeo slandered China-U.S. subnational and people-to-people friendly exchanges and mutually beneficial cooperation as 'united front work' and 'malign influence.' He obviously underestimated and insulted the kindness, intelligence and wisdom of the American people, only exposing his own inanity and incompetence," the organization said in a statement posted to its website. "We believe that the insightful people in the U.S. could clearly see and firmly oppose the 'political virus' spread by the like [*sic*] of Pompeo, strengthen friendly exchanges between the Chinese and American people, and drive forward subnational win-win cooperation so as to promote common development."

Sister city relationships have come under scrutiny from some of the United States' most outspoken right-wing China hawks, including Marsha Blackburn and Josh Hawley, who wrote a letter to the U.S. Conference of Mayors in October 2020 urging its members to reconsider the 157 sister relationships between U.S. and Chinese cities. They warned that sister city relationships may be "China's newest political weapon" and "may leave American communities vulnerable to Chinese espionage and economic coercion."

Chinese cities weren't the only sister cities helping to facilitate PPE donations. In June 2020, Yilan, a scenic city on Taiwan's northeast coast—to which I allude in chapter 3—donated nearly $65,000 worth of personal protective equipment to Rockville, Maryland, a city with a population of around 60,000 that sits on the outskirts of the greater Washington municipal area. Mayor Bridget Donnell Newton presided over a ceremony on June 5 thanking Taiwan for the donations, which were passed on to nursing homes and medical staff in Rockville.

Yilan and Rockville were sister cities, and this was one of numerous donations of PPE that cities near DC had received at that time from their sister cities in China and Taiwan. That same month, Montgomery County, Maryland, where Rockville is located, received 20,000 masks from its sister city, Xi'an, China, and the state of Maryland received 100,000 masks from China's Anhui Province, its sister state.

But the Yilan-Rockville donation could very easily have not occurred at all. This sister city relationship was very new, officially formed just the year before, and had almost been scuttled by a sustained campaign to block it, one that culminated in a dramatic showdown at an annual meeting at Rockville City Hall, a threat to vote out city officials who didn't support the "One China" policy, and, finally, an off-the-record visit by Chinese embassy officials to Mayor Newton's office.

It's a case study that demonstrates how the party's political control and dual-function strategy can impact U.S. society on a hyper-local level. Rockville's Taiwanese American community faced extreme difficulty in establishing a simple people-to-people exchange program. An intentionally nonpolitical organization became heavily politicized, thrusting the small nonprofit board that manages Rockville's sister city links into controversy it wasn't accustomed to handling. Only an extraordinary mobilization effort among Rockville's Taiwanese Americans, one of the largest Taiwanese diaspora communities in the United States, finally ended the drama and allowed the Rockville-Yilan sister city relationship to come into existence.

Kuan Lee of Rockville, Maryland, is tall and outgoing, with a confident smile and a firm handshake. He was born in the United States to parents who hailed from Yilan, Taiwan. Trained as a lawyer, Lee worked as a civil servant in the U.S. Social Security Administration. It was he who had first come up with the idea of forming a sister city relationship with Yilan. About a quarter of Rockville is Asian American; the city is home to both Taiwanese and Chinese diaspora communities of significant size. Lee thought a sister city relationship would be a great opportunity to celebrate Taiwanese culture in Rockville and to strengthen relationships between Americans and Taiwanese. In October 2017, he submitted a proposal to the Rockville Sister City Corporation (RSCC), which oversees international sister city relationships for Rockville, Maryland. The RSCC board was enthusiastic.

But a problem soon materialized. Rockville already had a friendship city agreement with Jiaxing, a city in the mainland Chinese province of Zhejiang, though the relationship between the two cities had been dormant for several years. According to emails, meeting minutes, and interviews with members of the RSCC board, two board members, Ying Chen and Bing-jib Huang, both longtime Maryland residents who had worked to facilitate the Jiaxing-Rockville relationship, were upset by the Yilan proposal and tried repeatedly to block it. Chen also said something that some people present at one February 2018 RSCC board meeting told me they took as a threat. As the minutes from that meeting state, "Ying also suggested that if Rockville elected officials move forward with a Rockville-Yilan relationship, Rockville residents of (non-Taiwanese) Chinese descent will vote to remove such elected officials from office."

The conflict reached a boiling point in September 2018, with the annual RSCC board election. The anti-Yilan faction on the board tried to put forward an alternate slate of candidates who would be able to gain a majority on the council and kill the proposed Taiwan sister city relationship. But the Taiwanese community in Rockville had mobilized to support the Yilan proposal, with more than fifty local Taiwanese residents applying for RSCC membership so they could vote in the election. The pro-Yilan vote carried the day.

Several months later, Rockville and Yilan formally signed a sister city agreement in a ceremony held in Rockville. Despite the region's large Taiwanese population, it was the first city in the entire Virginia/Maryland/DC area to form a relationship with a Taiwanese sister city.

The establishment of this sister city tie caught the attention of leaders in both Taipei and Beijing. On July 9, Taiwanese president Tsai Ing-wen sent a letter congratulating both Yilan and Rockville for the successful establishment of their sister city relationship. That same day, Ba Cuicui, a political secretary at the Chinese embassy in Washington, DC, sent an email to Rockville mayor Bridget Donnell Newton, requesting to meet "at her earliest possible date this week" to discuss "subnational cooperation between Rockville and China." Two embassy diplomats subsequently showed up, expressing "concerns" about Rockville's new relationship with

Yilan and offering to have the embassy introduce other mainland Chinese cities to Rockville for potential new sister city relationships.

Taiwanese Americans in Rockville were participating in a basic foundation of U.S. democracy, which is working with their local government on an initiative they cared about—but their attempt to have their voices heard in their own local government was almost stymied by the Chinese government's aggressive foreign policy moves, even on U.S. soil, and its promotion among its citizens of the belief that blocking Taiwan's participation in global society was a virtuous act.

The problem posed by the party's abuse of sister cities isn't that "Communist infiltration" is going to cause the collapse of the United States or the end of democracy or anything of such a dramatic nature. To cast the problem in such extreme terms, as some more hawkish U.S. politicians have done, does no one any favors. Rather, the party's behavior is gradually eroding the hard-earned trust built up over decades by people-to-people exchanges. And that distrust is contagious. When positive and beneficial China-linked activities come under suspicion because other, similar activities have been previously abused, the targets of this suspicion rightfully become angry and believe themselves to have been the victims of McCarthyism and even racism.

In his 1956 speech launching the sister cities program, Eisenhower presaged this problem. "The communist way is to subject everything to the control of the state," he said. "They do this in every walk of life in everything they do." The Chinese Communist Party's reassertion of control over sister city exchanges runs the risk of ruining everything those exchanges stand for.

The same is true of cross-border business and investment, ties that Chinese leaders since Deng Xiaoping have worked hard to cultivate—and which are now suffering from the same abuse overseas that Chinese organizations have long faced.

5

ZOOMING IN

On the evening of June 8, 2020, four days after the thirty-first anniversary of the Tiananmen Square Massacre, I received a message from Zhou Fengsuo, a student leader during the 1989 pro-democracy movement who now lives in New Jersey.

"Hi, Bethany, our Zoom account was closed with no explanation," he wrote. "We have emailed Zoom asking for the reason, but we haven't received a response." He wasn't the only one affected. Numerous other Chinese pro-democracy activists in both the United States and Hong Kong had seen their accounts closed in recent days and their virtual Tiananmen memorials disrupted, with no response from the videoconferencing company.

Zhou and I had known each other for several years through his work in the Chinese pro-democracy movement and the reporting I had done on human rights issues in China. He is gentle and soft-spoken, but he has a will of iron. After the June 4 massacre and subsequent crackdowns crushed the movement, he was thrown in prison for a year and then released but kept under close surveillance for several years. The Chinese government finally permitted him to leave China in the mid-1990s. He came to the United States, where he attended graduate school. He has long served as a leader of the Chinese dissident community abroad, and in 2007, he founded Humanitarian China, a nonprofit organization dedicated to helping political prisoners in China.

The Chinese Communist Party has sought to stamp out the memory of the Tiananmen pro-democracy movement through a smothering veil of censorship. Chinese children do not learn about the demonstrations or the subsequent military crackdown in school; mentions of it are filtered out of movies, television, books, and magazines; and every year on June 4, internet censors instantly delete even cryptic references to the anniversary, including the numerals 64 and references to the date May 35. Tiananmen survivors such as Zhou work to counteract this censorship by holding annual vigils to keep the spirit of the movement alive and to honor the memory of those who were murdered.

And despite the Covid-19 pandemic, 2020 was no different. Humanitarian China, together with several other Chinese pro-democracy organizations, did what millions of others had done amid the lockdowns and quarantines. They moved their event to Zoom.

The pandemic was an extraordinary windfall for Zoom, whose videoconferencing services quickly became part of this shared experience. Zoom was founded in 2011, in San Jose, California, by a China-born engineer named Eric Yuan who moved to the United States to work for Cisco's Webex and became a naturalized American citizen in 2007. At the end of 2019, the U.S. company had ten million daily users. By April 2020, that number had soared to more than three hundred million. In its April 30 filings, Zoom posted revenues of over $328 million—a 169 percent increase from the year before and nearly double its original projections of $203 million. And net income rose exponentially from a slim $198,000 to $27 million. Companies used Zoom for meetings, families held virtual weddings and reunions, and friends held online happy hours. Even numerous U.S. government agencies and offices, including the Pentagon, used Zoom's government service, hosted on a special, secure cloud, for official meetings. In May 2020, former Trump national security advisor H. R. McMaster joined Zoom's board.

But Zoom's good fortune represented a major opportunity to other organizations as well: China's security agencies. That's because, while Zoom is a U.S. company, one particular feature sets it apart from Cisco's Webex, Google Meet, and similar services from other companies. More than seven hundred of its employees (most of its research and development team) are based in China.

Zhou's message to me that day set into motion a chain of events that would culminate in a groundbreaking Department of Justice investigation proving that several worst-case scenarios about the reach of China's security state into U.S. businesses had already become reality—and in an indictment in which the DOJ drew a line in the sand, broadcasting for the first time that it would no longer tolerate Chinese government harassment of dissidents on U.S. soil.

———————

Zhou Fengsuo's Zoom troubles began on May 15. He and a group of other Chinese dissidents, mostly based around the East Coast, had begun planning the upcoming June 4 Tiananmen Square Massacre memorial, and on May 15, they held their first planning meeting, hosted through the personal Zoom account of Zhu Rikun, a well-known Chinese independent filmmaker.

They evaluated several options for a videoconferencing platform, eventually choosing Zoom for several reasons. Google Meet was blocked in China, but Zoom wasn't, and the latter was easy to use. People in China could simply scan a QR to get into the meeting without creating an account, thus limiting their manual input of personal information and reducing their online traceability. "The idea was to try to use an online platform to try to be inclusive, especially for people within China, so that they could have a good opportunity from within China, both as speakers and as listeners," Zhou told me.

But the dissidents ran into trouble almost immediately. As they tried to start their first planning meeting, Zhu found he couldn't dial in. It was the first time he had ever had trouble with his Zoom account. He and the other organizers immediately realized something was wrong.

Zhou had known that they might face trouble; he knew that Zoom had significant operations in China. The year before, he had experienced directly how the Chinese Communist Party strong-armed U.S. tech companies with operations in the mainland. In early January 2019, LinkedIn censored Zhou's profile, rendering it inaccessible in China.

In 2014, LinkedIn had struck a deal with the Chinese government that granted the professional networking platform access to the Chinese market after it agreed to implement state-mandated censorship on its Chinese-language website and after it granted a 7 percent stake of its China-based operation to Chinese venture capital firms.

LinkedIn had made these concessions for one obvious reason: profit. In 2014, there were an estimated 140 million working professionals in

China who might be interested in using such a platform. Getting an early start in such a huge market could pay dividends for years to come, while getting shut out could mean falling far behind global competitors. At that time, the Chinese government had already clearly communicated to foreign tech and internet firms that ignoring government internet censorship demands would mean expulsion from the Chinese market, as Google, Facebook, Twitter, and YouTube had already learned. "While we strongly support freedom of expression," LinkedIn spokesperson Hani Durzy said in 2014, "we recognized when we launched that we would need to adhere to the requirements of the Chinese government in order to operate in China."

As LinkedIn's China operations were built up and became more profitable over the next several years, a noticeable shift occurred in how LinkedIn executives talked about their relationship with the Chinese government. By 2019, LinkedIn had 44 million users in China, making it the platform's third-largest user base, after the United States at 150 million users and India at 52 million. In February 2019, a month after Zhou's profile was censored, Billy Huang, LinkedIn China's head of consumer marketing and communication, said in an interview that "the government is a key stakeholder for us. We are always looking for ways to help our stakeholders be successful."

The shift from reluctant justification to enthusiastic partnership is one that many companies have undergone and that the Chinese government—and Xi Jinping in particular—has actively cultivated. An element of emerging party-state capitalism in China isn't just growing political control over business decisions but also the understanding among business executives and entrepreneurs that working closely with the government is the key to success and profit.

LinkedIn restored Zhou's profile on January 4, 2019, just a day after his tweet about the censorship resulted in a media outcry. In a message to him, the company apologized and stated that his profile had been "blocked in error." Zhou knew, though, that there was no longer any guarantee that using an American platform while on U.S. soil meant the CCP couldn't censor him.

Even so, Zhu Rikun's difficulty logging on to Zoom that day in May 2020 wasn't expected. "It was a surprise that it could come so quick," Zhou Fengsuo told me. "This was a group of just five or six people."

Zhou decided to open a new Zoom account specifically for the purpose of hosting the upcoming June memorial. He and the other dissidents explored the features of the various tiers and, in the end, chose Zoom's most expensive paid account. "We paid the highest premium available. It was pretty expensive, in the hundreds just for one month. Knowing we might encounter some problem, we wanted to have the highest account," he said.

With the new account set up, Zhou began to plan in earnest for the June 4 memorial, coordinating with speakers inside and outside China. He knew that the Chinese government would likely try to sabotage the event through a number of widely known tactics, including hacking, denial-of-service attacks, or mobilizing loyal internet users to join the call only to disrupt it by posting or even shouting obscene content. To make sure the group was fully prepared to guard against these possibilities, Zhou held three rehearsals between May 20 and May 31, as the group practiced how to weed out suspicious-looking accounts and block people before they could disrupt the meeting.

Getting people located in China to agree to speak during the event was difficult. Many of the people whom Zhou's team contacted there declined to speak to them; some were contacted by Chinese police and warned not to participate in the conference. But some people in China displayed remarkable courage. Dong Shengkun, who had spent more than fifteen years in prison for his participation in the 1989 protests, prerecorded his speech despite police warnings and sent it to Zhou to be broadcast at the meeting.

Finally, on May 31, the group held the first-ever virtual Tiananmen Square Massacre vigil. It lasted from 9 to 11:30 a.m. Eastern Time. The online format also made it the first global commemoration. People in Taiwan, Hong Kong, mainland China, the United States, and other countries spoke about their memories of the event and its lasting legacy. One person in mainland China, Chen Yunfei, somehow dodged police and spoke live during the event. One of the Tiananmen mothers—one of the many women who lost a child during the massacre—gave a touching speech. And Zhou said he found Dong Shengkun's recorded broadcast "very courageous and inspiring because, after all these years, after all he went through, he is still holding on to his ideal."

The event attracted around 250 Zoom attendees, and more than 4,000 people streamed it on social media. The organizers had seen a few suspicious accounts but had used the paid account's advanced features to boot them out without a hassle. Zhou soon learned that police detained Chen Yunfei immediately after the conference, but he was released a few days later. Overall, the memorial had gone smoothly.

"After the conference, I was actually quite content," Zhou told me. "Even though I knew that people in China were paying a very high price for this—there were people arrested—but we were able to let them speak out. We were able to hear each other in a shared platform. This shows what technology can do. If there is such a platform that could penetrate the firewall and really connect people freely, how great would that be? So, I was hopeful."

This feeling of hopefulness, however, was not to last. On June 5, Zhou tried to log back on to the paid Zoom account to start making plans for an upcoming event in July on Chinese human rights lawyers, but he was unable to log on and soon realized the account had been shut down. After speaking with several other Chinese activists who had experienced the same thing in recent weeks, including U.S.-based activist Wang Dan and former Hong Kong lawmaker Lee Cheuk-yan, he realized that something was terribly wrong. That was when he decided to reach out to me.

As Zhou Fengsuo and numerous other Chinese pro-democracy activists were preparing to hold their first-ever online Tiananmen memorial, Julien Jin was hard at work thousands of miles away. The thirty-nine-year-old Chinese citizen was a Zoom employee serving as a "security technical leader" based in the company's offices at a technology park in Hangzhou, Zhejiang Province.

The address of Zoom's China headquarters is located in a rather nondescript office building known as Shuyu Daxia, or "Digital Entertainment Tower," in the heart of Hangzhou, just a few residential districts over from the city's scenic West Lake. The ground floor of Digital Entertainment Tower is home to several shops on the bustling street level; the approximately twelve floors rising above have dark tinted windows surrounded by thick metal beams. From the higher floors, office workers can look out south-facing windows, across a busy boulevard, to the picturesque campus of Zhejiang University of Finance and Economics, with its green lawns and large reflecting pool.

Jin's official job responsibilities included liaising with China's law enforcement and security services, including the Ministry of Public Security and the Ministry of State Security, the political security and intelligence arm of the Chinese government. Zoom had first hired him in 2016, but it was in 2019 that his activities began to evolve. That year's June 4 anniversary was particularly consequential, as it marked the thirty-year anniversary of the massacre. Online censorship was especially stringent, as China's armies of censors ensured that even the most cryptic of references, such as "May 35" or the posting of a candle emoji, were instantly scrubbed away. Security police made extra efforts to ensure that even small, in-home Tiananmen commemorations were nipped in the bud. In a rare public commentary on the occasion, the *Global Times* published an editorial calling the 1989 event a "vaccination" that would "greatly increase China's immunity against any major political turmoil in the future."

The year 2019 also saw the explosion of massive demonstrations in Hong Kong. The annual Tiananmen candlelight vigil in Hong Kong, which has often attracted thousands of participants to Victoria Park, has long been a fixture of the city's political freedoms and a sign that pro-democracy sentiment there remains strong. In 2019, the thirtieth anniversary of the massacre coincided with growing anger at a draft law, first proposed in February of that year, that could potentially allow the extradition of Hong Kong residents to mainland China; many in Hong Kong viewed the proposed law as an existential threat to the city's political freedoms. On June 4, Victoria Park was filled with not thousands, but tens of thousands of participants dressed in mourning black and holding up candles; estimates of the crowd size range from 40,000 to 180,000.

Days later, anger at Hong Kong's government over the proposed extradition law, and fear of the Chinese government's creeping political influence in the city, exploded in some of the largest protests the city had ever seen. On June 9, hundreds of thousands marched against the extradition bill. On June 17, 2019, almost two million people, roughly a quarter of Hong Kong's population, once again hit the streets in protest. It was the largest mass demonstration in the city's history.

It was right on the cusp of what party leaders in Beijing would come to view as an existential crisis that Julien Jin allegedly made his first known attempt to try to block a group of Zoom users who were planning to hold a Tiananmen-related event. On June 4, 2019, Jin messaged several Zoom employees to tell them he wanted to gather social media information on the users to prevent them from holding the meeting.

His efforts to shut down activities held on Zoom that the Chinese government opposed continued. According to U.S. government documents, in August he asked a U.S.-based Zoom employee to block the account of a Zoom user who Jin said was a member of a religious cult. The account was put into "quarantine" status, which limited its features.

Despite Jin's efforts to implement censorship at the company and to comply with Chinese government directives, in September 2019 the Chinese government blocked access to Zoom. In an instant, it became impossible for people using both free accounts and corporate paid accounts, the primary source of Zoom's revenues, to use the platform to communicate in China. Chinese government officials demanded that Zoom submit "rectification plans" to the Ministry of Public Security in Hangzhou detailing how the company would actively surveil activities conducted on its platform for any political or other content the Chinese government deemed unacceptable.

The demands that the Chinese government was suddenly making came as a shock. "Like many fast-growing companies, we were focused on building the best possible product and delighting our customers. We had not, at that point in our evolution, been forced to focus on societal or policy concerns outside of this relatively narrow frame of vision," the company said of the block in a later statement.

The block put Zoom in an "unfamiliar and uncomfortable position," the company said. "At that time, we were a much smaller company primarily serving businesses. The shutdown caused significant disruption for many of our multinational customers, who could not effectively communicate with their employees and partners in China. They urged us to take immediate action to get the service resumed."

The month after Zoom was blocked, Zoom executives flew to China to meet with government officials. The block would be lifted if Zoom agreed to fully abide by Chinese laws and regulations, officials told the Zoom employees.

So, Zoom agreed to the demands. According to U.S. government documents, the company drafted a rectification plan, agreed to proactively supervise and report "illegal" content, granted Chinese security authorities special access to its systems, agreed to migrate the data of one million "Chinese users" from U.S. servers to servers in China—it's unclear how "Chinese" was defined—and named Julien Jin as the liaison between Zoom and Chinese government authorities.

According to U.S. court documents, Yuan himself was closely involved in many discussions about the details of what would happen in Hangzhou. In late October, he was included in a series of messages in which Jin explained that the Hangzhou public security bureau had demanded that Jin "provide them with some detailed lists of our daily monitoring; such as Hong Kong demonstrations, illegal religions fund-raising, pyramid schemes, etc." The bureau also wanted to know how much Zoom intended to budget for "safety supervision."

Yuan was also told that Jin would be creating five Zoom accounts for use by officers affiliated with the Hangzhou public security bureau's cybersecurity department and that Zoom would exchange "secret" information with the Ministry of Public Security through both the Zoom employee messaging system and WeChat.

Zoom's efforts to placate Beijing seemed successful. On November 17, 2019, its services in China were unblocked.

————————

But Chinese security authorities weren't done with Zoom yet. The dramatic increase in the number of Zoom users in the early months of the pandemic coincided with increasingly stringent controls over the company's internal workings and with demands from Chinese security agencies to immediately block any activities on the teleconferencing platform, anywhere in the world, that authorities deemed illegal.

The enormous surge of Zoom users around the world also gave the Chinese government an unprecedented opportunity to try to disrupt political activities happening through the auspices of a company it had thoroughly cowed just months earlier.

Starting in April 2020, as the United States was in the early weeks of its first major lockdown, Jin began to go beyond the "rectification" to which Zoom had initially agreed, U.S. government documents allege. The Ministry of State Security (MSS) began tasking Jin to proactively target specific groups based abroad. In a message that month, Jin told one U.S.-based Zoom employee that the "[MSS] asked me to track down a bad organization overseas."

As Chinese security officials' demands grew, Jin began circumventing the regulations Zoom had in place to keep its China operations separate from those in the United States. At the Hangzhou public security bureau's request, he agreed to a "one-minute processing requirement"—the ability to shut down a meeting within one minute of the public security bureau's making the request. Zoom's chief compliance officer and U.S.-based chief operating officer told Jin that such a requirement would have to be reported to the U.S. compliance team. But Jin believed that this would violate the Chinese security agency's requirement that such requests be kept confidential.

The Ministry of State Security was, in other words, asking Jin to keep secrets from his own employer. On one occasion, Jin urged a U.S.-based Zoom employee to avoid putting a security-related request to Zoom higher-ups in an email but instead to convey the request in person. Another time, Jin said he couldn't document his actions in a company report because the issue had to be handled confidentially.

So, Jin tried to find a workaround himself. Shutting down an account within one minute of the security services' request required immediate access to the back end, so Jin worked with a U.S.-based Zoom employee to grant him access to U.S. servers. It was clearly Jin's intent to develop the capacity to shut down accounts based outside China. "Even abroad, political attacks on leaders are not allowed," Jin told another Zoom employee. "For example, including U.S. users, if the issue of June 4th is being discussed in a meeting, it must be handled within one minute," or else it would be deemed "security non-compliant."

The Chinese government and its security services were aware that their attempts to use Zoom for political censorship would be unpopular if they became public. The Shanghai branch of the Ministry of State Security came to Zoom's offices in Hangzhou and requested that Jin and others sign a nondisclosure agreement. As he explained to another employee, "What the MSS is asking for are mostly politics related, therefore they request that we cannot disclose it otherwise it will greatly impact our country's reputation."

The MSS also told Jin that it required the user information for all

Chinese participants from the Tiananmen memorial Zhou had hosted the day before. On June 1, Jin sent this request to Zoom employees in the United States. These employees shared with him the account holder's real name, email address, user ID, account ID, and account number and then closed the account. But that wasn't all. On Jin's request, one U.S. employee also shared the IP (internet protocol) addresses used by the account holder in any previous activity on Zoom and the IP addresses of everyone who attended the May 31 meeting, including several users with U.S. IP addresses, according to U.S. court documents. But Jin didn't have access to this data himself. He had to repeatedly ask U.S.-based Zoom employees to send this information to him. Several readily complied.

China's Ministry of Public Security told Jin that it wanted the Zoom account information for all users from Xinjiang, no matter where in the world the accounts had been opened or in which country the servers holding that data were stored. On June 1, Jin relayed this message to Zoom employees in the United States. They complied. Later that day, a Zoom employee in the United States sent a spreadsheet to Jin that contained account IDs and user IDs for 23,000 Zoom accounts deemed connected to people from Xinjiang.

The first pro-democracy activist to run into trouble on Zoom wasn't Zhou Fengsuo but, rather, the Hong Kong–based Lee Cheuk-yan. In his mid-sixties with salt-and-pepper hair, Lee speaks the perfectly crisp, British-accented English of a lifelong Hong Konger.

He began his life in mainland China, where he was born in 1957. When he was two years old, he moved with his family to Hong Kong, where they settled. Lee studied civil engineering at the University of Hong Kong.

Lee's political awakening came in 1989, when he was thirty-two years old. He saw the pro-democracy protests unfolding in Beijing, raised money in Hong Kong to support the demonstrators, and flew to Beijing to join them. Three days after the massacre, he felt drained; the experience would shape the rest of his life. "I am of the generation of the Tiananmen Square movement," he later explained. "I promised the people of

China that I would tell the truth about what happened in Tiananmen Square back in '89."

Lee has taken full advantage of the political freedoms enjoyed in Hong Kong, dedicating much of his adult life to pushing for full democracy there and keeping alive the memories of the Tiananmen protest movement. He served as an elected lawmaker in Hong Kong's Legislative Council from 1995 to 2016 and is one of the special administrative region's most prominent pro-democracy activists and a member of the Hong Kong Alliance. Established in 1989 in support of the Tiananmen protests in Beijing, the alliance has organized annual Tiananmen vigils ever since and also ran the city's June 4th Museum. (On June 1, 2021, Hong Kong authorities forced the museum to close; the staff then digitized the archives and exhibits and put them online.) "Our mandate," Lee told me in a phone call in February 2021, "is to keep the memory alive and to support the movement in China for democracy."

Every year before June 4, Lee and his organization hold a series of talks about the Tiananmen pro-democracy movement and China's record on human rights. In 2020, due to the pandemic, they decided to hold their event series online. Lee opened a paid Zoom account around February and planned a total of four educational events to be held simultaneously on Zoom and Facebook Live in the weeks leading up to that year's Tiananmen anniversary.

"The reason we opened our account on Zoom is that we learned that the Chinese people in the mainland can use Zoom," Lee told me. "Because lots of lectures in Hong Kong can use Zoom. Then those Chinese students in mainland can use Zoom to participate in lectures. The point is to reach out inside China and not just the Hong Kong audience."

The first event, held on May 15, went off without a hitch; Lee used his Zoom account to host a video meeting. The second event, scheduled for May 22, was about the Tiananmen pro-democracy movement and its relevance for the anti-extradition movement in Hong Kong that had set off protests the year before. But half an hour before the talk commenced, the group's plans were thrown into chaos when Lee saw that his Zoom account had been suddenly suspended. The organizers scrambled to communicate with participants and to ensure that they could still use Facebook Live to broadcast the event.

After the event, Lee emailed Zoom to figure out what had happened to his account. For months, he received no substantive reply.

Unbeknownst to him, Jin had been paying close attention to Lee's activities. He had learned about the May 15 meeting and knew that another, similar meeting would be held on May 22. Jin knew that the meeting would be hosted on Zoom's U.S. servers. Even so, on May 21, he sent the meeting identifiers and passwords for Lee's planned May 22 meeting to a Chinese law enforcement official, telling the official that the planned content of the meeting would abrogate Chinese law.

Then Jin messaged a group of U.S.-based Zoom employees about the May 22 meeting, telling them that the company would again be blocked in China if the meeting weren't stopped and the related account suspended. On May 22, shortly before the meeting began, Jin emailed Zoom's U.S.-based compliance officers and told them about the May 15 event that had already occurred; then, according to U.S. court documents, the U.S.-based employees discussed the "political" nature of the event.

On May 22, Zoom suspended Lee's account. Jin didn't have to fabricate evidence or circumvent Zoom's existing guidelines; his warning about the platform's potentially being blocked again had been sufficient. He then emailed his U.S.-based colleagues to thank them for protecting Zoom's operations in China.

Lee learned what had happened to his Zoom account only after its blocking became international news. Still, according to the email he provided to me, Zoom did not reply to his complaint until August 20, when a Zoom customer service employee apologized for the delay and said they were looking into the issue. Lee demanded a refund, which wasn't processed until September.

As it turns out, my February 2021 conversation with Lee would be the last time I would talk with him. Six weeks after our interview, he was sentenced to fourteen months in prison for his role in organizing several "unauthorized" assemblies during the 2019 anti–extradition law protests. Then, in September 2021, Hong Kong authorities charged him and two other Tiananmen activists with inciting subversion, a newly designated crime under the draconian national security law forced on the city in 2020—the subject of this book's ninth chapter. At the time of publication, Lee was still appealing the charges. His targeting by Zoom's law enforcement liaison shortly before this law was imposed in Hong Kong underscores how Chinese security agencies aim to use every means at their disposal to chase down and silence anyone whom the Chinese Communist Party sees as a threat.

The Tiananmen vigil that Zhou had hosted on May 31, just over a week after Lee's event, had gone off without a hitch. Perhaps Jin had learned about the event too late. But he did learn about it and, subsequently, took action.

On June 1, Zoom's Jin messaged several Zoom employees in the United States and asked them to provide him with details of the account that had hosted the meeting. One of the employees sent Jin the account information, including the real name and email address of the account owner and the IP address used to host the May 31 meeting. Another Zoom employee terminated the account. Jin was also provided with the names and IP addresses of all the participants at Zhou's Tiananmen memorial—including those in the United States.

Thus, when Zhou tried to log on to the Zoom account on June 5, he found it had been shut down. Jin's actions to disrupt Tiananmen memorials on Zoom had only just begun. His efforts would soon cross the line into conspiracy and fabrication of evidence.

On June 4, 2020—the thirty-first anniversary of the Tiananmen Square Massacre—Wang Dan logged onto Zoom from his home in Bethesda, Maryland. In 1989, like Zhou Fengsuo, Wang had been a prominent student activist in the pro-democracy movement, leading a ten-mile march from his university to Tiananmen Square and giving passionate speeches against government corruption. Some of the movement's most iconic photos feature Wang, with his fashionably shaggy hair and thick-rimmed glasses of the period, standing and clutching a microphone in front of thousands of students sitting cross-legged on the vast promenade of Tiananmen Square.

Wang had been resting in his dorm room at Beijing University when tanks rolled into downtown Beijing and soldiers opened fire. After several weeks in hiding, he was apprehended and spent much of the next nine years in jail. He was finally released in 1998 and permitted to leave China, settling in Boston for several years, where he completed a PhD in history at Harvard. Since then, he has sought to keep the memory of Tiananmen alive and worked to promote democracy in China.

This year, Wang was cohosting an online Tiananmen vigil from his living room, together with several friends who lived in New York City and had gathered in an apartment there. That apartment was located in a district under the jurisdiction of the U.S. District Court for the Eastern District of New York—the federal court where an FBI special agent would eventually file an arrest warrant for Julien Jin.

The organizers had advertised the Zoom memorial online, and several days beforehand, Wang had posted about the event to his two hundred thousand Twitter followers. The organizers were anticipating a large audience.

Just like Zhou, Wang and his fellow organizers expected trouble. They had chosen Zoom specifically because the platform wasn't blocked in China; they wanted anyone in China who wanted to join to be able to— despite knowing that, by making it open, they would be making it easy for the Chinese government to dispatch people to disrupt the meeting through abusive verbal outbursts, a method Chinese authorities had employed in the past. To guard against this, the organizers upgraded to paid accounts and arranged the settings so that only those called upon would be able to speak, with the other participants muted. They also arranged to screen participants to filter out suspicious-looking accounts.

Even so, Wang ran into problems almost immediately. Around five hundred people joined the call, but almost as soon as it began, Wang unexpectedly found himself kicked off the platform. The organizers scrambled and quickly created a new account, then invited the guests to rejoin the meeting there. Wang also posted the link to the account on Twitter. About three hundred people rejoined the call, and things went smoothly for a little while. But about forty-five minutes later, as Wu'er Kaixi, another well-known Tiananmen student leader, began speaking, Wang again found himself booted off the platform, as did the other organizers. And that was it. They had no choice but to cancel the rest of the event.

This time, to disrupt Wang's meeting, Jin hadn't simply asked Zoom employees to shut it down. Rather, he and a group of people—whom the FBI referred to in court filings as "co-conspirators"—allegedly created a set of dummy email accounts, which they used to email false complaints about the meeting to an official Zoom complaint in-box.

The complaints were accompanied by manufactured evidence that was almost laughably fake. One email claimed that the meeting was inciting "terrorism and violence." According to U.S. court documents, the email included screenshots of fabricated profiles for people who were supposedly participants in the Zoom meeting. One profile was listed as belonging to someone named "Kate Steve," who had uploaded photos to their Zoom account featuring imagery affiliated with the Basque separatist group Euskadi Ta Askatasuna, which was founded in 1959 and designated a terrorist group after numerous bombings and assassinations; the group accepted a cease-fire in 2010 and voluntarily dissolved in 2018. Another Zoom profile featured a photo of someone in a mask holding a flag that resembled the Islamic State's; yet another showed people holding guns while standing with Muslim clerics.

More emailed complaints rolled in, with screenshots of Zoom accounts that were supposedly participating in the June 4 meeting. One image featured a card dealer; another showed two naked women; and several others showed more militant Islamic content. Several emails alleged that the meeting was inciting "racial conflicts."

Anyone doing the slightest bit of due diligence on these complaints would likely have found it odd to see Basque separatists, Islamic State supporters, pornographers, gamblers, and racists joining a Zoom call about a massacre by the Chinese government that had happened more than thirty years before. It was clear that these specific complaints had been chosen not because they made narrative sense but because they ran the gamut of serious violations of Zoom's user guidelines.

To ensure quick action, Jin flagged the complaints to a group of Zoom employees and asked them to terminate both the meeting and the user account hosting it. His request was carried out.

Wang spent months wondering how exactly the Chinese government had been able to get to him. He thought the most likely scenario was that the account suspensions had come through someone with connections to Chinese authorities who lived in the United States and worked for Zoom. But when he learned later that the Zoom meetings had been disrupted by a Chinese national based in Hangzhou, he was shocked. "I think, *Wow. What a world it is,*" Wang told me. "Chinese authorities can even do something in the United States from China." He said it felt almost like a "technological invasion."

"What Chinese authorities did has already directly damaged the normal life of normal American people in the United States," he said. "It kind of hurt the democracy in the United States. It's not only an attack on Chinese dissidents. It's an attack on American society. Because Zoom is an American company."

Wang said that this episode impressed upon him that the Chinese Communist Party "can do anything they want to do, no matter where you live. That's really serious."

———————

For a while, it seemed that Jin and China's security state had won. Tiananmen memorials and subsequent meetings had been shut down, accounts outside China had been closed, and Zoom wasn't responding to emails from the Chinese activists who had been affected. There had certainly been a media storm, and some members of Congress had sent a letter to Zoom demanding accountability, but nothing had really happened. Zoom's profits and user base continued to grow.

Then, on August 10, 2020, Zhou Fengsuo's cell phone rang. It was a number he didn't recognize. When he answered, he heard a man's voice. It was FBI Special Agent Joseph Hugdahl, who, after introducing himself, asked Zhou if he would be able to meet him in a few days' time.

On August 13, on Hugdahl's instructions, Zhou drove to the Fairfield Inn and Suites just outside Newark Liberty International Airport. The cream-colored six-story building sits on a long strip of other nondescript hotels lining Interstate 78, which skirts the busy airport. With airplanes taking off and landing throughout the day, it was hardly a quiet spot—but it was private.

Zhou met Hugdahl and another agent in a room with two queen-size beds and a table at the front end. The three of them sat around the table for four hours as Hugdahl and his partner asked Zhou to tell them about what had happened in the days leading up to the Tiananmen memorial and what happened afterward.

Hugdahl and his colleagues at the FBI had, in fact, been busy for quite a while. In June, amid the media outcry, Zoom had received a grand jury subpoena from the U.S. Attorney's Office for the Eastern District of New York. The next month, Zoom's offices in San Francisco received subpoenas from both the U.S. Attorney's Office for the Northern District of California and the U.S. Securities and Exchange Commission. Agents interviewed Wang Dan in Maryland and others in the United States who had been affected by the account suspensions and meeting shutdowns.

As the investigation deepened, the FBI scrutinized thousands of emails, text messages, and other communications from dozens of Zoom employees, U.S. court documents show. Agents examined IP addresses, noted time stamps on emails sent to generic Zoom in-boxes, and compared them with communications to and from Julien Jin.

On November 18, 2020—as chance would have it, exactly one year after the Chinese government unblocked Zoom's servers in China after the company's thorough "rectification"—Hugdahl filed a forty-seven-page indictment against Zoom employee Julien Jin. A month later, on December 18, the Department of Justice unsealed the indictment and charged Jin with conspiracy to commit interstate harassment and unlawful conspiracy to transfer a means of identification.

To Zhou Fengsuo, the indictment was groundbreaking. For years, Chinese activists, Uyghurs, Tibetans, and others in the United States whose activities or very existence had attracted the ire of the Chinese government had reported similar incidents to the FBI, often to sympathetic agents, but little action had ever been taken. "This was the first time that law enforcement in the United States was paying attention to our suffering, to the injustice to us happening on U.S. soil," Zhou told me.

The charges against Jin were quite creative. The common wisdom among people who followed Beijing's extraterritorial censorship and its digital pursuit of Chinese activists abroad had long been that there was likely no legal or government recourse to stop these actions, given that they were perpetrated by Chinese state–linked actors located in China. Deeming what Jin did as interstate harassment was a "very unique charge under Title 18" of the U.S. criminal code, Joan Meyer, a former federal prosecutor and lawyer who specializes in global white-collar crime, told me. FBI investigators had carefully drawn out every thread tying Jin's actions to U.S. soil in some way, Meyer said.

The forty-seven-page document didn't just lay out Jin's illegal activities. In the first few paragraphs, the Department of Justice also issued a strong political statement that reads almost as an indictment of the Chinese government. It described China's government as a "one-party state" that "regards any political dissent as a threat not only to its own political interests, but also to the PRC's one-party system of government." The indictment described the way that Chinese authorities had turned access to China's markets into a highly effective form of political leverage, noting that "service providers who fail to adhere to the PRC government's censorship requirements risk being excluded from the PRC's market." It also acknowledged the extraterritorial censorship that the Chinese government had exerted with growing boldness, stating that Beijing's "efforts to censor political dissent do not end at the PRC's national borders."

The public statements issued by top Department of Justice officials at the time the indictment was unsealed make that position even clearer. "The allegations in the complaint lay bare the Faustian bargain that the PRC government demands of U.S. technology companies doing business within the PRC's borders, and the insider threat that those companies face from their own employees in the PRC," Acting U.S. Attorney Seth D. DuCharme said on December 18.

John C. Demers, assistant attorney general in charge of the DOJ's National Security Division, also said that no company with operations in China could be free from the "coercive power" of Beijing. "The Chinese Communist Party will use those within its reach to sap the tree of liberty, stifling free speech in China, the United States and elsewhere about the party's repression of the Chinese people," he said. "For companies with operations in China, like that here, this reality may mean executives being co-opted to further repressive activity at odds with the values that have allowed that company to flourish here."

Perhaps the most chilling part of the indictment, however, came in the final paragraph, on page forty-seven, right above Special Agent Hugdahl's signature: "When senior [Zoom] executives asked Jin to provide documentation detailing all of the PRC law enforcement requests he had received in connection with the action taken against accounts hosting Tiananmen Square anniversary meetings, Jin stated that there was no legal documentation for the PRC government requests to terminate the June 4th political accounts.'" Jin suggested that Zoom should give "incites terrorism and violence," a violation of Zoom's terms of service, as the reason for the account closures.

In other words, China's security services communicated with Jin in a manner that allowed certain communications to remain out of the hands of the company and anyone else. And Jin denied that Chinese law enforcement had asked him to censor political content in the United States.

This strongly suggests that China's security agencies had told Jin to keep their requests to him a secret—even from top Zoom executives and even in the face of a U.S. government investigation. If this is the case, it may be the first known example of the use of Article 7 of China's National Intelligence Law to obtain the assistance of a U.S. company employee in China.

The National Intelligence Law, enacted in 2017, raised deep consternation among security analysts and foreign businesses with operations in China. The latest in a raft of security laws passed during Xi Jinping's tenure, it gives legal standing to a wide array of intelligence activities and mandates that organizations and individuals comply with requests from China's security agencies. Article 7 in particular makes these demands clear: "Any organization or citizen shall support, assist and cooperate with the state intelligence work in accordance with the law, and shall protect national intelligence work secrets they are aware of." The law's vague language, meanwhile, allows for broad interpretation of what state requests and activities are permitted.

"Of special concern are signs that the Intelligence Law's drafters are trying to shift the balance of these legal obligations from intelligence 'defense' to 'offense,'" Murray Scot Tanner, an expert on Chinese law enforcement and internal security, wrote when the law was implemented. In other words, the law seemed to create "affirmative legal responsibilities for Chinese and, in some cases, foreign citizens, companies, or organizations operating in China to provide access, cooperation, or support for Beijing's intelligence-gathering activities."

Taken another way, the law requires that private companies or individual employees of those companies become temporary arms of China's security state whenever and however Chinese authorities require. "Companies are faced with draconian consequences," Meyer, the former federal prosecutor, told me. "If they want to operate in China, they have to comply with Chinese law, even if [it is] in conflict with their local jurisdiction. And if Chinese law enforcement begins making inquiries and alleging that a company could be in violation of Chinese national security law, what is the company to do? Are you violating a national security law in the PRC by protecting freedom of speech and the privacy interests of your employees and customers? And PRC laws are written so broadly, they can apply to activity and individuals both in and outside China as long as there is a nexus to China. It presents enormous hurdles to a foreign company if it wants to operate in China."

Jin's work on behalf of China's security agencies to obtain Zoom user data and to carry out repressive activities at the agencies' request, while apparently hiding some of these activities from Zoom executives, is a chilling example of what China's 2017 National Intelligence Law looks like in practice. The FBI's work to uncover exactly how Jin operated and at whose instructions, with direct implications for Americans trying to exercise their freedom of speech and assembly, demonstrates that the 2017 law is no longer a theoretical concern.

Meyer believes that the indictment served as a warning to U.S. tech companies with operations in China that "they [had] better monitor their PRC employees."

Before the FBI investigation, Zoom executives did not know the extent of Jin's activities on behalf of China's security agencies. But they did know that their operations in China entailed a significant security risk.

At the time, Zoom had more than seven hundred employees in China, many of them part of its research and development team. In its January 2020 filings to the U.S. Securities and Exchange Commission, the company stated that its "high concentration of research and development personnel in China" could "expose us to market scrutiny regarding the integrity of our solution or data security features. Any security compromise in our industry, whether actual or perceived, could harm our reputation, erode confidence in the effectiveness of our security measures, negatively affect our ability to attract new customers and hosts, cause existing customers to elect not to renew their subscriptions or subject us to third-party lawsuits, regulatory fines, or other action or liability, which could harm our business."

Despite this risk, Zoom's official position was that its China operations presented a "strategic advantage" because they allowed the company to "invest more in increasing our product capabilities in an efficient manner."

"If we had to relocate our product development team from China to another jurisdiction, we could experience, among other things, higher operating expenses, which would adversely impact our operating margins and harm our business," Zoom stated in its January 2020 filings. "In addition, we would need to spend considerable time and effort recruiting a new product development team, which would distract management and adversely impact our ability to continue improving our platform's features and functionality."

———————

Since the FBI investigation began, Zoom has taken numerous measures to try to regain trust and establish better protocols to protect its users. The company fired Jin and placed some other employees on administrative leave. It also established what it calls an Insider Threat Program to monitor for signs of suspicious activity by its employees.

"Going forward Zoom will not allow requests from the Chinese government to impact anyone outside of mainland China," the company wrote in a June 11, 2020, statement posted to its website. Zoom also said it would develop the capability to block users based on geography. "This will enable us to comply with requests from local authorities when they determine activity on our platform is illegal within their borders; however, we will also be able to protect these conversations for participants outside of those borders where the activity is allowed," the company added.

Zoom has since adopted other measures to increase transparency, including tracking requests from governments and publishing those requests on its website. "Since the beginning of 2021, there have been seven requests from China; all have been denied or withdrawn. Moreover, whether it involves the Chinese government or any other government, we do not facilitate government intercepts for Zoom meetings and webinars. These sorts of requests would be denied as a result, and the request and denial would be included in our transparency reporting," a Zoom spokesperson told me in December 2022. "Zoom is safe, secure, and protected by sophisticated encryption and data security protocols. We do not monitor our users' meetings."

But Zoom has not moved to close its research and development offices in China or to relocate those employees abroad. Zoom announced in May 2020 that it would open research-and-development centers in Phoenix and Pittsburgh, and in December 2020 added Singapore to that list. But when I asked in December 2022 if Zoom was planning to phase out its research-and-development team in China, the company provided no response.

———————

On January 13, 2021, I rounded the corner of the Department of Justice headquarters in downtown Washington, DC. It was a chilly Wednesday morning, a week after the insurrection at the U.S. Capitol on January 6, and the streets surrounding the National Mall were still closed to traffic for blocks in every direction.

I was scheduled to meet with John Demers, who at the time was the head of the National Security Division at the Department of Justice. He had overseen a shift in the department's priorities and had made China's economic espionage and other forms of covert operations a top area of focus.

Some career officials in the department viewed this move as long overdue. For years, people who worked on the department's China portfolio had seen the Chinese government's operations in the United States become ever more frequent, brazen, and consequential. But the resources dedicated to the issue did not grow apace, and the number of Chinese-speaking agents tasked to investigate remained pitifully small, particularly in FBI field offices but even in the Bureau's central headquarters. Even for those cases that were pursued, the department's goal was to disrupt the covert activity, not to make the nature of China's activities public. When operations were successfully disrupted, indictments were not issued, arrests were not made, and, thus, court documents were not filed. Whatever covert activity the Chinese government had attempted remained a secret.

As a result, there was a growing gap between what the U.S government knew China was attempting on U.S. soil and what the U.S. public knew—which was almost nothing. This was cause for increasing alarm within the department's ranks, especially because much of China's activities weren't traditional espionage, such as theft of state secrets like missile defense plans. Rather, Chinese party-state actors or proxies were increasingly involved in different forms of economic espionage and the use of economic leverage for political purposes (such as coercing companies into censoring content), activities that often take place in the private sector and don't lend themselves to prosecution with traditional espionage charges. The best defense against such activity isn't to prosecute it to death but, rather, to foster widespread awareness throughout society that such activity is taking place. But when most of the information about China's covert operations on U.S. soil remained classified, ensuring that awareness became impossible.

These two problems—lack of resources dedicated to countering China's covert activities and lack of public awareness—were addressed in the U.S. Strategic Framework for the Indo-Pacific, approved in February 2018 as part of the Trump administration's National Security Strategy. The Strategic Framework stated that the U.S. government should "expand and prioritize U.S. intelligence and law enforcement activities that counter Chinese influence operations" and "strengthen defensive and offensive counter-intelligence functions across the public and private sectors to neutralize China's growing intelligence advantages." The framework also called for "educating governments, businesses, universities, Chinese overseas students, news media, and general citizenries about China's coercive behavior and influence operations around the globe." The China Initiative, launched in November 2018, was aimed in part at accomplishing these objectives.

Sitting far across from each other at a large conference table, Demers and I wore masks for the duration of the hour-long interview. The U.S. national security community has tended to focus on questions of military power and traditional intelligence, but Demers displayed a clear grasp of China's economic statecraft. "Whenever I get asked what makes China different from Russia, from Iran, from North Korea, it's that they have a tremendous amount of economic power that those other countries don't have. And they are not hesitant to use that economic power to further their political goals," he told me.

The indictment of Julien Jin was another example of how difficult it is to do business in China without getting pressured to help the Chinese government, Demers said. (The Justice Department has never publicly confirmed that Zoom is the "Company-1" listed in the indictment, and neither did Demers.)

"One of the things we always try to do in these cases is educate," he explained. "We were concerned about people who might continue to be using this product, and making sure that they understand what the risks are when they use that product, whether the risk is surveillance or disruption. In some ways, if you're lucky, all they're doing is disrupting your meeting. If you're unlucky, they're surveilling it and then taking some action down the road that you may not even be able to link back to that surveillance."

I asked Demers if the Zoom case was representative, if it was just one of numerous similar cases the department might be working on. He didn't answer directly, saying instead that general statements about what Chinese law demands—in this case, providing assistance to Chinese intelligence agencies and keeping that assistance a secret—don't really penetrate the public consciousness. "What our indictments do," he replied, is "tell a story. As human beings, it's the stories that stick with us."

Every government in the world is facing the new and growing challenge of digital governance and national security in the internet age. It's no surprise that the Chinese government has also sought to beef up its cybersecurity and internet governance laws. Some of these measures address universal concerns of digital governance, privacy, and rights, such as China's push to prevent private actors from illegally obtaining and abusing internet user data.

But Beijing's approach here goes farther than what democracies have so far pursued and, in some ways, is fundamentally different. Chinese government regulators require electronic service communications providers operating within China's borders to monitor live communications, to block content deemed politically sensitive or illegal, to suspend accounts transmitting such content, and to hand over any related data and personal information upon request by a Chinese law enforcement or national security agency. The Cybersecurity Law that took effect in June 2017 required companies to store data for Chinese users on servers in China, strengthening Chinese state control over this information.

Beijing's approach to managing digital spaces is another manifestation of the Chinese Communist Party's emphasis on "rule by law." The phrase used in Chinese, *fazhiquan*, is also the translation for "rule of law," but scholars of Chinese law, such as Jerome Cohen, have long used the phrase "rule *by* law" to distinguish between what the party means by *fazhiquan* and what liberal democracies mean by "rule of law." "Rule *by* law" means using law to impose the government's will on society, whereas "rule *of* law" confers rights on citizens and, as often as not, means using the law to restrain the power of the government.

Written, codified law also conveys a sense of legitimacy and even pride. Two decades ago, the Chinese government, like plenty of its illiberal counterparts in other regions of the world, sometimes gave lip service to democracy and would deny that it was doing some of the clearly repressive things it was doing. Xi Jinping's push for rule by law, however, has enshrined into law many of the authoritarian practices Chinese government officials were already implementing—by definition, making those practices public and giving them the government's official stamp of approval. This change represents the confidence that party members now often have toward China's model of governance and a true belief that what they are doing is the right path.

Such restrictive laws would have backfired if they had been spearheaded by a country with a small economy. Foreign companies simply wouldn't bother. But China's economy is massive, and it's still a key growth market. Any foreign company that fails to comply with China's laws is shut out of the Chinese market. Facebook has refused to agree to these surveillance and censorship demands; as a result, its website has been blocked in China since at least 2009, and aside from an ad sales office in Shenzhen, it has little presence on Chinese soil. Zoom, like LinkedIn, saw what happened to Facebook and chose to take Beijing's proffered path.

As the Chinese government enshrines censorship, surveillance, and data usage into law, it provides foreign multinationals and U.S. tech companies with a ready-made excuse they can give their audiences back home when the companies censor on behalf of the Chinese government. Company after company has excused its behavior in this way. "Just like any global company, we must comply with applicable laws in the jurisdictions where we operate," a Zoom spokesperson told me in a statement in June 2020. "When a meeting is held across different countries, the participants within those countries are required to comply with their respective local laws. We aim to limit the actions we take to those necessary to comply with local law and continuously review and improve our process on these matters."

LinkedIn trotted out similar language after its concessions to the Chinese government in exchange for market access eventually got it into hot water. In February 2014, the company had agreed to China's demands for a filtered version of its professional networking platform, and in exchange, LinkedIn became one of the few U.S. social media companies with significant operations in that country. In March 2021, China's internet regulators punished LinkedIn, which had been acquired by Microsoft in 2016, for failing to censor political content on its China-based platform, suspending new sign-ups for a month and requiring the company to submit a review to the Cyberspace Administration of China. Three months later, LinkedIn began aggressively censoring the profiles of prominent academics and journalists outside China that mentioned politically sensitive topics, including the Tiananmen Square Massacre.

LinkedIn even encouraged users to censor their own profiles—though the word the platform chose to use was *update*, rather than *censor*. In emails to affected users, LinkedIn stated, "We will work with you to minimize the impact and can review your profile's accessibility within China if you update the Education section of your profile. But the decision whether to update your profile is yours." It was shocking to see a U.S company offering to assist American users—in one case, a congressional staffer—in making sure their profiles were sufficiently edited to fall in line with Chinese government censorship demands. It's an example of how organizational infrastructures are being built up in the United States to accommodate and proactively implement Chinese Communist Party censorship and to "help" users outside China implement that censorship, too.

"It's clear to us that in order to create value for our members in China and around the world, we will need to implement the Chinese government's restrictions on content, when and to the extent required," LinkedIn said in a statement amid media scrutiny of its behavior. Despite the extensive media coverage, the censored profiles were not restored.

After the passage of China's Cybersecurity Law in 2017, Apple agreed to Chinese government demands to store Chinese user data domestically. Prior to that, much of this data, including contacts, messages, and photos, had been stored outside China. The company built a new facility on the outskirts of Guiyang, the capital city of the historically impoverished inland province of Guizhou. The personal data of Chinese users was stored on a server run by a Chinese state–owned company, with Chinese government employees staffing the data center. Apple's encryption keys are also stored in that facility.

It's illegal for U.S. companies to hand over data to the Chinese government, but Apple took a wide berth around that law by ceding ownership of its data center in Guiyang to a Chinese company owned by the Guizhou provincial government. It also created an internal, U.S.-based bureaucracy for removing apps from its Chinese App Store that the Chinese government might consider sensitive or illegal.

Apple, too, cited China's laws to justify its behavior. "In China, the law stipulates that iCloud data belonging to its nationals must remain in the country. We comply with the law . . . We abide by the laws in all of the countries where we operate, including China, and our teams must remove apps that fail to comply with them. These decisions are not always easy, and we may not agree with the laws that shape them. But our priority remains creating the best user experience without violating the rules we are obligated to follow," the company said in a May 2021 statement.

Data localization laws are a growing trend everywhere, particularly among authoritarian countries, including Indonesia, Russia, Turkey, and Vietnam. Though most European countries and Australia and the United States have not passed such laws, in 2015, Germany updated a data storage law to add requirements that user data be stored domestically and automatically deleted after a period of time. In a 2016 report, the U.S.-based Information Technology and Innovation Foundation (ITIF) criticized Germany's law as "mercantilist" and compared it to laws in China, Russia, and Turkey. "Fully half of all global trade in services now depends on access to cross-border data flows," ITIF's Nigel Cory said. "Inhibiting the flow of this data, for both modern and traditional businesses which increasingly rely on data undermines their ability to leverage economies of scale in global markets to use to invest in further research and development."

But there's an important distinction. In Germany, the data localization law is intended to protect the *user*, and when local government access to their data is used for investigations, the country's strong rule of law means the government can't easily abuse that access for corrupt or politically coercive reasons. In China, data localization is primarily intended to strengthen the *state*, granting it direct access to the private user data of political targets or for any other purpose of its choosing. The prioritization of innovation and "economies of scale" over basic user protections in the face of expansive authoritarian regimes is an example of the distortions that can occur when profits are divorced from political values.

"Only inside Germany can high demands be comprehensively guaranteed and regularly checked," the German economy ministry said in a statement in 2017. "By storing data abroad it can't be ruled out that the foreign state will gain access to the data by dint of its interior law."

The statements that Apple, LinkedIn, and Zoom have made justifying their implementation of Chinese government security measures and censorship provide a clear look at what happens when companies are incentivized to put their public relations spin capabilities to work on behalf of an authoritarian government. Neither the Chinese government nor U.S. companies look good when their activities in support of political repression are revealed; thus, both Chinese authorities and the U.S. companies implementing their demands are incentivized to lie, deceive, spin, and cover up.

Several broader lessons can be drawn from Zoom's experience in China. First, by establishing a relationship with China's Ministry of State Security and cybersecurity authorities, any U.S. or foreign company is putting its operations and reputation at risk, even if, on paper, the relationship has clearly delineated boundaries. Julien Jin was a Zoom employee who was appointed by the company itself to be the liaison between Zoom and the Chinese government. But the secretive and ever-expanding demands of China's security police turned him from a Zoom employee first and foremost into a de facto embedded government agent in the company, with access to its systems and an unofficial ability to draw on company relationships to secretly expand his limited access. Jin's initial role wasn't a secret. According to U.S. government documents, even Zoom CEO Eric Yuan had direct knowledge of it and was in direct communication with Jin about the role.

Zoom has chosen to deal with this risk not by dismantling its China operations and cutting off all ties to Chinese security police but, rather, by doing the opposite: developing the capability to prevent China-based users from logging on to meetings outside China that China deems "illegal" or, as one Quartz headline put it, promising to "be better at censoring global calls at Beijing's request." Such a capability would involve working even more closely with the Chinese government and its security police to establish exactly how and where Chinese user data should be stored, exactly how fast Chinese authorities require responses, and what exactly those responses should be.

Zoom's Insider Threat Program is more a kind of doublespeak than a meaningful policy response. There is no insider threat; the threat comes directly from the government that Zoom has bent over backward to mollify and from the local laws Zoom has repeatedly and publicly promised to follow.

The second lesson from the Zoom-China case is that the Chinese government will take everything it can until clear boundaries are drawn—and even then, those boundaries must be defended against encroachment. When Chinese security officials asked Jin to transfer the Zoom user data of numerous U.S.-based individuals, this action was already illegal under U.S. law. Jin's actions to disrupt Zoom meetings held outside China violated the company's terms of service, but he was still able to accomplish what he wanted in spite of that. It was media coverage and a sweeping FBI investigation that finally got Zoom to fire him.

Beijing has articulated a vision of "internet sovereignty," a model that supports its right to remove any content from the internet within China's borders. This articulation of internet sovereignty is primarily defensive, a communication to the democratic world that its freewheeling information ecosystem isn't welcome in China. That iteration of an internet governance model would seem to suggest that Chinese authorities wouldn't try to extend their reach beyond the borders of China's own internet. But the Zoom case demonstrates that Chinese security authorities don't view themselves as bound by the concept of internet sovereignty to act only within China's digital borders. Rather, it was the forceful intervention of

U.S. federal law enforcement that stopped the local Ministry of Public Security bureau and Ministry of State Security bureau from using a Zoom employee to extend their reach into the United States' digital borders.

Third, journalism and civil society action increasingly will only have efficacy in halting the Chinese Communist Party's expanding authoritarianism to the extent to which those efforts result in U.S. government action. In the face of extremely compelling incentives in the form of market access and profits to simply ride out U.S. media storms related to China—and with the risk of a media counter-storm in China and state-fanned boycotts by Chinese consumers should the U.S. company do something to "hurt the feelings of the Chinese people"—U.S. companies have become less likely to reject Chinese government demands in response to popular scrutiny in the United States alone.

Zoom is a good example of this: the June 2020 media storm over its suspension of several accounts connected to Tiananmen memorials resulted, eventually, in the company's reinstating those accounts but also resulted in its decision to develop the capability to block Chinese users from attending meetings beyond China's borders, a further entrenchment of the Chinese government's desired model. It was the Department of Justice's decision to launch an investigation, the individual dedication of Special Agent Hugdahl and his colleagues, and the unprecedented decision to pursue creative charges and issue a public indictment that finally turned the screws on Zoom.

But even public knowledge of how China's security services could infiltrate Zoom meetings did not seem to significantly dent American enthusiasm for the teleconferencing platform. In June 2021, the company reported huge earnings and sales growth of 191 percent in the first quarter of that year. The U.S. government continued to use Zoom. As of March 2021, the Biden White House was still using Zoom's more secure government services for unclassified meetings. Universities and companies across the country still use it. "Even Harvard University is still using Zoom as a teaching platform. They all know Zoom is unsafe," Wang Dan told me in June 2021. "Most American people or companies aren't aware that this threat can be real. Maybe they think this only happens between Chinese dissidents. I think it's kind of naïve."

Sunlight and civil action work only as a means to an end: to try to force action on the part of those who hold real power. When national debates are focused on unrelated issues such as domestic political controversies; and when China's actions have become so common as to seem normal, media scrutiny, if it even exists, may have little effect. Concerted legal action by numerous democratic governments and sustained enforcement are the only ways to hold the line against the Chinese Communist Party's attempts to change the global narrative through coercion and to force government and private actors to behave in alignment with its illiberal and harmful goals.

Beijing is sensitive to public scrutiny and knows that anytime its secret activities become public, it takes a reputational hit. The Chinese Communist Party attempts to ameliorate this situation in several ways. In the short term, it tries to hide its behavior, using deception, coercion, and various covert means. If it can't hide its behavior, it will change its behavior to more closely comply with the established boundaries. But, in the long run, the Chinese Communist Party aims to slowly change the values that make such behavior considered beyond the pale. Beijing wants the world to accept its jurisdiction over ethnic Chinese living outside China. It wants the world to accept that criticizing Chinese government behavior is always a violation of China's sovereignty and, thus, a form of meddling in its domestic affairs. And Beijing wants its demands to be normalized on a global scale—for it to be widely known and accepted as an unavoidable reality that any action or activity outside China that the Chinese government strongly opposes will come at a high price—whereas preemptively halting these activities and accommodating the CCP's demands will reap rewards in the form of company profits or other incentives.

––––––––

U.S. tech companies with operations in China are increasingly facing one of two paths. They will either have to choose between the Chinese market and the U.S. market or they will have to create a firewall, isolating their China operations from their operations elsewhere. Companies that faced China's ax the earliest, such as Facebook, Twitter, and Google, who left the market or were blocked around 2009 and 2010, took the first path, choosing to stay out of China rather than reworking their operations to comply with the government's censorship demands. Companies that were later to the game, such as LinkedIn and Zoom, acceded to Beijing's demands, not just for censorship but increasingly for a much deeper integration with Chinese government security and surveillance institutions. (Chinese tech companies, by comparison, have only one possible path—doing everything the Chinese government says. Chinese tech company Bytedance, which as of March 2023 still owns the short video platform TikTok, has no democratic home base to retreat to.)

But Google seemed to regret its earlier decision to leave the market. Former Google CEO Eric Schmidt, who ran the company at that time, said in 2019 that he had disagreed with Google's exit from China in 2010. "I believed they would be better to stay in China, and help change China to be more open," he told the BBC in a 2019 interview.

In 2018, Google began a secret project to develop a bespoke search engine for the Chinese market. Code-named "Dragonfly," it was designed with a local Chinese company and would have Chinese government censorship baked right into it. To avoid scrutiny and keep the project a secret, project management circumvented Google's usual oversight mechanisms. The search engine would automatically have banned key Chinese-language search terms such as "Nobel Prize," "human rights," and "student protests."

After the news website the Intercept revealed the existence of Project Dragonfly, more than 1,400 Google employees signed an open letter calling on the company to cancel the project. "Dragonfly in China would establish a dangerous precedent at a volatile political moment, one that would make it harder for Google to deny other countries similar concessions," the employees wrote. "Dragonfly would also enable censorship and government-directed disinformation, and destabilize the ground truth on which popular deliberation and dissent rely. . . . Many of us accepted employment at Google with the company's values in mind, including its previous position on Chinese censorship and surveillance, and an understanding that Google was a company willing to place its values above its profits," the employees wrote. "We no longer believe this is the case. This is why we're taking a stand."

In October 2018, Google CEO Sundar Pichai was still defending Dragonfly proudly. He said at a public event that the program would be able to respond to "well over 99 percent" of queries, indicating that less than 1 percent of users would be blacklisted. And Dragonfly would be able to provide better information to Chinese users than they currently had access to, such as more reliable information about cancer treatments. "People don't understand fully, but you're always balancing a set of values," Pichai said. "But we also follow the rule of law in every country."

But later on in the interview, he provided a rather more honest answer for why Google had pursued the project: "Given how important the market is and how many users there are, we feel obliged to think hard about this problem and take a longer-term view."

In an October 2018 speech delivered at the Hudson Institute—the administration's opening salvo against China in what would become the defining foreign policy legacy of the Trump years—Vice President Mike Pence demanded that Google scrap Project Dragonfly, warning that such a product would "strengthen Communist Party censorship and compromise the privacy of Chinese customers." He also said that U.S. businesses were increasingly aware that operating in China could mean "turning over their intellectual property or abetting Beijing's oppression."

A Google executive confirmed in July 2019 that Dragonfly had been canceled—meaning it took over a year, through multiple internal leaks, wall-to-wall press coverage, an open letter signed by more than 1,400 employees, a threatened employee walkout, public urging from the U.S. vice president, and grilling in front of a U.S. congressional committee to get the project canceled. That kind of full-court mobilization of civil society resources can't and won't happen every time a big U.S. company tries to integrate Chinese government censorship into its operations. A stronger regulatory environment is required.

Zoom, for now, is pursuing the firewall approach, trying to split off its China operations from the rest of the world. But Jacob Helberg, who previously led Google's internal efforts to combat foreign interference and who worked, briefly, on Project Dragonfly, told me that is most likely a losing battle. "You have these global companies that are trying to straddle doing business in the free world and doing business in the autocratic world. And when we're talking about the autocratic world, we're really talking about China. Because they're the ones with the wherewithal to set rules," Helberg said.

The dilemma that companies like Zoom, Google, and Apple are facing is "how to be a company that has company values, and then trying to build products that are value agnostic," he said. "It's really hard to articulate and defend that. And it's even harder over time when you try to gerrymander the same product, where you make one version for one market, and another version for another market." What happens eventually, Helberg added, is that one system wins out over the other.

LinkedIn eventually made an about-face—one in which I was peripherally involved. On the morning of Tuesday, September 28, 2021, I received an email from LinkedIn customer support stating that due to "prohibited content," my profile could no longer be viewed in China, though it could still be viewed anywhere outside China. After I wrote about the block on Twitter, it became a national controversy. The LinkedIn profiles of two other journalists, Melissa Chan and Greg Bruno, had also been blocked in China. Members of Congress weighed in, calling on LinkedIn and its owner, Microsoft, to answer key questions about how our profiles had been blocked. Had the company taken it upon itself to implement a regime of self-censorship, tasking its own employees with reading through profiles and making educated guesses about which ones contained content the Chinese government might view as illegal? Or had Chinese government officials directly provided our names to LinkedIn? If so, which Chinese government office or bureau had communicated this to LinkedIn, and who at LinkedIn had been tasked to be their liaison? The answers to these important questions remain unknown.

My profile was not restored in China, but just over two weeks later, LinkedIn announced that it would shut down its app in China, citing "a significantly more challenging operating environment and greater compliance requirements in China." What the announcement didn't say was that LinkedIn hadn't lived up to its revenue expectations in the Chinese market; in 2020, less than 2 percent of its revenue came from that market. This suggests that, at least by LinkedIn's calculus, the political and reputational risks of complying with Chinese government demands had outpaced the rewards of doing so.

―――――――――

It is popular to blame Zoom, Apple, Google, and LinkedIn for implementing Chinese government repression, or to view them as complicit. But these companies are simply behaving according to the rule that U.S. society has laid out over the past several decades: maximize profit wherever you can without breaking laws. This behavioral expectation is embedded in an environment where corporate social responsibility, rather than concerted government action, is viewed as the appropriate path to better social values and outcomes. If a company fails to act rightly, then, it is the company's fault alone—not that of an inherently flawed social-political system that expects profits and markets to somehow create virtuous power structures.

But the Chinese Communist Party has learned how to game this system. Through consistent application of law, coercion, and rewards, it has forcibly changed the market experience to incentivize profit-seeking organizations to do whatever it says. If we continue to place blame at the feet of corporations, rather than examining the political ideas that have put corporations on a moral pedestal, we will simply be perpetuating the vulnerabilities and blind spots that the CCP has learned to exploit.

Market analysts tend to dismiss long-term concerns about this trend by suggesting that the Chinese government simply won't be able to keep up this kind of pressure without chasing away foreign businesses—i.e., overregulation in the form of political control will chase away capital and incentivize Beijing to change its policies—thus providing reassurance that market incentives will have the final word. But this simply isn't what has happened. Rather, the Chinese government seems to have recognized, long before Western observers caught on, that the potential riches at its command are so great that it can push almost as much as it wishes, and foreign business will still come knocking. If there is some loss of investment, China's leaders seem to view this as a political control "tax"—a small price to pay for a long-term investment in shaping global business, internet, and governance values in the CCP's favor.

The single most important takeaway from Zoom's experience in China is that there is no market-based solution to the problem of Chinese government coercion of U.S. businesses with operations on Chinese soil. Democratic societies cannot look to companies to fix this. The only alternative to a market-based solution is one of government action. All markets are shaped by government regulations; as any student of economic history knows, maintaining truly free markets requires a strong government hand.

At a minimum, the United States must better defend its "digital borders." No U.S. company can withstand China's security state on its own. Only the U.S. government has the ability to defend the rights of U.S.

companies and the freedoms of American citizens on U.S. soil and to provide the tools to allow U.S. companies to defend these rights. The United States must communicate clearly both to companies and to the Chinese government what is legal and what is illegal under U.S. law—and then impose consistent consequences when those laws are broken. So far, the U.S. and other democratic governments are still scrambling to figure out how to create a democratic digital governance framework for their own societies and have spent little energy on trying to create a more proactive and even offensive push to establish global democratic norms in digital and tech spaces.

Some top tech executives are coming around to this position as well. "China plays by a different set of rules that allow it to benefit from corporate espionage, illiberal surveillance, and a blurry line between its public and private sector," stated a January 2021 report—authored by, among others, Eric Schmidt, Jigsaw CEO Jared Cohen, and Center for a New American Security CEO Richard Fontaine—that circulated in the Biden administration and among National Security Council officials in 2020. The report's authors called for "bifurcation" between the United States and China tech sectors, and for closer cooperation between Silicon Valley and Washington.

6

WHO AND THE PARTY MAN

At first, World Health Organization director general Tedros Adhanom Ghebreyesus appeared to be Beijing's man in WHO. On multiple occasions, he made clear choices to help protect China's core interests, sometimes in ways that damaged global trust in the organization.

The Trump administration certainly viewed him that way. On April 14, 2020, after weeks of intensifying criticism of the organization, President Trump announced that the United States would halt funding of WHO, accusing it of "severely mismanaging and covering up the spread of the coronavirus."

But the former health minister of Ethiopia, a scholarly looking man with glasses and graying hair at his temples, proved to be more independent than he had at first appeared. Over the course of the next two years, he went from effusively praising the Chinese government's pandemic response and repeating Beijing's rhetoric, to directly stating that Beijing needed to be held accountable, to finding his words censored on China's internet—and finally, to directly criticizing China for withholding important data on the pandemic's possible origins.

To understand why Tedros acted the way he did, we must look not to his experience as health minister but rather to the powerful position he subsequently held for four years: as Ethiopia's foreign minister, in charge of shepherding the country's crucial relationship with China. The strategic partnership between Beijing and Ethiopia's former ruling party, the Ethiopian People's Revolutionary Democratic Front, reached its pinnacle during Tedros's tenure as foreign minister, as China sought to secure Ethiopia's friendship as the diplomatic gateway to Africa.

Tedros the health minister led WHO's global response, which public health experts generally agree he did with skill. It was Tedros the politician, however, who dealt with China. Tedros's career was forged in Ethiopia's authoritarian one-party state, which he learned to navigate with political savvy and an eye to achieving goals without stepping on the toes of party leaders. He was, in that sense, a party man. Tedros drew on those skills, and on the relationships he had built up in Beijing, as he tried to coax an authoritarian regime to open up to WHO.

His is a high-stakes case study that tested the efficacy of the Chinese Communist Party's decades-long attempts to cultivate African leaders and to impress upon them the sanctity of upholding China's core interests. The CCP has long sought to build close ties with African nations, at first as a revolutionary party joining hands with other revolutionary non-Western governments to throw off the yoke of imperialism and, then, decades later, as a pragmatic rising world power looking to scoop up natural resources and strengthen its geopolitical standing. Beijing has made vast inroads using economics, trade, politics, and diplomacy to construct networks of influence across developing nations. These efforts were particularly successful with Ethiopia's former ruling party, which one Chinese scholar has described as China's "best student."

But these investments don't always pay off the way the party hopes. Its foreign interlocutors have their own goals and loyalties and their own means of achieving them. Tedros demonstrated that, despite his years of commitment to preserving good ties with Beijing, his first loyalty as WHO chief was to public health. When Chinese leaders repeatedly showed that reputational damage control, rather than public health, was their top concern, Tedros stopped giving them the benefit of the doubt. It was a hopeful, if imperfect, outcome.

WHO followed normal protocol during the days after it first received initial reports of a new viral illness in Wuhan. On January 1, 2020, the organization activated incident management protocols and put regional offices on alert, and on January 5, it published its first disease outbreak report, stating that there were forty-four known cases in Wuhan.

But in the weeks to come, WHO public communications about the virus exhibited a notable deference to Beijing. On January 14, in a now-infamous tweet, WHO claimed that "preliminary investigations conducted by the Chinese authorities have found no clear evidence of human-to-human transmission of the novel #coronavirus." The statement amplified Chinese government misinformation more than two weeks after local authorities in Wuhan had arrested doctors who were trying to warn of a dangerous new virus they had seen in their patients. On January 29, following his visit to China, Tedros announced that he was "very encouraged and impressed by [President Xi Jinping's] knowledge of the outbreak and his personal involvement in the outbreak. This was for me a very rare leadership."

The next day, Tedros declared an international public health emergency and, in the same announcement, praised China's "commitment to transparency"—despite the cover-up, well known by that time, that had likely allowed the Wuhan outbreak to become an international public health emergency in the first place.

"Let me be clear: this declaration is not a vote of no confidence in China. On the contrary, WHO continues to have confidence in China's capacity to control the outbreak," the WHO chief said. "We would have seen many more cases outside China by now—and probably deaths—if it were not for the government's efforts, and the progress they have made to protect their own people and the people of the world." But his praise didn't stop there: "The speed with which China detected the outbreak, isolated the virus, sequenced the genome and shared it with WHO and the world are [sic] very impressive, and beyond words," he said. "In many ways, China is actually setting a new standard for outbreak response. It's not an exaggeration." For many onlookers, it was hard to reconcile Tedros's obvious omissions with what the world already knew to be true. It seemed as if he were simply reading from a script handed to him by Beijing. Of course, he wasn't alone. At this time, Trump, too, was praising Xi prematurely for having the situation under control.

As it turns out, in its negotiations with its Chinese interlocutors, the WHO team in China had made numerous compromises. They agreed not to interrogate China's early response to the virus and to "augment, rather than duplicate" the investigating that Chinese scientists and officials had already done up to that point.

The novel coronavirus emergency in Wuhan had receded enough by mid-February to allow WHO officials to visit, in a joint mission with Chinese participants. The organization's subsequent five-page report avoided the sensitive subject of the virus's origin, instead focusing on basic facts about the virus and how to combat it. Also absent was any mention of arrests of doctors, lab data destroyed, or other features of China's cover-up. In the five recommendations that the report offered to China, none included improving freedom of the press, removing restrictions on information flow, or improving the lack of civil society protections that had enabled the cover-up and the unchecked spread of the virus in the first place.

One thing the report didn't lack was an outpouring of praise for China. "In the face of a previously unknown virus, China has rolled out perhaps the most ambitious, agile and aggressive disease containment effort in history," the authors wrote, adding that "achieving China's exceptional coverage with an adherence to these containment measures has only been possible due to the deep commitment of the Chinese people to collective action in the face of this common threat." While all this was certainly true, the omissions were glaring.

This deference to Beijing was a clear departure from WHO's previous behavior. In 2003, after the Chinese government waited three months to report the outbreak of SARS and then withheld access and information from the organization, then director general Gro Harlem Brundtland criticized Chinese officials' cover-up of the outbreak. "It would have been definitely helpful if international expertise and WHO had been able to help at an earlier stage," she said. "I'm saying as the director-general of the World Health Organization: Next time something strange and new comes anywhere in the world, let us come in as quickly as possible."

But there were other reasons to think that Tedros had already submitted himself to Beijing's leadership. He had previously seemed willing to use WHO as an institution to flatter an authoritarian leader. One of his first moves after he became WHO chief was to nominate Robert Mugabe, longtime dictator of Zimbabwe, as a WHO goodwill ambassador. Tedros said that Mugabe had made Zimbabwe "a country that places universal health coverage and health promotion at the centre of its policies." In reality, Zimbabwe's healthcare system had collapsed under Mugabe and his economic policies, hospitals often lacked basic supplies, and healthcare workers sometimes went unpaid; Mugabe and other Zimbabwean leaders would leave the country to seek medical treatment. Beijing, too, had a special fondness for Mugabe: in 2015, the Chinese government had awarded him the Confucius Peace Prize, its human rights–neutral alternative to the Nobel Peace Prize.

In 2017, Tedros gave a speech hailing the creation of the "Health Silk Road," the international public health arm of China's Belt and Road Initiative. "President Xi's proposal for a Health Silk Road, which strengthens and renews ancient links between cultures and people, with health at its core, is indeed visionary," Tedros said. "If we are to secure the health of the billions of people represented here, we must seize the opportunities the Belt and Road Initiative provides."

Some who knew Tedros ascribed his almost fawning public remarks about China's leaders as part of a strategy for dealing with China, a country particularly sensitive to external meddling, rather than a capitulation to Beijing's demands. "His strategy is to coax China to transparency and international cooperation rather than criticizing the government," Lawrence Gostin, a professor of global health law at Georgetown University, told the BBC in May 2020. "I do worry quite a bit however that his effusive praise for China could in the long term tarnish the WHO's reputation as a trusted scientific authority willing to speak truth to power."

Unfortunately, Gostin's worry over a loss of trust in WHO materialized. Trump's April 14 announcement that the United States would halt its support of WHO elicited grave concern that the removal of U.S. funds would imperil the global effort to combat the pandemic. But Trump would not budge. On May 29, he proceeded to withdraw the United States from WHO, explicitly citing China's "total control" as the rationale. (The withdrawal was made official on July 6, but it wasn't to take effect until the following year. After defeating Trump in the 2020 presidential election, President Joe Biden reversed Trump's decision.)

It wasn't just the Trump administration that had lost faith in WHO. Many analysts felt the same. "Tedros' permanent and forceful endorsement of Chinese actions throughout the crisis has, of course, created a counter-reaction: the organization itself is now accused of having missed the opportunity to forestall a global pandemic," wrote François Godement, a French expert on Chinese and East Asian strategic and international affairs at the Carnegie Endowment for International Peace, in March 2020. The Chinese government "succeeded from the start in steering the World Health Organization," Hinnerk Feldwisch-Drentrup, Berlin-based founder of the magazine *MedWatch*, wrote in April.

"It might be easy to dismiss this move as trademark Trumpian blame deflection or saber-rattling or shortsighted isolationism," wrote Kristine Lee, an associate fellow in the Asia program at the Center for a New American Security, in Washington, DC, in *Politico* on April 15, the day after Trump announced that he would halt WHO funding. "But for people who've been watching China's growing activism in the United Nations closely, the WHO's deference to China is no surprise."

As Gostin suggested, it's not unreasonable to think that Tedros preferred to avoid publicly criticizing governments. But in at least one situation in the early months of the pandemic, he harshly and publicly criticized one government: that of Taiwan.

Here's how it unfolded. The pandemic exacerbated underlying racism in China. Some Chinese people, viewing African countries and their populaces as dirty and "uncivilized," believed wrongly that Africans were more likely to transmit the novel coronavirus. The week that Tedros criticized Taiwan, a nearly unprecedented wave of anger was rising across the continent of Africa, as Africans living in Chinese cities faced race-based discrimination from police, landlords, and medical authorities. African residents in Guangzhou were subjected to discriminatory coronavirus testing, forced into quarantine, and even evicted without cause. A McDonald's franchise in Guangzhou posted a notice reading, "We've been informed that from now on, black people are not allowed to enter the restaurant." McDonald's later apologized.

The scenes created an international uproar. About a dozen African governments summoned their respective Chinese ambassadors to express outrage over the treatment of their citizens in China. "The singling out of Africans for compulsory testing and quarantine, in our view, has no scientific or logical basis and amounts to racism towards Africans in China," wrote African ambassadors in Beijing in a joint letter sent to China's foreign ministry. The speaker of Nigeria's House of Representatives posted a video on Twitter of him showing the Chinese ambassador a viral clip of Nigerians being mistreated in China, then urging the ambassador to raise this issue with Beijing and report back "by Monday."

Chinese government officials responded by denying that anything serious was happening in Guangzhou. "It is harmful to sensationalize isolated incidents," the Chinese embassy in Zimbabwe wrote in an April 11 statement posted to Twitter. "To misrepresent this as tensions between nations and races is dangerous." The denials likely stemmed from fears that the incidents would undermine Beijing's attempts to rehabilitate its global image after its early handling of the coronavirus outbreak. "If they acknowledge the racist treatment that they have for Africans in Guangzhou, this would hurt the campaign to improve their image," said Guangzhi Huang, an assistant professor at Massachusetts College of Liberal Arts who researches anti-Black racism in China.

Tedros made no public comment about any of these events. He did not criticize the Chinese government for failing to protect the rights of Africans in China, nor did he urge Chinese diplomatic officials in Africa to listen more respectfully to the concerns of African citizens. What he did instead was blame Taiwan for racist attacks against him.

That week Taiwan, which is blocked from WHO membership by China, had accused the organization of ignoring its December 31 email warning of a mysterious new illness in Wuhan and withholding vital information about the pandemic, a claim WHO denied. In public remarks given in early April 2020, Tedros said he had been the subject of racist attacks, and he singled out Taiwan as the source. "This attack came from Taiwan. We need to be honest. I will be straight today. From Taiwan," he said. "And Taiwan, the Foreign Ministry also, they know the campaign. They didn't disassociate themselves. They even started criticizing me in the middle of all that insult and slur, but I didn't care." Taiwan called the comments "imaginary," reiterated its opposition to discrimination, and invited Tedros to visit.

Given the unprecedented wave of anger across Africa toward racism in China, it was yet another example of Tedros seeming to succumb to willful blindness over what was happening in China. The remarks also felt strikingly inappropriate, given Taiwan's extraordinarily rapid and effective domestic response to the novel coronavirus—as of April 2020, despite its proximity to China and the large volume of cross-Strait travel, it had recorded just 380 cases and 5 deaths—and its role in sending medical aid to other countries early in their fight against it. In fact, Tedros's criticism came just as Taiwanese officials were making their case that Taiwan should be admitted to WHO—a contention that, if implemented, could cross one of Beijing's major red lines—and that if they had already been members when the outbreak began, the world would have been better prepared.

Behind the scenes, however, WHO was deeply frustrated with China. According to an investigation by the Associated Press, officials at the organization bristled when China sat on releasing the genetic map of the virus for more than a week and then stalled for at least two more weeks before providing WHO information on cases and patients. "It's obvious that we could have saved more lives and avoided many, many deaths if China and the WHO had acted faster," Ali Mokdad, a professor at the Institute for Health Metrics and Evaluation at the University of Washington, told the Associated Press.

WHO's effusive praise of China could charitably be understood as a necessary strategic maneuver: a tougher approach might not have yielded any cooperation at all. If that's what it was, however, it's safe to conclude that the strategy didn't work as intended. China's tardiness had deadly consequences for the rest of the world and greatly damaged the credibility of the organization best positioned to address the crisis.

"Did [Tedros] go too far?" Adam Kamradt-Scott, a global health professor at the University of Sydney, told the AP. "I think the evidence on that is clear . . . It has led to so many questions about the relationship between China and WHO. It is perhaps a cautionary tale."

WHO's frustration would only grow. In January 2021, a year after the outbreak in Wuhan and after numerous delays, a WHO delegation returned to China on a fact-finding mission. Tedros himself offered his first public criticism of Chinese authorities during this time, saying he was "very disappointed" when the WHO team was at first not permitted to enter China on the eve of the planned trip. Once they were admitted for a visit that lasted just under a month—two weeks of which were spent under strict quarantine—the participants encountered resistance from Chinese officials who urged the visitors to adopt Beijing's perspective. The Chinese government refused to hand over raw data and detailed patient records that might have shed light on the virus's origins. In an interview with *Science* magazine following the delegation's return, WHO program manager Peter Ben Embarek, who led the mission, noted that "politics was always in the room" during their collaboration with Chinese counterparts.

WHO, though, still appeared willing to play along. In a February 9 press conference concluding the mission, the organization claimed that it was "extremely unlikely" that the virus had emerged in a Chinese laboratory and added that it may have, instead, arrived via frozen food—a theory that dovetails nicely with Beijing's preferred theory of the virus's origins.

Meanwhile, WHO received welcome news from the United States: Joe Biden, who had replaced Donald Trump as president on January 20, had reversed his predecessor's decision to withdraw from the organization. Still, it soon became clear that the new administration was deeply suspicious of China's influence on WHO. In March 2021, shortly before WHO published a report on the coronavirus's origins, Secretary of State Antony Blinken said that the United States had "real concerns about the methodology and process that went into the report, including the fact that the government in Beijing [had] apparently helped to write it."

China's evasions cost it one admirer: Dr. Tedros. At the press conference upon the release of the WHO-China joint report in March, he elaborated: "In my discussions with the team, they expressed the difficulties they encountered in accessing raw data," he said. "I expect future collaborative studies to include more timely and comprehensive data sharing." He also refused to rule out the controversial hypothesis that the novel coronavirus had emerged from a laboratory, a clear rebuke to China. "As far as WHO is concerned, all hypotheses are on the table."

Bill Bishop, a longtime China watcher and author of the influential *Sinocism* newsletter, wrote on March 30 that the WHO chief's remarks were "surprisingly critical of China and gave life to the lab leak hypothesis," which Tedros surely knew would drive leaders in Beijing absolutely crazy. "The WHO report is out, no one is happy, and we will probably never know the origins of COVID-19," Bishop wrote. To date, the answer to how, exactly, the coronavirus emerged remains elusive. In this sense at least, the Chinese government may have achieved its desired outcome.

Tedros's criticism of the Chinese government did not stop there. In May 2022, he said that China's zero-Covid strategy wasn't "sustainable." Chinese censors removed the video clip of these remarks from China's internet, and searches for Tedros's name on Chinese social media were temporarily disabled. In March 2023, after new information emerged suggesting a possible genetic link to raccoon dogs at the Wuhan wet market, Tedros accused China of withholding important data about possible origins of the pandemic. "This data could have, and should have, been shared three years ago," he said. "We continue to call on China to be transparent in sharing data and to conduct the necessary investigations and share results."

Tedros's refusal to criticize or even publicly mention the Chinese government's early cover-up of the novel coronavirus outbreak, while he evinced a perfect willingness to criticize other governments for a variety of reasons, was likely due to a combination of factors. His rise to political power in Ethiopia hinged on his ability to operate within an authoritarian context and to get things done behind the scenes. That experience is no weakness when dealing with an authoritarian government like China.

But for years, if not decades, Tedros had also had to abide by all the diplomatic rules that the foreign minister of a country dependent on China must follow in order to preserve the relationship. At the top of the list are: never criticize the Chinese government publicly and never side with Taiwan. During the decade or so leading up to 2020, not one African government with diplomatic relations with China commented negatively on any of China's core interests, including Taiwan, Hong Kong, the treatment of Muslim minorities, the South China Sea, and human rights.

Ethiopia is no exception. How Addis Ababa's top officials came to support Beijing requires a deeper look at the party that ruled Ethiopia from 1991 to 2018—as chance would have it, these years also mark the approximate span of Tedros's domestic political career—and its ties to the Chinese Communist Party. Ethiopia's experience reveals not only China's diplomatic ambitions for Africa but also its long-term strategies for establishing regional power bases, which Beijing can then use at crucial moments to support its global agenda.

Chinese officials have long publicly touted their kinship with African nations, which were some of the earliest in the world to recognize the newly formed Communist government in Beijing. In 1956, Egypt, under the nationalist leader Gamal Abdel Nasser, became the first country in

Africa to establish ties with Beijing. Chinese premier Zhou Enlai first visited Ethiopia in 1964, during his famous December 1963–February 1964 trip to ten African countries that came to be known as his "safari." Zhou met with Ethiopian emperor Haile Selassie, though the East African nation had not yet established diplomatic ties with Beijing. Unlike some of his contemporaries among the continent's more left-leaning governments, Ethiopia's emperor was not fond of Communist governments. And Beijing had given support to the militant independence movement in Eritrea, a state in Ethiopia's north.

Within a few years of Zhou's visit, the Chinese government agreed to uphold Ethiopia's claim to Eritrea, in exchange for the government in Addis Ababa's recognizing China's claim over Taiwan, thus paving the way for the establishment of diplomatic ties between China and Ethiopia in 1970. In 1971, Ethiopia supported China's bid for a seat in the United Nations, displacing Taiwan. In October of that year, Selassie visited Beijing. In 1974, however, a military junta known as the Derg overthrew the emperor and established a Marxist-Leninist state. This could have been great for China-Ethiopia relations, except that the Derg threw its lot in with the Soviet Union, putting Ethiopia on the other side of the Sino-Soviet split. The year 1991 was a major turning point for Addis Ababa and Beijing. That year, the Ethiopian People's Revolutionary Democratic Front (EPRDF), headed by Meles Zenawi, overthrew the Communist government of the People's Democratic Republic of Ethiopia and ruled Ethiopia for the next twenty-eight years. The EPRDF was still a Marxist party, even if it was less Communist than the government that preceded it. It comprised four main, smaller parties. Its vanguard party, the Tigray People's Liberation Front (TPLF), was founded in 1976 and, by 1991, had become a powerful armed force, dominating the coalition that formed the EPRDF. The fall of the Soviet Union, and of the pro-Soviet military dictatorship in Ethiopia, removed a major barrier that had kept China and Ethiopia at arm's length.

Still, it would be several years before Ethiopia's leaders made a clear move toward Beijing. The EPRDF was strongly anti-Western, but it didn't want to jeopardize its new hold on power by publicly committing itself to unsustainable ideological positions or partnerships. Prime Minister Meles wanted economic development, but not from the neoliberal model pushed through U.S.-led institutions like the International Monetary

Fund and the World Bank. "The neoliberal paradigm is a dead end incapable of bringing about the African renaissance," Meles wrote in an academic article published in 2011. "Historical practice has shown that state intervention has been critical in the development process. Economic theory has shown that developing countries are riddled with vicious circles and poverty traps that can only be removed by state action."

Meles viewed state control over important sectors and strong private-sector regulations—anathema to the developmental model championed by the IMF and the World Bank—as important tools of a developmental state. This made China's state-driven development model, and its tendency toward anti-Western posturing, an ideal fit for him. In 1995, EPRDF leaders began to move toward China as a counterweight to Western pressure, and in October of that year, Meles flew to China. In 1996, Chinese president Jiang Zemin returned the visit. The reciprocal visits marked the start of what would become one of the closest relationships between China and an African nation. An economic agreement the two countries inked that year was structured to renew every three years, and in 1998, the two countries created a joint economic commission that granted most-favored-nation status to Ethiopia. In 2000, Ethiopia joined the first Forum on China-Africa Cooperation, and in 2003, it became the first African nation to host the forum.

Ethiopia is not rich in natural resources, a typical target of Chinese interest in the continent. Seifudein Adem, a professor of political science at the State University of New York in Binghamton who previously taught at Addis Ababa University, wrote in 2012 that the reason for China's increased activities in Ethiopia lay in "Ethiopia's perceived diplomatic usefulness." The headquarters of the African Union is located in Addis Ababa, as are the offices of numerous regional and multilateral organizations.

Ethiopia was China's diplomatic door to the continent. "If China's relations with many African countries could be described as one of 'infrastructure for natural resources,'" Adem wrote, "the Sino-Ethiopian relationship can be described as 'infrastructure for diplomatic support.'"

We often think of China as a party-state—a government and a party inextricably intertwined. "Beijing" and "the Chinese government" and "the Chinese Communist Party" are used interchangeably to refer to the country's decision makers. But the Chinese Communist Party isn't the same thing as the Chinese government, and it often engages in activities around the world as a political party, not necessarily as a government. Nowhere is this clearer than in Africa, where for decades the party has led party-to-party events and training sessions with political parties across the continent.

In 2000, the Chinese Communist Party began pursuing close and direct party-to-party ties with the EPRDF. Dai Bingguo, who served as the director of the party's International Liaison Department at this time, visited Addis Ababa in February of that year, and numerous exchanges between party officials of both countries would occur over the next fifteen years or so. The two parties signed a memorandum of understanding in 2010, after which EPRDF officials began to participate in regular delegations to Beijing, including a training session at the Central Party School in Beijing.

"Party-to-party relations were the bedrock of China-Ethiopia relations," said Joshua Eisenman, a political scientist at the University of Notre Dame whose work focuses on China-Africa ties. Tsinghua University scholar Tang Xiaoyang has referred to Ethiopia's ruling party as China's "best student."

During these years, the EPRDF was solidifying the authoritarian state over which it presided, betraying hopes that it might bring to fruition the revolutionary democracy it had offered. In 2005, protests swept the capital amid concerns over the integrity of the May elections that kept Meles and the EPRDF in power. Meles cracked down. Security forces fired on protesters, the government banned demonstrations, and, outside the capital, human rights groups estimate that at least ten thousand people were arrested amid the protests. Over the course of the year, the government extended its campaign of political repression and arrested opposition figures, journalists, and elected politicians. Later, the country's leaders would go on to block websites and opposition blogs, crack down on independent journalism, and commit raids in rural areas.

As Meles detained and murdered the citizens of his own country, the international community shunned Ethiopia, driving the EPRDF more fully into China's sphere as leaders in Beijing threw Ethiopia an economic and diplomatic lifeline. Addis Ababa knew how to repay Beijing for its support. In 2005, Ethiopia publicly backed China's new Anti-Secession Law, which explicitly authorized the Chinese government to use military force against Taiwan if the island declared its independence. In 2007, Ethiopia, as a member of the UN Human Rights Council, was one of the governments that helped shield China from criticism as Beijing backed the Sudanese government despite the genocide it was committing in Darfur. Before his death in 2012, Meles visited China four times while serving as Ethiopia's leader.

Economic and trade relations between the two countries blossomed after 2005. According to a 2012 World Bank study, Chinese foreign direct investment in Ethiopia grew from almost zero in 2004 to $74 million in 2009. In 2011, China was Ethiopia's largest trading partner. "The economic cooperation between the two countries has also been facilitated by the strong political support from both governments," the World Bank study found. "It appears that China is now looking to anchor its African investment in Ethiopia," while "the Ethiopian government is very keen on looking for insights from the East Asian development model."

By the late 2000s, evidence of the close trade and diplomatic relationship between China and Ethiopia was everywhere. "There is no aspect of the life of people in the city which was untouched by China, mostly positively," the scholar Adem wrote of a trip he took to Addis Ababa in 2008:

> If one had boarded an Ethiopian Airlines flight from the Far East, one would eventually notice that the Ethiopian hostesses speak Mandarin Chinese. After arriving at the Bole International Airport in Addis Ababa, chances are that the taxi waiting to take the visitor to the downtown is made in China. If one uses a vehicle made in another country, one would certainly have to use a road constructed or renovated not just by China's loans but by Chinese construction workers. Driving through the city to a hotel, one would see conspicuous clusters of condominiums financed by Chinese loans and built by Chinese contractors. As the visitor proceeds to a hotel, s/he would likely come across a traffic signal where a middle-aged Chinese person, a member of the Chinese team doing road maintenance on that spot, gives hand signals for vehicles to pass in an orderly manner.

It was at the height of these flourishing economic and political ties that Tedros became Ethiopia's top foreign policy official. During his tenure, he would oversee the upgrading of Ethiopia-China relations to a "fully-fledged strategic partnership."

Tedros has always been a party man. He was twenty-seven years old when the EPRDF overthrew the previous regime, and he was already set up to go far: he had already joined the Tigray People's Liberation Front, the most powerful party within the EPRDF coalition. In the years that followed, he dedicated himself to climbing the ranks of the government.

The EPRDF governed in a top-down, authoritarian manner. Its leaders selected members from its four coalition parties to install in key positions around the bureaucracy, to give the party control over the functioning of government mechanisms. The EPRDF would keep these officials in line by punishing or firing them if they strayed too far from party policies. The top-down control was far weaker than that practiced by the Chinese Communist Party, and in Ethiopia, there were fewer of these party-instated officials and less party discipline. There was, in other words, more room to maneuver.

Tedros did this well. By the time he was forty, he had been appointed Ethiopia's health minister, a position he held from 2005 to 2012. It was during this time that former U.S. ambassador to Ethiopia David Shinn got to know Tedros. The ethnic Tigrayan was certainly a "party person," Shinn told me, "but he had an excellent reputation as health minister." As a member of the TPLF, Shinn explained, Tedros was in a much stronger position to influence the health ministry than if he had been a member of one of the weaker coalition parties. He left the health ministry with a very good reputation.

In November 2012, Tedros was appointed Ethiopia's foreign minister, a position he held for four years. It's clear that Ethiopian foreign ministers have been key to the maintenance of the country's close ties to China. Seyoum Mesfin, Ethiopia's long-serving foreign minister, who held the post from 1991 to 2010, became the country's ambassador to China in 2011 and held that position until 2017. (Seyoum was one of the founders of the Tigray People's Liberation Front. He was killed by the Ethiopian national army in 2021, during the civil war that pitted ethnic Tigrayans against the government in Addis Ababa—a fate that could have befallen

Tedros had he remained involved in Ethiopian politics instead of moving to Europe.)

The years 2012 to 2016 were the "height of relations" between Ethiopia and China, researcher Daniel Kibsgaard told me. In 2014, Tedros and Chinese foreign minister Wang Yi released a joint statement celebrating the advances made in Chinese-Ethiopian political and economic relations over the past decade and a half. They announced that the two countries would pursue "deepening and upgrading of our relationship."

Shinn's next encounter with Tedros was at the foreign ministry. "I felt that when he got to that position, he was much more political, that he had adopted the politics of the EPRF and TPLF," Shinn said.

This is evident from Tedros's public statements, which were very pro-EPRDF and sometimes quite anti-Western. At this time, he was at the height of his political power. He was a member of the EPRDF central committee. In 2013, he served as chairman of the African Union's executive council. That year, he accused the International Criminal Court of "targeting Africa and Africans." In 2014, he posted on Facebook that "EPRDF's strategies and policies are right for our country. That's why our Ethiopia is on the March."

———

In 2017, Tedros became the first African to head WHO. It's important to note that, in rising to this position, he enjoyed the support of the United States as well as China. It would not be accurate to claim, as some have, that he was "China's candidate" alone. There have been showdowns at multilateral institutions in which a Chinese-backed candidate challenged a Western-backed candidate, but the 2017 selection of the WHO director general was not one of them.

"It is a fact that he had a good relationship with China," Shinn told me. "I was not surprised when it was suggested early on in the Covid-19 crisis that he might have been a little bit gullible in terms of what the Chinese were telling him—that he might have been more willing to be more accepting of their version of events in China than perhaps the facts merited. And perhaps he didn't ask some of the tough questions of China . . . But to go so far as to suggest that he was a puppet of China is going too far."

Tedros displayed a learning curve over the course of the pandemic—a learning curve different, perhaps, from what Beijing would have hoped for the Ethiopian foreign minister who had previously championed his country's strategic partnership with China. He started with the traditional diplomatic playbook of effusive praise. When that did not work, however, he eventually transitioned to open and public criticism of Chinese authorities for denying crucial access to WHO. "He was trying to use his connections to get him what he wanted, and they were trying to use their connections to keep him quiet," said Eisenman. "It got to the point where he had to choose between being a friend of Beijing and his credibility as head of WHO."

At the end of the day, though perhaps belatedly, Tedros chose his credibility as a public health official. Despite the Chinese Communist Party's efforts and its long cultivation of close ties with Addis Ababa, it was Tedros the health minister who emerged on the other side of the pandemic tussle with Beijing.

This suggests the limitations the CCP faces as it tries to win global leaders and bureaucrats to its side. Domestically, the party can force cadres and business leaders to put party loyalty over facts. That is a major motivation behind Xi's drive to revive the party's dominance over every government, business, and social institution. And it's a major reason that, in Xi's China, any higher calling that could supersede party loyalty is suspect—whether that is religion, ethnic identity, or even commitment to the pursuit of truth, transparency, or knowledge.

But beyond China's borders, it's much more difficult to stamp out higher loyalties. Chinese leaders can offer trade deals, investment funding, and protection from human rights criticisms as carrots to bring foreign governments over to their side. They can also threaten to take these things away if those governments step out of line. Chinese leaders can even draw on anti-Western, anti-imperialism sentiment to find ideological common ground with people in formerly colonized nations. But what party leaders cannot control is the reality that some people with power on the international stage choose their jobs and their careers because they are committed to something higher than themselves. In some cases, their final loyalty simply cannot be bought.

7

CHINA ADOPTS RUSSIA'S DISINFORMATION PLAYBOOK

Common wisdom once held that Beijing simply wasn't in the business of disrupting information ecosystems abroad. Beijing was no Moscow. While the Chinese government projected stilted propaganda globally, its obsession with online information control more or less stopped at its own borders.

Russia's successful efforts to sow chaos and distrust amid the 2016 U.S. presidential election, and its similar campaigns across Europe, seem to have changed Beijing's calculus, however. The Kremlin showed the world that the online information space is a realm perfectly fit for asymmetric warfare, in which one side does not have the ability to control the information flow and must find other ways to tilt narratives in its favor. Putin and his officials perfected a playbook of power projection that Beijing simply couldn't resist.

The Chinese government debuted this playbook in a big way during the Covid-19 pandemic. Seeking to deflect blame for a global catastrophe that originated within its borders, Chinese officials and propaganda outlets began pushing a conspiracy theory that the U.S. military had planted the virus in Wuhan. On March 12, 2020, Chinese foreign ministry spokesperson Zhao Lijian, the original "wolf warrior" diplomat, made this mainstream, tweeting in English, "It might be US army who brought the epidemic to Wuhan." His words, which were retweeted more than four thousand times, marked the debut of China's "big lie" on the novel coronavirus pandemic—that it did not begin in China—which swiftly became a sweeping global disinformation strategy. It prefaced the joining of wolf warrior diplomacy with brazen disinformation—"big lies" that, in recent years, had characterized Russian government officials but that more demure and camera-shy Chinese diplomats had avoided.

Chinese diplomats, government officials, Beijing-aligned content farms and social media accounts, and state media outlets soon began touting Covid-19 origin conspiracy theories, even when they contradicted one another. Chinese state– and Russian state–linked social media accounts increasingly quoted and tweeted one another, amplifying one another's messages and demonstrating growing convergence between their ideologies and information strategies—a result, in part, of a secret agreement signed between Moscow and Beijing in July 2021 to cooperate on news coverage. Coordinated inauthentic behavior on Twitter and Facebook also promoted alternative theories for where the virus might have originated or how it might have entered China. Later on in the pandemic, Chinese state media headlines cast doubt on the efficacy and safety of Western-made vaccines, as Chinese-made vaccines, on which Beijing's soft power hopes were riding, failed to achieve comparable levels of efficacy. In the three years since Zhao's tweet, Beijing has made Russian-style online disinformation campaigns a standard weapon of its foreign policy.

China is now playing an even more ambitious game. Within a matter of just a few years, Beijing has copied and successfully used many of Russia's information warfare techniques. But unlike Russia, the Chinese government believes it has the ability and even the mandate to turn its domestic online surveillance apparatus outward, to disrupt and, perhaps eventually, even control global narratives in real time.

The Chinese state's big lie on Covid-19's origins, and its use of external-facing online disinformation to promote that lie, seemed like a striking departure from precedent. But the seeds of the Chinese government's propensity to use foreign social media platforms to engage in disinformation campaigns were planted years before, as was evident to anyone who cared enough to pay attention. As with so many of its influence tactics, Beijing's earliest online disinformation campaigns related to its core interests: in this case, public remembrance of the Tiananmen Square Massacre.

It was early June 2014. In Hong Kong, thousands of residents would soon be converging to commemorate the twenty-fifth anniversary of the crackdown on antigovernment protests in Beijing's Tiananmen Square that killed hundreds or perhaps thousands of student protesters. This would be the only public memorial on Chinese soil, where the ruling Communist Party had worked tirelessly for a quarter century to wipe the event from the historical record.

Unbeknownst to the participants, however, the commemoration was about to be infiltrated by dangerous Islamic terrorists—at least, according to Twitter. Six "terrorists hoping to participate in jihad" had just escaped police in the southern metropolis of Guangzhou and slipped into Hong Kong, read a widely shared Chinese-language Hong Kong police report posted on Twitter. It said that the terrorists "will probably dress in dark clothing and mingle at the candlelight vigil." Apparently seeking to warn participants, the user who posted the report wrote in Chinese that "brothers attending the activity tonight" should be careful. Shortly after the police statement appeared on Twitter, another user purporting to live-tweet from the vigil wrote that he had just glimpsed a man "five feet ten inches tall, weighing around 154 pounds, wearing a black headband just like us; a knife with jagged edges is protruding from his bag." In March of that year, a group of Uyghurs wielding knives had killed 31 civilians and injured 141 during a terrorist attack in the southwestern city of Kunming. The user concluded, "This is absolutely terrifying." That post was retweeted 315 times.

But there was one problem: the Hong Kong police report wasn't real. Nor did any mainstream media outlets report on the allegedly escaped Guangzhou terrorists. The Twitter account that posted the police report closely resembled the 138 accounts that retweeted it. The handles were either random numbers or letters, or two English names followed by numbers—such as with the accounts "ericashley1231" and "drewserenity10," both of which posted related tweets. The accounts were barely active, often with fewer than fifty tweets and fewer followers. Writing exclusively in Chinese, most of these accounts had posted their first tweet between March and June 2014. The 315 accounts that retweeted the report of the supposed knife-carrying terrorist fit a similar mold.

This was an early example of a coordinated, inauthentic attempt to disrupt a real-world event using a foreign social media platform that wasn't even accessible in mainland China. Though it's difficult to definitively attribute online disinformation campaigns to a state actor, this campaign was clearly aligned with Beijing's interests. This demonstrates the sensitivity of pro-democracy protests in Hong Kong, even before the "Umbrella Movement" that would occur later that year. But it wasn't until the 2019 protests that would engulf the city, when Chinese state–backed information operations debuted in a big way on major foreign platforms to target Hong Kong protest supporters, that Twitter, Facebook, and Google put resources toward tracing, attributing, and then, for the first time, publicly revealing that these campaigns were backed by Beijing.

The Tiananmen anniversary in 2014 was not the first time similar inauthentic Twitter accounts made what looked like a coordinated attempt to influence the site's China-focused community. In March 2012, a cybersecurity blogger named Brian Krebs had documented a case in which Twitter bots inundated a pro-Tibet hashtag with so many junk tweets that the pro-Tibet activists said the hashtag was no longer useful for tracking pro-Tibet tweets. In March 2014, a number of newly opened accounts with pro forma handles let loose a cascade of Chinese-language tweets denouncing New York–based Chinese blogger Wen Yunchao, an anticensorship activist with 124,000 Twitter followers, as a "traitor" and the "degenerate of all degenerates." Wen was again targeted in early June, with posts calling him "Traitor Wen" forwarded by the same set of accounts. Another burst of activity came in May 2014, after the U.S. Department of Justice had issued arrest warrants for five Chinese military hackers accused of cyber espionage against U.S. firms. August 2014 featured a smear campaign against Chinese dissident author Murong Xuecun, in which a series of Chinese essays assailing his character and sex life were collectively retweeted more than a thousand times by around one hundred accounts with matching characteristics.

In all these incidents, hundreds of nearly identical accounts attempted to influence Twitter's Chinese community in a direction that bolstered party interests. Wen told me in an email at the time that he had been the target of multiple cyberattacks in the two years leading up to that online campaign. He felt their goal was to "exert pressure" and force him to "shut his mouth" and to reduce his credibility in the public eye. Wen said he felt certain the assaults had "come from government-organized activity."

Another campaign that year targeted perceptions of Tibet. In July 2014, the London-based advocacy group Free Tibet identified close to one hundred accounts that regularly posted material presenting Tibetans as a contented and flourishing people, often linking to Chinese government-sponsored propaganda websites. The accounts, written primarily in English, paired English names with profile pictures that used stock images and photos of models. Twitter closed many of these fake accounts within twenty-four hours after the *New York Times* reported them.

At the time, these targeted attempts to shift Twitter's Chinese-language narrative seemed anomalous. The vast majority of China's internet users were not on Twitter—the platform was blocked in China—and common wisdom held that party repression was primarily aimed at ensuring domestic stability. But how could a social media platform that was unavailable to the average Chinese internet user be considered a political threat?

In retrospect, the answer is clear, as is the trend line: the Chinese party-state, which already did everything it could to shut down its real-world critics beyond its borders, was now trying its hand at translating that kind of interference into the virtual world. As we have seen with so many of Beijing's attempts to censor, control, and disrupt behavior beyond its borders, these efforts also seemed restricted to China's core interests: Hong Kong, Tibet, Uyghurs, and Chinese pro-democracy voices.

Twitter was a logical target. As censorship of mainland Chinese social media had become increasingly restrictive, Twitter became a kind of Chinese social media underground, concentrating many of the dissident and activist voices that Chinese authorities wished most strongly to suppress. Chinese dissidents were largely the stars of Chinese-language Twitter. In 2014, well-known artist Ai Weiwei's Twitter account had more than 250,000 followers; outspoken lawyer Teng Biao had 76,000 Twitter followers; and blind activist lawyer Chen Guangcheng had 17,000. Other well-known Chinese Twitterati included Tiananmen movement leader Zhou Fengsuo, Beijing-based dissident Hu Jia, U.S.-based activist Yaxue Cao, and anonymous bloggers who espouse support for freedom of speech and other democratic ideals. By comparison, some Chinese celebrities had Twitter accounts, but they commanded only a tiny fraction of the followers they had on Weibo. Fan accounts for mega-celebrities like best-selling author Han Han and Taiwanese singer Jay Chou had only relatively small followings, ranging from 4,000 to 17,000 followers.

In those days, official Chinese state–linked accounts had just a tiny sliver of the narrative pie on Twitter. Almost no individual Chinese diplomats had their own Twitter accounts. Chinese state media accounts made barely a blip. In 2014, state broadcaster Xinhua's Chinese-language Twitter account, first opened in 2012, had around 2,200 followers. The Chinese-language account of the *People's Daily*, the party's flagship newspaper, had around 3,300 Twitter followers in 2014.

But sometime around 2019, the Chinese government seemed to make a major recalculation regarding its policy of officially ignoring international social media platforms. This wasn't entirely a shock. Over the past several years, the follower counts of English-language Chinese state media accounts on U.S. social media had mysteriously skyrocketed. A 2015 snapshot of the Facebook fan base of Chinese Communist Party mouthpiece *People's Daily* reveals an inexplicably dramatic surge. The *People's Daily* Facebook page had around 3 million fans on April 6, 2015. By early July, just three months later, that number had almost doubled, to 5.7 million fans. "Either China is the new master of journalism or what we are seeing is evidence of something not quite right," Italian cybersecurity researcher Andrea Stroppa, author of a 2013 report on click farms, said at the time.

By 2021, the number of followers of the *People's Daily* English-language account was more than 6 million. That year, Xinhua's Twitter account ballooned to 12.3 million followers. As Stroppa had intimated, such numbers strongly suggested that Chinese state media outlets had paid to acquire more social media followers. But we don't have to rely on suggestion. In August 2019, the state-run China News Service posted a tender on a government website, advertising a $175,000 contract for adding 580,000 new followers to its Twitter account, targeting countries with relatively large Chinese diaspora populations and "English-speaking countries that pay attention to China's development."

"As China's international influence has grown, countries around the world, and especially overseas Chinese and foreign friends who are interested in China, have a growing demand to understand China," the state media outlet wrote on the tender. "China News Agency's Twitter account provides overseas Chinese with a good information bridge, and at the same time it has also strengthened the influence of China News Service abroad, especially among overseas Chinese. Given that Twitter is a news platform with a particularly large international influence in the world, China News Service is hereby conducting this bidding directed at Twitter overseas." The task seems to have been accomplished. As of August 2021, China News Service's Twitter account had approximately 635,000 followers.

The same year, Chinese authorities began tracking down, harassing, and detaining people in China who posted on Twitter. When Luo Daiqing, a Chinese student pursuing a degree at the University of Minnesota, returned to his hometown of Wuhan for summer break in 2019, he was arrested and jailed for six months for posting several tweets satirizing Xi Jinping from his anonymous Twitter account. Others in China were forced to delete their tweets or even saw them deleted by hackers. Between 2018 and early 2021, at least fifty people in China received prison sentences for content they posted to Twitter, according to an investigation by the *Wall Street Journal.*

In March 2019, another pro-democracy protest movement arose in Hong Kong, as demonstrators demanded that the proposed extradition law be shelved. This time, Chinese authorities went on a major Twitter offensive. In August 2019, Twitter revealed that it had discovered a Chinese state–backed covert information campaign operating on its platform and targeting the Hong Kong pro-democracy protests. Twitter characterized the activity as "covert, manipulative behaviors" that were "deliberately and specifically attempting to sow political discord in Hong Kong, including undermining the legitimacy and political positions of the protest movement on the ground." Twitter released archives for 936 of the most active accounts, but said that it had also suspended an additional 200,000 related accounts before they were able to engage in significant activity. Facebook subsequently announced that it, too, had identified a smaller network of Chinese government–linked accounts engaging in similar activity that it had disabled. Google banned more than 200 YouTube channels.

In recent years, government offices across China have spent large sums to build targeted social media followings on foreign social media platforms, especially on Facebook and Twitter. Government offices may also take advantage of social media followers for hire. In August 2019, the Guangxi International Expo Affairs Bureau aimed to garner followers to help promote the China-ASEAN (Association of Southeast Asian Nations) Expo, an event held annually in Guangxi Province since 2004 together with ten other ASEAN member countries. According to the tender, the contractor would be required to accumulate five hundred thousand Facebook users and thirty thousand Twitter followers, most of whom had to come from the event's target audience.

Local government agencies in China have frequently awarded contracts for the management of their accounts on foreign social media platforms. On January 15, 2021, the Anhui Province Culture and Tourism Department awarded an approximately two-million-yuan contract to the Xinhua News Agency's News and Information Center to operate the department's Facebook, Twitter, Instagram, YouTube, TikTok, and Douyin accounts for one year. The contract specifications require that the contractor increase the number of Twitter, Facebook, and Instagram followers by at least 10 percent by the end of the contract period.

It's not unusual for foreign governments in a variety of countries to hand the management of their social media accounts to outside firms. What's unusual about the China case, however, is that these foreign social media platforms are blocked domestically. The rise of Chinese government agencies officially building their presence on Twitter, Facebook, YouTube, and Instagram underscores the asymmetrical messaging—viewing the platforms as tools to project propaganda and other official rhetoric internationally while preventing information from flowing back home.

The contrast is particularly stark in the case of the city of Wuhan, which sought to use international social media to rehabilitate its image as the epicenter of the pandemic. On December 8, 2020, the Wuhan Culture and Tourism Bureau awarded a contract worth approximately $145,000 to Yingsai Baihui (Beijing) Culture Media Company to manage the bureau's YouTube and Instagram marketing for one year. The contract listed specific performance targets for each platform; for example, the contractor was required to upload videos to YouTube that received at least one million views over the course of the year and to grow the number of Instagram followers by at least fifty thousand during the same time period.

On April 8, 2021, Wuhan's tourism bureau issued another tender, this time for the management of its "Visit Wuhan" Facebook and Twitter accounts. According to the detailed requirements for the tender, the contractor must increase the number of Facebook followers from 400,000 to 600,000 and the number of Twitter followers from 150,000 to 195,000. In both cases, the Wuhan government stipulated that the increase must comprise primarily followers from major Western countries. On May 7, the bureau awarded this contract, too, to Yingsai Baihui, for approximately $265,000.

In order to amplify its desired messages to the world, the Chinese government also began to reverse another long-term trend—that of Chinese diplomats staying off Twitter and, overall, maintaining a low-key public profile. In October 2018, there were just seventeen Chinese diplomats with Twitter accounts. In late 2019, dozens of Chinese diplomats began to open Twitter accounts and to tweet or retweet messages that were often aggressively nationalist. By February 2020, there were more than eighty Chinese diplomatic Twitter accounts. Chinese foreign ministry spokesperson Hua Chunying made her very first tweet on February 14, 2020.

The sum total of all this was that, by early 2020, the tone of Twitter's China discourse had already begun to change. The U.S. social media platform was already starting to feel like a battleground. The once-dominant voices of the pro-democracy Chinese critics of Beijing were being increasingly drowned out by a large and growing network of pro-Beijing voices. At the outbreak of the pandemic, the Chinese government was well prepared to use Twitter and other foreign social media platforms to rewrite the narrative of Covid-19's spread and, later, to amplify the party line on Xinjiang, Taiwan, Russia's war in Ukraine, and whatever other messages it chose.

———————

The Chinese government did not start out by embracing coronavirus conspiracy theories. At the end of January 2020, when a Chinese social media post claiming that the United States had engineered the coronavirus went viral, Chinese authorities arrested its author for disseminating fake news, and the *People's Daily* published a photo of him in shackles, according to an investigation by the Associated Press.

But as the disease spread farther beyond China's borders and the body count rose, the international outrage peaked. In response, Beijing launched a global propaganda blitz. On February 3, Xi Jinping publicly called on Chinese media outlets to "tell good stories of China's fight against the epidemic." Xi also stated that handling the pandemic will "relate directly to overall economic and social stability," suggesting that the pandemic response was already being seen through the lens of politics and that "stability maintenance" measures, including censorship and propaganda, might be deployed.

Some of the messaging that resulted after this call to tell "good China" stories was the usual spin, a reframing of the narrative to make the Chinese government look better. China's foreign ministry claimed in a March 9, 2020, tweet that "China's endeavor to combating [*sic*] the epidemic has bought time for int'l preparedness," a refrain that Chinese state media and diplomatic Twitter accounts soon picked up. Some of the messaging, though, was the combative nationalism of wolf warrior diplomacy, such as that demonstrated by the tweet the Chinese embassy in Caracas, Venezuela, posted on March 18, 2020, telling Venezuelan officials who had referred to a "Wuhan" virus to "put on a face mask and shut up."

The CCP's preferred narrative, which it was soon to spread as far and wide as its massive propaganda apparatus and increasingly sophisticated disinformation campaigns could push it, made its first official appearance at a press conference on February 27: Zhong Nanshan, a Chinese pulmonologist helping lead the country's Covid-19 response, said in a press briefing that day that "though COVID-19 was first discovered in China, it does not mean that it originated from China"—an evidence-free assertion that served to cast doubt on the novel coronavirus's clear origins in China.

Chinese state media soon latched on to the idea that the pandemic may not have originated in China, and China's new battalion of verified diplomatic Twitter accounts began pushing it hard. It was a global campaign that quickly gathered steam.

But the nature of party messaging was soon to change dramatically. Among the earliest evidence of Chinese state support for conspiracy-level disinformation regarding the origins of the coronavirus was a February 22 article in the *People's Daily* that mentioned speculation over a possible U.S. military role in the pandemic. An investigation by the Associated Press found that the *People's Daily* also placed paid inserts with this content in newspapers around the world, including Finland's *Helsinki Times* and the *New Zealand Herald*. Chinese state media began featuring quotes from low-profile conspiracy theorists to boost narratives and circulating debunked fake stories that were also running in content farms. The idea that the United States had created the virus as a bioweapon had first ballooned in January among Russian media and Russia-linked proxy actors. But from February on, it was China that led the world in promoting this idea.

In March 2020, conspiracy theories about the coronavirus were rampant on the Chinese internet (and internet spaces elsewhere) but were only beginning to be embraced by Chinese state–run media—a situation reflected in a survey of internet users at the time. According to a survey conducted that month by researchers at the City University of Hong Kong, just over 50 percent of a representative sample of three thousand Chinese internet users believed that the coronavirus was a bioweapon developed by the United States. Use of the social media platform Weibo was positively correlated with belief in conspiracy theories about the virus, whereas consumption of government-run media was negatively correlated with such beliefs. "Go on WeChat, go on Weibo, look on Baidu search, and it's full of 'look at all the other countries getting sick,' or 'the virus came from the United States,' or all different levels of conspiracy theories," Xiao Qiang, founder of China Digital Times, a website that analyzes China's internet and social media, said.

Chinese foreign ministry spokesperson Zhao Lijian's March 12 tweet suggesting that the U.S. Army might be responsible for the pandemic changed all this.

Zhao was already rather infamous to China watchers on Twitter. He had previously spent several years as a diplomat in Pakistan and had been one of the earliest Chinese diplomats to use Twitter to air aggressively nationalist views. By using his position as Ministry of Foreign Affairs spokesperson to tweet this, he was signaling that China's official position was to promote skepticism about the virus's origins and to blame the United States.

Not everyone at China's foreign ministry was on board with promoting the idea that the U.S. military had engineered the novel coronavirus. Cui Tiankai, China's then ambassador to the United States, disowned the theory in a March 2020 interview with my Axios colleague Jonathan Swan, calling it "crazy." Cui, a stately, silver-haired diplomat who had served as the Chinese envoy to the United States since 2013, seemed to prefer the relatively more reserved style of China's traditional diplomacy; in China's tightly controlled foreign ministry bureaucracy, for an ambassador to criticize as "crazy" something that a Chinese foreign ministry spokesperson had said on Twitter was considered remarkably direct. Cui's comments led to speculation that the new "wolf warrior" style of diplomacy was receiving pushback within the foreign ministry.

Despite Cui's opposition, Chinese diplomats, embassies, and media outlets soon followed Zhao's lead in a huge, coordinated global push. In April, the Chinese embassy in France posted an article to its website claiming that the French government was letting elderly French citizens die in nursing homes. The French government summoned China's ambassador over the post.

In early May, the Chinese embassy in Berlin published a sixteen-point rebuttal of critical reporting on China's pandemic response. Written in a true-or-false, fact-checking style, the 4,600-word German-language post blended fact with propaganda in a sophisticated attempt to persuade German audiences that China's response to the novel coronavirus was blameless. Chinese embassies in Portugal and Brazil soon followed with nearly identical posts to their websites.

The following example demonstrates how the official embassy post recast facts to blur reality:

> *Myth #6: China arrested doctors who warned the world about the virus early on to cover up the outbreak.*
>
> *Fact: No doctor in China has been arrested for warning of an epidemic. Doctors who have reported a possible outbreak have been recognized by the government.*

Yet it is widely known, as discussed earlier, that eight Chinese doctors were detained and interrogated for sharing information about the new virus with colleagues. It is technically true that detention and interrogation are not arrest. And three months after medical whistleblowers were detained, several were belatedly recognized as national heroes, including Dr. Li Wenliang, who had died several weeks before.

A variation on the theme of the United States' being to blame for the coronavirus soon bubbled up, involving Fort Detrick, in Frederick, Maryland, home to the U.S. Army Medical Research Institute of Infectious Diseases. On May 1, the *People's Daily* published an article asking, "What on earth happened in the bioweapons lab in Fort Detrick, Maryland? When did the earliest COVID-19 infection happen in the United States, since a COVID-19 patient without travel history to China died on Feb. 6?" Disinformation researchers also found that Beijing-aligned content farms in Malaysia and elsewhere were also putting out articles with a variety of similar claims.

Beijing's dissemination of disinformation and wild conspiracy theories didn't stop with the end of Trump's presidency. Chinese foreign ministry officials and Chinese state media began heavily promoting the Fort Detrick hypothesis in the summer of 2021, as President Biden ordered an intelligence investigation into the origins of the novel coronavirus, as the Wuhan lab leak theory gained new traction in U.S. media, and as outbreaks of the Delta variant resulted in a new round of lockdowns in China. Life had been more or less back to normal in China for over a year, and the new outbreaks rattled both the government and the population.

Chinese diplomatic Twitter accounts amplified these messages far and wide. "The US should release the data concerning the sickened American military athletes who attended the World Military Games in Wuhan," the Chinese embassy in Zimbabwe tweeted on July 3, 2021. "In October 2019, the US sent more than 300 people to Wuhan for the Games. Was there anyone with symptoms similar to those of COVID-19? What illness did those reported military athletes have exactly? The cases should be made public as soon as possible."

At a press briefing on July 30, 2021, foreign ministry spokesperson Zhao Lijian called on the United States to invite WHO to investigate Fort Detrick. "The international community and the American public have long voiced concerns about the illegal, obscure and unsafe activities in Fort Detrick," Zhao said. "The Research Institute, long engaged in coronavirus studies and modification, had serious safety accidents and was shut down in 2019. Soon afterwards, a disease with similar symptoms with COVID-19 broke out in the US. On these questions, the US side has never given any explanations to its own people and the international community."

In July, the *Global Times* also promoted a petition that it claimed had been started by Chinese netizens to ask the World Health Organization to investigate Fort Detrick's role in the pandemic's origins. The *Global Times* later claimed that the petition had garnered 25 million signatures in just two weeks. Disinformation researchers later found that at least 13.3 million of those signatures showed signs of having been fabricated.

The state-run China News Service hired OneSight, a Beijing tech company, to promote Beijing-aligned propaganda about Covid-19 on Twitter. ProPublica obtained records of fake Twitter accounts in 2021 reaching out to Twitter profiles with large followings, including Chinese Australian political cartoonist Badiucao, offering to pay them to post Chinese state media videos.

In August 2021, British researchers at the Centre for Information Resilience (CIR) uncovered a network of "deep fake" profiles on Twitter, Facebook, and YouTube that were linked to the Chinese state and that promoted misinformation on Covid-19, gun laws in the United States, and racial issues in a "coordinated influence operation."

The evidence indicated a "deliberate effort to distort international perceptions on significant issues—in this case, in favor of China," said Benjamin Strick, CIR's director of investigations. "If we value the ability to have open and honest discussions and develop informed opinions on social media, then understanding who is trying to influence us, and how, is important."

A Swiss biologist named Wilson Edwards featured prominently in Chinese state media coverage around the end of July 2020. One July 31 Xinhua headline read, "Swiss Biologist Wilson Edward's Explosive Revelation: The Novel Coronavirus Originated as an American Tool to Attack the Chinese Government." China Central Television, the *People's Daily*, and many Chinese news sites carried similar headlines.

But Wilson Edwards didn't exist. The Swiss embassy tweeted on August 10 that Swiss citizenry records contained no such person and that there were no academic articles in biology journals under that name. In this case, the fake Western expert seemed to have been the creation of one news outlet, the Voice of South Pacific, in Fiji, a bilingual Chinese-English company launched in 2020 by Fiji Chinese Media—and his quotes were then widely aggregated by many other outlets. "Wilson Edwards" was not the product of a state-backed information operation, but China's foremost state media outlet's reprinting of quotes from a supposed expert without attempting to verify his existence demonstrates the eagerness with which Chinese state media was seizing on anything that might suggest the United States was behind the pandemic.

In some ways, in 2020, the Trump administration and top Chinese officials seemed to egg each other on, to bring out the worst in each other. The Chinese government responded in kind to the Trump administration's barrage of blame and suspicion. It was only after Trump and some of his top officials publicly suggested that the virus may have been engineered in a Wuhan lab that Chinese government officials and CCP's massive propaganda apparatus began seriously to promote the conspiracy theory that the United States had created the novel coronavirus as a bioweapon. This was, perhaps, an early precursor to the "reciprocalypse" that would soon follow—the tongue-in-cheek term was coined by China Digital Times editor Samuel Wade, and the concept was championed in particular by U.S. secretary of state Mike Pompeo—as the United States and China descended into a tit-for-tat battle over reciprocity in journalist visas, sanctions, and diplomatic access.

For Americans and Europeans who did not support Trump, and especially for those who were left of center, it felt at times like they were simply watching two bullies fighting each other, rather than seeing one side as right and the other as wrong. There were clear similarities between Trump's behavior and some of what we saw coming out of Beijing. The president regularly lied about the severity of the U.S. epidemic and threatened to withhold pandemic aid to states whose politics he didn't like. He used press briefings and his Twitter account to make wild and baseless claims intended to distract from his administration's failings or to discredit an opponent. Over his four years in office, he gained greater sway over government institutions by installing loyalists and consolidated power in the Republican Party by systematically destroying the positions and careers of any detractors and then rewarding those who repeated his falsehoods. The effect was a constant cascade of lies and half-truths mixed in with facts, making it extremely difficult for casual news consumers to distinguish reality from falsehood. Trump was greatly aided in this endeavor by a highly polarized media environment in which Fox News, Breitbart, Newsmax, and other conservative media outlets moved farther away from conscientious reporting and closer to what might be called party media.

Trump's abuse of his office in this way was harmful, embarrassing, and reminiscent of the growing tendency of authoritarian leaders in the twenty-first century to destabilize the information environment in order to control the population through cults of loyalty and distrust of institutions. But the Chinese government's embrace of disinformation, propaganda, and conspiracy theories as parts of a clear global strategy since the pandemic makes Trump's actions look like child's play. Trump was unable to rally the entire U.S. government, as civil servants continued to do their jobs, elected members of Congress impeached him twice, and media outlets freely fact-checked his every word. Beginning in March 2020, the Chinese party-state tasked its foreign ministry, its state media outlets, and its massive censorship infrastructure with promoting disinformation, lies, and propaganda regarding the novel coronavirus and, later, other topics. Despite his threats and anger, Trump was unable to achieve anything resembling this.

The U.S. government is, in fact, forbidden by law from the domestic dissemination of propaganda—defined as messaging intended to influence the public without revealing its government source. This law is by no means defunct. In December 2015, for example, the U.S. Government Accountability Office, a congressional auditor, found that the Environmental Protection Agency had engaged in illegal propaganda when it employed a coordinated social media campaign in which identical messages in support of a proposed environmental law under the Obama administration were posted across Twitter, Facebook, and YouTube without their author being revealed as the EPA.

U.S. intelligence agencies acting abroad are bound by different rules, and in wartime, the United States undertakes some activities abroad that it otherwise would not—including the use of covert propaganda. What makes the Chinese government different is that it uses these methods in peacetime, both domestically and abroad, as a matter of course. A book on military strategy published in 1999 by two senior Chinese Air Force colonels called such tactics "war without bounds" and "unrestricted warfare" (超限战)—defined as the use of political warfare, "lawfare," economic coercion, and other nonmilitary strategies to achieve geopolitical goals without the use of direct military force.

Pushing the idea that the novel coronavirus pandemic did not originate in China is an odd hill on which to die. The lie is Trumpian—or perhaps Orwellian—in its sheer boldness. To rehabilitate their image, China's leaders could easily have limited their efforts to things that were actually true, such as Beijing's genuine successes in fighting Covid-19 and the leading role China has worked very hard to play in sending medical assistance and, later, vaccines to countries in need. Or they could have stuck with comparing China's much more effective response to the United States' many failures.

It's unquestionable that the U.S. response to the novel coronavirus in 2020 was an unmitigated disaster. The United States had the world's highest number of known cases and the highest number of known deaths; it never managed to implement a comprehensive contact tracing system, though many other countries did; and basic scientific facts of the virus became so politicized that the very wearing of a mask became a political statement rather than a simple public health measure.

China hasn't just learned from Russia how to perfect its online disinformation techniques; Beijing and Moscow have also come to coordinate disinformation. This phenomenon developed rapidly from 2019 through 2021 and came into full-fledged maturity with the Russian invasion of Ukraine, when China used its information control and disinformation methods to amplify Russian disinformation about the war.

As soon as Russia's invasion began, Chinese censors began scrubbing online spaces of expressions of support for Ukraine and criticism of Russia. Chinese social media sites, which are subject to tight state control, amplified official Chinese state media posts about the war, many of which were aggregated from official Russian sites. One media directive ordered employees to avoid posting "anything unfavorable to Russia or pro-Western." Chinese state media even bought ads on Meta targeting users around the world and pushing Russian narratives about the war in Ukraine.

Beijing's turn toward disinformation as a global narrative tactic, inspired by Russia and first debuting with the Covid-19 pandemic, came full circle in March 2022, when, during a press conference, Chinese foreign ministry spokesperson Zhao Lijian accused the United States of operating "dangerous" biolabs in Ukraine and conducting experiments with coronaviruses there—a false claim that served as a dog whistle to anyone looking for a reason to absolve China and instead blame U.S. imperialism for the global pandemic.

8

"CHEWING GUM STUCK TO THE BOTTOM OF CHINA'S SHOE"

As the first year of the pandemic drew to a close, the China-Australia relationship was veering off a cliff. November 2020 saw the Chinese government levy tariffs on Australian wine and deliver the "Fourteen Grievances," a list of sweeping domestic and international political demands on Australia, including that its leaders suppress domestic free speech and criticism of China. Another of the stated grievances was that Australia had sided "with the US' anti-China campaign."

But Australia's turn against Beijing long predated Prime Minister Scott Morrison's call for an investigation into the origins of the novel coronavirus and, indeed, the U.S. government's own hawkish turn. By 2016, Australia had already become the first country in the world (with the exception of Taiwan) to publicly recognize and respond to the Chinese Communist Party's pattern of political and economic coercion.

In their anger at Canberra, China's leaders got at least one thing wrong. It wasn't Australia that was following the United States' lead. It was, in many respects, the other way around. Australia's experience helped pave the way for the Trump administration's evolving stance on China. Beijing also saw Australia as setting a dangerous example for other middle powers.

Australia's early awakening had come about in part because of the unique background of one man: a journalist turned intelligence official named John Garnaut. U.S. and Australian intelligence agencies had tracked the party's covert activities long enough to start sounding internal alarms about what they were seeing, but the political classes in both nations lacked the will to act on that information, knowing that the strategic and economic costs of confronting China would be great. Garnaut's work both in and out of government bridged the gap between what was already known in the intelligence world and what many Australian politicians were trying very hard to ignore—thus, forcing a public discussion and forging the political will finally to act.

Garnaut stepped off a plane at Dulles International Airport on a sunny day in June 2017. He had just arrived on a long flight from Canberra, Australia, a capital city more distant from DC than any other capital in the world, as it sits not far from DC's antipode on the other side of the globe. Garnaut had visited the U.S. capital before, as a journalist and tourist. But this time, it was government business that had brought him to Washington. He was on his way to the White House for a meeting with Trump's newly minted National Security Council Asia director, Matt Pottinger—a meeting that would help set in motion the United States' turn away from engagement with China and toward an entirely new approach of defending itself from party incursions on U.S. soil.

Garnaut has a charming smile and the confident air of a star athlete. From 2007 to 2013, he made a name for himself as China correspondent for the *Sydney Morning Herald*, demonstrating an almost uncanny ability to break news on factions, infighting, and corruption among Chinese Communist Party elites and princelings, the scions of the party's founding families. In 2009, he won a major journalism award in Australia for his scoop on China's detention of Australian citizen Stern Hu, who ran multinational mining giant Rio Tinto's iron ore business there, amid a major corruption scandal. In 2012, Garnaut published a book about the stunning rise and equally dramatic fall of Bo Xilai, a charismatic princeling and Politburo member who once rivaled Xi Jinping for leadership of the party. Garnaut's peerless sourcing was, perhaps, aided by the fact that he was the son of Ross Garnaut, a prominent economist who had served as Australia's ambassador to China in the 1980s; John Garnaut had spent part of his childhood in Beijing and spoke Chinese fluently.

Perhaps surprisingly, it was Garnaut's investigative reporting on party princelings that first drew his interest to China's political warfare, the topic he would eventually bring to the international spotlight. By the late 2000s, China's princelings had developed a reputation as Ferrari-driving, fast-living, inside-trading showmen. But Garnaut found that most of them weren't like this, at least in their exterior presentation. Rather, they tended to live somewhat humbly but exuded a deep sense of entitlement to speak of China and the party's interests, and to do so without being silenced. They did this by drawing on the lives and experiences of their fathers and mothers—all party heroes—to diagnose the problems of contemporary China and what they saw as China's pathway out.

But few of these princelings' parents had been heroes on the battlefield or had even ever carried guns. Rather, they had been underground operators, working for the United Front, the intelligence system, and the "Department of Enemy Work," later known as the International Liaison Department of the General Political Department of the People's Liberation Army, the military office tasked with covert political influence operations. This indicated to Garnaut that it was this kind of covert political work that was most highly prized by the Chinese Communist Party.

But political warfare, and the party departments tasked with carrying it out, had been overlooked for decades in Western scholarship on China. The last English-language book on the United Front Work Department had been published decades earlier. Almost no information was available in English on the party's efforts to extend censorship and political influence abroad or to silence dissent among Chinese diaspora communities. Yet, since the 1990s, the Chinese Communist Party had only upped its investment in political warfare abroad, cultivating friendly groups to lobby for party interests in foreign capitals while hiding the party's role in those activities. Party officials aimed to "win without fighting" by privately suggesting to foreign government officials that China might indeed have a democratic future, if only the West would open its markets and invest enough in the country—all the while knowing that the party had no such plans.

Beyond the firewall of classified Western intelligence, very little information was available about the International Liaison Department, which for years had operated almost openly in Western political circles. The Ministry of State Security was seen largely through the lens of domestic repression in China; its international activities were largely ignored except by a handful of government intelligence analysts, who had underestimated the dramatic modernization and expansion of the International Liaison Department's capabilities, which were well under way by 2010.

Even the "Communist" part of the Chinese Communist Party was dismissed with something of an eye roll by Western commentators, who were dazzled by the extreme capitalist successes manifested by China's soaring skyscrapers, charismatic billionaires, and Prada-toting urbanites.

That was a mistake.

In 2013, John Garnaut returned to Australia. His new focus, informed by his unique access to China's princelings, was China's political warfare abroad. He set out upon what would become a yearslong process of researching and reporting on the structures, methods, and evolution of the Chinese Communist Party's political warfare departments, trying to help fill in the gaps of Western knowledge of how the party exerted power and influence in the twenty-first century. Garnaut believed that an understanding of this was key to understanding the party and modern China. Without it, there was no way to gain a holistic picture of what was occurring.

Other researchers in Australia and neighboring New Zealand were also making major contributions to this effort around this time. In 2010, Australian journalist Richard McGregor published a book called *The Party: The Secret World of China's Communist Rulers*, which reintroduced the centrality of Leninism—top-down party discipline—as the key to understanding how the Chinese Communist Party exerted political control over China's government, courts, and officials. The book would go on to influence a generation of China journalists and emerging political scientists around the world.

In 2014, James Jiann Hua To, a brilliant New Zealand political scientist who has since retreated from the public eye, published *Qiaowu: Extra-Territorial Policies for the Overseas Chinese*, which drew on a trove of documents about the Chinese Communist Party's United Front Work Department and how it sought to influence, surveil, and stifle overseas Chinese diaspora communities. Australian academics Gerry Groot and John Fitzgerald delved into the party's United Front work, a comprehensive strategy used not just by the United Front Work Department but throughout the party's offices to marginalize dissent and amplify support in order to smooth the way to achieve party goals. In 2017, Anne-Marie Brady, the New Zealand political scientist who had helped train

To, would publish the enormously influential paper "Magic Weapons," which examined how United Front work was being employed to directly interfere in New Zealand society and domestic politics; the paper further developed some of the concepts Brady had introduced in her 2003 book, *Making the Foreign Serve China: Managing Foreigners in the People's Republic.*

In the early to mid-2010s, Garnaut wrote several key articles about the People's Liberation Army that would become particularly influential in Washington. In May 2013, he published a story about a PLA International Liaison Department front known as the China Association for International Friendly Contact (CAIFC), which was operating openly by casting itself as a social organization facilitating exchanges between Chinese and high-level Western political and business leaders. CAIFC had hosted a delegation of top Australian business leaders, including the heads of Australia's top banks, the head of the airline Qantas, and Geoff Raby, a former Australian ambassador to China. CAIFC did not disclose its affiliation with the PLA's International Liaison Department, even though the department's director, Xing Yunming, accompanied the group, and Xing did not disclose his PLA rank of lieutenant general.

The former Department of Enemy Work's name may have changed, but its aims had not. A 2003 PLA International Liaison Department manual Garnaut obtained stated that the department was tasked with "carrying out work of disintegrating the enemy and uniting with friendly military elements." These kinds of activities are vastly different from the diplomacy and state messaging any ministry of foreign affairs might normally facilitate. A closer analogue might be if a U.S. intelligence agency hid behind a front organization and brought a group of influential foreigners to Washington for the purpose of deceiving them about the U.S. government's true aims and co-opting them into helping fulfill those aims.

Garnaut soon began breaking story after story about the Chinese Communist Party's covert activities in Australia. In April 2014, he reported that Chinese intelligence officials were attempting to build "large covert informant networks" at Australian universities and that Chinese students in Australia felt harassed and frightened by these attempts. In 2015, Chinese security officials had entered Australia to pursue a Chinese citizen without asking for permission from Australian authorities, an example of China's increasingly brazen attitude of extraterritoriality over Chinese citizens anywhere in the world. Garnaut also reported on foreign-based political donations in Australia. Since 2009 Garnaut had followed Australia's top foreign-based political donor Chau Chak-wing, who had donated more than two million Australian dollars to Australian political parties while living in Guangzhou. Australia's laws at that time still permitted foreign nationals to make political donations.

As Garnaut's interest in China's covert political influence was growing, Canberra and Beijing were quite cozy. The economic relationship between the two countries was becoming ever closer, while Australia shied away from challenging Beijing's growing military ambitions. China had been Australia's top trade partner since 2008. That year, Prime Minister Kevin Rudd withdrew from the just-launched Quadrilateral Security Dialogue, or "Quad," an informal grouping of Australia, India, Japan, and the United States for the purpose of military cooperation in the Asia-Pacific region, after the Chinese government signaled its strong displeasure to the grouping. Australia's 2009 defense white paper had stated that "the pace, scope and structure of China's military modernisation have the potential to give its neighbours cause for concern"—but the next white paper, released in 2013, walked back this warning. Despite China's unilateral military buildup in the South China Sea over the preceding four years, the 2013 white paper called China's growing military strength "natural and legitimate" and stated that "Australia welcomes China's rise." In 2014, Xi Jinping addressed Australia's Parliament. The same year, the two countries also launched the annual China-Australia Strategic Economic Dialogue, and in 2015, after a decade of negotiations, they inked a free trade agreement.

When he became prime minister in September 2015, Malcolm Turnbull was no China hawk. That month, Garnaut published an article exploring the reasons Turnbull was considered "soft" on China, including rumors that his son Alex's wife might have ties to China's party elites, which the family has firmly denied. A columnist for the *Australian Financial Review* wrote that Turnbull had "healthy skepticism" for the intelligence community, a legacy of the loss of trust the United States' "Five Eyes" partners (Australia, Canada, New Zealand, and the United

Kingdom) had suffered after the George W. Bush administration insisted, wrongly, that it had intelligence proving that Saddam Hussein's Iraq had weapons of mass destruction, justifying an invasion. The director of an Australian foreign policy think tank said that Turnbull was "less prone to seeing the world through a security prism."

But Turnbull had previously served as Australia's minister for communications, which meant he was more attuned to concerns about Chinese telecommunications companies like Huawei than most Australian government officials during that time—who were focused primarily on the threat of terrorism. As prime minister, he had also assembled a team that didn't view Beijing through rose-colored glasses. He chose Justin Bassi as his national security adviser. Bassi had a background in cybersecurity and, thus, like Turnbull, had a frame of reference for seeing China not just as a trade partner but also, on some level, as a security concern. The prime minister first brought on John Garnaut to help handle the media and to write speeches on China and Asia affairs. Neither realized that Garnaut would become part of the major policy shift Turnbull would soon lead.

"Where Malcolm deserves a lot of credit is in being willing to listen to John and me in our security concerns," Bassi observed. "Malcolm was a reader of intelligence, and he was evolving his views based on the growing concerns of intelligence." This mattered because, Bassi told me, "it was the intelligence community that moved first, with a very slow and reticent policy community and a political class who could see the benefits of being close to Beijing." In fact, Turnbull would become the first leader in the Western world to issue a democratic call to arms in the face of China's expanding authoritarianism.

———

It was the speechwriting that ended up giving Garnaut input into national policy. Amid a busy ministerial daily schedule, the time he and Turnbull spent together hashing out ideas and crafting sentences was what gave Garnaut the greatest opportunity to share his knowledge and conclusions with the Australian leader. Turnbull wasn't inherently suspicious of Beijing, but those close to him say he was insatiably curious and impatient with unsatisfactory advice, always pushing his advisers to get more information and go deeper.

Over the next year, Turnbull, Garnaut, and Bassi came to the conclusion that while Australia's defense and intelligence system was doing a good job tracking twentieth-century-style defense issues, such as missiles, ships, traditional intelligence threats, the system was failing at understanding the gray spaces where Beijing did much of its security work. United Front work and political warfare are forms of influence that have no analogue in Western democratic government systems. Turnbull, Garnaut, and Bassi came to believe that Australia had to build a completely new paradigm and even a new lexicon—because there was nothing on the shelf that worked. As Turnbull would later say, it was clear that "our system as a whole had not grasped the nature and the magnitude of the threat."

At this point, Turnbull decided to initiate a classified investigation into foreign government coercion and interference in Australia's democratic political system. The investigation resulted in a classified report written under the auspices of the Australian Security Intelligence Organisation (ASIO), the country's national security arm. Turnbull offered the job of writing that report to Garnaut, who accepted while continuing to serve as Turnbull's speechwriter.

Two significant events during this time helped catalyze public debate over China's influence and intentions in Australia. In 2015, Chinese shipping conglomerate Landbridge Group secured a ninety-nine-year lease on Port Darwin, a small, aging wharf in northern Australia where U.S. Marines and Australian forces trained several months each year and that offered southern access to the South China Sea. The local government didn't have money to develop the port; Landbridge did. The Australian federal government had barely reviewed the deal before the local government signed. But once the deal was signed, U.S. and Australian intelligence officials warned the Australian government that Beijing could use the facility for military intelligence collection; analysts believe that Landbridge has close ties to China's military-industrial complex. Intelligence officials were stunned that a Chinese-owned company could circumvent Australia's federal government and work directly with a cash-strapped local government to gain access to sensitive and critical infrastructure.

The second significant event, the Sam Dastyari affair, occurred in June 2016, just as the Turnbull government was beginning to tackle China's political influence head-on. As the scandal unfolded, it provided the

Australian public with a clear and compelling example of how damaging such influence could be.

Dastyari was a senator from New South Wales and a member of the opposition Australian Labor Party. Beginning in 2016, a series of media investigations revealed that he had financial ties to a billionaire Chinese property developer, Huang Xiangmo, one of Australia's top political donors. In June 2016, during an election campaign conference one month before the federal election, at an event with a local Chinese community, Dastyari had pledged to support China's position in the South China Sea. That year, China had lost a ruling at a tribunal in The Hague, which found that most of Beijing's territorial claims in the maritime region had no basis in international law. The Australian Labor Party backed the tribunal's finding, meaning Dastyari was going against his own party's official stance on the issue. What's more, he made the pledge while standing next to Huang.

Huang was an Australian permanent resident but not a citizen; he had resided in Sydney since 2011. He owned a $12.8 million mansion in an affluent neighborhood, with an infinity pool and a large glass-enclosed balcony. Huang had given at least $2.7 million, through various organizations and associates, to both political parties. In 2015, he paid 55,000 Australian dollars to have lunch with Labor leader Bill Shorten. At the time, Australian law did not prohibit foreign citizens from donating to political campaigns. What's more, Huang was known to have close ties to Chinese Communist Party organizations in China and Australia. He also gave the founding donation to the Australia-China Relations Institute, a research institution that, predictably, publishes pro-Beijing viewpoints. In a clear sign of the reach of Huang's influence, former Australian minister of foreign affairs Bob Carr accepted the offer to serve as the institute's director.

Subsequent reporting revealed that Dastyari had urged the government office in charge of immigration to process Huang's citizenship application, which had stalled. He tipped off Huang that Australia's intelligence agency may have tapped his phone, leading some in the opposition to openly question Dastyari's loyalty to Australia. Dastyari also pressured Labor's foreign affairs spokesperson, Tanya Plibersek, not to meet with a prominent pro-democracy activist and Australian citizen in Hong Kong during her upcoming visit. Huang gave Dastyari five thousand Australian dollars to cover a legal bill. It also came to light, according to a Chinese-language media report in 2014, that Dastyari had said that the Australian government should abandon its opposition to the air defense identification zone (ADIZ) China had declared over the South China Sea. While not an explicit claim of sovereignty, the declaration of an area over land or water as an ADIZ requires aircraft transiting through that region to report in with the declaring country's air traffic controllers. An ADIZ can strengthen a country's territorial claims, and China's unilateral declaration of an ADIZ over the contested region was considered a destabilizing action. In September 2016, Turnbull condemned Dastyari's actions as a "cash for comment" affair and asked, "Is the Labor party's foreign policy for sale?"

From the Dastyari scandal onward, Australian journalists across several outlets began pursuing Beijing's influence as a key area of emphasis. Chinese government harassment and surveillance of Chinese students at Australian universities began to receive more attention. The award-winning television show *Secret City*, a political thriller depicting Chinese government–backed schemes in Australia, premiered in 2016. Nick McKenzie, one of Australia's top investigative journalists, turned his attention to the issue and wrote about China-linked corruption and political donations in a series of articles and in a *Four Corners* documentary. It was as if the floodgates had opened.

In his June 2017 address at the annual Shangri-La Dialogue security conference in Singapore, Turnbull became the first world leader to publicly warn of China's interference in the sovereignty of other nations, striking a new tone for relations between China and the democratic world. He warned that Beijing was becoming "coercive" in its approach to the world and that China would soon "find its neighbors resenting demands they cede their autonomy and strategic space, and look to counterweight Beijing's power by bolstering alliances and partnerships, between themselves and especially with the United States." It was a prediction that forecast what would become the exact strategy of first the Trump and then the Biden administrations.

Garnaut's ASIO report was completed in 2017. It identified the Chinese government as the top perpetrator of foreign political interference in Australia. The report remained classified, but its broad findings helped spur the foreign interference laws introduced in the Australian Parliament in December 2017. Those laws were modeled in part on the Foreign

Agents Registration Act (FARA), a U.S. law enacted in 1938 to counter-act Nazi-era propaganda. FARA requires that individuals and organiza-tions acting on behalf of a foreign entity register with a special office at the Department of Justice and file financial and other disclosures.

"Garnaut played a central and major role in getting the Australian sys-tem and public to take Chinese foreign interference seriously," said John Lee, who served as foreign policy adviser to Australian foreign minister Julie Bishop from 2016 to 2018. "There was always extensive intelligence on United Front activities in both the United States and Australia. How-ever, Garnaut played a major role in using this information and intelli-gence to offer a broader narrative about what the CCP was doing and also link United Front activities to broader CCP foreign policy."

In December 2017, as the foreign interference laws were being intro-duced, Turnbull spoke before Parliament about the Chinese Communist Party's "covert, coercive or corrupting" activities, such as punishing media outlets for criticism, using proxies to provide financial incentives to Aus-tralian political parties, and rewarding Australian business and political leaders for toeing party lines, that threatened Australia's sovereignty and democratic political system. It was the first time Turnbull publicly used the "three Cs" formulation to define China's influence tactics and distin-guish them from the usual diplomatic and economic activity of states. Hashed out by Turnbull, Garnaut, and Bassi, the phrase was later picked up by Trump-era U.S. officials and is now used by analysts around the world who are examining China's activities in their own countries. The "three Cs," Turnbull explained, could be combated by a counter foreign interference strategy built on the four pillars of "sunlight, enforcement, deterrence and capability."

Unsurprisingly, this speech played poorly in Beijing. China's foreign ministry said the prime minister's speech "poisons the atmosphere of the China-Australia relationship."

As Australia was sticking its neck out in 2017, the United States was say-ing very little. Despite Trump's tough-on-China campaign rhetoric, by mid-2017, senior U.S. officials had yet to give a single speech or publish an article outlining the administration's views on China.

But this belied changes in perspective that had been taking place behind closed doors in U.S. intelligence agencies spanning both backward in time for at least a decade and outward across oceans through the long-standing intelligence-sharing relationships among Cold War allies, namely the Five Eyes of Australia, Canada, New Zealand, the United Kingdom, and the United States.

In the late 2000s, the FBI Counterintelligence Program had just a handful of people working on issues related to China's political influence activities in the United States. Under President Obama, FBI counterintelligence investigations relating to China often focused on disrupting operations rather than pursuing indictments. This meant that if an operation was successfully disrupted, the U.S. public would never have any idea what the Chinese government had been attempting, because no records of the case would be made public.

Over the next several years, FBI personnel saw the amount and extent of China-linked espionage and influence activities on U.S. soil grow, but there was no corresponding growth in the number of cases made public through indictments or formal charges. Between 2013 and 2016, the Department of Justice issued zero indictments for espionage tied to China, yet, during this time, China's Ministry of State Security—traditionally more focused on domestic political security—dramatically increased the scale of its international political operations. The sheer number and significance of classified cases that remained out of the public eye were breathtaking, sources told me. As a result, there was a widening gap between what the U.S. government was beginning to understand about the CCP's aggressive interference and espionage activities and what the American public knew. This state of affairs was the source of frustration and growing alarm at the DOJ.

Throughout the 2010s, other U.S. intelligence agencies began to experience a similar sense of rising alarm across regions and sectors, as the Chinese government aggressively sought to increase its power and influence beyond its borders. In addition to interagency processes to share what they were seeing, U.S. agencies actively pursued exchanges with their Australian counterparts on this issue and invited Australian politicians, academics, and researchers to brief U.S. officials and meet with investigators.

In 2016 and 2017, U.S. government intelligence analysts became particularly interested in a series of investigations by Garnaut, published several years earlier, that described the Chinese military's political influence operations run by its International Liaison Department. In one 2013 article, Garnaut had laid out how one top Chinese military officer, Zhang Yang, the head of the PLA's Political Work Department, which is responsible for influencing the defense policy of foreign governments, was able to gain easy access to high-ranking former officials in the United States and Australia without arousing suspicion.

"Zhang holds one of the four most important positions in the Central Military Commission, but he is barely noticed by many Western military analysts because he has a job that does not exist in their home systems," Garnaut wrote. This key observation would come to underlie the discussions Garnaut would later have with Turnbull and with U.S. officials, including Pottinger, about how Western democracies had forgotten how to deal with or even talk about Communist parties.

This engagement with top Western government figures happened through the China Association for International Friendly Contact, the International Liaison Department's public-facing platform to engage with Western elites. CAIFC once had an expansive website that posted regular updates on its meetings with foreign officials and business leaders, the exchanges and programs it sponsored, and the visiting congressional delegations it received. Around 2016, after U.S. intelligence agencies began to take an interest in Garnaut's work and in CAIFC, the website was scrubbed of most content and today contains little information.

U.S. intelligence agencies weren't alone in tracking China's increasingly aggressive behavior abroad. There was also the Five Eyes, the intelligence-sharing partnership. The Five Eyes is not a single treaty but, rather, many different and overlapping agreements on the sharing of images, signals intelligence, human intelligence, and other kinds of information—a "spider's web on a spider's web on a spider's web" is how Richard Aldrich, a professor of international security at the University of Warwick and author of *GCHQ: The Uncensored Story of Britain's Most Secret Intelligence Agency*, describes it. "There will be agreements between departments that we don't even think of as part of intelligence." Because of quick shared access to the same pool of intelligence, the Five Eyes partners have a tendency to back one another up.

The Five Eyes was crucial during the constant spy games of the Cold War. After 9/11, the group again attained a new level of urgency in the global fight against terrorism. The intelligence failures that led up to 9/11—in particular, the dossiers on future 9/11 hijackers that sat gathering dust on desks—led to a sort of culture change among Five Eyes stakeholders. "We've moved from 'need to know' to 'need to share,'" Aldrich told me. "The attitude is: We don't want another 9/11 on our watch. No one wants to be sitting on the file that should have been shared."

But China remained low on the priority list. President Barack Obama's "pivot to Asia" was intended to help rebalance U.S. resources away from the Middle East and toward China, including the vast U.S. intelligence resources that had been redirected to the Middle East after 9/11, leaving China-related offices and capabilities underdeveloped. Obama's pivot never really got off the ground, however, and his foreign policy had remained mired largely in the Middle East, with the major exception of the creation of the U.S.-led Trans-Pacific Partnership in early 2016, an agreement between the United States and twelve Pacific Rim countries but, conspicuously, not China. The TPP marked the biggest multilateral trade agreement since the creation of the World Trade Organization and was widely viewed as a direct challenge to China's growing economic and political clout in the Asia-Pacific region. But overall, as alarm grew within the understaffed China sections of intelligence agencies, their warnings did not result in significant policy shifts.

From the perspective of Australian government officials dealing with the United States during this time, this U.S. retreat from challenging China was due in part to the rise of the Islamic State, which dominated global attention and security resources for several years, and also to changes in personnel. "Prior to 2016, there were some within the U.S. system who were actually worried about the direction Australia's China policy was heading in terms of becoming too naïve about some of the problems China presented," Lee told me. This had been particularly true while Hillary Clinton was secretary of state; John Kerry, who held that position during Obama's second term, brought a softer and less confrontational approach to dealing with China. "By the time I entered the Australian government in early 2016, there appeared to be insufficient American resolve and will to challenge aspects of China's behavior." This uncertainty, said Lee, had the effect of further weakening the strategic courage and creativity of allies such as Australia.

Change would soon come from a surprising direction. On the 2016 campaign trail, Donald Trump had railed against the U.S. trade deficit with China. After his surprising victory, it was clear that the United States under the new president wasn't going to be business as usual. This was particularly true on the China front. After Trump's election, analysts had debated if Trump would be tougher on China—he had, after all, campaigned on a trade war—or if his eagerness to sign a trade deal, his apparent affinity for dictators, and his wealthy friends on Wall Street would lead him to cozy up to Xi Jinping.

On Friday, December 2, 2016, I had lunch with a diplomat from the Taipei Economic and Cultural Representative Office, or TECRO, Taiwan's de facto embassy in Washington. I was heading to Taipei in just a few days to interview Taiwanese president Tsai Ing-wen, and the diplomat and I had arranged to meet before I left. I mentioned these concerns to her and asked if she and her colleagues were worried that Trump might sell out if Xi offered major trade concessions in exchange for U.S. abandonment of Taiwan.

She replied with surprising confidence that, no, she was not worried and that there were people close to Trump who were strong supporters of Taiwan. I wondered at her apparent certainty.

Hours later, I knew the reason for her confidence. That evening, the news came out that the president-elect had broken with decades of precedent and spoken with Tsai in a phone call earlier that very day. This action suggested that the incoming administration might be iconoclastic not just on trade but also on other fronts of the United States–China relationship.

But one of Trump's first actions as president belied such a simple conclusion. On January 24, 2017, he issued an executive order withdrawing the United States from the Trans-Pacific Partnership, surrendering U.S. economic leadership in the Asia-Pacific region in a self-inflicted wound from which the United States may never be able to recover. The TPP would have been the biggest regional trade agreement in history; negotiations had been ongoing for almost a decade. It would have not just reduced tariffs but also set progressive new standards in labor, intellectual property, human rights, governance, and environmental protections for member countries, which together comprised 40 percent of the global economy. The United States would have been by far the largest economy in the new trade bloc, obtaining strong economic and political sway in the Indo-Pacific and serving as a counterweight to China's pull in the region. In addition, the Obama administration had persuaded the leaders of member states to expend their own domestic capital to ensure their governments and populace supported the deal. By withdrawing, the United States didn't just dismantle the best tool in its arsenal to fight China's authoritarian economic statecraft; it also deeply damaged the trust that regional governments had previously had in the United States as a reliable partner.

Moreover, months of infighting among different factions close to Trump—his billionaire friends who preferred a closer (and more lucrative) relationship with Beijing versus White House adviser Steve Bannon and other über–China hawks—kept China policy frozen in place. As for Trump, he wasn't wedded to any particular moral platform when it came to China. In those early months, he focused on his personal relationship with Xi Jinping. The two leaders held their first summit in April 2017, at Mar-a-Lago, after which Trump commented that Xi was a "terrific person" and that they had "good chemistry" and "a very good relationship." The president's early attempts to negotiate with North Korea seemed to occupy the foremost place in the United States' Asia policy at this time.

As 2017 wore on, the Trump administration struggled to articulate a China policy at all. The opening salvos of the United States–China trade war were still a long way off. As an August 2017 analysis by Brookings Institution scholars found, the administration was "still in search of a strategy": "The Trump administration has not presented a coherent public explanation of how it views China, what kind of relationship it seeks to cultivate, or how it plans to do so."

———————

It was in the midst of these foreign policy doldrums in late June 2017 that Garnaut had flown to Washington. He was scheduled to talk with Matt Pottinger at 5 p.m. on a Friday afternoon, the slot in a public servant's schedule that often goes to unimportant meetings. The two met in one of the secure skiffs in the Eisenhower Executive Office Building, near the White House. But the meeting stretched on. Pottinger grilled Garnaut on Chinese elite politics and the history of Chinese Communist Party influence tactics. Six thirty p.m. came and went, and the two hadn't gotten past discussing the CCP's strategies during World War II.

So, Pottinger invited Garnaut for breakfast at his rented house in Cleveland Park the next morning. They sat at the kitchen counter and, over homemade blueberry waffles made by Pottinger's wife, Yen, talked for hours about democratic governments, the "gray zone" tactics of the CCP's contemporary influence machine, and traditional military and economic competition. Garnaut was impressed. He saw that Pottinger was strategic, driven, action-oriented, and not beholden to the pro-engagement status quo that had trapped three decades of China analysis. Like Turnbull, Pottinger showed insatiable curiosity about things that mattered, and he was impressed with how Garnaut had used his reporting experience to help craft a major policy shift in Australia. "John had a galvanizing effect. He got it done," Pottinger later told me.

The two also talked about their respective backgrounds, which were surprisingly similar. Pottinger had spent seven years in China as a reporter for the *Wall Street Journal* and had then returned to the United States and joined the U.S. Marines. In December 2016, Gen. Michael Flynn, Trump's first national security advisor, asked Pottinger to join Trump's fledgling China team as Asia adviser. This meant that both Garnaut and Pottinger had previously served as correspondents in China, returned to their respective home countries, and eventually taken government positions working on China strategy—a fairly unusual career path for former foreign correspondents. The two hadn't quite overlapped during their posts in Beijing, though they knew each other's names and work. But it's no coincidence that two former China correspondents both had a clear-eyed view of how the Chinese Communist Party actually worked. During his years as a correspondent in China, Pottinger had been assaulted and detained by Chinese police. And Garnaut, over the course of his reporting, had seen death, cover-ups, corruption, and bribery up close and personal; the Chinese party-state had even attempted to recruit him as one of their own.

This was their first meeting, but it was far from their last. Garnaut may not have known it, but Pottinger at this time was working with NSC advisor Nadia Schadlow to draft the Trump administration's National Security Strategy. In subsequent meetings, Pottinger had Garnaut give briefings to Schadlow and to national security advisor H. R. McMaster. When Garnaut brought along the findings from his classified ASIO report, Pottinger made sure that Secretary of Defense Jim Mattis read them.

The ASIO report's key findings were not publicly announced until May 2018, and the report's entire contents remain classified, but subsequent reports and publicly available documents outline what Mattis, Schadlow, and Pottinger were reading as they formulated the National Security Strategy. The report identified China as the primary state actor responsible for foreign political interference in Australia. Garnaut discussed the findings of the report, and the strategies Australia was pursuing in response, in public testimony presented to the U.S. House Armed Services Committee in March 2018. "The Chinese Communist Party manipulates incentives inside our countries in order to shape the conversation, manage perceptions and tilt the political and strategic landscape to its advantage," Garnaut told the gathered U.S. lawmakers. "Our challenge—the shared challenge of democracies across the world—is to work with the strengths and shore up the vulnerabilities of our open, multicultural, democratic systems in order to push back against authoritarian interference." Appropriate countermeasures to China's "three Cs" should require "sunlight, enforcement, deterrence and capability," Garnaut said. Such strategies should also be country-agnostic, designed to push back against the Chinese government's interference but also against that of any other authoritarian government.

John Lee, who was also interacting with Trump officials during this time, found those officials very receptive and more willing to consider "creative approaches" than their predecessors. "I would say that these key Trump figures were far more willing to seek and consider Australian views than the second-term Obama administration," Lee observed.

The U.S. National Security Strategy was released in December 2017. It was the first major U.S. strategy document to raise concerns around China's infringement on the political sovereignty of other nations, echoing Australian prime minister Turnbull's June 2017 speech at the Shangri-La Dialogue in Singapore. "For decades, U.S. policy was rooted in the belief that support for China's rise and for its integration into the post-war international order would liberalize China. Contrary to our hopes, China expanded its power at the expense of the sovereignty of others," the document stated. In February 2018, Trump approved the National Security Strategy's Indo-Pacific Framework, drafted in significant portion by Pottinger.

The expansive framework called for building an "international consensus that China's industrial policies and unfair trading practices are damaging the global trading system"; expanding U.S. counterintelligence and law enforcement to counter China's intelligence activities in the United States and expanding intelligence sharing with allies to help them do the same; developing military and asymmetric warfare strategies to help Taiwan in its tense relationship with China; strengthening national security reviews of Chinese investments into sensitive U.S. sectors; and working with allies and partners to try to "prevent Chinese acquisition of military and strategic capabilities," among numerous other measures.

The Indo-Pacific Framework also drew directly from Australia's experience under Turnbull, including a reference to a shorthand version of the "three Cs." The document stated that one of the "desired end states" of the National Security Strategy would be that "the United States and its partners on every continent are resistant to Chinese activities aimed at undermining their sovereignty, including through covert or coercive influence." One objective for achieving that was to "align U.S. Indo-Pacific strategy with those of Australia, India, and Japan" and to "expand and prioritize U.S. intelligence and law enforcement activities that counter Chinese influence operations."

A senior White House official confirmed to me in 2021 that the Australian experience had played a key role as the Trump administration formulated its China policies and the Indo-Pacific Framework in particular. "In many ways, they were ahead of the curve in understanding influence operations and interference in domestic systems," the official told me. "They were pioneers, and we have to give a lot of credit to Australia." The senior official gave special credit to John Garnaut and Anne-Marie Brady, specifically Brady's 2017 report "Magic Weapons." Brady had visited Washington, DC, several times over the past few years and briefed U.S. officials on New Zealand's experience with China's covert political influence. She paid a high personal cost for her outspokenness. Laptops and research materials were stolen from her home and office in New Zealand, though cash and valuables were untouched; her car was tampered with; and her sources in China were harassed, in what she described as a clear campaign of intimidation.

In late 2017, as Trump was still by turns complimenting and lambasting China's leaders, focusing almost exclusively on trade and North Korea, the Indo-Pacific Framework may have seemed like a wish list. But 2018 would see the emergence of an increasingly unified China strategy that would, over the next three years, track very closely with what Pottinger had laid out.

In February 2018, FBI director Christopher Wray's comments during a Senate hearing hinted at widespread concerns over China's espionage in the United States. Wray said that the FBI saw China's use of nontraditional collectors "in almost every field office that the FBI has around the country. It's not just in major cities. It's in small ones as well. It's across basically every discipline." He also warned that the Chinese government was using unconventional means to increase its power and influence around the world.

In March 2018, the Office of the U.S. Trade Representative (USTR), Robert Lighthizer, released the findings of its extensive Section 301 investigation into China's trade practices. The 215-page report documented the Chinese government's widespread and systemic abuse of an open trade system to gain unfair advantage, particularly by forced technology transfer. "The Chinese government reportedly uses a variety of tools, including opaque and discretionary administrative approval processes, joint venture requirements, foreign equity limitations, procurements, and other mechanisms to regulate or intervene in U.S. companies' operations in China, in order to require or pressure the transfer of technologies and intellectual property to Chinese companies," the USTR report stated in one of its key findings. The Section 301 report lent a clearly documented, factual basis for Trump's relentless excoriation of China's "unfair" trade practices

In May 2018, the United States renamed its Pacific Command (USPACOM), the unified combatant command based in Hawaii and overseeing the Asia-Pacific region, the "Indo-Pacific Command" (USINDOPACOM). It was a symbolic move that did not assign additional resources to the region, but it marked a strategic turn toward the region and an attempt to tie the United States more closely to India and other regional partners amid Beijing's growing sway.

The United States–China trade war, long threatened, officially began on July 5, 2018, as Trump announced $34 billion in tariffs on a range of Chinese goods. The Chinese government immediately retaliated with $34 billion in tariffs on U.S. goods. The next two years would see further rounds of tariffs and retaliations, dialogues that went nowhere fast, and more tariffs, as the U.S. government offered subsidies to help prop up industries damaged by the trade war.

In October 2018, Vice President Mike Pence stepped in front of a microphone at the Hudson Institute, a conservative Washington, DC, think tank, and launched into a forty-minute speech that would finally outline what became the Trump administration's China policy. "As we speak, Beijing is employing a whole-of-government approach, using political, economic, and military tools, as well as propaganda, to advance its influence and benefit its interests in the United States," Pence said. "China is also applying this power in more proactive ways than ever before, to exert influence and interfere in the domestic policy and politics of our country." He gave examples of the Chinese government exerting pressure on U.S. businesses, local and national politicians, tech companies, academia, and even Hollywood to toe the party line. "We will not stand down," Pence declared.

The speech hit top Chinese officials like a slap in the face. This wasn't Trump's Twitter foreign policy, with its ragging on Chinese trade policies one day and complimenting Xi the next. Rather, it marked, both in policy and tone, a substantive and comprehensive departure from the decades-long engagement era. Longtime *New York Times* China correspondent Jane Perlez described the speech as a "public indictment" of Beijing. Commentators on Chinese social media likened it to Churchill's "Iron Curtain" speech. If Turnbull's two speeches the year before had clearly signaled that Australia wanted to set a new tone for how democracies related to China, then Pence was giving that message the world's loudest megaphone.

In November 2018, the U.S. Department of Justice announced its China Initiative, a sweeping new focus on combating China's economic espionage in the United States. The initiative would also work with the DOJ's Foreign Agents Registration Act unit to "counter covert efforts to influence our leaders and the general public," U.S. attorney general Jeff Sessions said in his November 1 remarks. The initiative tracked clearly with the Indo-Pacific Framework approved nine months earlier, both in its emphasis on economic aspects of the Chinese Communist Party's attempts to use unfair practices to grow its global heft and in the stress it placed on covert influence, particularly the Indo-Pacific Framework's insistence on making major examples of China's foreign interference publicly known.

By the end of 2018, the U.S. and Australian governments were experiencing a high degree of public and private convergence in their assessment of the problems posed by the Chinese Communist Party and in the policies they were proposing in response. This bilateral convergence was just a beginning. As indicated in Turnbull's 2017 Shangri-La speech and in the 2018 U.S. Indo-Pacific Framework, getting more allies on board was a top priority. The Five Eyes began to focus more on China and to become more vocal about their joint efforts and their shared commitment to upholding democratic values and security.

In early 2018, Five Eyes governments also began sharing classified information relating to China's foreign influence activities with countries outside the coalition, including Germany and Japan. This marked an unofficial expansion of the Five Eyes alliance around the particular topic of foreign influence. The expanded sharing was "below the radar," according to one government official, and was usually conducted bilaterally.

"Consultations with our allies, with like-minded partners, on how to respond to China's assertive international strategy have been frequent and are gathering momentum," one U.S. official said of the expanded information sharing in late 2018. "What might have started as ad hoc discussions are now leading to more detailed consultations on best practices and further opportunities for cooperation." According to Bassi, "Australia going first meant no one could honestly say" that U.S. actions on China were just about cynical great-power rivalry. It helped ensure that the debate couldn't just be about the U.S. and China."

Australia's ban on Huawei was a particularly prominent example of this; the ban came almost a year earlier than the U.S. offensive against Huawei. In early 2018, hackers working at the Australian Signals Directorate played out a cyber war game testing the vulnerability of 5G networks. Their findings raised alarms within the directorate that, if Huawei became embedded in the country's 5G networks, they would essentially be indefensible. In high-level meetings in Washington in 2018, Turnbull raised the issue with top U.S. officials. Canberra quietly reached out to governments in western and Northern Europe to share their findings on Huawei and warned India of the risks as well. In August 2018, Australia banned Huawei and ZTE from providing 5G technology there.

It wasn't that the U.S. intelligence community didn't know Huawei was a problem, Bassi explained. It was that U.S. policy and public debate were far behind where intelligence agencies stood on the issue. It wasn't until May 2019 that the Trump administration blacklisted Huawei and began its push the get European allies to block it from their 5G networks as well.

In December 2020, the Office of the Director of National Intelligence said that it would boost spending on China spying by about 20 percent. Director of National Intelligence John Ratcliffe said that the increase in resources would involve both "money and manpower," and he also suggested that some analysts who had previously worked on counterterrorism would be reassigned to China-related work.

When the Hong Kong government disqualified elected legislators in November 2020 amid the city's deepening authoritarianism imposed by Beijing, the foreign ministers of the Five Eyes issued a joint statement urging authorities in Beijing to "re-consider their actions against Hong Kong's elected legislature and immediately reinstate the Legislative Council members." This prompted an especially foreboding response from China's foreign ministry: "No matter if they have five eyes or ten eyes, if they dare to harm China's sovereignty, security and development interests, they should beware of their eyes being poked and blinded," ministry spokesperson Zhao Lijian, former envoy to Pakistan and number one wolf warrior, said in response at a press briefing.

It was against this yearslong backdrop that Prime Minister Scott Morrison issued his call, in April 2020, for an independent investigation into the origins of the novel coronavirus. The Chinese government responded by launching a campaign of economic coercion against Australia, with 80 percent tariffs on Australian barley announced two weeks later and more tariffs targeting sugar, lobster, coal, copper ore, and cotton soon to follow.

"Australia is always messing around," Hu Xijin, then editor in chief of the nationalist tabloid *Global Times*, wrote on Weibo in April 2020. "I feel it is a bit like chewing gum stuck to the bottom of China's shoe. Sometimes you have to find a stone to scrape it off."

Beijing's pressure didn't stop at tariffs. In July 2020, China's Ministry of Foreign Affairs warned Chinese citizens against traveling to Australia, citing what it called a "marked increase in racial discrimination and violence in Australia," "anti-China" incitement by Australian media, and arbitrary searches of Chinese citizens by Australian law enforcement. Of course, Australia wasn't arbitrarily searching and seizing the property of Chinese citizens residing there; it had issued a travel advisory warning that Australian citizens traveling to China risked arbitrary detention. China's own statement was issued just a few days later, echoing the language of Australia's foreign ministry. This put a $28 billion industry in Australia at stake.

Chinese investment in Australia also plummeted by 62 percent in 2020. That's a 94 percent drop from 2016, when it peaked at $12.8 billion. That year, Australia tightened rules on foreign investment, which reduced it to some extent, but the dramatic drop in 2020 was an outlier.

In November 2020, the Chinese embassy in Canberra deliberately leaked a document to Australian news outlets that has come to be known as "the Fourteen Grievances." The list of complaints included Australia's: blocking of Chinese investment projects and banning Huawei and ZTE on national security grounds; enacting new foreign interference legislation; calling for an independent inquiry into the origins of the novel coronavirus; "interfering" in Xinjiang, Hong Kong, and Taiwan affairs; complaining at the United Nations about China's claims in the South China Sea; making efforts to "torpedo" Victoria's participation in China's Belt and Road Initiative; funding an unnamed "anti-China think tank" (a clear reference to the Australian Strategic Policy Institute, or ASPI, in Canberra); accusing China of cyberattacks; allowing "antagonistic" media reports about China; criticizing the CCP by Australian members of parliament; and tolerating racist attacks against Chinese people.

The *Sydney Morning Herald* called the list an "extraordinary attack on the Australian government." Kelsey Munro, a senior analyst at ASPI, called it a "helpfully unambiguous ransom note," one that demanded Australia choose between "sovereignty or friends with China, you decide."

Rush Doshi, director of the Brookings Institution's China Strategy Initiative in Washington, who would soon be asked to join President Biden's National Security Council as a China director, called the Fourteen Grievances "revealing." As he tweeted at the time, "It shows the PRC holds countries responsible for their free *civil societies* & serves as a template for illiberal order-building. . . . An old view was that China used economic coercion when core interests had been crossed. That's outdated."

With its list of grievances, Beijing was also punishing Australia for the actions of its citizens and demanding that the nation give up sovereignty in key areas. "The deployment of coercive economic leverage to shape Australian internal behavior is a kind of illiberal order-building," Doshi noted in the same tweet. "This list is a partial guide to the norms of that illiberal order." Those norms include curtailing domestic media and muzzling civil society at Beijing's demand, not reporting China's cyberattacks, allowing access to Chinese champions like Huawei, and permitting Beijing's interference in domestic politics.

The economic fallout in Australia could have been far worse. Australia is the world's top iron ore exporter, and China is its most important customer; in 2019, 82 percent of Australian iron ore exports went to China. If Beijing had decided to slap huge tariffs on Australian iron ore, the Australian economy would have taken a real beating.

But China is also heavily dependent on Australian ore, which comprises 60 percent of its iron ore imports. It is the world's largest iron consumer, as construction-heavy projects are still powering the country's development. It's no easy trick to find an immediate replacement—though Chinese companies are currently developing an ore mine in Simandou, Guinea, estimated to have one of the largest ore reserves in the world. Still, it makes sense that Beijing didn't place tariffs on Australian iron ore, and as a result, Australia's overall trade balance sheet with China didn't seem to reflect a dramatic drop over the course of 2020.

Global markets also tossed Australia something of a life preserver. In early 2021, iron ore prices soared due to a spike in demand from robust steel production in China amid reduced supply due to ongoing pandemic-related disruptions and complications from a 2019 dam collapse in Brazil, the only other country besides Australia that produces large quantities of iron ore. Even so, overall trade volumes aside, individual industries in Australia suffered heavily.

As a growing number of governments began to realize that the Chinese government could not be relied upon to keep national security from encroaching on what should have been siloed off as purely commercial activities, global trust in China plummeted. In December 2020, Australia appealed to the World Trade Organization, and in June 2021, Prime Minister Scott Morrison called for a binding dispute resolution mechanism in the WTO to address China's economic coercion.

"If you make China the enemy, China will be the enemy," a Chinese government official told an Australian reporter.

9

HONG KONG OUTLAWS GLOBAL ACTIVISM

The global crisis created by the Covid-19 pandemic gave Beijing the perfect opportunity to silence the tradition of free speech and protest that had long thwarted its plans for Hong Kong. Western countries were far too preoccupied to take serious countermeasures, and China's leaders knew it. Beijing's takeover of Hong Kong demonstrated the new confidence and ambition with which Xi now viewed the party's rule. That domination was now highly public, not hidden in the shadows of influence or corruption. In June 2020, Beijing asserted authoritarian rule over one of the world's most important financial hubs, with a clearly outlined plan to use control over financial assets to crush dissent. And its rule extended far beyond the city itself, with a powerful new law creating a foundation for waging lawfare on free civil societies around the world—including in the United States.

On the morning of July 31, 2020, Samuel Chu woke up when his cell phone rang. It was a friend of his, a journalist who worked for the BBC in Washington, DC.

"How are you *doing*?" the friend said, sounding concerned.

Chu was confused. It was 5 a.m. in Los Angeles, where he was based. The night before had been just like any normal night. He'd gone to bed after watching some episodes of *Law & Order*. "I'm sleeping!" he said.

"You better check the news," his friend said.

When Chu did, he was stunned. The Hong Kong government had just issued an arrest warrant for him and five other Hong Kong pro-democracy activists under the newly passed National Security Law, accusing them of "incitement to secession" and "collusion with foreign forces." It was the first time that the new law had been invoked to target people living outside Hong Kong.

But Chu had been an American citizen for almost twenty-five years and had spent much of the past twenty years as a community organizer in the United States; the Hong Kong advocacy work he had done was through a U.S.-registered, U.S.-based nonprofit that worked with U.S. lawmakers on Capitol Hill. The Beijing-backed government of Hong Kong was accusing an American of "colluding" with his own government by engaging in advocacy that is a right under U.S. law. It was a shot across the bow warning Beijing's critics that no matter where in the world they lived, the party was coming for them. It was also a direct attack on American civil society and political freedom, a clear message that Beijing believed its jurisdiction extended onto U.S. soil.

Two months earlier, in May 2020, as much of the world was buried deep in the first wave of Covid-19 lockdowns, Beijing had decided to take Hong Kong. It wasn't a military invasion: no tanks rolled down the streets of China's only free city. Instead, Beijing used the power of law to impose its will on Hong Kong's civil society, courts, police, universities, and streets, dismantling the city's celebrated political institutions and freedoms in a matter of months.

That month, the National People's Congress, China's rubber-stamp legislature, convened in Beijing for its annual two-week meeting. The session, usually held in March, had been delayed two months due to the coronavirus pandemic. On May 22, without prior notice, the NPC announced new national security legislation that it would insert into Annex III of Hong Kong's Basic Law, giving it legal force in Hong Kong. The text of the draft law was never released, but according to a report by state news agency Xinhua summarizing the draft law's contents, it cited "national security risks" in Hong Kong and the need for "law-based and forceful measures" to "prevent, stop and punish such activities."

This was a direct shot at the Sino-British Joint Declaration of 1984, the treaty outlining the 1997 handover in which China had agreed to grant Hong Kong a "high degree of autonomy, except in foreign and defense affairs," and to uphold a broad swath of rights and freedoms, including the freedoms of press, assembly, speech, strike, association, and academic research. According to the treaty, the laws governing Hong Kong were required to be drafted and passed in Hong Kong, using the city's own governance and legal traditions—not in Beijing.

Beijing justified its actions by saying that it was stepping in because the Hong Kong government had failed in its obligation to pass national security legislation, as was required under Article 23 of the Basic Law, which states: "The Hong Kong Special Administrative Region shall enact laws on its own to prohibit any act of treason, secession, sedition, subversion against the PRC government, or theft of state secrets, to prohibit foreign political organisations or bodies from conducting political activities in the Region, and to prohibit political organisations or bodies of the Region from establishing ties with foreign political organisations or bodies."

Beijing's move didn't come as a complete surprise. The Basic Law, Hong Kong's brief constitution, requires the city to adopt security laws, but no such legislation has ever been enacted—due, in large part, to the distrust Hong Kongers feel toward China's party rulers and what their true intentions for such legislation would likely be.

The Hong Kong government, whose chief executive is selected by an election committee structured to lean heavily pro-Beijing, had tried several times before to pass national security legislation but had been thwarted by mass demonstrations. In 2003, the last time it tried to pass such legislation, as many as half a million people flooded the streets in protest. The draft law was tabled.

Subsequent efforts to bring Hong Kong more firmly under the central government's control had been similarly stalled by popular protest. In September 2012, the Hong Kong government canceled plans to introduce a mandatory patriotic education curriculum in schools that extolled the virtues of CCP rule. But the idea of a national security law never completely faded from view. In 2015, following the National People's Congress's enactment of a national security law for the mainland, pro-Beijing academics and legislators called for Hong Kong to enact its own national security law before China legislated its own for the territory.

And in 2019, amid widespread protests sparked by a proposed law that would have allowed extradition of criminal suspects to mainland China, China's leaders again pressed for the imposition of a national security law. The protests were among the largest in Hong Kong's history;

on June 9, more than a million people attended a protest against the extradition bill, and subsequent protests also drew huge numbers. As the protests continued into the summer and fall, groups of radical protesters increasingly engaged in violence against targets perceived to be pro-Beijing, and police responded with force that the protesters often criticized as disproportionate.

State media in China uniformly condemned the protests, focusing on reported acts of violence and alleged foreign interference. A November 2019 *China Daily* editorial described protesters as "violent criminals" controlled by the United States and other foreign forces. Views of the protests in mainland China largely reflected these sentiments.

Even many educated Chinese people with access to unbiased information about the protests were unsympathetic, viewing them as a distraction from economic concerns in Hong Kong. Mainland Chinese students and those supporting the protests clashed on university campuses around the world, with some of these confrontations turning violent. At the University of Queensland in Brisbane, Australia, a scuffle broke out after pro-China students ripped up signs held by students supporting the protesters.

By the time the pandemic hit, these mass protests had already embroiled Hong Kong for months. Pandemic restrictions did what police batons, tear gas, and arrests could not: clear the streets of protesters. In March 2020, Hong Kong enacted a regulation banning public gatherings of more than four people, and Quartz reported that the Hong Kong Police Force was using the law to target protesters. For the first time in Hong Kong's history, the police banned the annual June 4 vigil commemorating the pro-democracy Tiananmen Square protests of 1989, after conveniently extending the restriction on gatherings to June 5.

Many in Hong Kong credited the solidarity forged during the 2019 protests with enabling a successful grassroots response to the pandemic in its early days, but the city's good fortune has not lasted. A spike in cases of Covid-19 in early 2022 drove Hong Kong's death rate, by early March, to the highest level in the developed world, as evidenced by grisly images of hospital wards packed with both the living and the dead. With the city's turn toward authoritarianism, it has become increasingly difficult to question or even understand the government's policies.

The National People's Congress announced the new draft law just as

China's leaders were using the occasion of the NPC's *lianghui*, or "two meetings," to declare victory over the domestic epidemic in mainland China. This presented a stark contrast to much of the Western world. While China had employed strict lockdowns to halt the spread of the virus, leaders in the United States and Europe were largely unwilling or unable to employ similar strategies. This had led to rising case counts and a crisis of confidence in the ability of Western democracies to respond to major crises.

"While the rest of the world is preoccupied with fighting Covid-19, [Xi Jinping] has in effect ripped up the Joint Declaration, a treaty lodged at the UN to guarantee Hong Kong's way of life till 2047," wrote Chris Patten, the final British governor of Hong Kong , who presided over the 1997 handover, in the *Financial Times* on May 24, 2020. Chinese leaders denied this, saying that the law fully respected "one country, two systems."

On June 30, just over a month since the draft legislation was first announced, the National People's Congress in Beijing voted unanimously to pass it—and implement it *the same day.* The full text of the law, which would be inserted directly into Annex III of Hong Kong's Basic Law, had not even been released. When it finally was—at midnight Hong Kong time on June 30, 2022, when most of the city was asleep—it was noon for me in Washington, DC. I spent the next several hours going through the Chinese-language text with a fine-tooth comb, the official English translation not having been released yet. The farther I read, the more alarmed I became.

The law prohibits secession, "terrorism," and "collusion" with foreign powers, leaving those terms vaguely defined and imposing harsh penalties, including up to life in prison. Article 54 calls for increased regulation of foreign and overseas organizations, including nongovernmental organizations and news organizations based in Hong Kong—what seems like a blank check to intervene in any meaningful area of civil society. Article 59 requires anyone with knowledge of any situation that constitutes a crime against national security to testify—meaning there is no right to remain silent. Article 65 gives the Standing Committee of the National People's Congress in Beijing the power to interpret this law—yet another blank check to achieve a politically expedient result. Each of these provisions marks another link in the chain with which Beijing hopes to shackle Hong Kong's freedoms.

But when I came to Article 38, my jaw dropped. I wondered if I was somehow misinterpreting the Chinese, though it seemed straightforward: "This Law shall apply to offences under this Law committed against the Hong Kong Special Administrative Region from outside the Region by a person who is not a permanent resident of the Region."

Everyone. Everywhere. The New National Security Law, which was already in effect, applied to everyone, everywhere in the world. This was de jure extraterritoriality, written into the law explicitly for everyone to see.

I quickly called up as many experts on Chinese and international law as I could find on short notice and spent the rest of the afternoon on the phone.

"It literally applies to every single person on the planet. This is how it reads," Wang Minyao, a Chinese American lawyer based in New York, told me. "If I appear at a congressional committee in DC and say something critical, that literally would be a violation of this law."

Nathan Law, a former Hong Kong lawmaker and leading pro-democracy activist, fled the city. He spoke to me a few days later from an undisclosed location (later revealed to be in the United Kingdom, where he would be granted asylum). "One of the main purposes of having the National Security Law is to quash the international front of the movement," Law told me. "For Hong Kong, we have to understand that it is the foreground of a very global fight, authoritarianism versus democracy."

When Article 38 is taken in combination with Article 32, which allows for the confiscation of property, "think about what that means for Amnesty International Hong Kong, or even HSBC Hong Kong," Alvin Cheung, a legal scholar at New York University who previously practiced law in Hong Kong, told me. "Their property is suddenly liable to be taken, depending on the whims of the state. That's a problem."

The National Security Law shocked Western observers. For many, it represented a final shattering of their long-held hopes that engagement with China might work. "I have to confess that, yesterday, I was questioning a lot of my prior assumptions about what kind of rising power China is," Susan Shirk, chair of the 21st Century China Center at the University of California San Diego and former deputy assistant secretary of state for East Asian affairs under Bill Clinton, said in an interview on PBS's *NewsHour* on July 2, 2020, the day after the National Security Law's full text was released. Shirk had long been a leading advocate for engaging diplomatically with China to resolve disputes, and she had pushed back fervently against the Trump administration's hawks. "But I am not sure how you deal with Xi Jinping's regime," she said. "And I am rethinking a lot of my premises about what—how the United States should really deal with this type of regime."

But in the mainland and among supporters of Beijing, the law was seen as heralding an overdue return to order in the city. There was even a degree of schadenfreude among mainland Chinese nationalists, who tended to view Hong Kongers as haughty, spoiled children in need of stronger discipline. The *New York Times* reported that a widely shared article titled "Can Hong Kong Be Saved," written by a mainland Chinese resident who had studied in Hong Kong and published during the 2019 protests, described Hong Kongers as stupid and easily deluded by Western values.

"Article 38 of the Hong Kong national security law targeting foreigners may be seen as returning the favor for Western extraterritoriality," Alex Lo, a stridently pro-Beijing columnist at the Hong Kong–based *South China Morning Post*, wrote in an opinion piece on July 4, 2020. Washington is "increasingly abusive" in its dominance of the global financial system, using sanctions to enforce U.S. law all over the world," Lo went on. "Beijing must be thinking: if the U.S. can do it on such an egregious scale, why can't we?"

On June 30, Samuel Chu was doing the same thing I was: sifting through the new law word by word. He, too, stopped short at Article 38. Chu flagged that portion of the law to his legal counsel, who, Chu told me, said, "I think they wrote it for you."

"We raised the point, what is this extraterritorial jurisdiction about?" Chu told me. "I didn't want to say, 'I think it's us.' But it really felt that way. I knew from the very beginning."

The arrest warrant targeting Chu was issued just one month later, confirming his and his lawyer's interpretation of Article 38. Chu was the first U.S. citizen to be charged under the National Security Law. In 2019, he had founded a U.S.-registered nonprofit called Hong Kong Democracy Council, based in Washington, DC, to advocate on behalf of Hong Kongers. The organization had played an important behind-the-scenes role in the passage of the Hong Kong Human Rights and Democracy Act of 2019, which requires the U.S. State Department to certify each year whether the political situation in Hong Kong justifies the special economic, judicial, and political arrangements the United States has granted it. The act also mandates the sanctioning of officials complicit in the deteriorating political and human rights conditions in the city.

The 2019 law outraged Chinese officials. Chinese foreign ministry spokesperson Geng Shuang said the bill represented a "naked double standard" and revealed "sinister intentions to undermine Hong Kong's prosperity and stability and contain China's development." On December 2, 2019, five days after President Trump signed the bill into law, the Chinese government issued retaliatory sanctions on groups based in the United States, including the National Endowment for Democracy, Human Rights Watch, and Freedom House, and halted U.S. naval vessels from docking in Hong Kong.

The arrest warrant "was probably personally the greatest validation of my work ever," Chu told me with a laugh. He would have had plenty of reasons to be gloomy. The warrant meant he could never go back to Hong Kong, his childhood home, where he would likely be arrested immediately and given a lengthy prison sentence. It also meant it would be wise for him to avoid traveling to countries with extradition treaties with Hong Kong or China, or to countries with close political relationships with Beijing. Chu's father, Chu Yiu-ming, a Baptist preacher and a pro-democracy activist, had been convicted just the year before on charges related to his work as a leader of the 2014 Umbrella Movement and was serving a suspended sentence in Hong Kong.

But an attitude of almost cheerful optimism seemed to characterize Chu's views of his own life and his approach to dealing with the Chinese Communist Party. I spent a couple of hours with Chu on a sunny but chilly morning in January 2022, when he was on a work trip to Washington, DC. We sat at a long table in a pandemic-empty WeWork space downtown, near K Street, where he often works when he visits.

Chu told me that his career was simply continuing the "family business," both pastoring and working as an activist and organizer. His father had been orphaned at a young age and lived on the streets for several years as a child in Hong Kong, before converting to Christianity, putting himself through college and seminary, and, eventually, becoming a pastor.

Chu Yiu-ming became active in the Tiananmen pro-democracy protests in 1989 and spent time with the protesters in Beijing. He narrowly missed the June 4 massacre, having flown back to Hong Kong the day before to officiate at a wedding. Soon after, he helped launch Operation Yellowbird, an underground network that smuggled Tiananmen activists out of China through Hong Kong and on to safer countries.

Together with his father, the younger Chu had attended the first million-strong march in Hong Kong, in May 1989, held in solidarity with the protesters in Beijing. He was eleven years old when the People's Liberation Army killed hundreds, perhaps even thousands, of student protesters in Beijing. As his father helped bring survivors to Hong Kong, the younger Chu spent a lot of time with them as they waited for their travel paperwork to come through.

The next year, Chu's parents sent him to boarding school in the United States, in part because they worried about the future of Hong Kong. Chu spent the rest of his childhood Stateside, became a U.S. citizen, went to seminary, and became a pastor. "I went from being a Southern Baptist kid in British colonial Hong Kong, where my dad started a church in a fishing village, to eight years pastoring at a Presbyterian church in Koreatown in Los Angeles that was attended mostly by undocumented immigrants from Latin America," Chu said with a chuckle. "But I think in some ways the very different landscape was the same, politically speaking."

That landscape led him to his first experience with community organizing, which was to become his career. His church was located in the Los Angeles Unified School District, one of the largest school districts in the country, and it had a major overcrowding issue. There simply weren't enough schools. Kids were bused here and there across the district, wherever they could fit, and schools ran on round-the-year calendars, which meant that families with multiple children might have kids on vacation at different times of the year. It was a logistical nightmare for working-class families. When Chu asked the people in his church what they wanted, "They said, 'We want more schools, we want more schools in our neighborhoods, we want schools that we can walk to,'" he told me. So, Chu helped organize a sponsoring committee, and over a period of about five years, the committee got hundreds of local churches, schools, and nonprofit organizations to join. The group successfully pushed for a bond program to fund an education construction program that built about 130 new schools in the district and remodeled around 400 existing ones.

Chu had found his calling. He ran registration drives in California for the Affordable Care Act, served as executive director of an LGBT advocacy organization, and worked for a Jewish national hunger relief organization to support a legislative effort in Minnesota to stop the practice of "lunch-shaming" public school students who couldn't pay for school lunches.

Chu cited Saul Alinsky, the controversial leftist political organizer whose 1970s philosophy of grassroots organizing and political advocacy was an early influence on Hillary Clinton and Barack Obama, as a major influence of his: "The idea was always, 'How do you build political power, as the main project?'" Chu said. "It's how I was trained and how I see the world."

None of this work involved Hong Kong. But as the political situation in the city of his birth deteriorated, and especially when his father was arrested in 2017, Chu began to think about applying his political organizing skills to help Hong Kong's pro-democracy movement. While he admired the Chinese pro-democracy movement, he felt that activists' attempts to achieve real political influence in the United States had been largely ineffective.

Chinese dissidents living in the United States "struggled to translate from protests to politics," Chu had observed, and functioned "more like mascots than political operatives," getting little more than photo ops with U.S. lawmakers rather than legislation or executive action. Pro-democracy activists based in Hong Kong, meanwhile, had done an effective job at establishing a broad base of grassroots support there, but they lacked a similar base in the United States. "No political capital is going to be created if they know you're just going to go back to Hong Kong. You don't vote," Chu said. A truly fruitful effort "has to be funded in the U.S., it has to be led in the U.S."

Chu believed he could change the current situation. "I realized I was in a unique position. I spent twenty years working in U.S. politics." With relationships with U.S. lawmakers already in place, he began working with House Speaker Nancy Pelosi, Democratic representative, and with co-chair of the Congressional-Executive Commission on China Jim Mc-Govern, and other lawmakers behind the scenes to push for the passage of the Hong Kong Human Rights and Democracy Act of 2019.

"I don't care about if a particular senator or particular party rhetoric is better than the other. That's not how politics works," Chu told me. "Politics is about getting someone to do something that they don't want to do."

Trump's signing of the Hong Kong Human Rights and Democracy Act was a perfect example of the success of this strategy, Chu said. Amid United States–China trade talks, the U.S. president had long avoided expressing either strong support for the pro-democracy protests in Hong Kong or strong condemnation of Beijing for its actions there. In an August 2019 tweet, Trump had called Xi a "good man" and wrote, "I have ZERO doubt that if President Xi wants to quickly and humanely solve the Hong Kong problem, he can do it." As the Hong Kong bill made its way through Congress, the White House refused to comment on whether the president would sign it. In the end, the president faced veto-proof majorities in Congress; he signed.

The anti-extradition law protest movement in 2019 brought greater urgency to Chu's advocacy. In September, he and New York–based activist Anna Yeung-Cheung founded the Hong Kong Democracy Council. The decision to register it as a U.S. nonprofit, and to have a U.S. citizen run it, wasn't an accident. The founders expected the Chinese government to come after Hong Kong activists as far as it could chase them.

As it turns out, the Chinese government aims to chase them onto U.S. soil. Chu's twenty years of experience in grassroots organizing in the United States demonstrate what is at stake. He is a U.S. citizen whose career has manifested the very essence of American democracy. This is precisely what Beijing, through the Hong Kong National Security Law, would deem to outlaw.

———————

Since the imposition of the National Security Law, Hong Kong's previously freewheeling political culture has been brought to heel. In March 2021, the National People's Congress passed a law giving a pro-Beijing committee the power to vet candidates for political office in Hong Kong, effectively barring pro-democracy candidates from running. Many leading pro-democracy figures have been criminally charged or imprisoned, and others forced into exile abroad. In June 2021, Bloomberg reported that at least 117 activists, journalists, and former lawmakers had been arrested since the law's enactment.

But the impact of the law has extended beyond political activists to every corner of Hong Kong's once-vibrant civil society. Teachers have been fired for educational content considered "subversive" under strict new regulations. Authorities have increasingly restricted press accreditation and denied visas to foreign journalists, which has led outlets such as the *New York Times* to relocate their operations outside Hong Kong. The National Security Law has even impacted the arts, as pro-Beijing elements in the city question whether exhibits violate the law and as individuals practice self-censorship to avoid running afoul of its vague provisions.

Article 38 has also made itself felt. It has had a chilling effect among Hong Kongers abroad who hope to maintain ties to the city, or who still have family there, or who live in countries with close political ties to China. People have closed their social media accounts, asked for anonymity, and stopped publishing.

"If you are not returning to Hong Kong and you are living in a country which has no extradition treaty with Hong Kong or China, you can still enjoy a degree of freedom to express or discuss Hong Kong," Eric Yan-ho Lai, the Hong Kong Law Fellow at Georgetown University, explained. "But the danger or risk would be in terms of surveillance by Chinese embassies or their agents."

For exiled Hong Kong activists, the idea of a new Cold War–style bloc of countries tied to Beijing isn't theoretical. There is a growing list of countries that aren't safe for them to visit. Frances Hui, an activist who left Hong Kong for the United States after the National Security Law was passed, helped organize a protest at the 2022 Beijing Winter Olympics torch-lighting ceremony held in Athens, Greece. But she couldn't attend in person because Greece has an extradition treaty with China. "Every time when I'm looking at foreign countries to visit, I would always look at which places are safer to go," Hui told me in an October 2021 interview. She and other activists avoid travel to countries with extradition treaties with Hong Kong or China and to countries like Thailand and Singapore, whose governments are close with Beijing. Even some EU countries weren't safe at the time. Belgium, Italy, and France have extradition treaties with China, and Portugal and the Czech Republic haven't suspended their extradition treaties with Hong Kong. In October 2022, however, the European Court of Human Rights blocked the extradition of a man from Poland to China, issuing a landmark ruling that will make it much more difficult for any of the forty-six member states of the Council of Europe to comply with any extradition request to China in the future.

The spirit of Article 38 has even been applied to journalism published outside Hong Kong in major international news outlets. In April 2021, the Hong Kong government made it illegal to urge people not to cast a vote, effectively outlawing a boycott movement. The new regulation amended an election ordinance originally implemented in 2000 to provide standard protections for voters and election integrity. City authorities then issued arrest warrants for Hong Kong activists based abroad who had called for a boycott of the election. The *Wall Street Journal* Editorial Board published an article on November 30 denouncing the move and calling the elections a "sham." Erick Tsang, Hong Kong's secretary for constitutional and mainland affairs, then sent a letter to the *Wall Street Journal* stating that "inciting another person not to vote" was illegal under Hong Kong law, even if the incitement happened abroad. "We reserve the right to take necessary action," Tsang told the *Journal*. Gilford Law, the director general of the Hong Kong Economic and Trade Office, in London, wrote a similarly worded letter, dated December 8, to the United Kingdom's *Sunday Times*, which had published an article on December 5 calling the Hong Kong elections a "mockery" of democracy and a "sham."

Compare this shrinking space for international free speech on Hong Kong—and the growing risks that those who do speak out now face—with the overseas narrative that Beijing would wish to impose. On May 31, 2020, just over a week after the National People's Congress announced that it would impose a national security law on Hong Kong, the Xinhua home page featured an article titled "Overseas Chinese Strongly Support the Hong Kong National Security Law Put Forward by the National People's Congress." The article included supporting statements from Chinese diaspora organizations in Cambodia, the Czech Republic, Malaysia, Mexico, Peru, Sri Lanka, Switzerland, Thailand, the United States, Venezuela, and elsewhere.

One diaspora organization, in Switzerland, said that the new legislation would "stop the forces of 'Hong Kong independence' from undermining the 'One Country, Two Systems' principle." Another, in Thailand, said that the National Security Law would "contribute to the long-term stability and prosperity of Hong Kong." A group in Malaysia said that "Hong Kong is China's Hong Kong." The Chilean Chinese Entrepreneurs Association said that the National People's Congress's "legitimacy is beyond doubt."

The Xinhua article presented these organizations as the authentic representatives of Chinese communities in these countries, suggesting that these were the genuine (and only) opinions held by the Chinese diaspora. But, in reality, most of the organizations that issued these statements were "peaceful unification associations"—the name is translated variously, but Beijing's preferred translation is "China Council for the Promotion of Peaceful National Reunification," or CCPPNR. The groups claim to be independent but, in fact, function as overseas outposts of the United Front Work Department, the party bureau tasked with ensuring that nonparty members inside China and key groups abroad such as the Chinese diaspora are all working toward party goals. Peaceful unification associations are branches of an organization by the same name based in Beijing, whose website lists more than seventy branches worldwide. Until 2017, the executive vice president of the Beijing-based CCPPNR was Sun Chunlan, a member of the powerful Politburo who also directed the United Front Work Department.

With this background knowledge, it's easy to see that the May 2020 Xinhua article was the result of a coordinated campaign by the Chinese Communist Party to manufacture the appearance of genuine support for its policies in Hong Kong by reaching out through the CCPPNR to compile statements of support from its many branches around the world and then feature them prominently on the home page of China's state news agency.

This kind of manufactured messaging has several goals:

First, it grants greater legitimacy to the National Security Law in the eyes of mainland Chinese citizens. Chinese people are generally aware that they live in a country with tight information controls and a government that hides the truth, and many understand that people outside China may enjoy freedom of information and higher standards of living.

Thus, residents of China have long viewed Chinese people living abroad as having a certain prestige. By putting forth these messages from the Chinese diaspora, the party wants to demonstrate to people in mainland China that "even" Chinese people abroad support Beijing's actions in Hong Kong.

Second, this kind of messaging can also carry an implicit threat: that no matter where you go in the world, Chinese people support the party, that there's nowhere to run. It's a deterrent for anyone inside China wondering if anti-party organizing might be possible abroad. And, increasingly, it represents the only kind of speech that is truly safe, whether in China or abroad.

Article 43 of the National Security Law gives authorities powerful new tools to target pro-democracy figures, including warrantless searches, covert surveillance, and asset freezes. In December 2020, the Hong Kong Police Force ordered multinational bank HSBC to freeze the assets of exiled pro-democracy legislator Ted Hui while they investigated suspected violations of the law. HSBC and other financial institutions have thus become instruments for imposing de facto financial sanctions on behalf of the Chinese government.

One of China's top targets was Jimmy Lai, a real estate tycoon and outspoken critic of Beijing who, in 1995, had founded the pro-democracy tabloid *Apple Daily*. In May 2021, Hong Kong police froze Lai's assets, amounting to about $64 million, including his controlling stake in *Apple Daily*. Lai was already in jail when his assets were frozen, serving fourteen months for his role in a 2019 protest. He was also facing charges under the National Security Law. That month, Hong Kong's security chief, John Lee—now the city's chief executive after Carrie Lam stepped down in June 2022—sent letters to HSBC and Citibank, threatening up to seven years in prison for any dealings involving Lai's accounts.

"This is the first time we know of that the national security law has been invoked to deprive an owner of his equity in a publicly traded company in Hong Kong," the *Wall Street Journal* Editorial Board wrote after city authorities froze Lai's assets. "So much for being a global financial center based on the rule of law."

The asset freeze applied also to Lai's shares in Next Digital, the publisher of *Apple Daily*. Days later, authorities froze the accounts of *Apple Daily* itself. Unable to pay its bills, the newspaper had no choice but to shut down at the end of June. According to Bloomberg, some cabdrivers and shopkeepers in Hong Kong continue to display its final print edition as a show of support for the democracy movement.

The anti-democracy asset freezes in one of the world's most important financial centers have placed banks in an untenable position and perhaps even put the U.S. and Chinese financial systems on a collision course. HSBC is one of the world's largest multinational banks and is uniquely tied to China. While it has been officially headquartered in London since 1993, it traces its origins to the establishment of the "Hongkong and Shanghai Banking Corporation" in 1865 and derives nearly 40 percent of its revenue from mainland China and Hong Kong.

Despite its China pedigree, in recent years HSBC has increasingly found itself caught in the middle of worsening relations between the United States and China. Reuters has reported that, since 2017, Chinese authorities have blackballed HSBC for a range of perceived offenses, ranging from its assistance with the U.S. investigation into Huawei executive Meng Wanzhou in 2017 to its belated public expression of support for the Hong Kong National Security Law in 2020.

HSBC's footing in China has grown only more difficult since 2020, as the United States and other Western countries have ramped up their sanctions on Chinese officials in connection with a range of human rights abuses in China—including Chinese officials who have undermined Hong Kong's autonomy and carried out mass detention and surveillance policies in Xinjiang. For example, in December 2020, the United States sanctioned fourteen vice-chairpersons of the Standing Committee of the National People's Congress over human rights abuses in Hong Kong.

In response to these sanctions, HSBC has attempted to placate both sides. The bank complied with a Hong Kong police request to freeze the accounts of former pro-democracy lawmaker Ted Hui in December 2020, but it also appeared to have cut off business with Hong Kong chief executive Carrie Lam in August 2020, following U.S. sanctions against her and other officials. However, the criticism has continued; in January 2021, the UK Parliament called HSBC's CEO to testify following outrage over the bank's freezing of Hui's accounts the previous month.

For foreign companies operating in China, this dilemma of balancing compliance with Chinese demands with adherence to Western expectations has always existed. According to Lester Ross, a partner in the Beijing office of the law firm WilmerHale, "China has had informal ways of punishing foreign companies for a long time, through informal boycotts, import restrictions, export restrictions, and other tools to express their displeasure." As long as these measures weren't clearly spelled out, foreign companies could rely on their positive relationships with Chinese officials to protect their interests in China while quietly complying with the more formal obligations established by Western countries.

However, in recent years—in line with President Xi Jinping's call in a February 2019 speech to "use the law as a weapon"—China has begun to change this calculus by formalizing many measures with extraterritorial impact as laws and regulations. A June 2021 analysis by the Berlin-based Mercator Institute for China Studies, Europe's most prominent China-focused research institution, noted provisions in a range of recent laws that allow for countermeasures against foreign laws that the Chinese government views as discriminatory. These provisions include a series of laws and regulations China has enacted since 2020 in response to the new sanctions from the West.

In September 2020, China's Ministry of Commerce created an "Unreliable Entity List" for foreign entities or individuals that enforce foreign sanctions. Entities on the UEL can be barred from investing in China or engaging in import and export activities, and their employees can be barred from entering China. While the Chinese government does not appear to have added any names to the UEL, analysts have compared it to the Entity List maintained by the United States.

In January 2021, the Ministry of Commerce enacted the "Rules on Counteracting Unjustified Extra–Territorial Application of Foreign Legislation and Other Measures." The Rules, for the first time, created a private right of action in Chinese courts, allowing Chinese entities and individuals harmed by foreign sanctions to sue the entities or individuals enforcing those sanctions. The Rules include a process through which foreign companies can apply for an exemption and thus avoid this liability.

China's efforts to block foreign sanctions culminated in the Anti–Foreign Sanctions Law, passed in June 2021. According to an August 2021 analysis by the law firm Davis Wright Tremaine, the Anti–Foreign

Sanctions Law codifies and expands the previous regulations in multiple ways. It creates a "Countermeasures List" that is effectively an enhanced version of the Unreliable Entity List, because it can include not only foreign entities and individuals that enforce foreign sanctions but also those who formulate the sanctions and their immediate family members, employees, and other related parties. Individuals or entities on the Countermeasures List can be denied entry into China and have their assets in China frozen, and Chinese companies can be barred from doing business with them. The Anti–Foreign Sanctions Law also enhances the private right of action by removing the exemption process provided for by the Rules.

China is not the first country to implement blocking statutes to nullify foreign sanctions. In 1996, the European Union adopted a blocking statute in response to U.S. sanctions on Cuba, Libya, and Iran. Following the passage of the AFSL, Chinese state media explicitly compared the law to the EU blocking statute and described it as primarily a defensive reaction to improper foreign sanctions.

However, while the EU statute is limited to protecting EU entities and individuals from needing to comply with a clearly defined list of restrictive measures imposed by foreign countries, the AFSL also provides for retaliatory sanctions against individuals and entities that formulate and enforce sanctions and for proactive sanctions against parties that threaten China's "national sovereignty, security, and development interests." An April 2021 explanation of the law indicates that counteracting independence movements in Taiwan, Hong Kong, Tibet, and Xinjiang is one of its purposes. According to Helena Legarda, a senior analyst at the Mercator Institute for China Studies, "because of its expansiveness and vagueness, the law could theoretically be used against almost anybody for a wide range of reasons."

If the Anti–Foreign Sanctions Law is ultimately used primarily to counteract foreign sanctions, it presents the greatest risk to financial institutions like HSBC. Many foreign sanctions specifically block financial transactions with sanctioned parties, placing banks squarely in the crosshairs of the AFSL if they comply. In addition, given the long-standing position of the United States as an economic powerhouse, banks everywhere rely on access to the U.S. financial system and a steady supply of dollars in order to operate. "It is hard to disconnect from the U.S. system," said

Julian Ku, a professor of law at Hofstra University. "[Banks] need currency transactions to have enough dollars around."

For now, however, the impact of the Anti–Foreign Sanctions Law on financial institutions has been limited, because the law does not yet apply in Hong Kong. In August 2021, in the face of concerns from the Hong Kong business community, the Chinese government temporarily shelved its plans to enact legislation to apply the AFSL to Hong Kong. According to Ku, "the Hong Kong business elite doesn't really care about civil liberties, but they see this as a real problem, because they think that Hong Kong or foreign banks can't comply with it."

However, it is likely only a matter of time before the law is applied to Hong Kong in some form. An early sign appeared in October 2022, when Hong Kong chief executive John Lee said the city would allow a yacht owned by sanctioned Russian oligarch and Putin ally Alexei Mordashov to dock there. Lee said that Hong Kong would not comply with "unilateral" sanctions.

The AFSL and its predecessor Blocking Rules make explicit the legal conflict between Chinese expectations and Western laws that before was merely tacitly understood. While they largely codify and strengthen the previous informal measures used by the Chinese government to punish foreign companies, these formal regulations create a de jure risk of legal exposure that, at least on paper, matches that of defying Western sanctions. "It creates a no-win situation for these companies, in the sense that by complying with one law, they can't comply with the other," said Ku.

Faced with the conflicting legal obligations created by the AFSL, foreign companies essentially have three options:

First, they can restructure their Chinese operations to make them legally separate from the rest of the company. However, given the broad nature of the AFSL, it is likely impossible for a company to restructure in a way that both shields it from legal exposure and allows it to continue operating in China in any meaningful sense.

Second, companies could also withdraw from China and move their operations to other countries in the region. However, many companies have become deeply embedded in China and cannot easily leave. During testimony before the UK Parliament in January 2021, HSBC CEO Noel Quinn reaffirmed the bank's commitment to Hong Kong, saying it was "too committed as an institution" to walk away.

Most companies, however, will likely choose the third option: silence. Caught between two legal imperatives, they will attempt to quietly comply with U.S. sanctions while not angering the Chinese government through overt actions or the public comments of their employees. "They have to try to thread this very difficult needle, by complying with U.S. sanctions in a nonpublic way," said Ku. To do so, these companies will likely seek to use their informal relationships with Chinese officials to determine where, in practice, the red lines are. At the same time, they will need to strengthen their internal controls over employee conduct to reduce the risk of inadvertently triggering liability under the law.

For the Chinese government, even if it rarely enforces formal countermeasures against foreign companies, this corporate self-censorship may be a victory in and of itself. The AFSL's mere existence effectively makes acquiescence to Chinese demands on human rights issues a formal condition of access to the Chinese economy. For companies like HSBC, this threatens to upend their delicate balancing act once and for all.

10

CHINA VACCINATES THE WORLD

While technology allowed the novel coronavirus to reach all corners of the globe faster than any other new disease in history, it also promised a panacea to end the pandemic: vaccines.

Chinese scientists first mapped the complete genome of the novel coronavirus in early January 2020 and shared their findings a week later by posting them publicly. With genetic data in hand, researchers needed only to start developing the lifesaving jabs. Decades of research on vaccines—particularly attempts to make one that worked against the virus that caused HIV/AIDS—had vastly shortened the amount of time needed to create an effective shot.

The race to develop a Covid-19 vaccine involved unprecedented international and science industry collaboration. Researchers at the University of Oxford worked with the British-Swedish company AstraZeneca, and the German company BioNTech collaborated with U.S. multinational firm Pfizer. Given that China's population had too few Covid-19 cases, Chinese companies formed partnerships with institutes in Brazil, Indonesia, Turkey, and elsewhere to help run clinical trials.

There was never really a doubt that one of the dozens of vaccines soon in development would end up proving both safe and effective in a record amount of time. The problem, public health experts knew, would be the geopolitical and logistical hurdles of getting those vaccines distributed equitably to everyone who needed them. Poorer countries didn't have the cash or clout to fight their way to the front of the line.

Equitable distribution wasn't important merely from a moral standpoint: it was the only way to end the pandemic, epidemiologists believed.

As long as there were places where the coronavirus was replicating quickly and freely through unvaccinated populations, it would continue mutating quickly, outpacing efforts to stop it through inoculations.

That's why the COVAX initiative was born. In early 2020, Gavin Yamey, a vaccine researcher at Duke University, participated in discussions about how to create what became COVAX, a joint initiative led by the Coalition for Epidemic Preparedness Innovations, the vaccine alliance Gavi, and the World Health Organization. The "beautiful idea," Yamey said, was that high-income countries would join the initiative and prepay for the vaccines they would receive through the initiative; ninety-two lower-income countries would receive grants to pay for their vaccines. And once vaccines were approved and manufactured, all countries participating in the program would be sent shipments of doses at the same rate.

But that's not what happened. Instead, high-income countries went directly to manufacturers, buying up most of the doses and leaving very little for global equitable distribution through COVAX. The Trump administration refused to join COVAX, though the Biden administration did join later. By May 2021, about 60 percent of the 1.5 billion doses administered worldwide were in just twenty high-income countries. "Rich countries behaved worse than anyone's worst nightmares," Yamey said.

The failures of COVAX drew scorching criticism around the world. "Today, ten countries have administered 75 percent of all COVID-19 vaccines, but, in poor countries, health workers and people with underlying conditions cannot access them. This is not only manifestly unjust, it is also self-defeating," UN secretary-general Antonio Guterres said at a June 2021 Gavi COVAX Advance Market Commitment Summit. World Trade Organization director general Ngozi Okonjo-Iweala said the hoarding of vaccines by wealthy countries was "morally unconscionable." By September 2021, though the number of doses worldwide had risen to 5.5 billion, just 1.8 percent of the populations of low-income countries had received them.

But China didn't hoard its own vaccines or buy up millions of doses made in other countries. In the early months of 2021, the country exported millions of doses to sixty-nine countries for free, and made commercial deals to provide millions more to an additional twenty-eight countries—a feat made technically possible by China's rapid advancements in science and technology and its efficient mass manufacturing and politically palatable domestically by China's highly effective pandemic response, which had frozen the early spread of the virus in its tracks and driven the infection rate down nearly to zero.

Thus, it was Chinese-made vaccines that were the first available in large quantities to people who didn't live in wealthy countries. China's decision to export its vaccines around the world held obvious strategic benefits. It allowed Beijing to fill a void left by the United States; China's leadership made this comparison explicit. In July 2021, Chinese foreign ministry spokesperson Zhao Lijian said that U.S. vaccine hoarding was "strangling" a lifeline that could have been used in developing countries. Beijing's relative generosity with vaccines also enabled it to deflect criticism for its initial cover-up of the existence of the novel coronavirus in the crucial days after its discovery in Wuhan.

The race to become the first country to develop a Covid-19 vaccine showed great-power competition at what was probably its best. Governments knew that the country whose scientific and industrial prowess created the world's first Covid-19 vaccine would enjoy a major soft-power boost, and shipping those vaccines around the world would be a windfall in diplomatic leverage—at least for those governments willing to use it that way.

But Xi Jinping took this accomplishment too far. He hitched his reputation, and that of the Chinese Communist Party, to the effectiveness of China's vaccines; Chinese diplomats and state media even spread disinformation about the supposed dangers of Western-made mRNA vaccines. When it later became clear that China's deactivated virus vaccines simply were not as effective against later Covid-19 strains as the mRNA vaccines, it was politically too difficult to change course. Xi refused to import Western-made mRNA vaccines. This left China's 1.4 billion people vulnerable to Omicron and other variant strains, creating the conditions for China's zero-Covid policy to persist, with economically and socially devastating lockdowns put in place long after other countries had opened up.

Soon after the novel coronavirus began to spread around the globe, the United States, China, Europe, and the United Kingdom entered the running. India and Russia, too, hoped to make a name for themselves. In June 2020, Russia became the first country in the world to register its Covid-19 vaccine, Sputnik V, which made it an early and surprising front-runner in the competition. In an apparent bid to demonstrate the vaccine's efficacy, Russian president Vladimir Putin announced that even his daughter had taken the shot. Russia's Ministry of Health authorized emergency use of Sputnik V in August 2020, before data from clinical trials had even been published—a decision some scientists criticized as "unethical." But this did little to dampen enthusiasm for the venture. According to one eastern European diplomat, the Russian-made vaccine offered "potentially the most powerful tool of soft power that Moscow has had in its hands for generations."

Despite the speedy approval, Russia suffered from a remarkably slow domestic rollout. That appears to be due at least in part to a high degree of vaccine hesitancy. In a July 2021 poll from the Levada Center in Moscow, 54 percent of respondents in Russia said they were not ready to get vaccinated.

Most doses of Sputnik V had, in any case, been earmarked for export. In March 2021, Putin said that 700 million doses of Sputnik V had been promised to other countries. At the time, less than 5 percent of the Russian population of approximately 144 million had been vaccinated. The Russian vaccine thus became an early alternative for middle-income countries that weren't able to obtain significant supplies of Western-made vaccines, including Brazil, Hungary, Mexico, the Philippines, and Turkey, all of which ordered doses. By mid-2021, almost seventy countries had approved Sputnik V for use.

Even so, the efficacy and safety of Russia's vaccine were still in question. WHO declined to approve Sputnik V, meaning that the vaccine couldn't be distributed through the COVAX initiative. In June 2021, WHO officials said there remained unresolved concerns regarding how Sputnik V vials were being filled in the Russian plant making them, a claim the plant denied. The European Medicines Agency also has yet to approve the vaccine. One year after Russia's Ministry of Health authorized emergency use of the vaccine, Sputnik V had failed to be the soft-power win Russia was hoping it would be.

China's efforts to leverage vaccine exports for soft power have proven to be far more successful. In the weeks after Covid-19 exploded across the world, Beijing mobilized twenty-two separate institutes and firms to work on seventeen vaccine development projects. By mid-March 2020, just as the virus began upending life in the United States, clinical trials began. And by midsummer, vaccines from Sinopharm and Sinovac had successfully entered phase three trials, an almost incomprehensibly fast process—and certainly a world record.

To accomplish this, China relied on the symbiotic relationship among its industry, military, and government. The successful suppression of the virus in early 2020 had presented an unintended consequence: there was simply too little coronavirus circulating through the population for scientists to conduct proper trials. So, Beijing permitted Sinopharm and Sinovac to combine phase one and phase two trials and offered experimental jabs to employees at PetroChina, a state-owned oil behemoth, who were working outside China. Chinese pharmaceutical companies also sought partnerships with research organizations in other countries with high rates of infection.

The ability of China, a middle-income country, to compete with the United States and Europe reflects Beijing's increasingly robust investment in research and development, which exceeded 2 percent of gross domestic product in 2019. It also became a potent symbol of national pride. Chen Wei, an epidemiologist, biologist, and major general tapped to spearhead China's vaccine efforts, said in May 2020 that "the successful entry of a vaccine with independent intellectual property rights into clinical trials is a manifestation of my country's scientific and technological progress, a manifestation of the image and responsibility of a great country, and a contribution to mankind."

From the start, and in pointed contrast to the United States, Beijing made it clear that it would not hoard its vaccines. "Covid-19 vaccine development and deployment, when available, will be made a global public good, which will be China's contribution to ensuring vaccine accessibility and affordability in developing countries," Xi Jinping said in May 2020. The structure of Sinovac's and Sinopharm's vaccines facilitated this. Because they were made from inactivated viral material—unlike the U.S.-developed Pfizer and Moderna vaccines, which are made from messenger RNA—the Chinese vaccines could be stored at regular refrigerator temperatures, which facilitated their use in developing countries that lacked the cold-storage infrastructure needed for the mRNA vaccines.

In early January 2021, Indonesia became the first country in the world, outside China, to approve the Sinovac vaccine. Trials there indicated that the vaccine offered 65 percent protection from infection. Indonesia had ordered 126 million doses, and its vaccination campaign began right away. Other countries—including Brazil, Chile, Mexico, Turkey, and Ukraine—soon followed suit. By early March, China had promised 500 million doses of lifesaving vaccines to approximately forty-five countries around the world, and Chinese companies projected that they would together be able to manufacture more than 2.6 billion jabs in 2021 alone.

WHO approved the Sinopharm vaccine on May 7, 2021, making it the first Covid-19 vaccine developed by a non-Western country to gain official regulatory approval by the organization—and the first Chinese-made vaccine of any kind to receive emergency approval from WHO. The next month, the organization also granted emergency approval to the Sinovac vaccine, stating that it prevented the development of Covid-19 infection in 51 percent of vaccinated people and serious illness in 100 percent of vaccinated people. WHO approval also meant that the Sinopharm and Sinovac doses could be distributed through COVAX, allowing millions more vaccine doses to enter the pipeline for people in low-income countries.

This made a huge difference in the lives of many people around the world, particularly in countries such as Iran, which, due to its diplomatic isolation and relative poverty, struggled to obtain Western vaccines. Iran was one of the earliest epicenters of the novel coronavirus outbreak outside China. By late January and early February 2020, the Chinese government had threatened retaliation against foreign governments that canceled flights originating in China due to the coronavirus outbreak in Wuhan and was pressuring its friends to maintain open travel. Iranian authorities felt they couldn't alienate one of their closest economic and political partners and chose to keep its borders open. By late February 2020, the country had among the highest case counts outside China. Iranian hospitals were soon overwhelmed with Covid-19 patients. Photos of hastily constructed medical tents and of nurses in full-body protective clothing were forwarded widely on Telegram, an encrypted messaging app popular in the country despite government attempts to ban it. Iranian universities and health officials warned of the possibility of fatalities in the hundreds of thousands or even millions if the outbreak was not contained.

Countless families in Iran suffered, both from Covid-19 infections and from the endless social isolation that was the only way to protect family members with compromised health. Ghaasem, a mechanical engineer living in Tehran with his wife and children, is a representative case. His mother-in-law had diabetes, which made her more vulnerable to serious complications if she became infected. When reports about the novel coronavirus began to filter into Iran in early 2020—and as case counts in the country soon began to spike—Ghaasem took strict precautions to protect his family's health, and they stopped visiting with his mother-in-law in person. Ghaasem's family stayed healthy, but they suffered emotionally. "My children couldn't see their grandmother, and they missed her," Ghaasem said. "Since my mother-in-law has diabetes, my wife was very worried about her. And this had an effect on her behavior, because my wife had a history of stress, and she also had bad headaches and earaches because of stress."

Western sanctions and Iran's isolation from global trade meant that, as the months went by, Iranians struggled to obtain the treatments for Covid-19 disease that were being swiftly developed by medical researchers around the world. Hospitals didn't have reliable stocks of intravenous immunoglobulin, a treatment used to combat multisystem inflammatory syndrome in children (MIS-C), a rare but serious condition caused by Covid-19 infection. Parents of children with MIS-C sometimes had to turn to the black market, paying hundreds of dollars (an enormous sum for an average salary earner in Iran) to purchase the drug and bringing it to the hospital themselves so their children could be treated.

As 2020 stretched on, the situation in Iran seemed bleak. "We no longer have orange and yellow. The entire country is red," a senior Iranian health official said in September, referring to the color classification system being used to designate which parts of the country had high case counts.

The rollout of vaccines abroad in early 2021 seemed to offer a glimmer of hope. But those lifesaving jabs were out of reach for most Iranians and for many outside the Western world. U.S. sanctions meant that the Iranian government didn't have the cash to buy foreign vaccines; it didn't help that Tehran implemented a largely symbolic ban on the importation of vaccines produced in the United States or Great Britain, seeking instead to produce its own domestic vaccine from the older technique of using the inactivated virus. The government did accept 10 million Chinese-made vaccines and 2.9 million doses of the AstraZeneca vaccine donated by Japan. Still, by August 2021, just 3.5 million Iranians out of a population of 80 million had been vaccinated.

Western vaccines remained out of reach for Ghaasem's family. Then, in December 2021, his mother-in-law was finally able to receive a Sinopharm vaccine. It made a dramatic difference for their family; Ghaasem's children and their grandmother could at last reunite. "After my mother-in-law and brother-in-law had their second dose of the vaccine, we were able to meet after months," Ghaasem said. "Furthermore, after my wife had her first dose, we were less worried, and we were able to travel to other cities to meet my family."

Vaccination in the Republic of Georgia, a small country in the Caucasus with little clout on the international stage, illustrated a similar success. Technically, Sinopharm was the third vaccine available in Georgia. In mid-March, the country received 43,200 doses of the AstraZeneca and 29,250 doses of the Pfizer vaccines, delivered by the COVAX initiative, available only to medical personnel and citizens over age fifty-five. Georgia's first choice would have been to administer vaccines made in a Western country; its hostile relationship with Russia forestalled any deal for Sputnik V, and Georgian health authorities preferred to wait for WHO's preliminary approval to ensure the effectiveness of Chinese vaccines.

"Georgian embassies worldwide were tasked to reach out to vaccine manufacturers, and our team in Washington had been in regular contact with the executives of Pfizer, Moderna, J and J, and Novavax," one Georgian diplomat in Washington, DC, told me. But those vaccines were difficult to secure.

It was China that ended up filling the gap. In April, Georgia received large shipments of the Sinopharm and Sinovac vaccines; one hundred thousand doses of the Sinovac vaccine were a humanitarian gift from the Chinese government, while the Sinopharm vaccines were purchased. On May 5, after an evidence assessment by WHO's Strategic Advisory Group of Experts, Georgia's National Center for Disease Control and Public Health decided to start vaccinating the population with the Sinopharm and Sinovac vaccines. In June and July 2021, the Georgian diplomat's own mother, stepfather, both grandmothers, and grandfather back in Georgia received doses of the Chinese-made vaccines. "I felt glad and relieved to see all my family members vaccinated, especially grandparents, as they are over seventy and in a high-risk group," the diplomat told me.

"The Chinese government has been increasingly attentive to China's image in the world. China's COVID-19 vaccine diplomacy was motivated in part by its determination to transform itself from an object of mistrust over its initial mishandling of the COVID-19 outbreak to a savior," wrote Seow Ting Lee, a professor of marketing and public relations at the University of Colorado Boulder. "This approach entails reframing its image as the country that accelerated the virus' spread through cover-ups to that of the magnanimous global power offering leadership at a time of international leadership disarray."

The stakes for China were significant. "Covid can be a real game changer for China," Jennifer Huang Bouey, an epidemiologist at the RAND Corporation, told the *Washington Post*. "They have never seen such large international demand for their pharmaceutical products."

Without question, Chinese vaccine exports were a tremendous humanitarian accomplishment. By January 2022, nearly 1.4 billion doses of Sinovac and Sinopharm vaccines had been delivered to 115 countries around the world, including 255 million doses to Indonesia, 95 million to Brazil, and 110 million each to Iran and Pakistan. Even at efficacy rates below those of Pfizer's and Moderna's vaccines, Chinese vaccines, it isn't difficult to conclude, have saved a substantial number of lives around the world.

But as more Chinese-made vaccines landed on tarmacs in developing countries, questions over their true efficacy rates began to arise. And the distribution of Western-made vaccines gradually caught up, blunting what proved to be a meaningful but relatively short-term soft-power boost for China.

It was in Brazil that concerns over Sinovac's data transparency first arose. The Butantan Institute, in São Paulo, which ran the Sinovac trials in that country, was originally due to release the results on December 15, 2020. But publication was delayed by a week, and then delayed again, as researchers said they needed more time to collect data from other trials. This did not go unnoticed. Denise Garrett, a well-known Washington,

DC–based epidemiologist, told the *Wall Street Journal* in early January 2021 that the delays were "extremely unusual." Garrett said they seemed to indicate a desire to present the results "in a more favorable way."

When the trial results were finally published on January 7, 2021, they showed an efficacy rate of 78 percent at preventing infections. This was a very good result, if slightly less effective than that for the Moderna and Pfizer vaccines, but Sinovac's ease of transport and storage helped compensate for the difference.

Days later, in a stunning about-face, updated results revealed that Sinovac vaccines appeared to have only around 50 percent efficacy in preventing infections—almost 30 percent lower than that reported just days before. This wasn't high enough to result in herd immunity, a major goal of vaccination campaigns.

By February 2021, China was receiving sustained criticism for a lack of transparency with regard to data on efficacy and safety. Others accused Chinese vaccine developers of cherry picking data instead of publishing full results of clinical trials. "Much of the developing world has only limited access to Western-made vaccines and will depend heavily on those produced in China," China analyst Eyck Freymann and oncologist Justin Stebbing wrote in *Foreign Affairs* that month. "The country's vaccine makers must not undermine confidence in their products at a time when so much of the world desperately needs them."

There have also been concerns about price gouging. In March 2021, Hungary signed a deal with Sinopharm for thirty-six dollars per dose. Compared with the approximately ten dollars per dose it agreed to pay for Sputnik V and the approximately two dollars per dose the European Union promised to AstraZeneca, the Hungarian deal with Sinopharm likely makes the Chinese-made vaccine the world's most expensive.

The situation in the Seychelles, where the government had acted with incredible speed to vaccinate almost the entire population of 98,000 within one month, brought further global scrutiny to Sinovac's underwhelming efficacy. Following an outbreak of Covid-19 cases there in May, it was revealed that more than a third of the country's positive cases were in fully vaccinated people—and more than half of those fully vaccinated had received Sinovac jabs. The outbreak was viewed as a setback among Seychelles residents, who had believed the vaccine would protect them from symptomatic illness.

The highly infectious Delta variant, first identified in India in April, further exposed the flaws of China's vaccines—particularly in Indonesia. In June 2021, at least twenty doctors who had received both doses of Sinovac died of Covid-19. So did Novilia Sjafri Bachtiar, the scientist who had led the country's Sinovac trials. In one town alone, five hundred fully vaccinated medical workers contracted Covid-19 disease within a two-week span. In the wake of Delta, countries that had relied heavily on Chinese vaccines shifted course. In July, the government of Thailand altered its policy to allow recipients of one Sinovac jab to receive the United Kingdom's AstraZeneca vaccine for its second shot. In the Philippines, a survey revealed that a sizable majority of Filipinos preferred U.S.-made vaccines; residents queued up until 2 a.m. to receive a jab of the Pfizer vaccine. And by the summer, people in Singapore originally inoculated with Sinovac began seeking booster shots of Pfizer and Moderna after blood tests showed low antibody counts.

This reversal of fortune diluted the soft-power potential of China's vaccine exports. In April 2021, Gao Fu, director general of the Chinese Center for Disease Control and Prevention, publicly admitted that China's domestic vaccines did not offer a high degree of protection from transmission of the coronavirus (though he later walked back this statement) and that mixing different vaccines might offer better protection. Gao had previously questioned the safety of the mRNA vaccines, a new technology used by Moderna and Pfizer-BioNTech in their Covid-19 vaccines. But at the April conference, he praised the vaccines' efficacy. Meanwhile, Sinopharm still hadn't released detailed information about its vaccine's ability to prevent infection.

"The current reality does present a stark contrast to the fanfare with which Beijing rolled out their vaccines and then insisted on their high efficacy, even when data was less available," Chong Ja Ian, a political scientist at the National University of Singapore, told the *Washington Post* in August 2021. He said that this demonstrates "how risky it is to try to make the current pandemic, and the very real dangers to human life, into a sort of propaganda tool."

"China's competitors worry that where Beijing's inoculations go, its influence will follow," wrote Yanzhong Huang, a senior fellow for global health at the Council on Foreign Relations, in March 2021. But "China has yet to prove that it can fulfill the role it has taken on or win the trust of those it has offered to aid."

As vaccine production revved up, and as populations in Western countries vaxxed up, Western vaccines soon became more widely available. By late 2021, the Republic of Georgia had enough Western-made shots to cover the whole eligible population after the United States donated half a million doses and the government in Tbilisi struck a deal with Pfizer to purchase a million; EU member states began to supply Georgia, too.

The emergence of the hyper-infectious Omicron variant in South Africa also put a major dent in the appeal of Chinese-made vaccines, which seemed to offer even less protection against Omicron than the mRNA vaccines. In December 2021, Xi Jinping announced that China would donate one billion doses of its vaccines to countries across Africa as news of Omicron raised alarms. But initial reports suggested that even those equipped with three shots from Sinovac and Sinopharm had only limited protection from infection from Omicron, though they still remained well protected against severe Covid-19 disease.

The relative inefficacy of Chinese-made vaccines wasn't the result of a flawed political system but of China's impressive but still-developing science and technology sector. Even so, at times, the Chinese government appeared to view vaccine shipments as a direct tool of political coercion, and perhaps most shamefully, China's propaganda apparatus made a sustained Kremlin-style effort to spread disinformation about Western-made vaccines in a cynical and dangerous attempt to blunt Western soft power.

Things came to a head in the early summer of 2021. The year before, Taiwan had successfully stopped the virus in its tracks and had almost no Covid-19 cases. But in April 2021, it experienced a significant outbreak, with more than five thousand cases and almost fifty deaths. President Tsai Ing-wen had secured deals for around 5 million doses of the Moderna vaccine, 10 million doses of the AstraZeneca, and an additional 4.76 million doses through the COVAX initiative. As Taiwan's outbreak deepened, however, only 700,000 of those doses had arrived. Just 2 percent of the population was vaccinated. Some observers described Taiwan as "vaccine-starved."

It was right in the midst of this crisis that China's politics got in the way. The Taiwanese government had signed a contract with BioNTech in January 2021 for a shipment of its Pfizer vaccines. But the German company had already reached an agreement with the Shanghai-based company Fosun Pharma for exclusive distribution rights in China, Hong Kong, Macau, and Taiwan—meaning that Taiwan would have to go through a Chinese company in order to get its vaccines. This created two related problems. First, Taiwan has a long-standing policy, far predating the coronavirus pandemic, that prohibits importing Chinese vaccines of any kind. To get the Pfizer jabs, it would have to circumvent Fosun and sign a contract with BioNTech directly. Second, BioNTech now had a close relationship with a Chinese entity. The German company returned the contract to Taiwan: before the deal could be made, the company said, Taiwanese officials had to remove a reference to Taiwan as a country. The Pfizer vaccine acquisition came to a grinding halt. In May 2021, Taiwan-ese president Tsai Ing-wen publicly accused the Chinese government of interfering with Taiwan's efforts to obtain vaccines for its population.

The Chinese government more or less openly acknowledged that po-litical conditions had been placed on Taiwan's ability to acquire vac-cines. When asked in a press briefing about the recent news that Japan was considering sending vaccines to Taiwan, Chinese foreign ministry spokesperson Wang Wenbin responded, "We are firmly against those who exploit the pandemic to put on political shows or even meddle in China's internal affairs." This response indicates that the Chinese government views other countries' sending vaccines to Taiwan as an infringement on China's sovereignty—thus, Beijing viewed blocking vaccine shipments to Taiwan as an important political interest.

Wang also demonstrated China's strategy of subnational engagement in a very unsubtle way: "Recently many counties, cities, and groups in the Taiwan region have been calling for early access to vaccines from the mainland, and some institutions have announced that they will re-ceive donations from the mainland. All this demonstrates the Taiwan people's confidence in mainland vaccines," Wang said. "However, the DPP [Democratic Progressive Party] authorities, proceeding from selfish political calculations, turned a blind eye to the goodwill of the mainland, and even resorted to malicious smears and various other means to thwart the shipment of vaccines from the mainland to the island. This is running roughshod over the life and health of our compatriots in Taiwan."

This was a fascinating and very public example of how China makes appeals to cities and states when the central government of a country is hostile to Beijing and then invokes those ties to undermine the legitimacy of a central government action Beijing does not like.

This wasn't the only example of the Chinese government appearing to view vaccines as a political tool. In April 2021, Taiwanese foreign minister Joseph Wu accused the Chinese government of pushing Paraguay, one of Taiwan's fifteen remaining allies, to switch diplomatic allegiance from Taiwan to China in exchange for Chinese-made vaccines. "The Chinese government was very active in saying if the Paraguay government is willing to sever diplomatic ties with Taiwan, they will be able to get quite a few million vaccine doses from China," Wu said. He also said that Taiwan had worked with India and other democracies to secure vaccines for Paraguay; India had sent 100,000 doses of its domestically developed vaccine and had promised an additional 100,000 doses.

On June 4, Japan sent 1.24 million doses of the AstraZeneca vaccine to Taiwan. Taiwan finally received a shipment of 930,000 doses of the Pfizer-BioNTech vaccine on September 1. Meanwhile, in late May 2021, China once again prevented Taiwan from attending the annual World Health Assembly. If the Chinese government were truly committed to a Covid-free world and a world in which governments worked together to prevent future pandemics, Beijing would not try to block Taiwan's participation in multilateral institutions or its population's access to vaccines.

By the end of the pandemic, global perceptions of China's political model seemed to have come full circle. Its early cover-up of the initial outbreak in Wuhan thrust the Chinese Communist Party into a domestic crisis of legitimacy and deeply damaged global trust in Beijing. China's highly effective "zero-Covid" pandemic response had been the envy of the world.

But as the calendar turned to 2022, China found itself the last country on earth committed to zero-Covid. There was no clear off-ramp. Xi had hitched his reputation, and that of his party, to the model of mass testing, quarantines, and localized lockdowns that had kept the number of deaths in China stunningly low over most of the course of the pandemic. But by that year, two factors were working together to make zero-Covid both untenable and imperative. First was the rise of the Omicron variant, which was so infectious that it simply could not be fully contained by previous measures, requiring ever-more-extreme lockdowns and quarantines—meaning that just as the rest of the world was opening back up, Chinese people were being thrust into a life of total health surveillance and random lockdowns that devastated the country's economy. By the middle of the year, the World Bank had projected that for the first time since 1990, China's economic growth would fall behind that for the rest of Asia.

The second factor was entirely self-inflicted. China's leaders had refused to approve Western mRNA vaccines for use in China. By viewing the vaccine race as a geopolitical competition over whose political model was best, and amplifying disinformation about the more effective vaccines, the party under Xi had painted itself into a corner. It would be an unacceptable political failure to have to admit defeat by importing Western vaccines. So China didn't. By the time Omicron arrived, the country's 1.4 billion people had only the protection of the Chinese-made jabs, which used an older technology and were less effective than mRNA vaccines against the new variants. If Xi abandoned zero-Covid, Omicron would sweep through the population, and hundreds of thousands of people, and likely more, would die. The ascendancy of politics over basic health considerations turned China's fight against Covid-19 from a soft-power victory into a cautionary tale and a source of international pity and fear.

The two-month-long lockdown in Shanghai in March and April 2022 was a breaking point. Millions of residents in one of the world's most modern and prosperous cities were locked inside their apartments for weeks. Supplies dwindled and food shortages began to dominate people's daily lives as they awaited government deliveries that came days late or bartered with neighbors for potatoes and bread.

That was when the party lost China's middle class. White-collar workers in Shanghai, who had long enjoyed the greatest benefits of the country's rapid economic development and were often able to sidestep the worst of its political system, began seeking ways to get their assets out of China and leave for good. An online neologism, "run xue," meaning "studying how to run" or leave the country, became popular as young people across the country felt they had no future there.

11

BUILDING A DEMOCRATIC ECONOMIC STATECRAFT

The Chinese government's deployment of coercive economic measures to achieve geopolitical ends represents a weaponizing of its market leverage—one that governments and international regulatory bodies have proven unprepared to counter effectively. There are numerous reasons for this, including a post–Cold War idealism that saw nonliberal countries admitted to international institutions in the hope that engagement would bring them closer to liberal democracy—resulting in the inclusion of some governments, like Beijing, that actively worked at times to undermine the very reasons for which those institutions had been created.

But a key underlying factor is the rise of neoliberalism in the United States and the international sphere. National and global economies based on varying shades of neoliberalism provide the ideal conditions for China's economic statecraft to shape the behavior of individual commercial actors abroad in ways that promote its own geopolitical and security goals while at times harming the values and security of democratic nations.

Unilateral neoliberalism—given that China's system certainly isn't neoliberal—is the perfect environment for a globalized economic statecraft like China's to flourish. When it is China versus individual actors in the market, the power is stacked in the Chinese Communist Party's favor. In many cases, companies and institutions have been more or less on their own in dealing with the weaponized politics that come with the Chinese market. In the realm of diplomacy, China prefers bilateral agreements over multilateral ones, because that guarantees it has the upper hand. A neoliberal trade environment can, at times, represent an even more extreme power balance: that of the Chinese Communist Party versus an individual company.

The equation of democracy and free-market capitalism in the American consciousness—a classic characteristic of a neoliberal worldview—has had another unforeseen side effect. It created a blind spot to the rise of China's authoritarian state capitalism, which was thought to be an existential impossibility according to the precepts of neoliberalism: authoritarianism and prosperous capitalism simply could not coexist for long, as one would eventually swallow the other. This belief contributed to a long-standing nonchalance in the West toward the rise of a clearly authoritarian and increasingly prosperous China. The Chinese Communist Party would surely fall as soon as China's middle class expanded, the thinking went; or else, the party's authoritarian policies would inevitably crush the country's economy. Either way, there was nothing to worry about in the long run.

Glorification of the market and the individual has also made it difficult for Americans to think creatively about possible solutions to the challenges posed by China. A philosophy of neoliberalism, especially when taken to extremes, often precludes government action. It's the reason that, for years, civil society responses—such as public shaming of companies, opt-in university codes of conduct, and legal measures promoting transparency but not prohibiting any particular actions—were considered the only democratic options to pushing back against China's authoritarian influence. Even now, amid a growing consensus that democratic governments must take firm and unified measures to hold the line against Beijing, most new legal and regulatory measures target unfair trade practices and national security threats from Chinese state–linked actors rather than proactively enforcing democratic guardrails on economic behavior.

The belief that companies have a moral right to bolster their profits by any legal means available has also contributed to decades of successful lobbying against government restrictions on trade with China. As Joseph Stiglitz, economics professor at Columbia University, wrote in 2020, "In a democracy where money matters—clearly true in this country—it is in the private interest of corporations to do what they can to make sure that the rules of the game serve their interests and not the interests of the public at large. And they often succeed."

Just as China is learning to wield its economic power for political means abroad, the U.S. government and society have become more vulnerable than ever to the raw sway of money. As economist Thomas Piketty points out in his book *Capital in the Twenty-First Century*, capital is more heavily concentrated in the hands of a very elite few than at any time since World War II. At the same time, our political and legal systems' current momentum is toward less regulation of corporations and of the wealthy, not more. Compared with western Europeans, Americans have been less willing to place such checks on the economy and have, in fact, moved in the opposite direction, toward even less regulation, a trend that accelerated under President Donald Trump. Deregulation has made it difficult for the U.S. government to conduct oversight or to put structural guardrails on company activities. Supreme Court decisions such as *Citizens United* have increased, not decreased, the power of corporations and individual wealthy donors in our political processes. Mass movements such as Occupy Wall Street, aimed at keeping corporations and the ultra-rich accountable, have failed. Billions of corporate lobbying dollars thrown at Congress drown out the voices of actual voters. The revolving door blends the interests of government bureaucrats and elected officials with the industries in which they once worked or plan to work.

The growing power of large companies also extends downward into the lives of those who work for them. In her book *Private Government*, American political philosopher Elizabeth Anderson argues that U.S. companies in the twenty-first century hold an almost dictatorial power over their employees, at times determining what they wear, what they say, when they use the bathroom, whom they can date, which doctors they can see, even which birth control they can use. Union busting in traditional industries, and the absence of union organizing in emerging industries such as in Silicon Valley, has greatly weakened the ability of employees to fight for their own interests and well-being in the workplace. A highly competitive job market means many employees have little job choice, making them more dependent on their current employers and further reducing their power over their own lives.

While there is now growing agreement in the United States that an unregulated and amoral approach to commerce can create problems—to those left of center, systemic inequality and environmental degradation, and to those right of center, the outsourcing of jobs and even of entire industries abroad—this line of inquiry has yet to be applied to the issue of systemic challenge to China's authoritarian economic statecraft.

Yet, all this means that the balance of power, in terms of who is making explicit demands on the holders of U.S. wealth, has shifted in the Chinese Communist Party's favor. American employees have little power to push back internally if they find that their company has chosen to act unethically due to China's political demands and have few protections to save their jobs if they choose to stage a protest, leak to the press, or otherwise push back. Companies serve as a de facto pro-Beijing lobby in Washington, pushing back against legislation that might close off China's markets—even if that means overlooking the Tiananmen Square Massacre, endemic labor violations, and the authoritarian takeover of Hong Kong. Former U.S. elected officials are hired to lobby on behalf of the same Chinese surveillance giants whose cameras blanket Xinjiang.

This has left transparency and American civil society—or the invocation of national security —as the primary means for pushing back against Chinese Communist Party pressure, through "naming and shaming" U.S. companies that choose to self-censor or that become actively complicit in repressive Chinese government initiatives. Up until recently, American civil society was not engaged enough to care—and it was certainly nowhere near as engaged as many online Chinese nationalists, whose indignation, fanned in part by a massive state propaganda and censorship apparatus, has helped force many Western companies to apologize and self-censor. And criticism from democratic publics frequently doesn't work. The opening of a new Tesla showroom in Urumqi, Xinjiang, in January 2022—after the United States had already designated the campaign of repression against Uyghurs there a genocide, and after a growing web of restrictions limited the import of products from Xinjiang—demonstrates the limits of naming and shaming when so much money in the Chinese market is on the line.

There's nothing wrong with shaming a U.S. company for investing in Xinjiang or self-censoring to please Beijing. But purely placing the blame on individual commercial actors for succumbing to the innovative economic statecraft of a trade superpower is misguided. By engaging the Chinese market and toeing the Chinese Communist Party line, companies are simply playing by the rules that the United States has set for forty years. To change their behavior, the United States and other liberal democratic nations must change the rules. Through new laws, regulations, and multilateral institutions, we need to relink economic and democratic rights, both domestically and internationally. On the international stage, that means walking back the Clinton-era delinking of trade and human rights. For just as the United States was delinking its trade policies from the political and civil values that the country claims to stand for, China under the party was doing the opposite. Only a democratic economic statecraft, linking our domestic and international systems, can effectively respond.

Every major power employs economic statecraft of some kind, and the United States is no exception. Tracing the emergence of a neoliberal-minded trend within U.S. economic statecraft can help us understand how we got to our current predicament.

The term *neoliberalism* means different things to different people. To some, it simply describes a political-economic model in which the government removes itself from as many economic decisions as possible, both domestically and in international trade and institutions. To others, it is a shrill catch-all used by critics to lambast the flaws of Western capitalism in its current iteration. British political activist George Monbiot, in a 2016 piece for the *Guardian* titled "Neoliberalism: The Ideology at the Root of All Our Problems," wrote that "neoliberalism sees competition as the defining characteristic of human relations. It redefines citizens as consumers, whose democratic choices are best exercised by buying and selling, a process that rewards merit and punishes inefficiency. It maintains that 'the market' delivers benefits that could never be achieved by planning."

Regardless of what term is used, it's clear that the past forty years differ markedly from the forty years that preceded them, and the changes that took place over the former weren't confined to domestic spheres alone. Beginning in the 1980s, U.S. liberal economic statecraft in some aspects gave way to a neoliberal economic statecraft, as the United States began to push neoliberal policies from within multilateral institutions as well. Washington implemented more public-private partnership programs within the World Bank and the IMF and made multilateral development loans contingent upon recipient governments' promising to privatize industries and implement other neoliberal reforms. Since then, the neoliberal liberalization of international trade policies, the weakening of regulatory systems, the erosion of labor protections, the rise of massive multinational corporations, and the disproportionate sway that monied interests have gained over U.S. elections and governance have created an environment in which it is nearly impossible to openly discuss, much less formulate a systematic response to, the challenge of China's authoritarian economic statecraft.

The United States has used its financial and economic dominance to shape international political and economic norms in two primary ways— first, through the creation of the Bretton Woods system (namely, the World Bank, the IMF, and the World Trade Organization) to promote economic interdependence, trade, and, increasingly since the 1980s, privatization and other neoliberal policies; and second, by leveraging U.S. dominance of the international financial system through the use of sanctions.

The Bretton Woods approach contrasts sharply with what came before: the nationalist economic policies pursued by Nazi Germany, the state-controlled economy of the Soviet Union, and the mercantilism that was common among European countries during the colonial and early modern period, in which governments sought to maximize state power through regulating their economies, such as by maximizing exports and reducing imports to build up gold reserves, in order to overpower their geopolitical rivals. Mercantilist policies were a significant factor contributing to European colonial expansion and wars; Nazi Germany's nationalist economic policies contributed to that country's early invasions of neighboring regions.

In the post–World War II period, the United States and its allies rejected mercantilism, communism, and economic nationalism. Instead, these countries sought to establish institutions and norms to promote economic liberalism (open markets and protections for private property) out of the belief that nations with close trade relationships were unlikely to go to war with each other, that economic liberalism was the best way to ensure the greatest prosperity for all, and that prosperous countries and populaces were unlikely to instigate violence. Western nations pursued this approach through the creation of the World Bank, the International Monetary Fund, and the General Agreement on Tariffs and Trade (GATT); and then, even more enthusiastically, in the post–Cold War period, when the fall of Soviet communism fed the belief that the world was converging toward a universalist system of political and economic liberalism and the United States and its allies sought to open up the international trade system to most countries in the world, creating the World Trade Organization as a successor to GATT to help make this a reality.

This form of economic statecraft is gradual and macrocosmic, focused on the creation of global norms and institutions that reduce perceived negative security externalities and promote positive ones. It also has a sharper edge. In recent decades, Western governments and the United Nations have also deployed an increasingly sophisticated precision tool of economic statecraft, the sanction, to police the borders of their international system. They levy sanctions against rogue governments, government officials, individuals, and nonstate actors such as Al Qaeda.

During the postwar period and up to the late 1970s, this international system along with domestic institutions in the United States, Britain, and Western Europe tended to balance protectionism with free trade in order to encourage economic growth while preserving employment and social safety nets. International institutions like the World Bank and the International Monetary Fund restricted capital controls. Sitaraman describes this era of liberalism as a period when "big institutions—big government, big corporations, big labor—cooperated to balance the needs of stakeholders in society." International relations scholar John Ruggie referred to this system as "embedded liberalism": the idea that markets should be "reconciled with the values of social community and domestic welfare."

But in the 1970s, amid chronic economic stagnation and inflation that plagued both sides of the Atlantic, critics of liberalism began to gain prominence. Economists Friedrich Hayek, Milton Friedman, and others helped popularize a new libertarian orthodoxy that championed free markets and opposed most government intervention.

A new philosophy of business was also beginning to take hold. In September 1970, Friedman published an essay called "The Social Responsibility of Business Is to Increase Its Profits," in which he argued that profit should be a corporation's only goal. Businesses cannot and should not have a "social conscience," Friedman wrote, and corporations are not responsible for larger social goals such as environmental protection, antidiscrimination, and a healthy job market. Friedman denounced the idea of corporate social responsibility as "pure and unadulterated socialism."

His essay soon became mandatory reading in many business schools in the United States. It would set the tone for the next half century of a certain style of American corporate governance and of the political zeitgeist that enabled it, which can be summarized by the catchphrase "greed is good."

Ronald Reagan's election in 1980 brought Friedman's ideas to the White House, as the conservative president cut taxes, reduced government spending, weakened unions, and deregulated sector after sector. Reagan's now-famous line from his 1981 inaugural address, "Government is not the solution to our problem; government is the problem," became the guiding mantra of the Republican Party for the next forty years. The era of embedded liberalism was over. Neoliberalism was ascendant.

If liberalism spread from the outside in—a conference of exhausted war victors looking to create an international system that would promote prosperous, peace-loving domestic systems and, thus, global harmony—neoliberalism spread from the inside out. It began as a set of ideas designed primarily to address domestic problems, with little thought given to the international system—at least at first.

But soon Reagan, and successive presidents, began to apply neoliberal principles to U.S. development initiatives and institutions. The International Monetary Fund and the World Bank began pressing governments receiving development loans to privatize major industries and liberalize their financial and trade policies.

These efforts greatly accelerated with the fall of the Soviet Union. The new independence of numerous post-Soviet countries across eastern Europe whose economies were transitioning out of communism created a whole new ecosystem of governments and societies desperate for a quick road out of poverty. "The acceleration of interest in privatization evident in the last two to three years is striking," wrote Mary Shirley, chief of the World Bank's public sector management and private sector development division, in a 1992 report. "Governments of very different political and ideological streams are bent on privatizing, and governments that are already privatizing are moving from selling small retail outlets and industries to selling larger mining and infrastructure enterprises."

The World Bank strongly supported these efforts. "The World Bank's interest in privatization stems from its fundamental goals—to help its borrowers achieve efficient growth with equity, while reducing poverty and protecting the environment. Privatization can be an important means to these ends," Shirley wrote. "There are virtually no limits on what can be privatized."

As capitalism prevailed over communism with the end of the Cold War, the precepts of neoliberalism increasingly became indistinguishable from those of a triumphalist vision of democracy. Democracy didn't just mean free elections and rule of law; it also meant free markets, private industry, and free trade. The two were inextricably linked, it was believed. Excessive government intervention in the economy was both a symptom of political unfreedom and, in and of itself, an impingement on freedom; while sweeping away government involvement in economic decisions would pave the way for political liberty.

Belief in the democratizing effect of participation in global free markets helped fuel support for expanding the GATT globally to create the World Trade Organization. It also helped lead to a great enthusiasm for "shock therapy" as a quick, if painful, way to transform post-Communist economies into prosperous democratic capitalist ones through abolishing price controls, adopting monetary policy, allowing private business, and opening the doors to foreign direct investment. Harvard professor Jeffrey Sachs, described in a 1993 *New York Times* article as "probably the most important economist in the world," was one of shock therapy's strongest proponents; that year he flew to Moscow to urge reformists there to immediately reduce government budgets to curb inflation and to worry about unemployment later. The end goal was democratic capitalism. As the *Times* article put it, "The first goal for reformers, Sachs says, is to get across the message that democracy and capitalism are inextricable."

The great democratizing project became largely indistinguishable from the great neoliberalizing project: one could be substituted for the other. Nowhere is this clearer than in President Bill Clinton's 1994 decision to delink human rights demands from trade with China. Clinton had come into office just a few years after the Tiananmen Square Massacre, as the United States was still implementing an array of tough sanctions on China. He had campaigned on taking a hard line against Beijing, promising to end the most-favored-nation status that granted China preferential trade privileges with the United States unless the Chinese government improved its human rights record. But, within two years of taking office, Clinton abandoned this stance:

> *Late in the afternoon of May 26, 1994, President Clinton stepped to the podium of the White House briefing room to formally delink human rights from trade. In a tone that struck some reporters there as defensive and almost apologetic, he said that China had failed to achieve "overall significant" progress in human rights, as his policy required. But even so, he would recommend continuing China's trade preference. His goal wasn't to isolate China by cutting off trade, he said, but rather "to engage the Chinese with not only economic contacts but with cultural, educational, and other contacts, and with a continuing aggressive effort in human rights"—a position that business groups had been advocating for months, and which became U.S. policy for every succeeding administration until Donald Trump took office.*

This was the essence of the U.S. engagement strategy, the idea that integrating China into global institutions and markets would expose the Chinese to democratic values and shape their institutions and society in ways that would inevitably draw them nearer to liberal democracy. Engagement involved more than just economics, but the neoliberal equivalence of economic freedom with political freedom helped provide the ideological justification for this conveniently pro-business approach.

It's hard to fault world leaders who embraced this post–Cold War vision. It was a compelling idea that presented a simple, unified approach to a global "end of history," as political scientist Francis Fukuyama famously dubbed it.

But in the grand scale of human history, we are still very early in our study of economics and political science. We are, as it were, still figuring things out. Just as the excesses of the once-seductive systems of mercantilism and national socialism led to their rejection and the subsequent embrace of liberalism—and just as the imperfections of liberalism contributed to stagnation by the 1970s, leading to new formulations of libertarianism and neoliberalism—the imbalances of neoliberalism also began to take their toll on societies around the globe.

Neoliberal reforms at first seemed to work well in developed Western countries, at least by some benchmarks. In the years after Margaret Thatcher became the United Kingdom's prime minister, some believe that her policies of privatization, austerity, and union busting brought much-needed change to a dysfunctional system and boosted productivity. But the reforms also caused high unemployment, with cuts to public support for former workers and reduced public investment in the long term. Inequality rose, and social mobility fell. Some former industrial towns never recovered.

The systemic failings of shock therapy in Russia and eastern Europe, too, were becoming apparent. Stagnant wages couldn't keep up with soaring inflation caused by the sudden removal of price controls, wiping out the life savings of a generation of workers. During the 1990s, standards of living for many people actually fell, resulting in nostalgia for the reliable, if modest, living standards of the Communist era. Weak institutions and rule of law funneled new wealth to the politically connected, fueling an epidemic of corruption and, eventually, entrenched kleptocracy. Democracy, at least in its neoliberal incarnation, failed to deliver on its promises. Russian president Vladimir Putin has capitalized on the loss of faith in democracy, reviving authoritarianism and fashioning himself as a strongman leader who blames the West for the country's problems and promises to make Russia great again. China managed to avoid shock therapy by ignoring Western neoliberal reformers such as Sachs and instead gradually liberalizing portions of its economy over time while maintaining state control over the "commanding heights" of certain key sectors.

Philip Alston, the UN special rapporteur on extreme poverty and human rights, has criticized the World Bank and the IMF's adoption of privatization as a requirement for loan recipients. In a 2018 report, Alston wrote that privatization, when applied aggressively and without consideration for those negatively affected, can result in the "systematic elimination of human rights protections and further marginalization of the interests of low-income earners and those living in poverty."

The first major rumblings of popular discontent in the United States began in the wake of the 2008 financial crisis, as grassroots movements and a growing body of research highlighted rising socioeconomic inequality and unchecked environmental devastation around the world. The year 2011 gave us Occupy Wall Street and the now-household term "the one percent." Thomas Piketty's 2014 book, *Capital in the Twenty-First Century*, brought us the U-curve to visualize the looming return of modern societies to the nineteenth-century reality in which most wealth was inherited, rather than earned, leading to a class of entrenched wealthy elites who more or less run everything.

The 2016 presidential campaign heralded the rise of a truly leftist wing of the Democratic Party, which openly rejected neoliberalism and, instead, championed structural economic reform while railing against corporations for distorting the United States' political process with campaign cash.

Remarkably, it wasn't just the American left that was starting to openly reject neoliberalism. The 2016 triumph of Donald Trump's far-right populism brought a critique of libertarian capitalism to the Republican Party, long an unshakable bastion of radical free-market ideology. This movement, however, was a critique not from the standpoint of classical liberal values but from that of a rising nationalism, a rejection of globalization, and a belief that immigrants and company outsourcing abroad were impoverishing Americans by stealing their jobs, a phenomenon painted as a symptom of free-market capitalism run amok. The movement also lambasted free trade, particularly with China, as economically harmful to Americans unless conducted with significant muscling. While anti-globalization was a key part of Trump's appeal among a broad base that poached some traditional Democratic and labor union support, with that came the rising idea that government could and should do more and that free markets simply weren't delivering.

Tucker Carlson, the conservative Fox News host, well summarized these sentiments in a January 2019 broadcast: "Republican leaders will have to acknowledge that market capitalism is not a religion. Market capitalism is a tool, like a staple gun or a toaster. You'd have to be a fool to worship it. Our system was created by human beings for the benefit of human beings. We do not exist to serve markets. Just the opposite." The Fox News host skewered the unresponsiveness of American political elites who, in his view, had created the conditions resulting in the high unemployment, the opioid epidemic, and the high single-parent birth rate that were decimating families in rural white America. "One of the biggest lies our leaders tell us is that you can separate economics from everything else that matters. . . . Both parties believe this," Carlson continued. "The idea that families are being crushed by market forces never seemed to occur to them . . . Questioning markets feels like apostasy."

In some ways, then, the United States' left-wing and right-wing discontents have met in the middle—in rough agreement that "the business of business is business" is no longer tenable. And the corporate world seems to have sensed which way the winds are blowing. With the growing embrace of ESG (environmental, social, and governance) factors when making investment decisions, companies have started at least to go through the motions of concern about more than just profit. "Just look where the obsession with maximizing profits for shareholders has brought us: terrible economic, racial and health inequalities; the catastrophe of climate change," Marc Benioff, the CEO of Salesforce, said in September 2020.

Jeffrey Sachs, the great shock therapy economist who equated capitalism and democracy, became the perfect example of how this uncritical equivalence can backfire. After championing China's successes in lifting its population out of poverty, Sachs has repeatedly downplayed the severity of the Chinese government's genocide in Xinjiang, arguing that it isn't genocide and saying that the United States should not put Xinjiang at the center of its foreign policy with China.

The annual Human Freedom Index—co-published by the Cato Institute, in Washington, DC, and Canada's Fraser Institute, both think tanks that promote libertarianism—also highlights the absurdity of viewing a low corporate tax rate as on par with political freedom. The index measures "personal, civil, and economic" freedom, defining freedom as the "absence of coercive constraint." The ranking published in 2021 was based on data from 2018, long after the Chinese government in Beijing had blocked Hong Kong from implementing universal suffrage, after leaders of peaceful protests, including Nathan Law, an elected lawmaker in Hong Kong, had been jailed, after Chinese agents had kidnapped a Hong Kong bookseller, and after rising police brutality. Even so, the index ranked Hong Kong among the freest places in the world, placing it third on a list of 162 countries, above every European democracy except Switzerland.

As a predictive indicator of the guarantee of future freedoms, the ranking was clearly an abject failure. Six months before it was published, Beijing forced its draconian National Security Law on Hong Kong, destroying the city's political traditions and effectively absorbing it into the mainland's established authoritarianism.

The neoliberal state, writes political economist Isabella Weber, "is neither small nor weak, but strong. Its purpose is to fortify the market." It also takes a strong and proactive state to establish and defend a politically free market. The neoliberal state should now use the significant resources it has historically wielded to preserve an economically free market, to also build a politically free market—one that is structurally resilient in the face of China's authoritarian economic statecraft. Of course, by doing so, the neoliberal state would cease to be neoliberal.

Countering China's Authoritarian Economic Statecraft

First under the Trump administration and continuing under the Biden administration, the United States has made swift progress toward insulating certain aspects of its economy from some of the more egregious aspects of China's abuses, with Europe tagging along behind. The Biden administration has also focused on building coalitions with other democratic countries and encouraging like-minded countries to act in concert. These measures are a very good start and have already challenged or even rejected several neoliberal assumptions. But some of the most difficult work has yet to be attempted, including reforming or replacing compromised international institutions such as the World Trade Organization and—most crucially in the U.S. context—reforming purely domestic structures that make our body politic vulnerable to the pull of Beijing's will.

In this book, I have focused on economic coercion aimed at achieving illiberal geopolitical goals rather than simply enriching China or boosting its competitive edge—though, in many cases, this is a false distinction, as the Chinese Communist Party often uses the greater economic power it gains through unfair trade practices to then further bolster other forms of economic coercion intended to achieve authoritarian geopolitical ends. For example, China's widespread and sometimes state-supported economic and industrial espionage targeting U.S. businesses and research institutions is unfair and harmful and goes against the spirit of the open international system, but it isn't directly aimed at shutting down dissent or shaping the world into a more illiberal place.

Even so, the sharp competitive edge that such massive transfers of technology have given to Chinese companies in some sectors—and, thus, to the illiberal state that increasingly uses the power of companies for geopolitical ends—has strengthened the coercive power of China's economic statecraft.

Most economic measures that the United States has taken so far are intended to strengthen U.S. national security, as traditionally defined, and to combat Chinese espionage, surveillance, military buildup, and unfair trade practices. The use of the U.S. Entity List, a trade restriction under the Commerce Department's Bureau of Industry and Security, to blacklist Chinese companies and other entities is a clear-cut example of this; the list requires that U.S. companies and federal government offices first obtain a license before exporting products or technologies to any entity on the list. It is not a ban or a sanction; countries on the list are still permitted to use U.S. financial institutions and sell products in the United States. Even so, the use of the Entity List demonstrates clear recognition in Washington that U.S. government action is necessary when the Chinese government uses ostensibly private companies to further its national security goals. Chinese telecommunications companies Huawei and ZTE, both determined to have potential links to the Chinese military, and some other Chinese entities have now been added to the list.

Most innovatively—and most promising, from the perspective of putting democratic guardrails on economic behavior—Chinese companies and other entities deemed complicit in Xinjiang human rights abuses have also now been added to the Entity List. The 2021 passage of the Uyghur Forced Labor Prevention Act, which bans the importation of all products from Xinjiang unless it can be proven that they were not made with forced labor, marks one of the biggest steps the United States has taken in decades toward relinking trade and human rights.

This is the avenue that more U.S. and European measures need to take—a clear and explicit focus on asserting legal force to defend liberal democratic values and systems, including human rights and political rights. The world is already well on its way toward insulating domestic economies and sensitive infrastructure from geopolitical risk associated with China. And, in many cases, selective decoupling to bolster national security—as in the case of banning Huawei from 5G networks—can support and achieve some of the same goals as a directly values-based approach. If a government hasn't allowed Huawei into its networks, Beijing can never threaten to turn the 5G switch off or use it as some other form of leverage to force that government to go along with its illiberal agenda.

Even so, distinguishing between democratic countermeasures aimed at blunting authoritarian statecraft specifically and measures intended to support free markets and national security without reference to democratic values still matters. Censorship provides a good example of why this is so. It has swiftly become an accepted norm that U.S. companies must obey Chinese censorship laws within the Chinese market because, the thinking goes, this is a technical issue of sovereignty; we generally expect companies to abide by the local laws and regulations of the countries where they operate. But the entire premise of international human rights law and conventions is that there must be exceptions to this principle. Indeed, that's the very reason that the Chinese government has sought to undermine human rights protection mechanisms in international organizations; Beijing views such laws and standards as a violation of its sovereignty. But liberal democratic nations accept that sovereignty does not extend to human rights violations.

What many commentators seem to have forgotten is that international human rights norms also enshrine free access to information as a right. Article 19 of the International Covenant on Civil and Political Rights specifies as a right the "freedom to seek, receive and impart information and ideas of all kinds, regardless of frontiers, either orally, in writing or in print, in the form of art, or through any other media."

Censorship on the scale implemented by China is an egregious human rights violation. Foreign companies that accede to Chinese government demands to censor their content within the Chinese market are actively complicit in a violation affecting 20 percent of the world's population. But customary discussions of foreign corporate complicity in censorship in China are often dominated by market-related language—censorship "within the Chinese market" and abiding by "local laws" is a normal prerequisite for "access" to this market.

It is beyond clear that Beijing believes it has both the power and the right to extend its censorship as far beyond its borders as possible, and it has used the full extent of every channel of its power to accomplish this. If liberal democracies refuse to push back with the full force of their power, including the force of their laws, Beijing will continue to shrink the international space for free debate over its actions and even over basic scientific facts.

A To-Do List for Democracies

Liberal democracies should have two goals in their response to China's authoritarian economic statecraft. The first goal is to strengthen democratic guardrails on economic behavior. Very few steps have been taken toward this, because it is not directly related to security in any sense and thus cannot benefit from the general bipartisan consensus that national security concerns should supersede domestic divisions.

Many of the measures I recommend involve massive reform and restructuring of the U.S. economic, legal, and regulatory systems. It is important to state these as goals; it's also important to be realistic about what may actually be accomplished in our highly polarized society and often dysfunctional political system. To that end, I will also suggest modified measures that have less impact but are more feasible.

The second goal is to bolster economic security explicitly as a form of national security—the goal toward which the United States, Europe, and Japan have already made the most progress. That includes taking measures to support supply chain resilience, inbound investment screening, export controls, telecommunications security, and diversifying trade relationships. Even so, there is still much to be done, so the second section explores how democratic allies can work together to promote individual and collective economic security in the face of authoritarian challenge.

Strengthening Democratic Guardrails on Economic Behavior

One key direction to push reform aimed at weakening China's authoritarian economic statecraft is to reduce the power of billionaires and corporations to shape our political system and dictate our rights.

Eliminate corporate campaign contributions. To be fair, this is almost impossible for the United States to achieve anytime in the near future. The Supreme Court's 2010 decision in *Citizens United v. FEC* held that campaign contributions by corporations are a form of free speech and thus cannot be restricted. The current Supreme Court is significantly more conservative than the 2010 Court and is unlikely to consider overturning that decision.

- A more viable, though less impactful, policy measure would be to establish a public-funding option for candidates in federal, state, and local elections. Some states and municipalities in the United States have options for public funding for candidates; more states could work toward adopting similar laws.
- In the long run, *Citizens United v. FEC* should be overturned.

Make it illegal to lobby on behalf of authoritarian foreign governments.
- It's not hard to ban former public officials from doing this. The Trump administration briefly imposed such a rule, then revoked it. The Biden administration then implemented a two-year ban. Such a rule should be codified into law by Congress, rather than through executive order or other executive rule change.
- But it's extremely difficult to ban average U.S. citizens and residents from lobbying on behalf of whomever they choose; it's considered a free-speech issue and has other thorny legal implications. An alternative would be to strengthen lobbying disclosure requirements by mandating companies and individuals to file far more extensive disclosures about the nature of their activities and their conversations with public officials.
- An even easier way to mitigate the influence of lobbying on behalf of foreign authoritarian governments would be to make the DOJ Foreign Agents Registration Act online database easier to use and search.

Create a regulatory framework making it illegal or costly for U.S. companies to acquiesce to foreign government censorship demands. The Preventing Foreign CENSORSHIP in America Act (Preventing the Foreign Coercive Export of Non-Consensual Speech and Orwellian Restrictions by Superpowers Hoping to Intimidate People in America Act) was one attempt at this. It was introduced in 2020 but was not passed into law. The draft bill would:

- Prohibit companies from firing or retaliating against employees or contractors because they spoke up about sensitive topics countries such as China seek to censor;
- Prohibit companies from firing or retaliating against employees who refuse to help their employers facilitate the human rights violations or propaganda efforts of designated geopolitical rivals;
- Prohibit employment contracts from requiring workers, even when they are off the clock, from staying silent on topics designated countries seek to censor;
- Create federal, state, and private enforcement mechanisms to ensure these rights are upheld and that victims of extraterritorial censorship can have their day in court; and
- Establish meaningful reporting requirements to name and shame companies that give in to the censorship or self-censorship efforts of geopolitical rivals.

One weakness of this draft law, however, is that it would create a list of "NATO and non-NATO allies" to whom the censorship ban would not apply. This seems tacked on purely to protect anti-BDS laws (Boycott, Divest, Sanction—a civil society movement that encourages people to support Palestine by severing all financial ties to Israel), which numerous Republican-dominated states have adopted to penalize government employees for boycotting Israel. This strategy is an obvious violation of the First Amendment but has yet to be struck down by courts. A fundamental problem with the approach taken in this draft bill is that it is constitutionally incoherent to create a legislative environment that sets up carve-outs for bans on anti-Israel speech while explicitly protecting anti-China speech.

Strengthen legal protections for private whistleblowers and mandate for-cause termination. Whistleblower protections already exist for government whistleblowers but there are few if any such protections for whistleblowers in most private industries. There can only be whistleblowers if there are regulations that are being violated. Regulatory frameworks such as those listed in this section must first be enacted.

Strengthen unions. Unions are, in essence, intracompany democracy. They allow the employees within a company to challenge the power wielded by wealthy executives. Unionizing in Silicon Valley could help employees push back against unethical policies. For example, Google employees were considering staging a walkout to protest Project Dragonfly; they turned to crowdsourcing as a guarantee for a financial cushion had employees been fired over their internal protests. No U.S. employees should have to use GoFundMe to help protect their livelihoods if they want to protest authoritarian government censorship.

Strengthen public oversight over social media platforms, which are the twenty-first-century version of the town square. Of course, U.S. society and politics are heavily polarized over this issue. At this time, any attempt at public oversight either would be entirely derailed or would be captured by one side of the political spectrum or the other to push its domestic speech priorities. As it currently stands, our town squares are for-profit corporations subject to the whims of the billionaires that own them.

- Pass a national data privacy law, modeled on the European Union's, as well as laws modeled on Europe's Digital Services Act and the Digital Markets Act, which mandate transparency for social media content algorithms.
- Reinstate a twenty-first-century version of the Fairness Doctrine, a 1949 regulation enforced by the Federal Communications Commission that required news outlets to present the opinion of both sides of an issue in a fair manner. The doctrine was abolished under President Ronald Reagan in 1987. An updated version of the Fairness Doctrine would apply to social media platforms and would require their algorithms to prioritize fair and fact-based content, to fact-check misinformation, to remove state-sponsored disinformation content, and to clearly label government-linked accounts and content.
- Pass a law requiring social media companies to establish in-house insider threat programs to ensure that employees have not been recruited or co-opted by foreign authoritarian governments to secretly spy on users, hand over user data, or implement censorship on behalf of authoritarian regimes.

Ensure that U.S. trade negotiations with China don't prioritize the concerns of big business in gaining access to the Chinese market. Instead, the United States should strive to open access in ways that help workers and increase wages. This would accomplish two things: First, it would decline to cater to the power of big companies while simultaneously reducing the future leverage that China would gain over them if even more of their revenue came from the Chinese market. Second, it would represent structural action to help readjust the economy in favor of wage earners.

Create mechanisms that legally prohibit transacting with entities that censor on behalf of an authoritarian foreign government. If freedom of information is a human right, then censorship is a violation of a human right, and we can use similar government mechanisms already in play for other forms of rights violations, such as forced labor.

- Entities that censor on behalf of an authoritarian government, such as Chinese social media companies and internet search engines, could be placed on the Federal Entity List, which would prohibit U.S. companies from transacting with them without first obtaining a license.
- Sanctions under the Global Magnitsky Act could be placed on top Chinese government officials responsible for implementing and expanding censorship, and on CEOs of major companies that abide by Chinese government censorship requirements, such as Baidu and Tencent.
- Congress could pass a law, modeled on the Uyghur Forced Labor Prevention Act, that prohibits U.S. companies from forming partnerships with Chinese companies unless they are able to prove that those companies do not censor.

Strengthen transparency requirements for any U.S. companies with operations in China. These measures will not only increase transparency and accountability for U.S. companies but will also convey a powerful message to Chinese authorities that their U.S. counterparts are legally prevented from keeping Beijing's demands secret. This could temper the expectations of Chinese authorities and help U.S. companies feel safer to make better and more democratic decisions.

- Require U.S. companies to publicly disclose if they have ongoing communications with any office or liaison of Chinese law enforcement or security services, and to disclose specifically which offices they are in communication with.

- Require U.S. companies to disclose if there is an employee of the U.S. company who is tasked with doing outreach and liaison work with Chinese security services, broadly defined.
- Require U.S. companies to publicly disclose any Chinese government demands to censor public-facing political content as well as any actions taken to satisfy these demands.

Create FARA requirements and publicly searchable databases on the state level, for every state. FARA is an incredible tool for holding lobbyists to account and understanding how foreign government money might be influencing our politics and debate. But there are no FARA laws or databases on the state level. Yet Chinese companies and officials do extensive lobbying work at the state and local level in the United States, and work with U.S. counterparts on the subnational level. This is a clear and obvious fix, and states should work hard to pass FARA-type laws as soon as possible.

Bolstering Individual and Collective Economic Security*

There are two broad avenues for countering coercive economic provocations. The first avenue is deterrence by denial, which means robbing these actions of their power and boosting the resiliency of those targeted. This includes measures to soothe the sting of boycotts and denial of market access, such as providing financial compensation to companies and individuals losing revenue as a result of China's actions. It also includes short-term efforts to diminish or remove the threat, such as diversifying trade routes and supply chains and making long-term strategic shifts to retain national competitive advantages and reshore manufacturing of key products. Democratic governments should take measures to enhance both short-term defense and longer-term resiliency and resistance to economic coercion.

The second avenue is to punish economic coercion. Punitive countermeasures can be unilateral or multilateral. Countries can hit back with

---

* Emily Walz contributed significantly to the research, analysis, and drafting of the final portion of this chapter.

retaliatory tariffs or levies, tools that are likely most effective when affixed to products upon which Beijing relies. Countries can also retaliate in diplomatic, law enforcement, military, or other domains.

Given the globalized nature of the international economic system—and China's documented history of dividing nations and targeting less powerful actors—any preventative or retaliatory action is more likely to succeed with united international support. So, government responses need to focus on drawing affected actors together, pulling companies under the protective shield of government, and banding governments together.

Pursuing a coordinated response also means building institutions. Domestic institution-building must be accompanied by moves to create international collective compacts to deter China's economic coercion and coordinate multilateral responses to it. Countries must also move to implement concrete measures to support affected entities and deter and punish authoritarian economic coercion. A bipartisan group of U.S. lawmakers introduced a bill in the U.S. House of Representatives in February 2023 that, if passed into law, would give the president new authorities to support allies and partners affected by authoritarian economic coercion. Those new authorities would include asking Congress to provide direct financial assistance to the targeted country, reducing import duties on affected products from the targeted country, and increasing import duties on certain products from the state perpetrating the coercion.

The Countering China's Economic Coercion Act, introduced in the U.S. House of Representatives in October 2021, proposes establishing an interagency task force under the leadership of the National Security Council with assistant secretary–level principals from relevant government bodies. The purpose of the bipartisan-sponsored bill is to streamline means for addressing China's economic coercion and to expand cooperation both with the private sector and with other allied and partner governments, with the goal of raising awareness and holding Beijing accountable.

International Action: Alliances of Democracies Acting Collectively

Multilateral coordination is the linchpin of combating China's economic coercion globally. Small countries, like individual companies, are vulnerable to a divide-and-conquer strategy.

Many already recognize the better prospects that banding together offers, with frequent proposals for "like-minded countries" (generally understood as liberal democracies) to stand together in opposing Chinese pressure. The U.S. government's foreign policy apparatus itself holds this general view: in March 2021, U.S. Secretary of State Antony Blinken called for like-minded countries to band together to stand up to economic coercion. The participation of the world's biggest economy, the United States, in a coordinated response is consequential. The most general recommendation for "banding together" suggests using a collective to leverage "joint pressure" against economic coercion. While options like joint statements calling out China's economic coercion are relatively milquetoast, in many cases China's actions have not provoked a significant or coordinated response, which, at a baseline, would raise the reputational costs of such actions.

The European Council on Foreign Relations also highlights the strength that comes with collective action, noting that strong U.S.-EU and global relations would undermine the effectiveness of Chinese economic coercion. China's deployment of secondary sanctions makes collective action more complicated and more urgent, particularly in Europe; under pressure, German companies began to push Lithuania's leaders to de-escalate the situation with China, with the German-Baltic Chamber of Commerce warning that some firms may have to leave China. For its part, Lithuania's deputy foreign minister, Mantas Adomėnas, has criticized the German approach, *Wandel durch Handel*, or "change through trade," as ineffective, saying, "When we are facing an era where our geopolitical considerations will come to the fore, economic interpenetration can become a liability, or something that can be exploited, instrumentalized or even weaponized."

Collective Economic Defense Pact

Both the North Atlantic Treaty Organization and the U.S.-Japan Security Treaty have an Article 5 that triggers mutual support measures in the event of an attack. Jonas Parello-Plesner, a former Danish diplomat, has proposed that a broad "alliance of democracies" establish an "economic article 5" that would formalize a commitment to respond to economic coercion. An explicit agreement would itself become a deterrent to autocracies considering coercive economic measures. Others have since proposed that this economic mutual defense compact would be more effective at binding a smaller cohort, such as the Five Eyes countries, arguing that the highest levels of solidarity are required to forgo the potential economic benefits that countries might gain from standing as a substitute trade partner in place of the member China is targeting.

The European Union offers another possible bloc that could enact a mutual economic defense mechanism. Europe relies on its ability to export to many markets simultaneously; it has also made the most progress toward a formalized mechanism for countering economic coercion. In December 2021, the European Commission unveiled its proposal for an anti-coercion instrument, a tool that could be established under the auspices of the European Union's common commercial policy. Initially designed (rather ironically) as a bulwark against sanctions overreach by the United States—specifically, Trump-era sanctions on Iran—it offers a clear, if still theoretical, mechanism to counter Beijing's actions. The proposed instrument is not dependent upon unanimity—an advantage, given China's attempts to use economic coercion to drive a wedge between countries with diverging economic interests—and it offers a compensation mechanism for collateral damage.

Alignment between countries and their companies becomes key here. While some commentators argue that companies ought to be "on the front line defending the rules-based international order," companies are not states, and when put into conflict with a nation-state power, they generally stand at a disadvantage. Agreeing not to sell to a foreign market is also potentially complicated if companies can be sued by their shareholders for forgoing opportunities to increase profits, at least in the absence of legal prohibitions. One approach toward defending against economic coercion is to force companies to internalize the risk of operating in China or to reprice that risk after many years of mispricing it. One Australian think tank argues that "foreign companies with business operations in China need to factor in the increasing risk to trade flows, supply chains and market share" and calls the risk "significant enough to warrant board-level attention" that comes with an established pattern of economic coercion, noting that it "will no doubt be a standing topic in audit committees because of its bottom-line impact." Board involvement would protect shareholder value and require closer company-policymaker collaboration. To prompt broader market caution, entities like the U.S. Department of Commerce could also issue business advisories.

Appeals to International Institutional Referees

Existing international institutional referees are poorly equipped to police China's actions. The preeminent international body governing trade is the World Trade Organization, an entity with two primary flaws. On a tactical level, the WTO has only a trade dispute mechanism, and the slow speed of the arbitration process renders it irrelevant to the immediate pain of coercive economic actions. On an organizational level, the body's consensus-driven design renders unlikely any agreement among nations as to what constitutes economic coercion—never mind determining when coercion has been used and what consequences ought to follow. At the very least, the WTO would likely need an overhaul before it becomes effective at deterring coercive economic actions. One *Japan Times* editorial proposed strengthening WTO rules and ceasing to block appointments to the appellate body.

To overcome the absence of a WTO provision for collective sanctions, some suggest that individual countries take their cases to the WTO—at which point other countries could join their appeals on the grounds that the cases raise questions about the integrity of the global trading system. Other proposals for WTO action include the idea that "like-minded countries" could start a debate on the topic with a position paper or begin discussion at committee levels. One trade law professor notes that "while this would not lead to hard [legal] rules on economic coercion, it would be a 'soft' approach highlighting concerns in a formal setting and attempting to change member behaviour."

In lieu of the WTO, others have proposed use of the G7 or the G10 as global forums where economic countermeasure principles could be hashed out; though others note that existing bodies like the Financial Action Task Force would likely not prove a successful forum in which to coordinate coercive sanction actions.

Some researchers argue that gaps in existing trade agreements, such as the Wassenaar Arrangement's narrow conception of national security risk, make it impossible to use these legal regimes to address economic coercion and suggest that a plurilateral export control agreement would be an important first step to aligning legal regimes across nations and creating agreed-upon norms and rules.

The nuclear option here would be for like-minded countries to create an entirely new trade body to function alongside the WTO in a way that promotes democratic and liberal values. There are major problems with this approach, of course. The first is that doing so, and then using that body to establish and act upon new trade norms, would violate WTO standards. So the two bodies would become rivals. Second, a mass democratic exodus from the WTO would leave it in the hands of authoritarian governments. That would strengthen their institutional, narrative, and likely moral sway over international trade norms.

Undermining Economic Coercion: Relief and Resilience

A primary defense against economic coercion is to undermine its effectiveness, denying China its objective by removing its leverage. The most immediate relief is to redirect exports to new markets or, conversely, source imports from other suppliers, and in the absence of that, to replace lost revenue. An interim step toward strengthening resilience and avoiding the disruption that buyer and supplier shifts cause is to secure minimum inventory levels.

There are several proposed variations on the idea of providing compensation or starting funds to support affected countries and companies. Countries could construct unilateral relief mechanisms in advance of coercive action, stipulating that if a company is subject to revenue loss as a result of Chinese government actions, it can apply and receive aid automatically. In the United States, this might be structured like the recent Covid-19 relief Paycheck Protection Program loans and grants. One Canadian proposal suggests supporting affected commodity farmers by expanding existing insurance programs, possibly through diversion of the country's capital share in the Asia Infrastructure Investment Bank (AIIB).

As an example of this kind of unilateral approach toward compensating affected actors, Australia announced in December 2020 the formation of an Agri-Business Expansion Initiative to support Australian businesses impacted by China's trade restrictions with funding of 85.9 million Australian dollars. The initiative comprises four key elements, supporting market expansion, in-country engagement, work on technical market access, and greater collection and delivery of market intelligence to exporters. A fifth element would be in the form of scaled-up business support services to more than two thousand agri-food exporters annually. These measures are not expected to be sufficient to fully offset the damage of Chinese economic actions, but they will mitigate economic coercion in the long term.

A few proposals suggest expanding compensation funds to a multilateral model. One Japanese opinion writer proposed a "Freedom Alliance Fund" comprising "like-minded countries sharing the same values," "with each country paying premiums in proportion to the depth of its economic relationship with China" and funded by their respective national companies involved with China. This is perhaps unlikely if relatively small economies heavily dependent on China lack the funds to pay proportionately higher premiums and given a general reluctance on the part of nations to invest in international organizations. The writer's answer is for companies to foot the bill, but that seems likely to be unpopular.

Communicating for Effective Deterrence

A precursor to effective action is the collection and sharing of information. Raising awareness across governments and publics and establishing communication channels are both necessary for collective action. There must be a shared understanding of what China's concerning behaviors are, agreement on how to assess them in real time, and consensus on how to respond.

But China's economic coercion is hard to measure by design. In Lithuania's case, after Lithuania said it would allow Taiwan to open an unofficial representative's office in Vilnius, the Chinese government moved rapidly to decimate bilateral trade and to pressure third-party countries to cease using Lithuanian components, all without declaring any official sanctions or other punitive measures. "Global Times is their main tool of communication with us," said Lithuania's deputy economy minister. Actions such as removing Lithuania from China's customs list of origin countries eligible for a specific duty rate amount to de facto sanctions and state-backed commercial retaliation against companies taking stances Beijing finds disagreeable are cloaked in the guise of "popular boycotts," as when fashion retailer H&M was removed from Chinese commerce platforms after releasing a statement expressing concerns about human rights violations in Xinjiang Province. The slippery nature of this coercion means that documenting related actions and quantifying their impact are both necessary to illuminate patterns and build the case for why countering and defending against economic coercion are important.

In the case of the United States, documenting and analyzing authoritarian economic coercion could be accomplished by developing designated government agency capabilities, such as housing at the Central Intelligence Agency any government agency intelligence and analysis capabilities focused on Chinese sanctions doctrine and practice.

To expand this idea internationally, the Australian Strategic Policy Institute suggests requiring the foreign ministries of democratic countries to track coercive diplomacy, use data to identify potential coalitions, and encourage research institutions also to track coercive diplomacy. The European Union has proposed the creation of an "EU Resilience Office" to identify when China is deploying obscured coercion. The work of the Resilience Office would also pinpoint the costs of these coercive policies and assess and offset their impact.

Reducing Medium- and Long-Term Risk

Future immunity to economic coercion comes in the form of risk reduction, specifically in avoiding asymmetries and excessive dependence on China. Similar to the short-term rerouting of products and the search for new suppliers, reducing medium-term risk means taking more deliberate actions to diversify trade, while the long-term requires maintaining footholds in competitive and strategic production areas. Supply chain security should include a combination of reshoring production and concluding nation-to-nation agreements not to restrict exports even in crises.

China moved to reduce supply chain vulnerabilities after the May 2019 listing of several Chinese technology companies on the BIS Entity List, effectively cutting off the nation's semiconductor supply. Supply chain security and science and technology innovation are the focus of China's Fourteenth Five-Year Plan (2021–25). In 2020, Xi Jinping vowed to build "production chains and supply chains that are independently controllable, secure, and reliable" and highlighted the need to ensure at least one alternative source for important products and supply channels, "forming the necessary industrial backup system." This suggests a blueprint that other nations could follow to avoid vulnerability to economic coercion.

Redirecting exports and diversifying trade routes have historically had some success. Expanding alternate markets and foreign direct investment (FDI) destinations can also serve to circumvent sanctions, as was the case with Norwegian salmon, which was indirectly imported into China via Vietnam. This could preserve the market while offering some insulation against the threat of economic sanction.

Australia has been caught in China's economic crosshairs for some time, which has forced the country to pursue several innovations. These range from a campaign on the part of the Inter-Parliamentary Alliance on China to boost consumption of Australian wine to longer-term trade access and diversification measures, including a free trade agreement with the United Kingdom and "ongoing efforts to negotiate FTAs with major global economies such as India and the European Union."

Taiwan has worked for years to reduce its trade dependence on China. In 2016, it launched its "New Southbound Policy" (新南向政策) to increase economic ties with a slate of countries in South Asia, Southeast Asia, and Australasia following a series of previous Taiwanese "Go South" policies initiated under other administrations. Taiwan has seen some success in the years under the New Southbound Policy, especially with ASEAN nations. Total trade between Taiwan and ASEAN moved from a negative growth rate of 10.9 percent during Ma Ying-jeou's Kuomintang administration (2012–16) to 13.6 percent annual growth in Tsai Ingwen's first term (2016–20), up to $89 billion, with "significant gains" from Singapore, Vietnam, Brunei, and Malaysia, though trade with South Asia fell over the same period. Trade to all eighteen target countries covered under the New Southbound Policy hit a historic high in 2021. Other steps included a signed investment deal with the Philippines (2017) along with memoranda of understanding on economic cooperation with Indonesia and Malaysia.

Another avenue for reducing vulnerability is to strengthen multilateral trading agreements and partnerships. This proposal gained some traction in midsize economic powers like Japan, especially during the Trump administration's "America First" policy stance in the United States. Japan has pushed forward a new incarnation of the Trans-Pacific Partnership, resurrected as the Comprehensive and Progressive Agreement for

Trans-Pacific Partnership (CPTPP), and pursued the Japan–European Union Economic Partnership as a second significant multilateral trade agreement. The *Japan Times* argues that Japan also needs to find a path to include India in the Regional Comprehensive Economic Partnership; that U.S. participation in the CPTPP would induce China to reform itself and eventually join the first-tier trading agreement; and that middle powers must shoulder the burden of building multilateral cooperation, supporting one another and the rules-based order.

Improving Public-Private Coordination for Resilience

Because coercive economic actions often take aim at individual companies, specific industries, and dependent sectors, improved public-private coordination is also a key preparatory measure. Companies singled out for Beijing-backed pressure have had few options beyond compliance with or withdrawal from the Chinese market. If they had acted in concert or with government backing, they might have been able to effectively resist. In 2018, China gained a rhetorical victory, targeting individual U.S. airlines to demand they comply with Chinese restrictions against "separatism" by removing from their websites and other public-facing content any references to Taiwan, Hong Kong, and Macau as independent countries. This action followed a similar press against hotel chains. A more robust business–government communication channel would, in the event of coordinated action against companies, allow individual companies to elevate disputes to the state level and participate in organized resistance. Anticipating future actions along these lines, national governments should also work with business groups to develop potential responses.

Domestic Steps: Increasing Institutional Capacity

Unilateral action offers the advantage of customizing a response to a nation's particular issue set. Existing institutional mechanisms could be adapted to respond specifically to economic coercion. The Department of Commerce's Bureau of Industry and Security (BIS), keeper of the department's Entity List, could use a similar blacklist mechanism to subject Chinese individuals or companies involved in economic coercion to licensing requirements for the export, re-export, or transfer of in-country items subject to U.S. Export Administration Regulations. As I will discuss in more detail in these next pages, governments could also move unilaterally to institute compensatory mechanisms to offset the economic pressure on individuals and companies.

As early as 2012, Eurasia Group founder Ian Bremmer proposed the creation of a "Department of Economic Statecraft" to manage global industrial policy and promote America's economic interests. Clyde Prestowitz, who served as counselor to the commerce secretary in the Reagan administration, has also recommended the creation of a "Department of Competitiveness," merging many of the functions of the departments of commerce, energy, and transportation, in order to "achieve U.S. and free world leadership in all major technologies and industries."

Deterrence: Future Fireproofing by Design

Maintaining a competitive edge and leverage must be the focus of long-term efforts, something that involves both protecting sensitive and valuable technologies and investing in new research and development in key areas. Investment regulation offers a path toward ensuring national economic security and safeguarding traditional national defense in cases where companies pursuing profit alone may not adequately safeguard these national priorities. While the interagency Committee on Foreign Investment in the United States (CFIUS) is charged with reviewing the national security implications of foreign investment in U.S. companies and operations, there is currently no mechanism to review outbound U.S. investment and block transactions that would weaken the national security or economic competitiveness of the United States, though the idea has been proposed with more frequency in recent years.

One such proposal is housed within the 2022 omnibus America COMPETES Act (aka the U.S. Innovation and Competition Act), which incorporated the text of the earlier National Critical Capabilities Defense Act of 2021. This text proposes amending the Trade Act of 1974 to establish a National Critical Capabilities Committee (NCCC), modeled on the structure of the CFIUS but focused on countries of concern and possibly nonmarket economies rather than a country-agnostic screening. The NCCC would consider transactions with bearing on the "long-term strategic economic, national security, and crisis preparedness interests of the United States" and on the "history of distortive or predatory trade practices" of the foreign countries where individuals party to the transaction are domiciled and their impact on domestic industry. The NCCC would be chaired by the U.S. trade representative and its membership would be drawn from the Office of Science and Technology Policy and the Departments of Commerce, Treasury, Homeland Security, Defense, State, Justice, Energy, Health and Human Services, Agriculture, Labor, and any other federal agency. Nonvoting members—from the Office of the Director of National Intelligence, the Federal Emergency Management Agency (FEMA), the National Institute of Standards and Technology, the Centers for Disease Control and Prevention, the National Institute of Allergy and Infectious Diseases, the Federal Communications Commission, the Securities and Exchange Commission, the Commodity Futures Trading Commission, and the Federal Aviation Administration—would be tasked with determining supply chain risks, with greatest attention reserved for "articles the supply chains for which are housed wholly or in part in countries of concern or from an entity of concern and for which substitute production is unavailable elsewhere at required scale." The act directs the NCCC to review industries that FEMA identifies as emergency support functions. If enacted, it would be the first outbound investment screening process in a major Western economy.

Other policy safeguards that can provide early warning and insulate against future coercion include overall efforts to reduce the power of money in the system, including extending the Foreign Agents Registration Act to include state-level activity in the United States beyond the current federal registry. It should also include stronger union protections for workers, including protections for speaking out and private-sector whistleblower protections.

U.S. economic sanctions stand to be less powerful with China's increasing economic strength and the growth of digital currencies. The U.S.-led global financial system, with its traditional channels, favors the dollar, something cryptocurrencies could upend. Designing a digital currency to compete with the digital renminbi would keep pace with a European proposal for a digital euro.

Deterrence by Punishment

Cross-domain retaliation offers additional tools for punishment. Diplomatic countermeasures include expulsions of select foreign government officials, while information countermeasures could include cyber actions that fall short of use of force. Options could also include financial sanctions on Chinese state–owned enterprises, increased law enforcement actions against Chinese companies, such as requiring monthly audits of companies operating overseas, and a mechanism similar to the EU human rights sanctions regime. Existing proposals suggest financial and diplomatic sanctions, such as freezing the assets of or imposing diplomatic sanctions on relevant officials. A Canadian commentary goes farther, with a suggestion to ban Huawei from national 5G wireless networks on national security grounds, register and scrutinize all research and development funding from China and sever those that aim to steal intellectual property, and withdraw from the AIIB as explicit counter–economic coercion measures.

Deterrence by punishment is most commonly proposed in the economic realm, answering the coercive action in kind. Economic countermeasure options include retaliatory tariffs, export and import bans, market access restrictions (including quotas and trading licenses), a truncating of intellectual property rights, recovery of losses, trade and investment restrictions, divestment in certain sectors, and restrictions on access to public procurement markets.

Countering economic coercion with responsive, proportionate action is the most frequent proposal. An intuitive suggestion is to extract a cost equal to the cost of the coercive act as an offset to distribute to affected producers. However, many assert that this would announce that countries were no longer bound by Annex 2 of the World Trade Organization's Uruguay Round Agreement, which obligates countries to follow the multilateral dispute resolution process and agree not to take unilateral action. Others still suggest that sanctions or the private threat of them from an economy with leverage over China like the United States may have some deterrent effect, or that countries could impose levies on products the Chinese government values, such as one politician's proposal concerning Australian iron ore.

China's "dual circulation" (双循环) strategy and its efforts to insulate itself from dependence on the global market seem to anticipate this, or aim to proactively minimize the risk, along with sanctions law.

Conclusion

These recommendations may seem overwhelming. Many of them, particularly domestic reforms in support of democratic goals, feel impossible to accomplish. But if we have learned anything since 2016, it's that the zeitgeist can change on a dime. The story of the Covid pandemic, and how it affected the world's understanding of China, is testament to the reality that facts do matter and that long-held assumptions can be changed. Democracies, and people who value them, should take heart. The path laid out to minimize the effects of China's authoritarian economic statecraft is clear. All that's left is getting down to business.

ACKNOWLEDGMENTS

This book is a culmination of years of research, reporting, and thinking. But even more than that, it's a testament to the many brilliant and kind people whom I have been lucky enough to get to know along the way. The book would not exist without my sharp and upbeat agent, Gillian MacKenzie, and my incisive editor at HarperCollins, Jonathan Jao. I am so grateful for their encouragement, patience, and, above all, the faith they placed in my ideas.

There are many excellent journalists, academics, and researchers whose work has helped inform and shape my ideas, including Zach Dorfman, Joanna Chiu, Joshua Eisenman, Peter Mattis, Alex Joske, Anne-Marie Brady, Vicky Xiuzhong Xu, James Jiann-Hua To, James Palmer, Matt Schrader, Chris Buckley, Dexter Tiff Roberts, Michael Forsythe, Li Yuan, Nick McKenzie, Erika Kinetz, Peter Martin, and many more.

The world owes an enormous debt to the courageous journalists and citizen journalists who were reporting on the ground during the earliest weeks of the Covid-19 pandemic in China: Gao Yu, Xiao Hui, Ding Gang, Bao Zhiming, Alice Su, Emily Feng, Gerry Shih, Jeremy Page, Chao Deng, Zhang Zhan, Chen Qiushi, and many others. Their careful and compassionate reporting informed my understanding both of life in Wuhan during the pandemic and of the response of Chinese authorities.

Friends, including Mara Hvistendahl, Nick Monaco, Charles Edel, Jonathan Swan, Sebastian Kjeldtoft, and Jonas Parello-Plesner gave generously of their time by reading portions of the manuscript and offering insightful feedback. Isaiah Schrader, Dana Lutenegger, Matt Schiavenza, Emily Walz, and Miranda Jarrett assisted with research, drafting, and citations; their remarkable skill, talent, and hard work saved my sanity on multiple occasions.

Zach Dorfman and I together reported and published for Axios the story of suspected Chinese intelligence operative Christine Fang and her activities in California and elsewhere. Zach graciously allowed me to use our reporting to write a more detailed narrative version of that investigation for chapter 4. Joshua Eisenman shared with me his groundbreaking research and publications on relations between the Chinese Communist Party and Ethiopia's former governing party. These were invaluable to me as I wrote chapter 6, which looks at WHO chief Tedros Adhanom Ghebreyesus's political career in his home country of Ethiopia. Emily Walz and I worked together on the final chapter; her expertise in theory and policy contributed greatly to the text there. Any shortcomings are mine alone.

My career as a journalist has spanned nearly a decade, and I am deeply grateful for the inspiration, support, and training I've received along the way. *Foreign Policy* magazine was my first home in DC, and I benefited greatly from a host of talented editors and colleagues there. David Wertime gave me my first chance at journalism and taught me, with the patience of a saint, how to write an article. Ben Pauker taught me how to dream up big new ideas. Sharon Weinberger believed in me and showed me how to become the journalist I am today. Isaac Stone Fish shared some of the most useful advice I've ever received as a journalist. James Palmer's winning combination of compassion and brilliance makes him one of the best editors I have ever known, and I feel lucky also to be able to call him a friend.

Axios has been a true serendipity. Working there has been one of the most unexpectedly joyful and rejuvenating experiences of my life. Alison Snyder, Sara Kaulani Goo, Nick Johnston, Mike Allen, Margaret Talev, Jonathan Swan, Dave Lawler, Shawna Chen, Sara Fischer, Ina Fried, Felix Salmon, and so many others aren't just talented colleagues; they are all, to a person, wonderful human beings. Alison's kindness, compassion, and gentle intelligence have made a huge difference in my life, and I consider myself incredibly fortunate to be able to work with her. Axios managers granted me four crucial months of book leave in the summer of 2021—a remarkable gift to an employee of less than eighteen months. I am grateful for the trust they have continually placed in me.

A special thanks to G., wherever you are. I hope you found some apple pie.

The past few years haven't always been easy—working full-time, parenting a young child, moving abroad, and writing a book all at the same time is a poor life plan—but I've been blessed with friends who have encouraged me, offered advice, and made me laugh. A heartfelt thank-you to Felicia Sonmez, Vanessa Larson, Christina Larson, Alexa Olesen, Tabitha Mallory, Jane Tang, Azeem Ibrahim, Julie Zauzmer Weil, Emily Rauhala, Emily Tamkin, Johanna Smallwood, Julia King, Megan Maluatoga, Mei Fong, and Melissa Chan.

My deepest love, gratitude, admiration, and affection go to my mom and dad. Having two parents who love you is like waking up to Christmas every morning. Their support at key times in my life has made all the difference. I am certain that without their unconditional love, this book would not exist. If I can model the love and selflessness that they have shown, I will consider my life a success. Everything else is window dressing.

Finally, this book would not have been possible without Jemima, Fara, and R., whose time and care gave me the hours to write.

NOTES

Introduction

ix   There are more viruses on earth: Katherine J. Wu, "There Are More Viruses than Stars in the Universe. Why Do Only Some Infect Us?" *National Geographic*, April 15, 2020, https://www.nationalgeographic.com/science/article/factors-allow-viruses-infect-humans-coronavirus.

ix   Wei Guixian thought she was coming down with a cold: Jeremy Page, Wenxin Fan, and Natasha Khan, "How It All Started: China's Early Coronavirus Missteps," *Wall Street Journal*, March 6, 2020, https://www.wsj.com/articles/how-it-all-started-chinas-early-coronavirus-missteps-11583508932.

ix   On December 16, a sixty-five-year-old man: Page, Fan, and Khan, "How It All Started."

x   health officials in Wuhan learned: Gerry Shih, Emily Rauhala, and Lena H. Sun, "Early Missteps and State Secrecy in China Probably Allowed the Coronavirus to Spread Farther and Faster," *Washington Post*, February 1, 2020, https://www.washingtonpost.com/world/2020/02/01/early-missteps-state-secrecy-china-likely-allowed-coronavirus-spread-farther-faster/.

x   a delay that would ultimately have immense consequences: Shih, Rauhala, and Sun, "Early Missteps and State Secrecy in China Probably Allowed the Coronavirus to Spread Farther and Faster."

x   "If I had known what was to happen": Lily Kuo, "Coronavirus: Wuhan Doctor Speaks Out Against Authorities," *The Guardian*, March 11, 2020, https://www.theguardian.com/world/2020/mar/11/coronavirus-wuhan-doctor-ai-fen-speaks-out-against-authorities.

x   eight doctors were called in for questioning: "Several Arrested in China for Spreading False Information About Pneumonia Cases," Channel NewsAsia, January 2, 2020, YouTube, https://www.youtube.com/watch?v=hTpwyMZTh6g.

x   the World Health Organization's China office: Shih, Rauhala, and Sun, "Early Missteps and State Secrecy in China Probably Allowed the Coronavirus to Spread Farther and Faster."

x   began to screen passengers arriving from Wuhan: Mandy Zuo et al., "Hong Kong Takes Emergency Measures as Mystery 'Pneumonia' Infects Dozens in China's Wuhan City," *South China Morning Post*, December 31, 2019, https://www.scmp.com/news/china/politics/article/3044050/mystery-illness-hits-chinas-wuhan-city-nearly-30-hospitalised.

xi   stop testing and destroy samples: Gao Yu et al., "How Early Signs of the Coronavirus Were Spotted, Spread and Throttled in China," *Straits Times*, February 28, 2020, https://www.straitstimes.com/asia/east-asia/how-early-signs-of-the-coronavirus-were-spotted-spread-and-throttled-in-china.

xi   Chinese president Xi Jinping began directly managing: Amy Qin, "China's Leader, Under Fire, Says He Led Coronavirus Fight Early On," *New York Times*, February 15, 2020, https://www.nytimes.com/2020/02/15/world/asia/xi-china-coronavirus.html.

xi   "no clear evidence" of human-to-human transmission: @WHO, "Preliminary Investigations Conducted by the Chinese Authorities Have Found No Clear Evidence of Human-to-Human Transmission of the Novel #coronavirus (2019-nCoV) identified in #Wuhan, #China ▇▇." Twitter, January 14, 2020, 6:18 am, twitter.com/WHO/status/1217043229427761152.

xi   "Everything was down to not collecting cases": Shih, Rauhala, and Sun, "Early Missteps and State Secrecy in China Probably Allowed the Coronavirus to Spread Farther and Faster."

xi   a patient in Thailand tested positive for the virus: "Novel Coronavirus—Thailand (ex-China)," World Health Organization, January 14, 2020, https://www.who.int/emergencies/disease-outbreak-news/item/2020-DON234.

xi   Two days later, a person infected with the virus: Bethany Allen-Ebrahimian, "Timeline: The Early Days of China's Coronavirus Outbreak and Cover-Up," Axios, March 19, 2020, https://www.axios.com/2020/03/18/timeline-the-early-days-of-chinas-coronavirus-outbreak-and-cover-up.

xi   On January 19, Beijing dispatched epidemiologists: Allen-Ebrahimian, "Timeline: The Early Days of China's Coronavirus Outbreak and Cover-Up."

xi   Zhong Nanshan, a leading pulmonologist: Lily Kuo, "China Confirms Human-to-Human Transmission of Coronavirus," *The Guardian*, January 21, 2020, https://www.theguardian.com /world/2020/jan/20/coronavirus-spreads-to-beijing-as-china-confirms-new-cases.

xi   authorities announced lockdowns in Wuhan: "Coronavirus Death Toll Jumps to 41 in China as Lockdown Expands to Unprecedented 36 Million People," Associated Press, January 25, 2020, https://www.chicagotribune.com/nation-world/ct-nw-china-coronavirus-wuhan-china-20200124 -cqweccz5tzhxzdg3rse25puxqa-story.html.

xi   More than five million residents had already fled: Josephine Ma and Zhuang Pinghui, "5 Million Left Wuhan Before Lockdown, 1,000 New Coronavirus Cases Expected in City," *South China Morning Post*, January 26, 2020, https://www.scmp.com/news/china/society/article/3047720 /chinese-premier-li-keqiang-head-coronavirus-crisis-team-outbreak.

xi   "we have passed the golden period of control and prevention": " 'This Time I'm Scared': Experts Fear Too Late for China Virus Lockdown," Agence France-Presse, January 24, 2020, https:// www.yahoo.com/now/time-im-scared-experts-fear-too-china-virus-103855664.html.

xii   cases could have been reduced by 95 percent: Shengjie Lai et al., "Effect of Non-pharmaceutical Interventions for Containing the COVID-19 Outbreak: An Observational and Modelling Study," *Nature* 585 (March 3, 2020), https://www.nature.com/articles/s41586-020-22 93-x#citeas.

xii   "reactions that are probably going to be disproportionate": Simon Kuper, "Why Does Davos Man Get It So Wrong?" *Financial Times*, January 21, 2021, https://www.ft.com/content/a9395f9b -33de-45f6-a5ff-249d578676a7.

xiii   "Openness is a trademark of today's China": "Vice-Premier Renews China's Commitment to Globalism," World Economic Forum, January 21, 2020, https://www.weforum.org/press/2020/01 /vice-premier-renews-china-s-commitment-to-globalism/.

xiii   On Friday, January 24, the forum's final day: Allen-Ebrahimian, "Timeline: The Early Days of China's Coronavirus Outbreak and Cover-Up."

xiii   He decided he needed to warn colleagues: Zhuang Pinghui, "Dr. Li Wenliang: Who Was He and How Did He Become a Coronavirus 'Hero'?" *South China Morning Post*, February 7, 2020, https://www.scmp.com/news/china/society/article/3049561/dr-li-wenliang-who-was-he-and-how -did-he-become-coronavirus-hero.

xiii   eight doctors who were called to the local police bureau: Shih, Rauhala, and Sun, "Early Missteps and State Secrecy in China Probably Allowed the Coronavirus to Spread Farther and Faster."

xiii   "making false comments": "Li Wenliang: Coronavirus Kills Chinese Whistleblower Doctor," BBC News, February 7, 2020, https://www.bbc.com/news/world-asia-china-51403795.

xiii   "believed this virus was not confirmed to be SARS": "He Warned of Coronavirus. Here's What He Told Us Before He Died," *New York Times*, February 7, 2020, https://www.nytimes.com /2020/02/07/world/asia/Li-Wenliang-china-coronavirus.html.

xiv   authorities completely closed off transportation: Emma Graham-Harrison and Lily Kuo, "China's Coronavirus Lockdown Strategy: Brutal but Effective," *The Guardian*, March 19, 2020, https://www.theguardian.com/world/2020/mar/19/chinas-coronavirus-lockdown-strategy-brutal -but-effective.

xiv   major cities in Hubei Province were locked down: Vivian Wang and Sui-Lee Wee, "China to Ease Coronavirus Lockdown on Hubei 2 Months After Imposing It," *New York Times*, March 24, 2020, https://www.nytimes.com/2020/03/24/world/asia/china-coronavirus-lockdown-hubei.html.

xiv   The hashtag #LiWenliangDies: Barbara Demick, "China Declares Victory over Both the Coronavirus and Critics of the Communist Party at the Biggest Political Event of the Year," *The New Yorker*, May 22, 2020, https://www.newyorker.com/news/daily-comment/china-declares-victory -over-both-the-coronavirus-and-critics-of-the-communist-party-at-the-biggest-political-event-of-the -year.

xv   "The delay of China to act is probably responsible": David Cyranoski, "What China's Coronavirus Response Can Teach the Rest of the World," *Nature*, March 17, 2020, https://www.nature .com/articles/d41586-020-00741-x.

xv   the party's "Chernobyl moment": Filip Noubel, "Is the Coronavirus Epidemic China's 'Chernobyl Moment'?" GlobalVoices, February 14, 2020, https://globalvoices.org/2020/02/14/is -the-coronavirus-epidemic-chinas-chernobyl-moment/.

xv   determined to wage a total "people's war" on Covid-19: Steven Lee Myers et al., "Power,

Patriotism and 1.4 Billion People: How China Beat the Virus and Roared Back," *New York Times*, February 5, 2021, https://www.nytimes.com/2021/02/05/world/asia/china-covid-economy.html.

xvi massive new centralized quarantine facilities: Myers et al., "Power, Patriotism and 1.4 Billion People."

xvi The government developed smartphone apps: Raymond Zhong and Paul Mozur, "To Tame Coronavirus, Mao-Style Social Control Blankets China," *New York Times*, February 15, 2020, https://www.nytimes.com/2020/02/15/business/china-coronavirus-lockdown.html.

xvi true number of Covid-19 cases was somewhat questionable: Ken Moritsugu, "How Accurate Are China's Virus Numbers?" *NewsHour*, PBS, April 1, 2020, https://www.pbs.org/newshour/world/how-accurate-are-chinas-virus-numbers.

xvi astonishment at the virus's virtual disappearance: Cyranoski, "What China's Coronavirus Response Can Teach the Rest of the World."

xvi "most ambitious, agile, and aggressive disease containment effort": *Report of the WHO-China Joint Mission on Coronavirus Disease 2019 (COVID-19)*, World Health Organization, February 16–24, 2020, https://www.who.int/docs/default-source/coronaviruse/who-china-joint-mission-on-covid-19-final-report.pdf.

xvi China's army of censors went into overdrive: Raymond Zhong et al., "No 'Negative' News: How China Censored the Coronavirus," *New York Times* and ProPublica, December 19, 2020, https://www.nytimes.com/2020/12/19/technology/china-coronavirus-censorship.html.

xvii highest case count in the world: COVID Data Tracker, Centers for Disease Control and Prevention, n.d., https://covid.cdc.gov/covid-data-tracker/#datatracker-home.

xvii withdrew the United States from the World Health Organization: Zachary Cohen et al., "Trump Administration Begins Formal Withdrawal from World Health Organization," CNN, July 8, 2020, https://edition.cnn.com/2020/07/07/politics/us-withdrawing-world-health-organization/index.html.

xvii disparaged his own top adviser: Kaitlan Collins and Kevin Liptak, "Trump Trashes Fauci and Makes Baseless Coronavirus Claims in Campaign Call," CNN, October 20, 2020, https://www.cnn.com/2020/10/19/politics/donald-trump-anthony-fauci-coronavirus/index.html.

xvii "We used to look to the U.S. for democratic governance inspiration": Hannah Beech, "'I Feel Sorry for Americans': A Baffled World Watches the U.S.," *New York Times*, November 14, 2020, https://www.nytimes.com/2020/09/25/world/asia/trump-united-states.html.

xviii The 2008 financial crisis was a "decisive moment": @elyratner, Twitter, https://twitter.com/elyratner/status/1237719334413361152 (since deleted).

xviii "when they quarantined people, they were spraying shit in the streets": Greg James, "'I Want No Smoke with the Chinese': Cardi B Wins Fans in China with Coronavirus Rants," China Project, March 26, 2020, https://thechinaproject.com/2020/03/26/i-want-no-smoke-with-the-chinese-cardi-b-wins-fans-in-china-with-coronavirus-rants/.

xviii "Daring to fight and daring to win": Vivian Wang, "China's Coronavirus Battle Is Waning. Its Propaganda Fight Is Not," *New York Times*, April 8, 2020, https://www.nytimes.com/2020/04/08/world/asia/coronavirus-china-narrative.html

xviii By year's end, more than three hundred thousand Americans: Rashida Kamal, "300,000 Americans Have Died from Covid-19. This Is the Tragic Story in Numbers," *The Guardian*, December 14, 2020, https://www.theguardian.com/world/2020/dec/14/300000-americans-died-covid-facts-figures.

xviii Chinese people began to feel a strong sense of superiority: Hiroshi Murayama, "Chinese Netizens Flip from Anger to Praise for Virus Response," Nikkei Asia, March 8, 2020, https://asia.nikkei.com/Spotlight/Comment/Chinese-netizens-flip-from-anger-to-praise-for-virus-response.

xix "profound adjustment in the international balance of power": 中国共产党第十九届中央委员会第五次全体会议公报 ("Communiqué of the Fifth Plenary Session of the Nineteenth Central Committee of the Communist Party of China"), Xinhua, October 29, 2020, http://www.xinhuanet.com/politics/2020-10/29/c_1126674147.htm.

xix only major economy in the world to expand in 2020: Jonathan Cheng, "China Is the Only Major Economy to Report Economic Growth for 2020," *Wall Street Journal*, January 18, 2021, https://www.wsj.com/articles/china-is-the-only-major-economy-to-report-economic-growth-for-2020-11610936187.

xix "Western media said that the coronavirus would be China's Chernobyl": https://mp.weixin.qq.com/s/erCJHZVLEtnZ4wWbkgij3g.

xx "state manipulation of international economic activities": William Norris, *Chinese Economic Statecraft: Commercial Actors, Grand Strategy, and State Control* (Ithaca, NY: Cornell University Press, 2016), 3.

xx   It's the international extension of what some scholars: Margaret Pearson, Meg Rithmire, and Kellee S. Tsai, "Party-State Capitalism in China," *Current History* 120, no. 827 (2021): 207–13.

xxiii   The rise of neoliberalism: The term *neoliberalism* means different things to different people: There are a number of different ways of expressing the basic concept relayed by the word *neoliberalism*; all are imperfect. I've chosen the definition described in *The Great Democracy*, a 2019 book by Ganesh Sitaraman, a legal scholar at Vanderbilt University and a longtime adviser to Senator Elizabeth Warren. Sitaraman defines *neoliberalism* as deregulation, privatization, liberalization, and austerity and describes it as a system in which "individuals are on their own and should be responsible for themselves. Instead of governments, corporations, and unions balancing the interests of all stakeholders, the primary regulator of social interests should be the marketplace." Neoliberalism has leftist overtones; I would prefer a more neutral term but haven't found a better one. To distinguish, in brief, the terms *libertarian* and *neoliberal*, both of which enshrine the primacy of the free market, I'll turn to a useful formulation by online commentator Alexander Albrecht: "Neoliberalism wants to aim the wealth generated by markets at specific social goals using some government mechanism, whilst libertarianism focuses on letting the wealth created by free markets flow where it pleases."

xxiii   privatization, deregulation, and minimal government intervention in markets: Ganesh Sitaraman, *The Great Democracy: How to Fix Our Politics, Unrig the Economy, and Unite America* (New York: Basic Books, 2019), 9–26.

xxiii   "By joining the WTO, China is not simply": Bob Davis and Lingling Wei, *Superpower Showdown: How the Battle Between Trump and Xi Threatens a New Cold War* (New York: Harper Business, 2020), 83.

xxiv   "Today, people often speak in the language of markets": Sitaraman, *The Great Democracy*, 27.

xxv   "intense strategic competition with China": Bethany Allen-Ebrahimian and Dave Lawler, "Biden Holds First Call as President with China's Xi Jinping," Axios, February 11, 2021, https://www.axios.com/2021/02/11/biden-holds-first-call-as-president-with-chinas-xi-jinping.

xxvi   Growing awareness of the political demands: Margaret M. Pearson, Meg Rithmire, and Kellee S. Tsai, "The New China Shock: How Beijing's Party-State Capitalism Is Changing the Global Economy," *Foreign Affairs*, December 8, 2022, https://www.foreignaffairs.com/china/new-china-shock.

xxviii   negative views of China and its leaders reached historic levels: Laura Silver, Kat Devlin, and Christine Huang, "Unfavorable Views of China Reach Historic Highs in Many Countries," Pew Research Center, October 6, 2020, www.pewresearch.org/global/2020/10/06/unfavorable-views-of-china-reach-historic-highs-in-many-countries/.

xxviii   China also saw a rise in xenophobia: Vivian Wang and Amy Qin, "As Coronavirus Fades in China, Nationalism and Xenophobia Flare," *New York Times*, April 16, 2020, https://www.nytimes.com/2020/04/16/world/asia/coronavirus-china-nationalism.html.

xxviii   Pew Research Center found that unfavorable sentiment toward China: Laura Silver, Christine Huang, and Laura Clancy, "How Global Public Opinion of China Has Shifted in the Xi Era," Pew Research Center, September 28, 2022, https://www.pewresearch.org/global/2022/09/28/how-global-public-opinion-of-china-has-shifted-in-the-xi-era/.

1: The Rise of China's Authoritarian Economic Statecraft

1   a very convincing Willie Wonka: Glenn Harris, "Australia's Willie Wonka of Wine, Chester Osborne [*sic*] of d'Arenberg Wine and the McLaren Vale," JustLuxe, May 14, 2020, https://www.justluxe.com/lifestyle/dining/feature-1969955.php.

1   The company was founded by his great-grandfather: D'Arenberg company, https://www.darenberg.com.au/.

1   Osborn's mother carried him around the winery: Rebecca Gibb, "Q&A: Chester Osborn, d'Arenberg Winery, McLaren Vale," Wine-Searcher, July 23, 2012, https://www.wine-searcher.com/m/2012/07/chester-osborn-q-and-a.

1   "the best restaurant in Australia": Lucy Shaw, "Osborn to Open 'Australia's Best Restaurant,'" Drinks Business, July 25, 2016, https://www.thedrinksbusiness.com/2016/07/chester-osborn-to-open-australias-best-restaurant/.

1   certainly achieved national prominence: Jane Llewellyn and John Neylon, "The Great d'Arenberg Cube Debate," *Adelaide Review*, March 29, 2018, https://www.adelaidereview.com.au/latest/2018/03/29/the-darenberg-cube-just-another-big-thing-or-a-work-of-art/.

1   multimillion-dollar Salvador Dalí art exhibition: "Dalí at d'Arenberg: Salvador Dalí Exhibition," d'Arenberg wine company, https://www.darenberg.com.au/dali-at-darenberg.

1   "China was our biggest market": Author interview with Chester Osborn, October 2021.

2   the fifth largest market: Vicky [no surname], "Deciphering the Chinese Wine Market," Cellar Asia, November 29, 2019, https://cellar.asia/wine/china-wine-market-analysis/.

2   Australia's wine exports to China had exploded: Trish Gleeson, Donkor Addai, and Liangyue Cao, *Australian Wine in China: Impact of China's Anti-Dumping Duties*, PDF of report, Australian Bureau of Agricultural and Resource Economics and Sciences, July 2021, https://daff.ent.sirsidynix .net.au/client/en_AU/search/asset/1032321/0.

2   the company made 11 percent of its sales: Author interview with Chester Osborn.

2   "a lot of thirsty people there": Cara Waters, "'A Lot of Thirsty People over There': Australia Shipping 234 Million Bottles of Wine a Year to China," *Sydney Morning Herald*, November 11, 2018, https://www.smh.com.au/business/small-business/a-lot-of-thirsty-people-over-there-australia -shipping-234-million-bottles-of-wine-a-year-to-china-20181105-p50e51.html.

2   the Chinese government permitted a team of WHO scientists: *Report of the WHO-China Joint Mission on Coronavirus Disease 2019 (COVID-19)*.

3   "we're equally vulnerable in future": Selam Gebrekidan et al., "In Hunt for Virus Source, W.H.O. Let China Take Charge," *New York Times*, November 2, 2020, https://www.nytimes.com /2020/11/02/world/who-china-coronavirus.html.

3   the Chinese government continued to stymie researchers: Gebrekidan et al., "In Hunt for Virus Source, W.H.O. Let China Take Charge."

3   2.5 million infections and 177,500 deaths: Andrew Probyn, "Scott Morrison Lobbies Donald Trump, Others for Greater World Health Oversight to Prevent Another Pandemic," Australian Broadcasting Corporation, April 22, 2020, https://www.abc.net.au/news/2020-04-22/morrison-to -push-for-anti-pandemic-inspection-powers/12173806.

3   On April 23, he publicly called for an investigation: Kirsty Needham, "Australia to Pursue Coronavirus Investigation at World Health Assembly," Reuters, April 23, 2020, https://www.reuters .com/article/us-health-coronavirus-australia-china/australia-to-pursue-coronavirus-investigation-at -world-health-assembly-idUSKCN2251G7.

3   be given "weapons inspector" powers: Andrew Tillett and Phillip Coorey, "PM Wants Weapons Inspector-Like Powers for WHO," *Australian Financial Review*, April 22, 2020, https://www .afr.com/politics/federal/pm-wants-weapons-inspector-like-powers-for-world-health-organisation -20200422-p54m5x.

3   "We'd like the world to be safer when it comes to viruses": "Press Conference—Australian Parliament House, ACT," Australian Department of the Prime Minister and Cabinet, April 23, 2020, https://pmtranscripts.pmc.gov.au/release/transcript-42793.

3   "so-called independent inquiry": Colin Packham, "Australia Says All WHO Members Should Back Coronavirus Inquiry," Reuters, April 22, 2020, https://www.reuters.com/article/us-health -coronavirus-australia/australia-says-all-who-members-should-back-coronavirus-inquiry-idUS KCN225041.

3   boycott of Australian goods might be forthcoming: Andrew Tillett, "China Consumer Backlash Looms over Morrison's Coronavirus Probe," *Australian Financial Review*, April 26, 2020, https://www.afr.com/politics/federal/china-consumer-backlash-looms-over-morrison-s-coronavirus -probe-20200423-p54mpl.

4   denounced the statement as "economic coercion": Andrew Tillett, "Australia Hits Back at China's 'Economic Coercion,'" *Australian Financial Review*, April 27, 2020, https://www.afr.com /politics/federal/payne-blasts-beijing-s-economic-coercion-over-virus-probe-push-20200427-p54nig.

4   China banned meat: Kirsty Needham and Colin Packham, "China Halts Beef Imports from Four Australian Firms as COVID-19 Spat Sours Trade," Reuters, May 12, 2020, https://www .reuters.com/article/us-australia-china-beef/china-halts-beef-imports-from-four-australian-firms-as -covid-19-spat-sours-trade-idUSKBN22O0FB.

4   Then it placed 80 percent tariffs on Australian barley: Dan Conifer, "China Imposes 80pc Tariff on Australian Barley for Next Five Years amid Global Push for Coronavirus Investigation," Australian Broadcasting Corporation, May 18, 2020, https://www.abc.net.au/news/2020-05-18 /china-to-impose-tariffs-on-australian-barley/12261108.

4   Soon, more import barriers followed: "Timeline: Tension Between China and Australia over Commodities Trade," Reuters, November 4, 2020, https://www.reuters.com/article/us-australia -trade-china-commodities-tim-idUKKBN27K0FH.

4   announced preliminary anti-dumping tariffs: "China Slaps Up to 200% Tariffs on Australian Wine," BBC News, November 27, 2020, https://www.bbc.com/news/business-55097100.

4   tariffs were later confirmed by Chinese authorities: "China Sets Duties on Australia Wine for 5 Years as Ties Sour," Bloomberg, March 26, 2021, https://www.bloomberg.com/news

/articles/2021-03-26/china-s-tariffs-on-australian-wine-to-last-5-years-as-ties-sour?leadSource=uver
ify%20wall.

4   one of China's "Fourteen Grievances" against Australia: Jonathan Kearsley, "China Shows Official List of Reasons for Anger with Australia," 9News, November 18, 2020, https://www.9news .com.au/national/china-australia-tensions-beijing-government-grievance-list-with-canberra /adc10554-e4e9-4a19-970e-81949501a1ad.

4   exported just $9 million worth of wine to China: Byron Kaye, "Australia Wine Exports to China Fall 96% as Tariffs Turn Producers Away," Reuters, April 28, 2021, https://www.reuters com/article/china-australia-wine/corrected-australia-wine-exports-to-china-fall-96-as-tariffs-turn -producers-away-idUSL1N2MM05B.

4   estimated to have cost Australia $19 billion: Daniel Hurst, "Australia Cannot Walk Away from Its Free Trade Agreement with China, Labor Says," *The Guardian*, December 2, 2020, https:// www.theguardian.com/australia-news/2020/dec/03/australia-cannot-walk-away-from-its-free -trade-agreement-with-china-labor-says.

7   levied sanctions against International Criminal Court chief prosecutor: Laurel Wamsley, "Trump Administration Sanctions ICC Prosecutor Investigating Alleged U.S. War Crimes," NPR, September 2, 2020, https://www.npr.org/2020/09/02/908896108/trump-administration-sanctions -icc-prosecutor-investigating-alleged-u-s-war-crim.

7   the Biden administration ended these sanctions: Antony J. Blinken, Secretary of State, "Ending Sanctions and Visa Restrictions Against Personnel of the International Criminal Court," Press Statement, U.S. Department of State, April 2, 2021, https://www.state.gov/ending-sanctions -and-visa-restrictions-against-personnel-of-the-international-criminal-court/.

8   the "primary regulator of social interests is the marketplace": Sitaraman, *The Great Democracy*, 3.

8   responded by imposing a five-year ban: Sharon Waxman, "China Bans Work with Film Studios," *Washington Post*, November 1, 1997, https://www.washingtonpost.com/archive/lifestyle/1997 /11/01/china-bans-work-with-film-studios/9f3a23e3-4d83-4749-898c-bd1fef276f03/.

9   it had been a "stupid mistake": David Barboza and Brooks Barnes, "How China Won the Keys to Disney's Magic Kingdom," *New York Times*, June 14, 2016, https://www.nytimes.com /2016/06/15/business/international/china-disney.html.

9   Chinese cinemas packed with moviegoers: Zhang Rui, "China Officially the World's Biggest Film Market," *China News*, October 20, 2020, http://www.china.org.cn/arts/2020-10/20/con tent_76824488.htm.

9   "For 10 years, you haven't seen any bad Chinese guys": Bethany Allen-Ebrahimian, "China Is Censoring Hollywood's Imagination," Axios, September 1, 2020, https://www.axios.com/2020 /09/01/china-censor-hollywood-films.

9   *World War Z* changed the location: Lucas Shaw, "Fearing Chinese Censors, Paramount Changes 'World War Z,'" The Wrap, March 31, 2013, https://www.thewrap.com/fearing-chinese -censors-paramount-changes-world-war-z-exclusive-83316/.

9   "an origin story for my fictional pandemic": Max Brooks, "China Barred My Dystopian Novel About How Its System Enables Epidemics," *Washington Post*, February 27, 2020, https:// www.washingtonpost.com/outlook/china-barred-my-dystopian-novel-about-how-its-system -enables-epidemics/2020/02/27/cc0446f0-58e5-11ea-9000-f3cffee23036_story.html.

10   "we don't have Chinese villains in Hollywood films": Allen-Ebrahimian, "China Is Censoring Hollywood's Imagination."

10   NBA is estimated to have lost two hundred million dollars: Kevin Arnovitz, "Inside the Longest, Most Unpredictable Year in NBA History," ESPN, September 29, 2020, https://www .espn.com/nba/story/_/id/29992879/nba-year-review-hong-kong-kobe-bryant-zion-williamson -pandemic-bubble.

11   Norwegian salmon exports did not return: "Norway Signs Deal to Help Resume Salmon Exports to China," Reuters, May 23, 2017, https://www.reuters.com/article/us-norway-china-salmon /norway-signs-deal-to-help-resume-salmon-exports-to-china-idUSKBN18J0YT.

11   "attaches high importance to China's core interests": Sewell Chan, "Norway and China Restore Ties, 6 Years After Nobel Prize Dispute," December 19, 2016, https://www.nytimes .com/2016/12/19/world/europe/china-norway-nobel-liu-xiaobo.html.

11   "China's firm determination against any external intervention": 社评：挪威用6年搞懂了" 不应惹中国" ("Editorial: It took Norway 6 years to figure out not to mess with China"), *Global Times*, December 20, 2016, https://opinion.huanqiu.com/article/9CaKrnJZfNy.

11   Chinese authorities said the bananas had an insect infestation: "Philippines Seeks New

Markets amid Sea Dispute with China," Reuters, May 17, 2012, https://www.reuters.com/article/uk-philippines-china/philippines-seeks-new-markets-amid-sea-dispute-with-china-idUSLNE84G02520120517.

11   "we should have been diversifying our exports": "Philippines Seeks New Markets Amid Sea Dispute with China."

12   punish numerous sectors of the South Korean economy: Jack Kim, "South Korea, U.S. to Deploy THAAD Missile Defense, Drawing China Rebuke," Reuters, July 7, 2016, https://www.reuters.com/article/us-southkorea-usa-thaad/south-korea-u-s-to-deploy-thaad-missile-defense-drawing-china-rebuke-idUSKCN0ZO084.

12   South Korean retail conglomerate Lotte Mart's: Cynthia Kim and Hyunjoo Jin, "With China Dream Shattered over Missile Land Deal, Lotte Faces Costly Overhaul," Reuters, October 24, 2017, https://www.reuters.com/article/us-lotte-china-analysis/with-china-dream-shattered-over-missile-land-deal-lotte-faces-costly-overhaul-idUSKBN1CT35Y.

12   deal with the Chinese market largely alone: Kim and Jin, "With China Dream Shattered over Missile Land Deal, Lotte Faces Costly Overhaul."

12   celebrities cut ties with H&M: "Nike, H&M face China Fury over Xinjiang Cotton 'Concerns,'" BBC News, March 25, 2021, https://www.bbc.com/news/world-asia-china-56519411.

12   H&M's sales in China dropped 23 percent: "H&M: Fashion Giant Sees China Sales Slump After Xinjiang Boycott," BBC News, July 2, 2021, https://www.bbc.com/news/business-57691415.

13   not be permitted to enter China's airspace: Lasley Lui, Regina Chen, and Gloria Li, "Clipping Their Wings: How White Terror Gripped Hong Kong's Aviation Industry," *Hong Kong Free Press*, January 4, 2020, https://hongkongfp.com/2020/01/04/clipping-wings-white-terror-gripped-hong-kongs-aviation-industry/.

13   China threatened retaliation against Czech companies: Raphael Satter and Nick Carey, "China Threatened to Harm Czech Companies over Taiwan Visit: Letter," Reuters, February 19, 2020, https://www.reuters.com/article/us-china-czech-taiwan-idUSKBN20D0G3.

13   suspended a $23.8 million order of the Czech-made pianos: Yin Yeping, "Piano Firms Expect Hit After Czech Senate Speaker's Taiwan Visit," *Global Times*, September 7, 2020, https://www.globaltimes.cn/content/1200167.shtml.

13   Klavir Petrof sold around five thousand pianos in China: "Výrobce klavírů Petrof cítí napětí v česko-čínských vztazích [Piano Manufacturer Petrof Feels Tense in Czech-Chinese Relations]," OperaPlus, January 1, 2020, https://operaplus.cz/vyrobce-klaviru-petrof-citi-napeti-v-cesko-cinskych-vztazich/.

13   A Czech billionaire intervened: Bethany Allen-Ebrahimian, "Czech Billionaire Saves Piano Company Threatened by Chinese Retaliation," Axios, September 22, 2020, https://www.axios.com/2020/09/22/czech-piano-china.

13   forty-three of the fifty-three countries that had expressed support for Beijing: Dave Lawler, "The 53 Countries Supporting China's Crackdown on Hong Kong," Axios, July 3, 2020, https://www.axios.com/2020/07/02/countries-supporting-china-hong-kong-law.

14   publicly distanced itself from the Tibetan spiritual leader: "Mongolia Pledges to Halt Visits by the Dalai Lama," *South China Morning Post*, December 22, 2016, https://www.scmp.com/news/china/diplomacy-defence/article/2056498/mongolia-pledges-halt-visits-dalai-lama.

14   "part of a near-global collapse in diplomatic capacity": Edward Wong, "Mongolia, with Deep Ties to Dalai Lama, Turns from Him Toward China," *New York Times*, December 30, 2016, www.nytimes.com/2016/12/30/world/asia/china-mongolia-dalai-lama.html.

15   the Australian government announced its JobKeeper program: "Media Release," Prime Minister of Australia, March 30, 2020, www.pm.gov.au/media/130-billion-jobkeeper-payment-keep-australians-job.

15   the UK market grew by 30 percent: Hugh Hogan and Bridget Murphy, "Australian Wineries Cracking New Markets, Including United Kingdom, Following China Tariff Hit," Australian Broadcasting Corporation, June 24, 2021, https://www.abc.net.au/news/rural/2021-06-25/wine-exports-australia-china-untied-kingdom-volume-increase/100241724.

15   made up 80 percent of its former revenue: Author interview with Bruce Tyrrell, October 2021.

16   were unable to shift to other markets: Author interview with Tony Battaglene, October 2021, updated comments from October 2022.

16   "China turned the whole thing political": Author interview with Bruce Tyrrell.

16   the Australian industry will make up 60 percent: Gleeson, Addai, and Cao, *Australian Wine in China: Impact of China's Anti-Dumping Duties*.

16   "We were victims of a bigger game": Author interview with Tony Battaglene.

2: The Global Rush for Masks

17   cases were first reported among soldiers in Kansas: John Barry, *The Great Influenza: The Story of the Deadliest Pandemic in History* (New York: Penguin Books, 2004), 1–9.

17   had to use tape to repair disposable face masks for reuse: Chris Buckley, Sui-Lee Wee, and Amy Qin, "China's Doctors, Fighting the Coronavirus, Beg for Masks," *New York Times*, February 14, 2020, www.nytimes.com/2020/02/14/world/asia/china-coronavirus-doctors.html.

18   orient them toward producing PPE: 国务院办公厅关于组织做好疫情防控重点物资生产企业复工复产和调度安排工作的紧急通知 ("General Office of the State Council: Urgent Notice on the Proper Organization of the Resumption of Work and Scheduling Arrangements for Key Materials Production Companies during Epidemic Prevention and Control"), Central People's Government of the People's Republic of China, January 1, 2020, www.gov.cn/zhengce/content /2020-01/30/content_5473087.htm.

18   Xinxing Cathay International Group: Liu Zhiqiang, "Chinese Enterprise Inject Power into Global Fight Against COVID-19 Pandemic," Alwihda Info, April 10, 2020, https://www.alwihdainfo .com/Chinese-enterprise-inject-power-into-global-fight-against-COVID-19-pandemic_a85577.html.

19   PPE production increased dramatically: 国务院新闻办就新冠肺炎疫情防控救治进展情况举行发布会 ("The State Council Information Office Held a Briefing on the Current Progress of the Prevention, Control, and Treatment of the Novel Coronavirus Pneumonia Outbreak"), Central People's Government of the People's Republic of China, March 6, 2020, www.gov.cn/xin wen/2020-03/06/content_5488021.htm.

19   exports of masks and respirators declined: Chad P. Bown, "How COVID-19 Medical Supply Shortages Led to Extraordinary Trade and Industrial Policy," first published July 29, 2021, *Asian Economic Policy Review* 17, No. 1 (January 2022): 114–35.

19   Many developing countries were almost totally reliant: Chad P. Bown, "China Should Export More Medical Gear to Battle COVID-19," Peterson Institute for International Economics, May 5, 2020, https://www.piie.com/blogs/trade-and-investment-policy-watch/china-should-export -more-medical-gear-battle-covid-19.

19   Chinese government had instituted a de facto export ban: Pamela Boykoff and Clare Sebastian, "With No Shipments from China, Medical Mask Suppliers Have to Choose Whom to Supply," CNN, March 6, 2020, https://www.cnn.com/2020/03/06/business/medical-masks-china -shortage-suppliers/index.html.

19   denied reports of an export ban: 商务部召开网上例行新闻发布会 ("The Ministry of Commerce Held a Routine Online Press Conference"), Ministry of Commerce of the People's Republic of China, March 5, 2020, http://www.mofcom.gov.cn/article/ae/ah/diaocd/202003 /20200302944083.shtml.

20   declined even in areas that were relatively unaffected: Bown, "How COVID-19 Medical Supply Shortages Led to Extraordinary Trade and Industrial Policy."

20   reduced its export of PPE and increased its import: "New Analytic Technique Indicates China Likely Hid Severity of COVID-19 from the International Community While It Stockpiled Medical Supplies," Department of Homeland Security, May 1, 2020, https://www.dhs.gov/sites /default/files/publications/china_and_covid-19.pdf.

20   established successful businesses: J&C Corporation, http://www.j-and-c.co.jp/english/c /company/familynetwork/.

20   built a business empire selling spring roll skins: https://mysgdaily.com/?p=news&newsid=2598.

21   an import-export company that leveraged connections to Wei: J&C Corporation, http:// www.j-and-c.co.jp/english/c/company/familynetwork/.

21   chosen to emphasize his connection to his home country: http://www.chinaqw.com/hqhr.

21   "Let's become a bridge between Japan and China": J&C Corporation, http://www.j-and-c. co.jp/english/c/company/familynetwork/.

21   Wei was the honorary vice president: 校友会简介, Fuqing Huaqiao High School Alumni Association in Japan, https://fqqz-aa-japan.com/about-old/jianjie/.

21   president of the Fujian Economic and Cultural Exchange Association: "日本闽籍华侨华人捐赠抗疫物资 98 箱物资再抵 ("Overseas Fujianese in Japan again donated 98 boxes of anti-epidemic supplies to Fujian Province"), China News, February 17, 2020, http://www.fj.chinanews .com.cn/news/fj_zxyc/2020/2020-02-17/460362.html.

21   attributed the shortage to manufacturing slowdowns: "李彤 刘卿 欧阳易佳，"医疗物资卡在哪？原材料、用工短缺等问题待解决" ("Where are the medical supplies stuck? Shortage of labour and raw materials and other such problems are awaiting resolution"), *People's Daily*, January 29, 2020, http://health.people.cn/n1/2020/0129/c14739-31564246.html.

21   asked to wear diapers over their faces instead of protective suits: Joyce Huang, "Health Workers in Wuhan Under Growing Risk as Medical Supplies Run Low," *Voice of America*, January 27, 2020, www.voanews.com/a/science-health_coronavirus-outbreak_health-workers-wuhan -under-growing-risk-medical-supplies-run/6183263.html.

21   founding ceremony in November 2019: 驻名古屋总领事刘晓军出席日本福建经济文 化交流会成立大会 ("Consul General in Nagoya Liu Xiaojun attends the inaugural meeting of Fujian Economy and Culture Promotion Association in Japan"), Consul-General of the People's Republic in Nagoya, November 12, 2019, https://www.mfa.gov.cn/ce/cgngy//chn/lsfw/lsxx/t1715137.htm.

21   attend the organization's annual meeting in July 2021: http://nagoya.china-consulate.org /chn/zlgyw/t1893111.htm.

21   Wei had met with members of the Ōbaku Cultural Promotion Association: "日领侨领魏 成炳：致力推动中日民间友好" ("Leader of overseas Chinese in Japan Wei Chengbing dedicated to promoting Sino-Japanese friendship"), China News, January 20, 2020, http://www.fj.chinanews .com.cn/news/fj_qlxdb/2020/2020-01-20/458804.html.

21   has close ties to local offices for Overseas Chinese Affairs: https://www.chinaqw.com/m /qx/2020/06-19/260320.sh.

22   a call for all overseas Chinese to donate funds and medical supplies: 榕籍海外乡亲积极 行动 共同助援抗击防范疫情 ("Overseas Fuzhou natives spring into action, banding together to help fight the epidemic"), All-China Federation of Returned Overseas Chinese, January 29, 2020, http://web.archive.org/web/20220212160608/http:/www.chinaql.org/n1/2020/0129/c431599 -31564126.html.

22   the Fujian association was raising funds to purchase two hundred thousand masks: All-China Federation of Returned Overseas Chinese, January 29, 2020.

22   Wei immediately organized a group of thirty-six Fujian association members: "Overseas Fujianese in Japan again donated 98 boxes of anti-epidemic supplies to Fujian Province."

22   scour pharmacies in Nagoya for any available masks: "在祖国需要时区这群福建人闷声干 了件大事," 泉州经济技术开发区新闻网" ("In our motherland's hour of need, this group of Fujianese quietly accomplished something big"), January 31, 2020, http://www.qzkfqnews.com/2020-01 /31/content_952780.htm.

22   Association members gathered a total of seven hundred thousand masks: "Overseas Fujianese in Japan again donated 98 boxes of anti-epidemic supplies to Fujian Province."

22   Wei credited branches of the United Front Work Department: "In our motherland's hour of need, this group of Fujianese quietly accomplished something big."

22   The Fujian association also donated about $73,000 to fight the pandemic: "Overseas Fujianese in Japan again donated 98 boxes of anti-epidemic supplies to Fujian Province."

22   Chinese state media provided glowing coverage of similar efforts: "榕籍海外乡亲凝聚 起驰援战"疫"的磅礴力量" ("Overseas Fuzhou natives mustered boundless strength in their rush to fight the epidemic"), Xinhua Net, February 2, 2020, http://m.xinhuanet.com/fj/2020-02 /03/c_1125524940.htm.

23   sent to China 2.5 billion items of PPE valued at $1.2 billion: Sheridan Prasso, "China's Epic Dash for PPE Left the World Short on Masks," Bloomberg, September 17, 2020, https://www .bloomberg.com/news/articles/2020-09-17/behind-china-s-epic-dash-for-ppe-that-left-the-world -short-on-masks?leadSource=uverify%20wall.

23   sent hundreds of thousands of masks and other PPE back to China: Kate McClymont, "Second Developer Flew 82 Tonnes of Medical Supplies to China," *Sydney Morning Herald*, March 26, 2020, https://www.smh.com.au/national/second-developer-flies-82-tonnes-of-medical-supplies-to -china-20200326-p54e8n.html.

23   desperately needed by residents caught in bushfires: Kate McClymont and Royce Millar, "Billions of Face Masks Sent to China During Australian Bushfire Crisis," *Sydney Morning Herald*, April 2, 2020, https://www.smh.com.au/national/billions-of-face-masks-sent-to-china-during -australian-bushfire-crisis-20200402-p54gjh.html.

23   search local pharmacies and stores for masks to send back to China: Kate McClymont, "Chinese-Backed Company's Mission to Source Australian Medical Supplies," *Sydney Morning Herald*, March 26, 2020, https://www.smh.com.au/national/chinese-backed-company-s-mission-to -source-australian-medical-supplies-20200325-p54du8.html.

23   led the Australian Medical Association to warn: Anne Davies, "Coronavirus: Medical Association Warns Australia Must Protect Medical Supplies amid Reports of Stockpiling by China-Backed Firm in February," *The Guardian*, March 26, 2020, https://www.theguardian.com/world/2020

/mar/26/coronavirus-doctors-issue-protective-equipment-warning-after-report-china-backed-firm
-sourced-bulk-supplies-from-sydney.

23   left "the world naked with no supply of PPE": Sam Cooper, "United Front Groups in
Canada Helped Beijing Stockpile Coronavirus Safety Supplies," Global News, April 30, 2020,
https://globalnews.ca/news/6858818/coronavirus-china-united-front-canada-protective-equipment
-shortage/.

23   In 2008, Chinese community groups in the United States: David Pierson, "L.A.'s Chinese
Mobilize for Quake Relief," Los Angeles Times, May 14, 2008, https://www.latimes.com/archives
/la-xpm-2008-may-14-me-quakereact14-story.html.

23   In 2021, Indian student groups in the United States: Lakshmi Gandhi, "As Covid Rav-
ages India, the Diaspora Pledges Help," NBC, May 4, 2021, https://www.nbcnews.com/news/asian
-america/covid-ravages-india-diaspora-pledges-help-rcna822.

24   In January and early February, it was difficult for anyone to foresee: Prasso, "China's Epic
Dash for PPE Left the World Short on Masks."

25   White House trade adviser Peter Navarro: Jonathan Swan and Margaret Talev, "Navarro
Memos Warning of Mass Coronavirus Death Circulated in January," Axios, April 7, 2020, https://
www.axios.com/2020/04/07/exclusive-navarro-deaths-coronavirus-memos-january.

25   Despite warnings from the World Health Organization: Ursula Perano, "10 Times Trump
and His Administration Were Warned About Coronavirus," Axios, April 12, 2020, https://www
.axios.com/2020/04/12/trump-coronavirus-warnings.

25   intelligence agencies: Ayesha Rascoe and Colin Dwyer, "Trump Received Intelligence
Briefings on Coronavirus Twice in January," NPR, May 2, 2020, https://www.npr.org/sections
/coronavirus-live-updates/2020/05/02/849619486/trump-received-intelligence-briefings-on
-coronavirus-twice-in-january.

25   3,607 healthcare workers died: Jane Spencer and Christina Jewett, "Twelve Months of
Trauma: More than 3,600 US Health Workers Died in Covid's First Year," The Guardian, April 8,
2021, https://www.theguardian.com/us-news/2021/apr/08/us-health-workers-deaths-covid-lost-on
-the-frontline.

25   many who lacked adequate PPE: Alastair Gee, "Texas Doctor, 28, Dies of Covid: 'She Wore
the Same Mask for Weeks, If Not Months,'" The Guardian, October 7, 2020, https://www.theguard
ian.com/us-news/2020/oct/07/texas-doctor-adeline-fagan-covid-coronavirus.

25   His first book, published in 1984: Peter Navarro, Policy Game: How Special Interests and
Ideologues Are Stealing America (Hoboken, NJ: John Wiley, 1984).

25   The Economist to describe him as a "China-bashing eccentric": "Peter Navarro Is About to
Become One of the World's Most Powerful Economists," The Economist, January 21, 2017, https://
web.archive.org/web/20180612150909/https:/www.economist.com/briefing/2017/01/21/peter
-navarro-is-about-to-become-one-of-the-worlds-most-powerful-economists.

25   "bring attention to Peter's anti-China agenda": Swan and Talev, "Navarro Memos Warning
of Mass Coronavirus Death Circulated in January."

25   a move that drew criticism: Stephen Sorace, "Fauci, Who Opposed China Travel Ban and
Praised Their Transparency, Criticizes Trump Response," Fox News, March 11, 2021, https://www
.foxnews.com/politics/fauci-china-travel-ban-coronavirus-transparency-criticizes-trump-response.

25   Trump critics tended to view: "Coronavirus: Immigration to US to Be Suspended amid
Pandemic, Trump Says," BBC News, April 21, 2020, https://www.bbc.com/news/world-us-canada
-52363852.

26   the pandemic would have "a very good ending for us": Swan and Talev, "Navarro Memos
Warning of Mass Coronavirus Death Circulated in January."

26   "we made about 500 million nitrile gloves [a year] in America": Bown, "How COVID-19
Medical Supply Shortages Led to Extraordinary Trade and Industrial Policy," 3.

26   U.S. imports of PPE from China declined: Chad P. Bown, "COVID-19: Trump's Curbs on
Exports of Medical Gear Put Americans and Others at Risk," Peterson Institute for International
Economics, April 9, 2020, https://www.piie.com/blogs/trade-and-investment-policy-watch/covid
-19-trumps-curbs-exports-medical-gear-put-americans.

26   Another reason for the United States' dire shortage of PPE: Patrice Taddonio, "Depleted
National Stockpile Contributed to COVID PPE Shortage: 'You Can't Be Prepared If You're Not
Funded to Be Prepared,'" Frontline, PBS, October 6, 2020, https://www.pbs.org/wgbh/frontline
/article/depleted-national-stockpile-contributed-to-covid-ppe-shortage/.

27   company representatives described these meetings as largely informational: Chairwoman of
House Committee on Oversight and Reform Carolyn B. Maloney, Memorandum on "Information

Provided by Medical Distribution Companies on Challenges with White House Supply Chain Task Force and Project Airbridge," July 2, 2020, https://oversight.house.gov/sites/democrats.oversight .house.gov/files/documents/Project%20Airbridge%20Memo%2007-02-20.pdf.

27 AdvaMed, another industry group, sent a letter to the Trump administration: Bown, "How COVID-19 Medical Supply Shortages Led to Extraordinary Trade and Industrial Policy."

27 believing that procurement was the responsibility of the states: Katherine Eban, " 'That's Their Problem': How Jared Kushner Let the Markets Decide America's COVID-19 Fate," *Vanity Fair*, September 17, 2020, https://www.vanityfair.com/news/2020/09/jared-kushner-let-the-mar kets-decide-covid-19-fate.

27 "We're not a shipping clerk": Quint Forgey, "Trump Tells Governors to Step Up Efforts to Get Medical Supplies," Politico, March 19, 2020, https://www.politico.com/news/2020/03/19 /trump-governors-coronavirus-medical-supplies-137658.

27 acquire PPE through Chinese brokers: "Memorandum," House Committee on Oversight and Reform, July 2, 2020.

27 the Trump administration launched Project Airbridge: Rob Noel, "Project Airbridge," *State Magazine*, July 7, 2020, https://statemag.lab.prod.getusinfo.com/2020/07/0720feat07/.

27 David Hale sent an urgent email to embassies in Europe and Asia: Robbie Garner, "U.S. Appeals to Aid Recipients for Help in Fighting Coronavirus," *Foreign Policy*, March 23, 2020, https:// foreignpolicy.com/2020/03/23/us-medical-supplies-coronavirus-appeal-aid/.

27 the administration phased out Project Airbridge: "FEMA Phasing Out Project Airbridge," Press Release, U.S. Department of Homeland Security, June 18, 2020, https://www.fema.gov/press -release/20210318/fema-phasing-out-project-airbridge.

27 Michigan alone requested 20 million N95 respirators: Priscilla Alvarez and Leyla Santiago, "Trump Administration Heralded Its Private-Public Partnership to Get Supplies to the US. It Was a Drop in the Bucket," CNN, May 27, 2020, https://edition.cnn.com/2020/05/27/politics/fema -project-airbridge/index.html.

27 EU officials initially viewed the pandemic as a Chinese problem: Ben Stockton, Céline Schoen, and Laura Margottini, "Crisis at the Commission: Inside Europe's Response to the Coronavirus Outbreak," Bureau of Investigative Journalism, July 15, 2020, https://www.thebureauinvest igates.com/stories/2020-07-15/crisis-at-the-commission-inside-europes-response-to-the-corona virus-outbreak.

28 the European Commission instituted a ban: Lili Bayer et al., "EU Moves to Limit Exports of Medical Equipment Outside the Bloc," Politico, March 15, 2020, https://www.politico.eu/article /coronavirus-eu-limit-exports-medical-equipment/.

28 As Raphaël Glucksmann, a French member of the European Parliament, would later tell me: Hudson Institute event, "Exploring the Effects of Chinese Sanctions on European MEPs," July 9, 2021.

28 he would consider invoking the Defense Production Act: Noah Weiland and Emily Cochrane, "Government Eyes War Powers to Speed Medical Manufacturing Ahead of Virus," *New York Times*, February 28, 2020, https://www.nytimes.com/2020/02/28/us/politics/trump-coronavirus .html.

28 "a lot of the raw materials": Ted Hesson and Alexandra Alper, "Exclusive: U.S. Mulls Using Sweeping Powers to Ramp Up Production of Coronavirus Protective Gear," Reuters, February 28, 2020, https://www.reuters.com/article/us-china-health-usa-production-exclusive-idUSKC N20L2S0.

28 ordering General Motors to produce ventilators: Michael Wayland and Christina Wilkie, "Trump Orders General Motors to Make Ventilators Under Defense Production Act," CNBC, March 27, 2020, https://www.cnbc.com/2020/03/27/trump-orders-general-motors-to-make-vent ilators-under-defense-production-act.html.

28 another directive, requiring additional companies to produce ventilators: "Trump Invokes Defense Production Act for Ventilator Manufacturing," Reuters, April 2, 2020, https://www.reuters .com/article/us-health-coronavirus-usa-ventilators/trump-invokes-defense-production-act-for-vent ilator-manufacturing-idUSKBN21K39R.

28 "The COVID-19 pandemic, with its disruptions of supply chains": Robert D. Atkinson, "The Case for a National Industrial Strategy to Counter China's Technological Rise," Information Technology and Innovation Foundation, April 13, 2020, https://itif.org/publications/2020/04/13 /case-national-industrial-strategy-counter-chinas-technological-rise/.

29 proposed $37 billion in subsidies: Bob Davis, Asa Fitch, and Kate O'Keeffe, "Semiconductor Industry to Lobby for Billions to Boost U.S. Manufacturing," *Wall Street Journal*, May 31, 2020,

https://www.wsj.com/articles/semiconductor-industry-to-lobby-for-billions-to-boost-u-s-manufact
uring-11590919201.

29   "Debates like this weren't happening two years ago": @DEricSayers, "Debates like this weren't happening two years ago. As the US-China have opened a new front in tech competition, semiconductors have joined telecomm/5G as the most important. Exciting to see the range of Democrats/Republicans coming together on this issue," https://wsj.com/articles/semiconductor-industry-to-lobby-for-billions-to-boost-u-s-manufacturing-11590919201, Twitter, May 31, 2020, https://twitter.com/DEricSayers/status/1267084629863010304.

30   "we must take control of our supply chain": "Rubio, Warren Introduce Legislation to Study the Effects of America's Overreliance on Foreign Countries and Foreign Direct Investment in Its Pharmaceutical Supply Chain," Press Release, Marco Rubio, U.S. Senator for Florida, June 30, 2020, https://www.rubio.senate.gov/public/index.cfm/2020/6/rubio-warren-introduce-legislation-to-study-the-effects-of-america-s-overreliance-on-foreign-countries-and-foreign-direct-investment-in-its-pharmaceutical-supply-chain.

30   "Industrial policy has been the Lord Voldemort of terms": Remarks by Ganesh Sitaraman, German Marshall Fund, Washington, DC, October 8, 2020, https://www.gmfus.org/event/great-democracy-how-fix-our-politics-unrig-economy-and-unite-america.

31   federal government ordered 50,000 artillery pieces from domestic manufacturers: Thomas D. Morgan, "The Industrial Mobilization of World War II: America Goes to War," *Army History* 30 (Spring 1994): 31–35.

31   called for national defense mobilization: "Proclamation 2352—Proclaiming a National Emergency in Connection with the Observance, Safeguarding, and Enforcement of Neutrality and the Strengthening of the National Defense Within the Limits of Peace-Time Authorizations," The American Presidency Project, University of California at Santa Barbara, September 8, 1939, https://www.presidency.ucsb.edu/documents/proclamation-2352-proclaiming-national-emergency-connection-with-the-observance.

31   The commission's final report: "The Report of the President's Commission on National Goals," November 1960, https://babel.hathitrust.org/cgi/pt?id=mdp.49015000077488&view=1up&seq=3.

31   U.S. industrial policy during the 1950s and '60s was predominantly Keynesian: Robert E. Baldwin, "The Changing Nature of U.S. Trade Policy Since World War II," in *The Structure and Evolution of Recent U.S. Trade Policy* (Chicago: University of Chicago Press, 1984), https://www.nber.org/system/files/chapters/c5828/c5828.pdf.

32   He believed that inflation and unemployment would not resolve automatically: Sidney Blumenthal, "Drafting a Democratic Industrial Plan," *New York Times Magazine*, August 28, 1983, https://www.nytimes.com/1983/08/28/magazine/drafting-a-democratic-industrial-plan.html.

32   "Japan Inc. needs to be met with U.S.A. Inc.": Blumenthal, "Drafting a Democratic Industrial Plan."

32   the Balanced Growth and Economic Planning Act: "Balanced Growth and Economic Planning Act," May 21, 1975, S.1795, 94th Congress (1975–1976), https://www.congress.gov/bill/94th-congress/senate-bill/1795.

32   Congress ultimately passed: Aaron Steelman, "Full Employment and Balanced Growth Act of 1978 (Humphrey-Hawkins)," Federal Reserve History, https://www.federalreservehistory.org/essays/humphrey-hawkins-act.

32   an impassioned call for an industrial policy: Robert B. Reich, "Why the U.S. Needs an Industrial Policy," *Harvard Business Review*, January 1982, https://hbr.org/1982/01/why-the-us-needs-an-industrial-policy.

33   pursued an economic policy focused on liquidity, limited spending, and free trade: Jeff Faux, "Industrial Policy: The Road Not Taken," *American Prospect*, December 21, 2009, https://prospect.org/special-report/industrial-policy-road-taken/.

34   Though Huawei has claimed: Arjun Kharpal, "Huawei Says It Would Never Hand Data to China's Government. Experts Say It Wouldn't Have a Choice," CNBC, March 5, 2019, https://www.cnbc.com/2019/03/05/huawei-would-have-to-give-data-to-china-government-if-asked-experts.html.

34   China's 2017 National Intelligence Law: Murray Scot Tanner, "Beijing's New National Intelligence Law: From Defense to Offense," Lawfare, July 20, 2017, https://www.lawfareblog.com/beijings-new-national-intelligence-law-defense-offense.

35   the company had received as much as $75 billion in government support: Chuin-Wei Yap, "State Support Helped Fuel Huawei's Global Rise," *Wall Street Journal*, December 25, 2019, https://www.wsj.com/articles/state-support-helped-fuel-huaweis-global-rise-11577280736.

35   the U.S. House Intelligence Committee had pushed to block: Jim Wolf, "U.S. Lawmakers Seek to Block China Huawei, ZTE U.S. Inroads," Reuters, October 8, 2012, https://www.reuters.com/article/us-usa-china-huawei-zte-idUSBRE8960NH20121008.

36   "We're losing $500 billion in trade": Katie Zezima, "Trump: 'Who the Hell Cares If There's a Trade War?'" *Washington Post*, May 20, 2016, https://www.washingtonpost.com/news/post-politics/wp/2016/05/20/trump-who-the-hell-cares-if-theres-a-trade-war/.

36   China policy doldrums: Josh Rogin, *Chaos Under Heaven: Trump, Xi, and the Battle for the 21st Century* (Boston: Houghton Mifflin Harcourt, 2021), 70–89.

36   policymakers could no longer rely on free markets alone: David Lauter and Jonathan Kaiman, "Trump's China Tariffs Get Bipartisan Support, Reflecting Widespread U.S. Disillusionment with Beijing," *Los Angeles Times*, March 22, 2018, https://www.latimes.com/politics/la-na-pol-trump-china-tariffs-20180322-story.html.

36   The trade war more or less ended: Chad P. Bown, "Anatomy of a Flop: Why Trump's US-China Phase One Trade Deal Fell Short," Peterson Institute for International Economics, February 8, 2021, https://www.piie.com/blogs/trade-and-investment-policy-watch/anatomy-flop-why-trumps-us-china-phase-one-trade-deal-fell.

37   In January 2018, U.S. Air Force Brig. Gen. Rob Spalding: Josh Rogin, "National Security Council Official Behind 5G Memo Leaves White House," *Washington Post*, February 2, 2018, https://www.washingtonpost.com/news/josh-rogin/wp/2018/02/02/national-security-council-official-behind-5g-memo-leaves-white-house/.

37   China's "dominant position in the manufacture and operation of network infrastructure": Jonathan Swan et al., "Scoop: Trump Team Considers Nationalizing 5G Network," Axios, January 28, 2018, https://www.axios.com/2018/01/28/trump-team-debates-nationalizing-5g-network.

37   "incentivize the U.S. private sector to reignite": "U.S. Strategic Framework for the Indo-Pacific," Trump White House Archives, n.d., https://trumpwhitehouse.archives.gov/wp-content/uploads/2021/01/IPS-Final-Declass.pdf.

37   "The pandemic has certainly highlighted the prescience of this strategy": Bethany Allen-Ebrahimian, and Zach Dorfman, "Newly Declassified Report Lays Out U.S. Strategy in Asia," Axios, January 12, 2021, https://www.axios.com/2021/01/12/indo-pacific-strategy-trump-administration-china.

38   minimum domestic manufacturing capacities: *Post Covid-19 Value Chains: Options for Reshoring Production Back to Europe in a Globalised Economy*, Policy Department for External Relations, Directorate-General for External Policies of the Union, European Parliament, March 2021, https://www.europarl.europa.eu/RegData/etudes/STUD/2021/653626/EXPO_STU(2021)653626_EN.pdf.

39 $1.2 billion in subsidies to domestic manufacturers of PPE: Bown, "How COVID-19 Medical Supply Shortages Led to Extraordinary Trade and Industrial Policy."

39   In a July 2020 letter: Bob Fredericks, "Sen. Lindsey Graham Calls to Stop China's 'Domination' of PPE Market," *New York Post*, July 16, 2020, https://nypost.com/2020/07/16/sen-lindsey-graham-calls-for-legislation-on-us-made-ppes/.

39   global supply chains for PPE are centered on lower-income countries: *Post Covid-19 Value Chains.*

3: Dual-Function Strategy and China's Core Interests

40   sixty million people of Chinese heritage: Zhuang Guotu, "The Overseas Chinese: A Long History," *UNESCO Courier*, October–December 2021, https://en.unesco.org/courier/2021-4/overseas-chinese-long-history#:~:text=There%20are%20more%20than%2010.7,Organization%20for%20Migration%20(IOM%20).

40   The United Front Work Department, after spending decades virtually unknown: Matt Schrader, "Friends and Enemies: A Framework for Understanding Chinese Political Interference in Democratic Countries," Alliance for Securing Democracy, April 22, 2020, https://securingdemocracy.gmfus.org/friends-and-enemies-a-framework-for-understanding-chinese-political-interference-in-democratic-countries/.

40   The department is tasked with reaching out to all levels: Marcel Angliviel de la Beaumelle, "The United Front Work Department: 'Magic Weapon' at Home and Abroad," China Brief, Jamestown Foundation, July 6, 2017, https://jamestown.org/program/united-front-work-department-magic-weapon-home-abroad/.

40   United Front work, on a grassroots level, harnesses the organizing power: Peter Mattis and Alex Joske, "The Third Magic Weapon: Reforming China's United Front," War on the Rocks,

June 24, 2019, https://warontherocks.com/2019/06the-third-magic-weapon-reforming-chinas-united-front/.

41   Party-affiliated organizations in China can offer a meaningful outlet: Anne-Marie Brady, "Magic Weapons: China's Political Influence Activities Under Xi Jinping," Wilson Center, September 18, 2017, https://www.wilsoncenter.org/article/magic-weapons-chinas-political-influence-activities-under-xi-jinping; and de la Beaumelle, "The United Front Work Department."

41   United Front work co-opts true civil society: Alex Joske, "The Party Speaks for You," Australian Strategic Policy Institute, June 9, 2020, https://www.aspi.org.au/report/party-speaks-you.

41   Chinese reformist and revolutionary groups: Bethany Allen-Ebrahimian, "The Chinese Communist Party Is Still Afraid of Sun Yat-sen's Shadow," *Foreign Policy*, March 8, 2019, https://foreignpolicy.com/2019/03/08/the-chinese-communist-party-is-still-afraid-of-sun-yat-sens-shadow/.

42   leaders in Beijing made a huge new push: Larry Diamond, ed., *China's Influence and American Interests*, Hoover Institution, November 29, 2018, https://www.hoover.org/research/chinas-influence-american-interests-promoting-constructive-vigilance.

42   various Beijing-aligned organizations: Bethany Allen-Ebrahimian, "How China Built an Army of Influence Agents," Daily Beast, July 28, 2018, https://www.thedailybeast.com/how-china-built-an-army-of-influence-agents-in-the-us.

43   United Front work has increasingly become: "China's Overseas United Front Work: Background and Implications for the United States," U.S.-China Economic and Security Review Commission, August 24, 2018, https://www.uscc.gov/research/chinas-overseas-united-front-work-background-and-implications-united-states.

43   United Front Work Department was reorganized: Alex Joske, "Reorganizing the United Front Work Department: New Structures for a New Era of Diaspora and Religious Affairs Work," China Brief, Jamestown Foundation, May 9, 2019, https://web.archive.org/web/20190721191900/https:/jamestown.org/program/reorganizing-the-united-front-work-department-new-structures-for-a-new-era-of-diaspora-and-religious-affairs-work/.

43   compiled budget documents for key organizations: Ryan Fedasiuk, "Putting Money in the Party's Mouth: How China Mobilizes Funding for United Front Work," China Brief, Jamestown Foundation, September 16, 2020, https://jamestown.org/program/putting-money-in-the-partys-mouth-how-china-mobilizes-funding-for-united-front-work/?mc_cid=d6244ae8ec&mc_eid=4831433c4a.

43   "This isn't necessarily representative of Chinese diaspora communities": Prasso, "China's Epic Dash for PPE Left the World Short on Masks."

44   a global humanitarian campaign involving these groups: Prasso, "China's Epic Dash for PPE Left the World Short on Masks."

45   party committees in cities across China: Chao Deng, "In Wuhan, China's Virus Outbreak Overwhelms Residential Committees," *Wall Street Journal*, February 14, 2020, https://www.wsj.com/articles/in-wuhan-chinas-residential-committees-fight-outbreak-on-front-line-11581717012.

4: Spies and Sister Cities

47   If Fang could build trusting relationships: This chapter would not have been possible without the extensive reporting and writing contributed by Zach Dorfman, national security reporter extraordinaire and an even better friend.

48   "using the local to surround the center": Bethany Allen-Ebrahimian, "Between the Lines on Chinese Strategy: Use the Local to Surround the Center," Axios, February 12, 2020, https://www.axios.com/2020/02/12/china-strategy-local-government-between-lines.

48   "It's got politics of the highest stakes": Dan Bobkoff, "Axios Investigates: A Suspected Chinese Spy," Axios, December 8, 2020, https://www.axios.com/2020/12/08/axios-investigates-chinese-spy-espionage-politics-swalwell.

49   spent more than a year tracking Fang down: Much of this chapter is adapted from the Axios investigation in Bethany Allen-Ebrahimian and Zach Dorfman, "Exclusive: Suspected Chinese Spy Targeted California Politicians," Axios, December 8, 2020, https://www.axios.com/2020/12/08/china-spy-california-politicians.

49   Chinese airlines have a history of alleged involvement: Jana Winter and Zach Dorfman, "DHS Eyes Chinese Airline Employees Suspected of Spying," Yahoo News, December 3, 2021, https://news.yahoo.com/dhs-eyes-chinese-airline-employees-suspected-of-spying-195725473.html.

50   had almost five thousand registered members: Chinese Students and Scholars Association at the University of California Berkeley, http://web.archive.org/web/20201217121512/https://callink.berkeley.edu/organization/bcssa.

52   charged her with serving as a double agent: Brian Ross and Vic Walter, "FBI Knew About Alleged Spy 12 Years Ago," ABC News, January 7, 2006, https://abcnews.go.com/WNT/story?id=129711&page=1.

52   Leung had championed the participation of Asian Americans: John Wildermuth, "Arrest of Asian American Activist May Curtail Political Involvement," SFGate, April 12, 2003, https://www.sfgate.com/politics/article/Arrest-of-Asian-American-activist-may-curtail-2655771.php.

52   Harrison told me in a phone call: Author interview with Bill Harrison, August 11, 2020.

53   he saw Fang on at least two different occasions: Author interview with Mark Stodola, August 28, 2020.

53   attend the U.S.-China Sister Cities Conference: "Sister Cities International & Chinese People's Association for Friendship with Foreign Countries to Host U.S.-China Sister Cities Conference," Sister Cities International, March, 2014, https://sistercities.org/sister-cities-international-chinese-peoples-association-for-friendship-with-foreign-countries-to-host-u-s-china-sister-cities-conference/.

53   Fang would later send two other photos: 邹于思思, "Christine Fang: 促进中美政治文化交流的新女性" ("Christine Fang: The new woman promoting political and cultural exchanges between China and the United States"), Moguz.com, April 1, 2015, http://web.archive.org/web/20170416124839/https:/moguz.us/t/1558/.

54   "I saw her as a young, attractive Chinese lady": Zach Dorfman interview with Gilbert Wong, August 20, 2020.

54   "widen every possible chink in the Iron Curtain": "Remarks at the People-to-People Conference," American Presidency Project, University of California at Santa Barbara, https://www.presidency.ucsb.edu/documents/remarks-the-people-people-conference.

54   Eisenhower said in a speech at the White House: "The Birth of the People-to-People Program," Video, Sister Cities International, https://www.sistercities.org/1956/09/11/birth-people-people-program/.

55   facilitates international local-to-local partnerships: "The Birth of the People-to-People Program."

55   more than 1,800 partnerships across 138 countries: "Where We Are (U.S. Partnerships Worldwide)," Sister Cities International, November 2019, https://sistercities.org/wp-content/uploads/2019/11/2019-SCI-maps-Where-We-Are-U.S.-Partnerships-Worldwide.pdf.

55   Since the normalization of Sino-American relations in 1978: "Sister Cities: Siblings' Relations Are Changing," *China Daily USA*, November 6, 2020, http://usa.chinadaily.com.cn/2015-11/06/content_22393869.htm.

55   China maintained friendship relationships with 1,247 cities: "友好城市" ("Friendship Cities"), CPAFFC, https://web.archive.org/web/20191230093722/http:/www.gov.cn/test/2005-06/02/content_18213.htm.

56   Xi's father, Xi Zhongxun, led a group: Sarah Lande, "Our Sister Cities: Muscatine's Friendship with China Runs Deep," *Quad-City Times*, January 30, 2016, https://qctimes.com/news/local/muscatine/our-sister-cities-muscatines-friendship-with-china-runs-deep/article_eec3b298-7e87-5a38-b497-2ca887486920.html.

56   "I was eager for them to come to Muscatine": Lande, "Our Sister Cities: Muscatine's Friendship with China Runs Deep."

56   future CCP general secretary's first visit to the United States: Lande, "Our Sister Cities: Muscatine's Friendship with China Runs Deep."

57   "implement[ing] China's independent foreign policy of peace": "About us," CPAFFC, https://cpaffc.org.cn/index/xiehui/xiehui_list/cate/12/lang/2.html.

57   should "serve the overall diplomacy of a country": 广州 国际朋友圈 越来越大 40年来与56个国家的81个城市建立了友好关系" ("Guangzhou's international friend circle gets bigger and bigger: Friendly relations with 81 cities in 56 countries established over the past 40 years"), *Guangzhou Daily*, November 1, 2019, http://www.guangzhou.gov.cn/201911/01/156098_52897855.htm.

57   CPAFFC vice president Xie Yuan gave a keynote speech: "Vice President Xie Yuan Attended Commemorative Meeting of 40 Years of International Sister Cities in Guangzhou," CPAFFC, November 1, 2019, https://cpaffc.org.cn/index/news/detail/id/5617/lang/2.html.

57   entire parallel track of events on a Silk Road theme: *2018 Annual Cities Leading the Way*, Souvenir Program Book, Sister Cities International, July 2018, https://sistercities.org/wp-content/uploads/2018/07/2018-SCI-program-guide-FINAL.pdf.

58   "all part of the ancient Silk Road and Water-Ways": Albuquerque Sister Cities, *Albuquerque*

Sister Cities Foundation, Newsletter, January 2019, https://www.abqsistercities.org/wp-content/up loads/2021/02/ASCF-January-2019.pdf.

58   has worked with the organization for decades: Author interview with Kathleen Roche-Tansey, June 26, 2020.

58   How a country manages its sister city relationships: Author interview with Kathleen Roche-Tansey.

59   "important channels to implement the BRI": Li Jing, "Sister City Relations Promote Co-operation," *China Daily*, April 26, 2020, http://www.chinadaily.com.cn/global/2019-04/26/con tent_37462677.htm.

59   Shanghai canceled its sister city relationship with Prague: Jessie Yeung, "Prague's Tryst with Taipei Sees Shanghai Spurned in Sister City Love Triangle," CNN, January 15, 2020, https://www .cnn.com/2020/01/15/asia/prague-taiwan-china-intl-hnk-scli/index.html.

59   a new head of CPAFFC was announced: 李小林退休 ("Lin Xiaolin retires"), *Beijing News*, April 14, 2020, https://web.archive.org/web/20200718205128/http://www.bjnews.com.cn /feature/2020/04/14/716536.html.

60   suggesting the coronavirus might not have originated in China: Henry Austin and Alexander Smith, "Coronavirus: Chinese Official Suggests U.S. Army to Blame for Outbreak," NBC News, March 13, 2020, https://www.nbcnews.com/news/world/coronavirus-chinese-official-suggests-u-s -army-blame-outbreak-n1157826.

60   defending China's repressive policies: Eric Olander, "China's New Twitter Diplomacy in Africa Used to Challenge US Critics," Africa Report, December 19, 2020, https://www.theafricareport .com/21507/chinas-new-twitter-diplomacy-in-africa-used-to-challenge-us-critics/.

60   "a community with a shared future for mankind": "Remarks by Our President," CPAFFC, https://cpaffc.org.cn/index/xiehui/xiehui_list/cate/11/lang/2.html.

60   dozens of Chinese student associations at campuses around the United States: Bethany Allen-Ebrahimian, "China's Long Arm Reaches into American Campuses," *Foreign Policy*, March 7, 2018, https://foreignpolicy.com/2018/03/07/chinas-long-arm-reaches-into-american-campuses-chinese -students-scholars-association-university-communist-party/.

61   "communication bridge between students and the Chinese consulate": "邹于思思,"Christine Fang: 促进中美政治文化交流的新女性" ("Christine Fang: The new woman promoting political and cultural exchanges between China and the United States").

62   Swalwell has never publicly denied having a sexual relationship with Fang: Ashley Collman, "Rep. Eric Swalwell Refused to Say If He Had Sex with a Suspected Chinese Spy Who Slept with 2 Mayors for an Intelligence Campaign," Business Insider, December 10, 2020, https://www.business insider.com/eric-swalwell-christine-fang-suspected-chinese-spy-2020-12?r=US&IR=T.

62   She was supposed to attend the opening ceremony: Author interview on background.

62   "people talking about this person who had just disappeared": Author interview with Steven Tavares, October 2021.

63   Rodney Faraon worked on China: "Former CIA Analyst Rodney Faraon on Transferring Skills from CIA to Disney," CBS News, September 2, 2020, https://www.cbsnews.com/news /former-cia-analyst-rodney-faraon-on-transferring-skills-from-cia-to-disney/.

63   subsequent Department of Justice investigation found: Bob Woodward and Brian Duffy, "Chinese Embassy Role in Contributions Probed," *Washington Post*, February 13, 1997, https:// www.washingtonpost.com/wp-srv/politics/special/campfin/stories/china1.htm.

64   Yah Lin "Charlie" Trie, had leveraged his political connections: Woodward and Duffy, "Chinese Embassy Role in Contributions Probed."

64   former DNC fund-raiser Johnny Chung admitted: Roberto Suro, "Not Chinese Agent, Chung Says," *Washington Post*, May 12, 1999, https://www.washingtonpost.com/wp-srv/politics /special/campfin/stories/chung051299.htm.

64   his first thought when I told him about Fang: Author interview with Rodney Faraon, December 1, 2020.

64   In October 2019, James Tong: Angela Ruggiero, "East Bay Developer Sentenced for Illegal Swalwell Campaign Donations," *Mercury News*, January 24, 2020, https://www.mercurynews. com/2020/01/24/east-bay-developer-convicted-of-illegal-congressional-campaign-donations-sent-to-prison/.

65   "The undercurrent of local buzz about Fang": "She Came Out of Nowhere. Then She Was Gone: The Local Angle on Swalwell's Ties to an Alleged Chinese Spy," *East Bay Citizen*, December 9, 2020, https://ebcitizen.com/2020/12/09/she-came-out-of-nowhere-then-she-was-gone-the-local -angle-on-swalwells-ties-to-an-alleged-chinese-spy/.

67   students in Norfolk video-chatted with students in Ningbo: Liu Yinmeng, "US Sister Cities Get Help from Chinese Friends in Virus Fight," *China Daily*, April 22, 2020, http://global.china daily.com.cn/a/202004/22/WS5e9fbcb6a3105d50a3d18050.html.

67   Ningbo-Beilun municipal government donated two thousand masks: Liu, "US Sister Cities Get Help from Chinese Friends in Virus Fight."

68   "These acts of compassionate exchange": Liu, "US Sister Cities Get Help from Chinese Friends in Virus Fight."

68   China sent six doctors on an Airbus A330 plane to Serbia: "Serbian President Kisses Chinese Flag as Support Team Arrives," CGTN, March 22, 2020, https://news.cgtn.com/news/20 20-03-22/Serbian-president-kisses-Chinese-flag-as-support-team-arrives--P3FlpiEMBa/index .html.

68   repeatedly visited Belgrade's airport: Angel Petrov, "Serbia's Vaccine Diplomacy in China's Shadow," Al Jazeera, March 17, 2021, https://www.aljazeera.com/opinions/2021/3/17/serbias-vac cine-diplomacy-in-chinas-shadow.

69   "China will give all kinds of technical and financial support": "Ali Asif Shawon, China Wants 'Sister Cities' in Bangladesh," *Dhaka Tribune*, May 19, 2020, https://archive.dhakatribune .com/bangladesh/2020/05/19/china-wants-sister-cities-in-bangladesh.

69   "a larger geostrategic objective": Joyeeta Bhattacharjee, "Chinese Proposal to Bangladesh for Sister-City Alliance," Observer Research Foundation, June 12, 2020, https://www.orfonline.org /expert-speak/chinese-proposal-bangladesh-sister-city-alliance-67725/.

69   three Swedish cities terminated their relationships: "Multiple Swedish Cities Terminated Sister City Agreement with China," Radio France Internationale, April 20, 2020, http://chinascope .org/archives/22968.

69   "Jackals, we welcome with shotguns": "How Sweden Copes with Chinese Bullying," *The Economist*, February 20, 2020, https://www.economist.com/europe/2020/02/20/how-sweden-copes -with-chinese-bullying.

70   "not a vehicle for people-to-people exchange": Designation of the National Association for China's Peaceful Unification (NACPU) as a Foreign Mission of the PRC," October 28, 2020, U.S. Department of State Archive, https://2017-2021.state.gov/designation-of-the-national-association -for-chinas-peaceful-unification-nacpu-as-a-foreign-mission-of-the-prc/index.html.

70   designated the peaceful reunification associations a foreign agent: "U.S. Designates Chinese Body a Foreign Mission, Quits Local Cooperation Agreement," Reuters, October 28, 2020, https:// www.reuters.com/article/us-usa-china-pompeo/u-s-designates-chinese-body-a-foreign-mission -quits-local-cooperation-agreement-idUSKBN27D305.

70   "subnational win-win cooperation": "The Regressive Behavior of Pompeo Led the U.S. Down the Wrong Path," CPAFFC, October 29, 2020, https://cpaffc.org.cn/index/news/detail /id/7094/lang/2.html.

70   "China's newest political weapon": "Blackburn & Hawley: Sister-City Partnerships May Be China's Newest Political Weapon," Senator Marsha Blackburn, U.S. Senator for Tennessee, October 8, 2020, https://www.blackburn.senate.gov/2020/10/blackburn-hawley-sister-city-partnerships -may-be-china-s-newest-political-weapon.

70   donated nearly $65,000 worth of personal protective equipment: "Rockville's Sister City in Taiwan Donates 10,000 Surgical Masks," *Bethesda Magazine*, June 8, 2020, https://bethesda magazine.com/2020/06/08/rockvilles-sister-city-in-taiwan-donates-10000-surgical-masks/.

71   received 20,000 masks from its sister city, Xi'an: Shennekia Grimshaw, "China Donates 20K Masks to Montgomery County, Maryland," DC News, June 24, 2020, https://www.dcnewsnow .com/news/china-donates-20k-masks-to-montgomery-county-maryland/.

71   Maryland received 100,000 masks: "Maryland Was Overjoyed to Receive over 100,000 Masks from Our Sister State Anhui Province China," Sister States Maryland, May 26, 2020, https:// www.marylandsisterstates.org/2020/05/26/maryland-was-overjoyed-to-receive-over-100000- masks-from-our-sister-state-anhui-province-china/.

72   Taiwanese president Tsai Ing-wen sent a letter congratulating: Sean Lin, "KMT Slams Tsai over 'Taiwan (ROC)' Title," *Taipei Times*, July 10, 2019, https://www.taipeitimes.com/News/taiwan /archives/2019/07/10/2003718420.

72   "at her earliest possible date": Email from Ba Cuicui to Rockville mayor's office, Subject line "Meeting request by Chinese embassy," July 9, 2019. Obtained via Maryland Public Information Act request.

73   "subject everything to the control of the state": "Remarks at the People-to-People Conference."

5: Zooming In

75 internet censors instantly delete even cryptic references: Kuang Keng Kuek Ser, "How China Has Censored Words Relating to the Tiananmen Square Anniversary," *The World*, June 4, 2016, https://theworld.org/stories/2016-06-03/how-china-has-censored-words-relating-tiananmen -square-anniversary.

75 ten million daily users: Eric S. Yuan, "A Message to Our Users," *Zoom Blog*, April 1, 2020, https://blog.zoom.us/a-message-to-our-users/.

75 that number had soared to more than three hundred million: "90-Day Security Plan Progress Report: April 22," *Zoom Blog*, April 22, 2020, https://blog.zoom.us/90-day-security-plan-progress -report-april-22/.

75 In its April 30 filings, Zoom posted revenues: Alex Wilhelm, "Remote Work Helps Zoom Grow 169% in One Year, Posting $328.2M in Q1 Revenue," TechCrunch, June 3, 2020, https:// techcrunch.com/2020/06/02/remote-work-helps-zoom-grow-169-in-one-year-posting-328-2m -q1-revenue/.

75 U.S. government agencies and offices, including the Pentagon: Patrick Tucker, "The Pentagon Is Using Zoom. Is It Safe?" Defense One, April 6, 2020, https://www.defenseone.com/technol ogy/2020/04/pentagon-using-zoom-it-safe/164402/.

75 former Trump national security advisor: Cristiano Lima, "Zoom Taps Former Trump National Security Advisor H. R. McMaster for Board," Politico, April 6, 2020, https://www.po litico.com/news/2020/05/06/zoom-taps-former-trump-national-security-adviser-hr-mcmaster-for -board-239996.

75 More than seven hundred of its employees: Bethany Allen-Ebrahimian, "U.S. Charges Against Zoom Executive Highlight Tech's China Problem," Axios, December 22, 2020, https:// www.axios.com/2020/12/22/china-zoom-charges-influence.

76 "try to be inclusive, especially for people within China": Author interview with Zhou Feng-suo, June 2021.

76 LinkedIn censored Zhou's profile: Megha Rajagopalan, "LinkedIn Censored a Pro-Democracy Activist's Profile in China," BuzzFeed, January 4, 2019, https://www.buzzfeednews.com /article/meghara/china-linkedin-zhou-fengsuo.

76 In 2014, Linkedin had struck a deal with the Chinese government: Paul Mozur and Vindu Goel, "To Reach China, LinkedIn Plays by Local Rules," *New York Times*, October 5, 2014, https:// www.nytimes.com/2014/10/06/technology/to-reach-china-linkedin-plays-by-local-rules.html.

76 an estimated 140 million working professionals: Paul Carsten, "In China, LinkedIn Must Beat Local Rivals, Win Over 'Loser' Workforce to Avoid Google Syndrome," Reuters, June 15, 2014, https://www.reuters.com/article/us-linkedin-china/in-china-linkedin-must-beat-local-rivals -win-over-loser-workforce-to-avoid-google-syndrome-idUKKBN0EQ16N20140615.

77 "While we strongly support freedom of expression": Mozur and Goel, "To Reach China, LinkedIn Plays by Local Rules."

77 By 2019, LinkedIn had 44 million users in China: Sarah Feldman, "The Countries with the Most LinkedIn Members," Statista, April 9, 2019, https://www.statista.com/chart/16265/linkedin -country-members/.

77 "the government is a key stakeholder for us": Wina Huang, "How LinkedIn China Operates—Exclusive Interview," *China Tech Blog*, February 4, 2019, https://www.chinatechblog .org/blog/how-linkedin-china-operates-exclusive-interview

77 the company apologized: @ZhouFengSuo, Twitter, January 3, 2019: "Update, @LinkedIn just apologized and reversed the decision which was deemed an error. I applaud the prompt and correct response by LinkedIn. I hope other companies would do the right job and avoid such error in the future. Thanks to @owenschurchill for the quick follow up," https://twitter.com/ZhouFengSuo /status/1080954055059480576.

78 "very courageous and inspiring": Author interview with Zhou Fengsuo.

79 "security technical leader": United States v. Xinjiang Jin, Case 1:20-mj-01103-RER (United States District Court, Eastern District of New York, 2020).

80 Jin's official job responsibilities: United States v. Xinjiang Jin.

80 calling the 1989 event a "vaccination": Ben Westcott, "Tiananmen Massacre a 'Vaccination' Against Turmoil: Chinese State Media," CNN, June 3, 2019, https://edition.cnn.com/2019/06/03 /asia/china-tiananmen-anniversary-vaccination-intl/index.html.

80 filled with not thousands, but tens of thousands of participants: "Tiananmen 30th Anniversary: Thousands Hold Huge Vigil in Hong Kong," BBC News, June 4, 2019, https://www.bbc.com /news/world-asia-china-48516455.

80   largest mass demonstration in the city's history: "Hong Kong Protest: 'Nearly Two Million' Join Demonstration," BBC, June 17, 2019, https://www.bbc.com/news/world-asia-china-48656471.

81   The account was put into "quarantine" status: United States v. Xinjiang Jin.

81   the Chinese government blocked access to Zoom: Emma Lee, "China Blocks US Video-Conferencing Tool Zoom," TechNode, September 9, 2019, https://technode.com/2019/09/09/china-blocks-us-video-conferencing-tool-zoom/.

81   demanded that Zoom submit "rectification plans": United States v. Xinjiang Jin.

81   "Like many fast-growing companies": "Our Perspective on the DOJ Complaint," *Zoom Blog*, December 18, 2020, https://blog.zoom.us/our-perspective-on-the-doj-complaint/.

81   Zoom agreed to the demands: United States v. Xinjiang Jin.

83   "Even abroad, political attacks on leaders are not allowed": United States v. Xinjiang Jin.

83   "What the MSS is asking for": United States v. Xinjiang Jin.

84   "I am of the generation of the Tiananmen Square movement": "Lee Cheuk-Yan's Lifetime Struggle for Democracy," *Lives and Times Blog*, December 27, 2019, https://livesandtimesblog.com/2019/12/27/lee-cheuk-yans-lifetime-struggle-for-democracy/.

85   Hong Kong authorities forced the museum to close: Lilit Marcus, "Hong Kong's Tiananmen Square Museum Moves Online Following June Closure," CNN, August 4, 2021, https://edition.cnn.com/travel/article/june-fourth-museum-tiananmen-square-hong-kong-cmd/index.html.

85   "to keep the memory alive and to support the movement": Author interview with Lee Cheuk Yan, February 2021.

85   "The reason we opened our account on Zoom": Author interview with Lee Cheuk Yan.

86   On May 22, Zoom suspended Lee's account: United States v. Xinjiang Jin.

87   Wang had been a prominent student leader in the pro-democracy movement: Wang Dan, "What I Learned Leading the Tiananmen Protests," *New York Times*, June 1, 2019, https://www.nytimes.com/2019/06/01/opinion/sunday/tiananmen-protests-china-wang-dan.html.

87   Wang had been resting in his dorm room: Author interview with Wang Dan, June 2021.

88   Just like Zhou, Wang and his fellow organizers expected trouble: Author interview with Wang Dan.

89   The complaints were accompanied by manufactured evidence: United States v. Xinjiang Jin.

90   "I think, *Wow. What a world it is*": Author interview with Wang Dan.

90   some members of Congress had sent a letter to Zoom: Bethany Allen-Ebrahimian, "Lawmakers Demand Answers from Zoom CEO Eric Yuan," Axios, June 12, 2020, https://www.axios.com/2020/06/12/lawmakers-demand-answers-from-zoom-ceo-eric-yuan.

90   Then, on August 10, 2020, Zhou Fengsuo's cell phone rang: Author interview with Zhou Fengsuo.

91   charged Jin with conspiracy to commit interstate harassment: Office of Public Affairs, "China-Based Executive at U.S. Telecommunications Company Charged with Disrupting Video Meetings Commemorating Tiananmen Square Massacre," Press Release, U.S. Department of Justice, December 18, 2020, https://www.justice.gov/opa/pr/china-based-executive-us-telecommunications-company-charged-disrupting-video-meetings.

91   "the United States was paying attention to our suffering": Author interview with Zhou Fengsuo.

91   a "very unique charge under Title 18": Author interview with Joan Meyer, June 15, 2021.

92   the Department of Justice also issued a strong political statement: United States v. Xinjiang Jin.

92   "The allegations in the complaint lay bare the Faustian bargain": Office of Public Affairs, "China-Based Executive at U.S. Telecommunications Company Charged with Disrupting Video Meetings Commemorating Tiananmen Square Massacre."

92   "sap the tree of liberty": Office of Public Affairs, "China-Based Executive at U.S. Telecommunications Company Charged with Disrupting Video Meetings Commemorating Tiananmen Square Massacre."

92   Perhaps the most chilling part of the indictment: United States v. Xinjiang Jin.

93   The National Intelligence Law, enacted in 2017: Tanner, "Beijing's New National Intelligence Law."

93   Article 7 in particular makes these demands clear: "National Intelligence Law of the P.R.C. (2017)," China Law Translate, June 27, 2016, https://www.chinalawtranslate.com/en/national-intelligence-law-of-the-p-r-c-2017/.

93   "trying to shift the balance of these legal obligations": Tanner, "Beijing's New National Intelligence Law."

93   "Companies are faced with draconian consequences": Author interview with Joan Meyer.

94   "expose us to market scrutiny regarding the integrity of our solution": Zoom Video

Communications, "Form 10-K for Fiscal Year Ended January 21, 2020," United States Securities and Exchange Commission, Washington, DC, https://investors.zoom.us/static-files/09a01665-5f33 -4007-8e90-de02219886aa.

95 "would adversely impact our operating margins and harm our business": Zoom Video Communications, "Form 10-K for Fiscal Year Ended January 21, 2020."

95 Insider Threat Program: "Our Perspective on the DOJ Complaint."

95 "Going forward Zoom will not allow requests": "Improving Our Policies as We Continue to Enable Global Collaboration," *Zoom Blog*, June 11, 2020, https://blog.zoom.us/improving-our -policies-as-we-continue-to-enable-global-collaboration/.

97 the U.S. Strategic Framework for the Indo-Pacific: "U.S. Strategic Framework for the Indo-Pacific."

97 "not hesitant to use that economic power to further their political goals": Author interview with John Demers, January 13, 2021.

98 "they understand what the risks are when they use that product": Author interview with John Demers.

99 "rule *by* law": Jerome A. Cohen, " 'Rule of Law' with Chinese Characteristics: Evolution and Manipulation," *International Journal of Constitutional Law* 19, no. 5 (2021): 1882–87, https://doi .org/10.1093/icon/moab085.

99 has little presence on Chinese soil: Paul Mozur and Lin Qiqing, "How Facebook's Tiny China Sales Floor Helps Generate Big Ad Money," *New York Times*, February 7, 2019, https://www .nytimes.com/2019/02/07/technology/facebook-china-internet.html.

100 "required to comply with their respective local laws": Email from Zoom spokesperson to Bethany Allen-Ebrahimian, June 10, 2020, 5:05 p.m.

100 China's internet regulators punished LinkedIn: Paul Mozur, Raymond Zhong, and Steve Lohr, "China Punishes Microsoft's LinkedIn over Lax Censorship," *New York Times*, March 18, 2021, https://www.nytimes.com/2021/03/18/technology/china-linkedin-censorship.html.

100 LinkedIn began aggressively censoring: Helen Davidson, "LinkedIn Blocks Profiles from View in China If Sensitive Topics Mentioned," *The Guardian*, June 18, 2021, https://www.theguard ian.com/world/2021/jun/18/linkedin-blocks-profiles-from-view-in-china-if-sensitive-topics -mentioned.

100 LinkedIn even encouraged users to censor their own profiles: Davidson, "LinkedIn Blocks Profiles from View in China If Sensitive Topics Mentioned."

100 "we will need to implement the Chinese government's restrictions": Davidson, "LinkedIn Blocks Profiles from View in China If Sensitive Topics Mentioned."

101 Apple agreed to Chinese government demands: Jack Nicas, Raymond Zhong, and Daisuke Wakabayashi, "Censorship, Surveillance and Profits: A Hard Bargain for Apple in China," *New York Times*, May 17, 2021, https://www.nytimes.com/2021/05/17/technology/apple-china-censorship -data.html.

101 Apple, too, cited China's laws to justify its behavior: Nicas, Zhong, and Wakabayashi, "Censorship, Surveillance and Profits."

101 Data localization laws are a growing trend everywhere: Paul Mozur, Daisuke Wakabayashi, and Nick Wingfield, "Apple Opening Data Center in China to Comply with Cybersecurity Law," *New York Times*, July 12, 2017, https://www.nytimes.com/2017/07/12/business/apple-china-data -center-cybersecurity.html.

101 in 2015, Germany updated a data storage law: Ben Knight, "German Data Storage Laws 'Threaten Free Trade,'" Deutsche Welle, January 12, 2017, https://www.dw.com/en/german-data -storage-laws-threaten-free-trade/a-37110699#:~:text=Under%20German%20law%2C%20com panies%20must,location%20data%20for%20four%20weeks.

101 criticized Germany's law as "mercantilist": Nigel Cory, "The Worst Innovation Mercantilist Policies of 2016," Information Technology and Innovation Foundation, January 9, 2017, https://itif .org/publications/2017/01/09/worst-innovation-mercantilist-policies-2016.

102 "it can't be ruled out that the foreign state will gain access": Knight, "German Data Storage Laws 'Threaten Free Trade.'"

103 would involve working even more closely with the Chinese government: Jane Li, "Zoom Promised to Be Better at Censoring Global Calls at Beijing's Request," Quartz, June 12, 2020, https://www.yahoo.com/now/zoom-promised-better-censoring-global-091046376.html.

103 Beijing has articulated a vision of "internet sovereignty": Eduard Saakashvili, "The Global Rise of Internet Sovereignty," The Intercept, March 21, 2019, https://www.codastory.com/auth oritarian-tech/global-rise-internet-sovereignty/.

104   In June 2021, the company reported huge earnings: Jordan Novet, "Zoom Reports Blowout Earnings but Warns of a Coming Slowdown," CNBC, June 1, 2021, https://www.cnbc .com/2021/06/01/zoom-zm-earnings-q1-2022.html.

104   White House was still using Zoom's more secure government services: Josh Rogin, "The White House's Use of Zoom for Meetings Raises China-Related Security Concerns," *Washington Post*, March 3, 2021, https://www.washingtonpost.com/opinions/2021/03/03/white-house-zoom -biden-meetings-china-cybersecurity/.

104   "Even Harvard University is still using Zoom": Author interview with Wang Dan.

106   "I believed they would be better to stay in China": "Ex-Google Boss Defends Multiple Controversies," BBC News, May 13, 2019, https://www.bbc.com/news/technology-48262148.

106   a secret project to develop a bespoke search engine: Ryan Gallagher, "Google's Censored Search Engine Would Help China 'Be More Open,' Said Ex-CEO Eric Schmidt," The Intercept, May 14, 2019, https://theintercept.com/2019/05/14/google-search-china-eric-schmidt-comments/.

106   more than 1,400 Google employees signed an open letter: Julia Carrie Wong, "Google Employees Sign Letter Against Censored Search Engine for China," *The Guardian*, November 27, 2018, https://www.theguardian.com/technology/2018/nov/27/google-employees-letter-censored-search -engine-china-project-dragonfly.

106   "would establish a dangerous precedent at a volatile political moment": "We Are Google Employees. Google Must Drop Dragonfly," Medium, November 27, 2018, https://medium.com /@googlersagainstdragonfly/we-are-google-employees-google-must-drop-dragonfly-4c8a30c5e5eb.

106   Pichai was still defending Dragonfly proudly: Nitasha Tiku, "Google's CEO Says Tests of Censored Chinese Search Engine Turned Out Great," *Wired*, October 15, 2018, https://www.wired .com/story/wired-25-sundar-pichai-china-censored-search-engine/.

107   "abetting Beijing's oppression": "Vice President Mike Pence's Remarks on the Administration's Policy Towards China," Hudson Institute, October 4, 2018, https://www.hudson.org/events /1610-vice-president-mike-pence-s-remarks-on-the-administration-s-policy-towards-china10 2018.

107   "You have these global companies": Bethany Allen-Ebrahimian, "Zoom Walks U.S.-China Tightrope," Axios, June 16, 2020, https://www.axios.com/2020/06/16/zoom-us-china.

107   "trying to build products that are value agnostic": Allen-Ebrahimian, "Zoom Walks U.S.-China Tightrope."

108   On the morning of Tuesday, September 28, 2021, I received an email: Bethany Allen-Ebrahimian, "LinkedIn Blocks U.S. Journalists' Profiles in China," Axios, September 30, 2021, https://www.axios.com/2021/09/30/linkedin-blocks-us-journalists-profiles-in-china.

108   Members of Congress weighed in: Jacob Knutson and Alayna Treene, "First Look: Rick Scott Probes LinkedIn, Microsoft on Censoring U.S. Journalists in China," Axios, September 30, 2021, https://www.axios.com/2021/09/30/scott-linkedin-microsoft-china-journalist-profile.

108   The answers to these important questions remain unknown: Bethany Allen-Ebrahimian, "LinkedIn's Unanswered Questions About China Censorship," Axios, October 12, 2021, https:// www.axios.com/2021/10/12/linkedin-unanswered-questions-china-censorship.

108   but just over two weeks later, LinkedIn announced: Sara Fischer, "LinkedIn to Shut Down App in China Following Censorship Controversy," Axios, October 14, 2021, https://www.axios .com/2021/10/14/linkedin-china-new-app-censorship-controversy.

108   in 2020, less than 2 percent of its revenue: Karen Weise and Paul Mozur, "LinkedIn to Shut Down Service in China, Citing 'Challenging' Environment," *New York Times*, October 14, 2021, https://www.nytimes.com/2021/10/14/technology/linkedin-china-microsoft.html.

110   "China plays by a different set of rules": Bethany Allen-Ebrahimian, "Former Google CEO and Others Call for U.S.-China Tech 'Bifurcation,'" Axios, January 26, 2021, https://www.axios .com/2021/01/26/scoop-former-google-ceo-and-others-call-for-us-china-tech-bifurcation.

6: WHO and the Party Man

111   "severely mismanaging and covering up": Alice Miranda Ollstein, "Trump Halts Funding to World Health Organization," April 14, 2020, https://www.politico.com/news/2020/04/14/trump -world-health-organization-funding-186786.

112   China's "best student": Joshua Eisenman and David Shinn, *China's Relations with Africa: A New Era of Political and Security Engagement* (New York: Columbia University Press, 2023).

112   WHO followed normal protocol: "COVID-19—China," World Health Organization, January 5, 2020, https://www.who.int/emergencies/disease-outbreak-news/item/2020-DON229.

113   "no clear evidence of human-to-human transmission": @WHO, "Preliminary Investigations

Conducted by the Chinese Authorities Have Found No Clear Evidence of Human-to-Human Transmission."

113 "very encouraged and impressed": Stephanie Nebehay and Emma Farge, "WHO Lauds Chinese Response to Virus, Says World 'at Important Juncture,'" Reuters, January 29, 2020, https://www.reuters.com/article/us-china-health-who/who-lauds-chinese-response-to-virus-says-world-at-important-juncture-idUSKBN1ZS2EE.

113 "this declaration is not a vote of no confidence in China": "WHO Director-General's Statement on IHR Emergency Committee on Novel Coronavirus (2019-nCoV)," World Health Organization, January 30, 2020, https://www.who.int/director-general/speeches/detail/who-director-general-s-statement-on-ihr-emergency-committee-on-novel-coronavirus-(2019-ncov).

113 agreed not to interrogate China's early response: Gebrekidan et al., "In Hunt for Virus Source, W.H.O. Let China Take Charge."

114 five-page report avoided the sensitive subject of the virus's origin: *Report of the WHO-China Joint Mission on Coronavirus Disease 2019 (COVID-19)*.

114 Brundtland criticized Chinese officials' cover-up: Thomas Crampton, "W.H.O. Criticizes China over Handling of Mystery Disease," *New York Times*, April 7, 2003, https://www.nytimes.com/2003/04/07/international/asia/who-criticizes-china-over-handling-of-mystery-disease.html.

114 "health promotion at the centre of its policies": "Robert Mugabe's WHO Appointment Condemned as 'an Insult,'" BBC News, October 21, 2017, https://www.bbc.com/news/world-africa-41702662.

115 awarded him the Confucius Peace Prize: Tom Phillips, "Zimbabwe's Robert Mugabe Awarded 'China's Nobel Peace Prize,'" *The Guardian*, October 22, 2015, https://www.theguardian.com/world/2015/oct/22/zimbabwes-robert-mugabe-awarded-chinas-nobel-peace-prize.

115 hailing the creation of the "Health Silk Road": "Towards a Health Silk Road," World Health Organization, August 18, 2017, https://www.who.int/director-general/speeches/detail/towards-a-health-silk-road.

115 "His strategy is to coax China": Imogen Foulkes, "Tedros Adhanom Ghebreyesus: The Ethiopian at the Heart of the Coronavirus Fight," BBC News, May 7, 2020, https://www.bbc.com/news/world-africa-51720184.

115 withdraw the United States from WHO: "Remarks by President Trump on Actions Against China," Trump White House Archive, May 29, 2020, https://trumpwhitehouse.archives.gov/briefings-statements/remarks-president-trump-actions-china/.

115 wasn't to take effect until the following year: Drew Hinshaw and Stephanie Armour, "Trump Moves to Pull U.S. Out of World Health Organization in Midst of Covid-19 Pandemic," *Wall Street Journal*, July 7, 2020, https://www.wsj.com/articles/white-house-says-u-s-has-pulled-out-of-the-world-health-organization-11594150928.

115 "missed the opportunity to forestall a global pandemic": François Godement, "Fighting the Coronavirus Pandemic: China's Influence at the World Health Organization," Carnegie Endowment for International Peace, March 23, 2020, https://carnegieendowment.org/2020/03/23/fighting-coronavirus-pandemic-china-s-influence-at-world-health-organization-pub-81405.

115 "succeeded from the start in steering the World Health Organization": Hinnerk Feldwisch-Drentrup, "How WHO Became China's Coronavirus Accomplice," *Foreign Policy*, April 2, 2020, https://foreignpolicy.com/2020/04/02/china-coronavirus-who-health-soft-power/.

116 "WHO's deference to China is no surprise": Kristine Lee, "It's Not Just the WHO: How China Is Moving on the Whole U.N.," Politico, April 15, 2020, https://www.politico.com/news/magazine/2020/04/15/its-not-just-the-who-how-china-is-moving-on-the-whole-un-189029.

116 believed wrongly that Africans were more likely to transmit the novel coronavirus: Zahra Baitie, "A Chinese Exhibit Comparing Africans to Animals Shows the Problematic Racial Attitudes in China," Quartz, October 24, 2017, https://qz.com/africa/1110191/africans-in-china-an-exhibit-comparing-africans-to-animals-shows-the-chinese-problematic-racial-attitudes/.

116 were subjected to discriminatory coronavirus testing: "African Nationals 'Mistreated, Evicted' in China over Coronavirus," Al Jazeera, April 12, 2020, https://www.aljazeera.com/news/2020/4/12/african-nationals-mistreated-evicted-in-china-over-coronavirus.

116 "black people are not allowed to enter the restaurant": "African Nationals 'Mistreated, Evicted' in China over Coronavirus."

116 McDonald's later apologized: "China McDonald's Apologises for Guangzhou Ban on Black People," BBC News, April 14, 2020, https://www.bbc.com/news/world-asia-china-52274326.

116 "amounts to racism towards Africans in China": Chun Han Wong, Joe Parkinson, and Nicholas Bariyo, "African Countries Complain of Racism in Chinese City's Pandemic Controls,"

April 14, 2020, www.wsj.com/articles/african-countries-complain-of-racism-in-chinese-citys-pandemic-controls-11586808397.

116 a viral clip of Nigerians being mistreated in China: @femigbaja, "Today I met with the Chinese ▨ Ambassador to Nigeria on the disturbing allegation of ill treatment of Nigerian citizens in China. I showed him the video clip that had made the rounds. He promised to look into it and get back to my office on Tuesday," Twitter, April 10, 2020, twitter.com/femigbaja/status/1248698266889457664.

116 "It is harmful to sensationalize isolated incidents": @ChineseZimbabwe, Twitter, April 11, 2020, https://twitter.com/ChineseZimbabwe/status/1248998324482564098.

117 "If they acknowledge the racist treatment": Bethany Allen-Ebrahimian, "Complaints of Racism Mar China's Global Image," Axios, April 15, 2020, https://www.axios.com/2020/04/15/coronavirus-racism-discrimination-africa-china.

117 accused the organization of ignoring its December 31 email: "Taiwan Says WHO Ignored Its Coronavirus Questions at Start of Outbreak," Reuters, March 24, 2020, https://www.reuters.com/article/us-health-coronavirus-taiwan/taiwan-says-who-ignored-its-coronavirus-questions-at-start-of-outbreak-idUSKBN21B160.

117 "This attack came from Taiwan": Will Feuer, "WHO Chief Addresses Death Threats, Racist Insults: 'I Don't Give a Damn,'" CNBC, April 9, 2020, https://www.cnbc.com/2020/04/08/who-chief-addresses-death-threats-racist-insults-i-dont-give-a-damn.html.

117 Taiwan called the comments "imaginary": "Coronavirus: WHO Chief and Taiwan in Row over 'Racist' Comments," BBC News, April 9, 2020, https://www.bbc.com/news/world-asia-52230833.

117 Taiwan's extraordinarily rapid and effective domestic response: "Coronavirus: WHO Chief and Taiwan in Row over 'Racist' Comments."

118 "we could have saved more lives": "China Delayed Releasing Coronavirus Info, Frustrating WHO," Associated Press, June 2, 2020, https://apnews.com/article/united-nations-health-ap-top-news-virus-outbreak-public-health-3c061794970661042b18d5aeaaed9fae.

118 "Did [Tedros] go too far?": "China Delayed Releasing Coronavirus Info, Frustrating WHO."

118 Tedros himself offered his first public criticism of Chinese authorities: "WHO's Tedros 'Very Disappointed' China Hasn't Granted Entry to Coronavirus Experts," Reuters, January 5, 2021, https://www.reuters.com/article/us-health-coronavirus-who-china/whos-tedros-very-disappointed-china-hasnt-granted-entry-to-coronavirus-experts-idUSKBN29A28B.

118 encountered resistance from Chinese officials: Javier C. Hernández and James Gorman, "On W.H.O. Trip, China Refused to Hand over Important Data," *New York Times*, February 12, 2021, https://www.nytimes.com/2021/02/12/world/asia/china-world-health-organization-coronavirus.html.

119 "politics was always in the room": Quoted in Kai Kupferschmidt, "'Politics Was Always in the Room.' WHO Mission Chief Reflects on China Trip Seeking COVID-19's Origin," *Science*, February 14, 2021, https://www.science.org/content/article/politics-was-always-room-who-mission-chief-reflects-china-trip-seeking-covid-19-s.

119 "extremely unlikely" that the virus had emerged in a Chinese laboratory: Kupferschmidt, "'Politics Was Always in the Room.'"

119 "real concerns about the methodology and process": Javier C. Hernández, "The U.S. Is Concerned About China's Influence over a Report on the Pandemic's Origins," *New York Times*, March 29, 2021, https://www.nytimes.com/2021/03/29/world/the-us-is-concerned-about-chinas-influence-over-a-report-on-the-pandemics-origins.html.

119 a clear rebuke to China: "WHO Director-General's Remarks at the Member State Briefing on the Report of the International Team Studying the Origins of SARS-CoV-2," World Health Organization, March 30, 2021, https://www.who.int/director-general/speeches/detail/who-director-general-s-remarks-at-the-member-state-briefing-on-the-report-of-the-international-team-studying-the-origins-of-sars-cov-2.

119 "gave life to the lab leak hypothesis": Bill Bishop, *Sinocism*, May 24, 2021.

119 remains elusive: Amy Maxmen, "Scientists Struggle to Probe COVID's Origins amid Sparse Data from China," *Nature*, March 17, 2022, https://www.nature.com/articles/d41586-022-00732-0.

119 Chinese censors removed the video clip: Rachel Liang, "China Censors WHO Chief's Call to End Covid-19 Strategy Dubbed Unsustainable," *Wall Street Journal*, May 11, 2022, https://www.wsj.com/articles/china-censors-who-chiefs-call-to-end-unsustainable-covid-19-strategy-11652270048.

120 "This data could have, and should have, been shared": Brenda Goodman, "Scientists Parse

Another Clue to Possible Origins of Covid-19 as WHO Says All Possibilities 'Remain on the Table,'" CNN, March 17, 2023, https://edition.cnn.com/2023/03/17/health/covid-origins-raccoon-dogs/index.html.

120 During the decade or so leading up to 2020: David Shinn and Joshua Eisenman, "Evolving Principles and Guiding Concepts: How China Gains African Support for Its Core National Interests," *Orbis* 64, no. 2 (Spring 2020): 281.

120 the first country in Africa to establish ties with Beijing: "China and Egypt," Ministry of Foreign Affairs of the People's Republic of China, https://www.fmprc.gov.cn/mfa_eng/wjb_66330 4/zzjg_663340/xybfs_663590/gjlb_663594/2813_663616/#:~:text=The%20Arab%20Repub lic%20of%20Egypt,countries%20maintained%20close%20political%20contact.

121 his famous December 1963–February 1964 trip to ten African countries: "Premier Zhou Enlai's Three Tours of Asian and African Countries," Ministry of Foreign Affairs of the People's Republic of China, https://www.fmprc.gov.cn/mfa_eng/ziliao_665539/3602_665543 /3604_665547/200011/t20001117_697814.html.

121 Zhou met with Ethiopian emperor Haile Selassie: Jean-Pierre Cabestan, "China and Ethiopia: Authoritarian Affinities and Economic Cooperation," *China Perspectives* 4, no. 92 (2012): 53–62.

121 several years before Ethiopia's leaders made a clear move: Seifudein Adem, "China in Ethiopia: Diplomacy and Economics of Sino-Optimism," *African Studies Review* 55, no. 1 (April 2012): 143–60.

122 "The neoliberal paradigm is a dead end": Meles Zenawi, "States and Markets: Neoliberal Limitations and the Case for a Developmental State," in Akbar Noman et al., eds., *Good Growth and Governance in Africa: Rethinking Development Strategies* (Oxford: Oxford University Press, 2011).

122 important tools of a developmental state: Daniel Kibsgaard, "Sino-Ethiopian Relations from Meles Zenawi to Abiy Ahmed: The Political Economy of a Strategic Partnership," China Research Center, June 3, 2020, http://www.chinacenter.net/2020/china_currents/19-2/sino-ethiopian-relations -from-meles-zenawi-to-abiy-ahmed-the-political-economy-of-a-strategic-partnership/.

122 An economic agreement the two countries inked: Cabestan, "China and Ethiopia: Authoritarian Affinities and Economic Cooperation," 53–62.

122 "Ethiopia's perceived diplomatic usefulness": Adem, "China in Ethiopia," 143–60.

122 "'infrastructure for diplomatic support'": Adem, "China in Ethiopia," 143–60.

123 direct party-to-party ties with the EPRDF: Cabestan, "China and Ethiopia: Authoritarian Affinities and Economic Cooperation," 53–62.

123 The two parties signed a memorandum of understanding in 2010: Eisenman and Shinn, *China's Relations with Africa.*

123 referred to Ethiopia's ruling party as China's "best student": Eisenman and Shinn, *China's Relations with Africa.*

123 Meles cracked down: Sarah Left, "22 Killed as Ethiopian Forces Fire on Protesters," *The Guardian*, June 8, 2005, https://www.theguardian.com/world/2005/jun/08/sarahleft.

123 ten thousand people were arrested amid the protests: "Human Rights Watch World Report 2007—Ethiopia," Refworld, January 11, 2007, https://www.refworld.org/docid/45aca29e1a.html.

123 Ethiopia publicly backed China's new Anti-Secession Law: "Ethiopia's Parliament Backs China's Anti-Secession Law," *Addis Tribune*, March 18, 2005, AllAfrica, https://allafrica.com /stories/200503180627.html.

123 authorized the Chinese government to use military force: Edward Cody, "China Sends Warning to Taiwan with Anti-Secession Law," *Washington Post*, March 8, 2005, https://www .washingtonpost.com/archive/politics/2005/03/08/china-sends-warning-to-taiwan-with-anti -secession-law/5dcdfae8-4523-4350-9d45-77a85f6b240f/.

124 Beijing backed the government of Sudan: Nicholas Kristof, "China's Genocide Olympics," *New York Times*, January 24, 2008, https://www.nytimes.com/2008/01/24/opinion/24kristof.html.

124 Meles visited China four times: Cabestan, "China and Ethiopia: Authoritarian Affinities and Economic Cooperation," 53–62.

124 foreign direct investment in Ethiopia grew: *Chinese FDI in Ethiopia: A World Bank Survey*, World Bank, November, 2012, https://openknowledge.worldbank.org/bitstream/handle/109 86/26772/NonAsciiFileName0.pdf;sequence=1.

124 "The economic cooperation between the two countries": *Chinese FDI in Ethiopia.*

124 "There is no aspect of the life of people in the city which was untouched by China": Seufudein Adem, "The Logic of China's Diplomacy in Ethiopia," in Seufudein Adem, *China's Diplomacy in Eastern and Southern Africa* (New York: Routledge, 2014).

125 "fully-fledged strategic partnership": "China-Ethiopia Relations: An Excellent Model for South-South Cooperation," Embassy of the People's Republic of China to the Federal Democratic Republic of Ethiopia, December 2, 2014, http://et.china-embassy.gov.cn/eng/zagx/201412/t20141202_7130871.htm.

125 The EPRDF governed in a top-down, authoritarian manner: Author interview with David Shinn, November 21, 2020.

125 The ethnic Tigrayan was certainly a "party person": Author interview with David Shinn.

125 became the country's ambassador to China in 2011: Cabestan, "China and Ethiopia: Authoritarian Affinities and Economic Cooperation," 53–62.

126 "height of relations" between Ethiopia and China: Author interview with Daniel Kibsgaard, November 28, 2020.

126 Tedros and Chinese foreign minister Wang Yi released a joint statement: "China-Ethiopia Relations."

126 "he had adopted the politics of the EPRF and TPLF": Author interview with David Shinn.

126 "targeting Africa and Africans": "African Union Condemns 'Unfair' ICC," BBC News, October 11, 2013, https://www.bbc.co.uk/news/world-africa-24489059.

126 "EPRDF's strategies and policies are right for our country": Tedros Adhanom Ghebreyesus, "Hi Zelalem. EPRDF's strategies and policies are right for our country. That's why our Ethiopia is on the March. It's [sic] future is bright! The changes I see makes me up and running everday[sic]—the source of my energy. Nothing more satisfying than seeing our country progressing. Please open your eyes. Together we can make it. Don't you agree?," Facebook, March 15, 2014, https://www.facebook.com/DrTedros.Official/posts/593652597370903.

126 "China's candidate" alone: Lawrence Freedman, "Organisation's Failure to Challenge China over Coronavirus Cost Us Dearly," *New Statesman*, April 5, 2020, https://www.newstatesman.com/long-reads/2020/04/how-world-health-organisation-s-failure-challenge-china-over-coronavirus-cost-us.

126 "he had a good relationship with China": Author interview with David Shinn.

127 "It got to the point where he had to choose": Author interview with Joshua Eisenman, December 9, 2022.

7: China Adopts Russia's Disinformation Playbook

128 "It might be US army who brought the epidemic to Wuhan": @zlj517, "2/2 CDC was caught on the spot. When did patient zero begin in US? How many people are infected? What are the names of the hospitals? It might be US army who brought the epidemic to Wuhan. Be transparent! Make public your data! US owe us an explanation!," Twitter, March 12, 2020, 10:37 am, https://twitter.com/zlj517/status/1238111898828066823 (hereafter: @zlj517, "2/2 CDC was caught on the spot").

129 Chinese diplomats, government officials, Beijing-aligned content farms: Jeff Kao and Mia Shuang Li, "How China Built a Twitter Propaganda Machine Then Let It Loose on Coronavirus," ProPublica, March 26, 2020, https://www.propublica.org/article/how-china-built-a-twitter-propaganda-machine-then-let-it-loose-on-coronavirus.

129 a result, in part, of a secret agreement: Mara Hvistendahl, Alexey Kovalev, "Hacked Russian Files Reveal Propaganda Agreement with China," *The Intercept*, December 30, 2022, https://theintercept.com/2022/12/30/russia-china-news-media-agreement/.

129 Chinese state– and Russian state–linked social media accounts: Julian E. Barnes, Matthew Rosenberg, and Edward Wong, "As Virus Spreads, China and Russia See Openings for Disinformation," *New York Times*, March 28, 2020, https://www.nytimes.com/2020/03/28/us/politics/china-russia-coronavirus-disinformation.html.

129 Chinese state media headlines cast doubt on the efficacy: Gerry Shih, "China Turbocharges Bid to Discredit Western Vaccines, Spread Virus Conspiracy Theories," *Washington Post*, January 20, 2021, https://www.washingtonpost.com/world/asia_pacific/vaccines-coronavirus-china-conspiracy-theories/2021/01/20/89bd3d2a-5a2d-11eb-a849-6f9423a75ffd_story.html.

129 In Hong Kong, thousands of residents: Tony Cheung and Ernest Kao, "Thousands of Hongkongers March in Memory of June 4 on Hottest Day of Year," *South China Morning Post*, June 1, 2014, https://www.scmp.com/news/hong-kong/article/1523332/thousands-hongkongers-march-memory-june-4-hottest-day-year.

130 Unbeknownst to the participants, however, the vigil was about to be infiltrated: Taken from research I conducted in 2014, shortly after the incident occurred.

131 In March 2012, a cybersecurity blogger: Brian Krebs, "Twitter Bots Target Tibetan Protests,"

Krebs on Security, March 20, 2012, https://krebsonsecurity.com/2012/03/twitter-bots-target-tib etan-protests/.

131 material presenting Tibetans as a contented and flourishing people: Andrew Jacobs, "It's Another Perfect Day in Tibet!" *New York Times*, July 21, 2014, https://www.nytimes.com/2014/07/22 /world/asia/trending-attractive-people-sharing-upbeat-news-about-tibet-.html.

133 almost doubled, to 5.7 million fans: Alexa Olesen, "Where Did Chinese State Media Get All Those Facebook Followers?" *Foreign Policy*, July 7, 2015, https://foreignpolicy.com/2015/07/07 /china-facebook-peoples-daily-media-soft-power/.

133 "Either China is the new master of journalism": Olesen, "Where Did Chinese State Media Get All Those Facebook Followers?"

133 2013 report on click farms: Nicole Perlroth, "Fake Twitter Followers Become Multimillion-Dollar Business," *New York Times*, April 5, 2013, https://archive.nytimes.com/bits.blogs.nytimes .com/2013/04/05/fake-twitter-followers-becomes-multimillion-dollar-business/.

133 $175,000 contract for adding 580,000 new followers: Daniel Wood, Sean McMinn, and Emily Feng, "China Used Twitter to Disrupt Hong Kong Protests, but Efforts Began Years Earlier," NPR, September 17, 2019, https://www.npr.org/2019/09/17/758146019/china-used-twitter-to -disrupt-hong-kong-protests-but-efforts-began-years-earlier.

133 approximately 635,000 followers: @Echinanews, Twitter, https://twitter.com/echinanews.

134 Chinese authorities began tracking down: Paul Mozur, "Twitter Users in China Face Detention and Threats in New Beijing Crackdown," *New York Times*, January 10, 2019, https://www .nytimes.com/2019/01/10/business/china-twitter-censorship-online.html.

134 jailed for six months for posting several tweets satirizing Xi: Bethany Allen-Ebrahimian, "University of Minnesota Student Jailed in China over Tweets," Axios, January 22, 2020, https:// www.axios.com/2020/01/23/china-arrests-university-minnesota-twitter.

134 saw them deleted by hackers: Mozur, "Twitter Users in China Face Detention and Threats in New Beijing Crackdown."

134 received prison sentences for content they posted to Twitter: Chun Han Wong, "China Is Now Sending Twitter Users to Prison for Posts Most Chinese Can't See," *Wall Street Journal*, January 29, 2021, https://www.wsj.com/articles/china-is-now-sending-twitter-users-to-prison-for-posts -most-chinese-cant-see-11611932917.

134 Twitter characterized the activity as "covert, manipulative behaviors": "Information operations directed at Hong Kong," *Twitter Blog*, August 19, 2019, https://blog.twitter.com/en_us/topics /company/2019/information_operations_directed_at_Hong_Kong.

134 Facebook subsequently announced: Dave Lee, "Hong Kong Protests: Twitter and Facebook Remove Chinese Accounts," BBC News, August 20, 2019, https://www.bbc.com/news/technology -49402222.

134 Google banned more than 200 YouTube channels: Shane Huntley, "Maintaining the Integrity of Our Platforms," *Google Blog*, August 22, 2019, https://blog.google/outreach-initiatives /public-policy/maintaining-integrity-our-platforms/.

134 Guangxi International Expo Affairs Bureau aimed to garner followers: Wood, McMinn, and Feng, "China Used Twitter to Disrupt Hong Kong Protests, but Efforts Began Years Earlier."

135 two-million-yuan contract to the Xinhua News Agency's News and Information Center: 2021年度安徽省文化和旅游厅境外新媒体平台及国内抖音平台账号整合运营服务项目 中标公告("Anhui Culture and Tourism Department: Announcement of Winning Bid for Overseas New Media Platforms and Domestic Douyin Accounts Integrated Operation Services Project"), Province Culture and Tourism Office, January 15, 2021, Anhui, https://web.archive.org /web/20210830211702/https:/ct.ah.gov.cn/public/6595841/8463085.html.

135 increase the number of Twitter, Facebook, and Instagram followers by at least 10 percent: 2021年度安徽省文化和旅游厅境外新媒体平台及国内抖音平台账号整合运营服务项目 ("Anhui Culture and Tourism Department Overseas New Media Platforms and Domestic Douyin Accounts Integrated Services Project") Anhui Provincial Department of Culture and Tourism, December 2020, https://web.archive.org/web/20210830211940/https:/ct.ah.gov.cn/group2/ M00/00/7C/wKg8FGABYMGAYUiaAAHL0fZHC20628.zip.

135 On December 8, 2020, the Wuhan Culture and Tourism Bureau awarded: 2020–2021武 汉文旅海外宣传Youtube&Instagram;平台营销项目合同及中标通知书("Wuhan Culture and Tourism Overseas Publicity on Youtube and Instagram 2020–2021: Online Marketing Project Contract and Notice of Award"), Wuhan Culture and Tourism Bureau, December 16, 2020, https:// web.archive.org/web/20210830212540/http:/wlj.wuhan.gov.cn/zfxxgk/fdzdgknr/zfcg/202012 /t20201216_1559348.shtml.

135   On April 8, 2021, Wuhan's tourism bureau issued another tender: 武汉市文化和旅游局 2020–2021武汉文旅海外宣传平台运营招标公告("Wuhan Culture and Tourism Bureau: Announcement of Tender for the Operation of Wuhan Culture and Tourism Overseas Publicity Platforms 2020–2021"), Wuhan Culture and Tourism Bureau, April 8, 2021, https://web.archive.org/web/20210830210904/http:/wlj.wuhan.gov.cn/zfxxgk/fdzdgknr/zfcg/202104/t20210408_1664082.shtml.

135   On May 7, 2021, the bureau awarded: 武汉市文化和旅游局2020–2021武汉文旅海外宣传平台运营中标（成交）结果公告("Wuhan Culture and Tourism Bureau: Announcement of the Winning Bid for the Operation of Wuhan Culture and Tourism Overseas Publicity Platforms 2020–2021"), Wuhan Culture and Tourism Bureau, May 7, 2021, https://web.archive.org/web/20210830211322/http:/wlj.wuhan.gov.cn/zfxxgk/fdzdgknr/zfcg/202105/t20210507_1681403.shtml.

136   dozens of Chinese diplomats began to open Twitter accounts: "China Finds a Use Abroad for Twitter, a Medium It Fears at Home," *The Economist*, February 20, 2020, https://www.economist.com/china/2020/02/20/china-finds-a-use-abroad-for-twitter-a-medium-it-fears-at-home.

136   Chinese authorities arrested its author for disseminating fake news: Erika Kinetz, "Anatomy of a Conspiracy: With Covid, China Took a Leading Role," Associated Press, February 15, 2021, https://apnews.com/article/pandemics-beijing-only-on-ap-epidemics-media-122b73e134b780919cc1808f3f6f16e8.

136   "tell good stories of China's fight against the epidemic": 中共中央政治局常务委员会召开会议 研究加强新型冠状病毒感染的肺炎疫情防控工作 中共中央总书记习近平主持会议 ("The Politburo Standing Committee of the Central Committee of the Chinese Communist Party Held a Meeting to Investigate Strengthening the Prevention and Control of the Epidemic of Pneumonia Caused by Infection with the Novel Coronavirus—General Secretary of the Central Committee of the Chinese Communist Party Xi Jinping Presided over the Meeting"), Xinhua, February 3, 2020, https://web.archive.org/web/20210815180022/http:/www.xinhuanet.com/politics/leaders/2020-02/03/c_1125527334.htm.

137   "bought time for int'l preparedness": @MFA_China, "China has been updating the WHO & other countries including the US on #COVID19 in an open, transparent & timely manner. China's endeavor to combating the epidemic has bought time for int'l preparedness. Our contribution is there for all to see. @WHO," Twitter, March 9, 2020, https://twitter.com/MFA_China/status/1237000481219571713.

137   "put on a face mask and shut up": Bethany Allen-Ebrahimian, "China's 'Wolf Warrior Diplomacy' Comes to Twitter," Axios, April 22, 2020, https://www.axios.com/2020/04/22/china-diplomacy-twitter.

137   "it does not mean that it originated from China": "Confident Novel Coronavirus Outbreak Under Control by Late April: Health Expert," En.people.cn, February 28, 2020, http://en.people.cn/n3/2020/0227/c90000-9662778.html.

137   diplomatic Twitter accounts began pushing it hard: @ChinaAmbSA, "Although the epidemic first broke out in China, it did not necessarily mean that the virus is originated from China, let alone 'made in China,'" Twitter, March 7, 2020, https://twitter.com/ChinaAmbSA/status/1236322524281044993.

137   Chinese state media began featuring quotes from low-profile conspiracy theorists: Nick Monaco, "No Rest for the Sick: Coronavirus Disinformation from Chinese Users Targets Taiwan," Medium, March 6, 2020, https://medium.com/digintel/china-coronavirus-disinfo-targets-taiwan-2490d99ce6a9.

137   The idea that the United States had created the virus: Kinetz, "Anatomy of a Conspiracy."

138   three thousand Chinese internet users believed that the coronavirus was a bioweapon: "Chris" Fei Shen, "Who Believed in COVID-19 Conspiracies in China?," Digital Asia Hub, January 28, 2021, https://www.digitalasiahub.org/2021/01/28/who-believed-in-covid-19-conspiracies-in-china/.

138   "all different levels of conspiracy theories": Gerry Shih, "Conspiracy Theorists Blame U.S. for Coronavirus. China Is Happy to Encourage Them," *Washington Post*, March 5, 2020, https://www.washingtonpost.com/world/asia_pacific/conspiracy-theorists-blame-the-us-for-coronavirus-china-is-happy-to-encourage-them/2020/03/05/50875458-5dc8-11ea-ac50-18701e14e06d_story.html.

138   China's then ambassador to the United States, disowned the theory: Jonathan Swan and Bethany Allen-Ebrahimian, "Top Chinese Official Disowns U.S. Military Lab Coronavirus Conspiracy," Axios, March 22, 2020, https://www.axios.com/2020/03/22/china-coronavirus-ambassador-cui-tiankai.

139 In April, the Chinese embassy in France: John Irish, "Outraged French Lawmakers Demand Answers on 'Fake' Chinese Embassy Accusations," Reuters, April 16, 2020, https://www.reuters .com/article/us-health-coronavirus-france-china-idUSKCN21X30C.

139 In early May, the Chinese embassy in Berlin published: Bethany Allen-Ebrahimian, "Chinese Embassy Publishes 16-Point Coronavirus Rebuttal," Axios, May 1, 2020, https://www.axios .com/2020/05/01/china-embassy-coronavirus-disinformation-propaganda.

139 eight Chinese doctors were detained and interrogated: Gerry Shih and Hannah Knowles, "A Chinese Doctor Was One of the First to Warn About Coronavirus. He Got Detained—and Infected," *Washington Post*, February 4, 2020, https://www.washingtonpost.com/world/2020/02/04 /chinese-doctor-has-coronavirus/.

139 "What on earth happened in the bioweapons lab in Fort Detrick, Maryland?": "这10个 追问，美国必须回答" ("The U.S. Must Answer These 10 Follow-Up Questions"), *People's Daily*, May 1, 2020, http://world.people.com.cn/n1/2020/0501/c1002-31695371.html.

139 Disinformation researchers also found that Beijing-aligned content farms: Nick Monaco, "Detecting Digital Fingerprints: Tracing Chinese Disinformation in Taiwan," joint publication of the Institute for the Future, Graphika, and the International Republican Institute, August 25, 2020, https://legacy.iftf.org/disinfo-in-taiwan/.

140 Chinese foreign ministry officials and Chinese state media began heavily promoting: Michael D. Shear et al., "Biden Orders Intelligence Inquiry into Origins of Virus," *New York Times*, May 26, 2021, https://www.nytimes.com/2021/05/26/us/politics/biden-coronavirus-origins.html.

140 "What illness did those reported military athletes have exactly?": @ChineseZimbabwe, "The US should release the data concerning the sickened American military athletes who attended the World Military Games in Wuhan. In October 2019, the US sent more than 300 people to Wuhan for the Games. What illness did those reported military athletes have exactly?" Twitter, July 31, 2021, 3:59 am, https://www.trendsmap.com/twitter/tweet/1421380031885025280.

140 Zhao Lijian called on the United States to invite WHO to investigate Fort Detrick: "Foreign Ministry Spokesperson Zhao Lijian's Regular Press Conference on July 30, 2021," Ministry of Foreign Affairs of the People's Republic of China, July 30, 2021, https://www.fmprc.gov.cn /mfa_eng/xwfw_665399/s2510_665401/2511_665403/202107/t20210730_9170797.html.

140 In July, the *Global Times* also promoted a petition: "Global Times invites you to sign the joint letter," *Global Times*, https://vote.huanqiu.com/af96c/?sign=false.

140 Disinformation researchers later found that at least 13.3 million: Nick Monaco, "2+2=5: Signatures from Chinese COVID-19 WeChat Petition to the WHO Show Signs of Manipulation," Miburo Substack, February 3, 2022, https://miburo.substack.com/p/china-who-petition-mani pulation.

140 ProPublica obtained records of fake Twitter accounts: Kao and Li, "How China Built a Twitter Propaganda Machine Then Let It Loose on Coronavirus."

141 a network of "deep fake" profiles on Twitter, Facebook, and YouTube: Benjamin Strick, "Revealed: Coordinated Attempt to Push Pro-China, Anti-Western Narratives on Social Media," Centre for Information Resilience, August 5, 2021, https://www.info-res.org/post/revealed-coordinated -attempt-to-push-pro-china-anti-western-narratives-on-social-media.

141 "deliberate effort to distort international perceptions": Jane Tang, "Researchers Spot Deep Fake Profile Photos Linked to Pro-China Twitter Accounts," Radio Free Asia, August 12, 2021, https://www.rfa.org/english/news/china/fake-08122021090719.html.

141 "Swiss Biologist Wilson Edward's Explosive Revelation": @idzhang3, "Wilson Edwards是 典型英伦名字，本来就小概率是瑞士人。众志成城之下，传播路线明确了：央视、新华 社、人民日报、环球时报均抄自新华社主管主办的参考消息7月31日报道。参考消息7 月31日报道抄自已被删除的观察者网7月28日报道，并把斐济改成美国。斐济的那个所 谓南太之声是中国人办的" ("Wilson Edwards is a typical British name that would have a small probability of being Swiss. Unity is strength and the line of communication here is clear: CCTV, Xinhua News Agency, People's Daily, and Global Times all copied the same July 31 report from Reference News, which itself is run by Xinhua. The July 31 report from Reference News had been lifted from a deleted July 28 report published by Guancha, and then changed from Fiji to the United States. Fiji's so-called Voice of the South Pacific is run by the Chinese."), Twitter, August 10, 2021, https://twitter.com/idzhang3/status/1425076834547511296.

141 Swiss citizenry records contained no such person: @SwissEmbChina, "Looking for Wilson Edwards, alleged 🇨🇭 biologist, cited in press and social media in China over the last several days. If you exist, we would like to meet you! But it is more likely that this is a fake news, and we call on the

Chinese press and netizens to take down the posts," Twitter, August 10, 2021, https://twitter.com /SwissEmbChina/status/1425042973289504770.

143   Environmental Protection Agency had engaged in illegal propaganda: "Environmental Protection Agency—Application of Publicity or Propaganda and Anti-Lobbying Provisions," U.S. Government Accountability Office, Washington, DC, December 14, 2015, https://www.gao.gov/pro ducts/b-326944.

143   A book on military strategy published in 1999: Qiao Liang and Wang Xiangsui, *Unrestricted Warfare* (People's Liberation Army Literature and Arts Publishing House, 1999).

144   The United States had the world's highest number of known cases: Benjamin Rosenberg, Tim Ryan Williams, and Christina Animashaun, "50 Million World Covid-19 Cases: The Biggest Outbreaks, Explained," Vox, November 9, 2020, https://www.vox.com/2020/11/8/21550345/50 -million-confirmed-cases-covid-19-worldwide.

144   Chinese censors began scrubbing online spaces: Bethany Allen-Ebrahimian, "Beijing Is Rewriting the Ukraine Narrative," Axios, March 8, 2022, https://www.axios.com/2022/03/08/bei jings-ukraine-censorship.

144   "anything unfavorable to Russia or pro-Western": Samuel Wade, "Minitrue: Keep Weibo Posts on Ukraine Favorable to Russia; Control Comments," *China Digital Times*, February 22, 2022, https://chinadigitaltimes.net/2022/02/minitrue-keep-weibo-posts-on-ukraine-favorable-to-russia -control-comments/.

144   Chinese state media even bought ads on Meta: Ashley Gold, "China's State Media Buys Meta Ads Pushing Russia's Line on War," Axios, March 9, 2022, https://www.axios.com/2022/03/09 /chinas-state-media-meta-facebook-ads-russia.

144   Zhao Lijian accused the United States of operating "dangerous" biolabs in Ukraine: "China Pushes Conspiracy Theory About U.S. Labs in Ukraine," Bloomberg, March 8, 2022, https://www .bloomberg.com/news/articles/2022-03-08/china-pushes-russia-conspiracy-theory-about-u-s-labs -in-ukraine?leadSource=uverify%20wall.

8: "Chewing Gum Stuck to the Bottom of China's Shoe"

147   they had been underground operators, working for the United Front: John Garnaut, *The Rise and Fall of the House of Bo: How a Murder Exposed the Cracks in China's Leadership* (New York: Penguin, 2012).

148   James Jiann Hua To, a brilliant New Zealand political scientist: "Writing China: James Jiann Hua To, 'Qiaowu: Extra-Territorial Policies for the Overseas Chinese,'" *Wall Street Journal*, August 15, 2021, https://www.wsj.com/articles/BL-CJB-23602.

148 · In 2017, Anne-Marie Brady, the New Zealand political scientist: Brady, "Magic Weapons."

149   he published a story about a PLA International Liaison Department front: John Garnaut, "Chinese Military Woos Big Business," *Sydney Morning Herald*, May 25, 2013, https://www.smh .com.au/business/chinese-military-woos-big-business-20130524-2k6r1.html.

149   A 2003 PLA International Liaison Department manual Garnaut obtained: Garnaut, "Chinese Military Woos Big Business."

149   "large covert informant networks" at Australian universities: John Garnaut, "Chinese Spies at Sydney University," *Sydney Morning Herald*, April 21, 2014, https://www.smh.com.au/national /chinese-spies-at-sydney-university-20140420-36ywk.html.

149   entered Australia to pursue a Chinese citizen: John Garnaut and Philip Wen, "Chinese Police Pursued a Man to Australia on a 'Fox Hunt' Without Permission," *Sydney Morning Herald*, April 15, 2015, https://www w.smh.com.au/nationalhinesee-police-pursued-a-man-to-australia-on-a -fox-hunt-without-permission-20150415-1mlum2.html.

150   China had been Australia's top trade partner: Hannah Reale, "Australia and China Aren't Backing Down," *The Wire*, June 6, 2021, https://www.thewirechina.com/2021/06/06/australia-and -china-arent-backing-down/.

150   withdrew from the just-launched Quadrilateral Security Dialogue: Indrani Bagchi, "Australia to Pull Out of 'Quad' That Excludes China," *Times of India*, February 6, 2008, https://timesofin dia.indiatimes.com/india/australia-to-pull-out-of-quad-that-excludes-china/articleshow/27601 09.cms.

150   "the potential to give its neighbours cause for concern": "2016 Defence White Paper," Department of Defense, Australian Government, June 2020, https://www.defence.gov.au/about/public ations/2016-defence-white-paper.

150   "natural and legitimate": "2016 Defence White Paper."

150   In 2014, Xi Jinping addressed Australia's Parliament: "2016 Defence White Paper."

150   Turnbull was considered "soft" on China: John Garnaut, "Is Malcolm Turnbull 'Soft' on China Because of His Family Connections?" *Sydney Morning Herald*, September 15, 2015, https://www.smh.com.au/national/is-malcolm-turnbull-soft-on-china-because-of-his-family-connections-20150915-gjnbz8.html.

150   Turnbull had "healthy skepticism" for the intelligence community: Christopher Joye, "Liberal Leadership: Malcolm Turnbull the Most Gifted PM Since Menzies," *Australian Financial Review*, September 15, 2015, https://www.afr.com/politics/liberal-leadership-malcolm-turnbull-the-most-gifted-pm-since-menzies-20150915-gjmphr.

151   "less prone to seeing the world through a security prism": Michelle Innis, "Malcolm Turnbull Defeats Tony Abbott to Become Prime Minister of Australia," *New York Times*, September 14, 2015, https://www.nytimes.com/2015/09/15/world/asia/tony-abbott-liberal-party-australia.html.

151   "it was the intelligence community that moved first": Author interview with Justin Bassi, September 30, 2022.

151   Turnbull wasn't inherently suspicious of Beijing: Author interview with Justin Bassi.

152   "our system as a whole had not grasped the nature and the magnitude of the threat": "Speech Introducing the National Security Legislation Amendment (Espionage and Foreign Interference) Bill 2017," Malcolm Turnbull personal website, December 7, 2017, https://www.malcolmturnbull.com.au/media/speech-introducing-the-national-security-legislation-amendment-espionage-an.

153   Dastyari had pledged to support China's position: Primrose Riordan, "Sam Dastyari Pledges to Support China on South China Sea Beside Labor Donor," *Australian Financial Review*, August 31, 2016, https://www.afr.com/politics/sam-dastyari-pledges-to-support-china-on-south-china-sea-beside-labor-donor-20160831-gr5mwk.

153   He tipped off Huang: Katharine Murphy, "Sam Dastyari's Loyalty to Australia Questioned After He Tipped Off Chinese Donor," *The Guardian*, November 29, 2019, https://www.theguardian.com/australia-news/2017/nov/29/sam-dastyaris-loyalty-to-australia-questioned-after-he-tipped-off-chinese-donor.

153   pressured Labor's foreign affairs spokesperson: Quentin McDermott, "Sam Dastyari 'Tried to Pressure' Tanya Plibersek Not to Meet with Chinese Activist," Australian Broadcasting Corporation, December 10, 2017, https://www.abc.net.au/news/2017-12-11/dastyari-tried-to-pressure-plibesek-over-chinese-meeting/9244600.

153   five thousand Australian dollars to cover a legal bill: James Massola, "Chinese Donor the Yuhu Group Steps in to Help Sam Dastyari," *Sydney Morning Herald*, March 27, 2015, https://www.smh.com.au/politics/federal/chinese-donor-the-yuhu-group-steps-in-to-help-sam-dastyari-20150327-1m9be2.html.

154   abandon its opposition to the air defense identification zone: Riordan, "Sam Dastyari Pledges to Support China on South China Sea Beside Labor Donor."

154   "Is the Labor party's foreign policy for sale?": "Sam Dastyari's Expenses Scandal a 'Cash for Comment' Moment, Says Turnbull," *The Guardian*, September 2, 2016, https://www.theguardian.com/australia-news/2016/sep/02/sam-dastyaris-expenses-scandal-a-cash-for-comment-moment-says-turnbull.

154   Beijing was becoming "coercive" in its approach: "Keynote Address at the 16th IISS Asia Security Summit, Shangri-La Dialogue," Malcolm Turnbull personal website, June 3, 2017, https://www.malcolmturnbull.com.au/media/keynote-address-at-the-16th-iiss-asia-security-summit-shangri-la-dialogue.

154   It identified the Chinese government as the top perpetrator: Chris Uhlman, "Top-Secret Report Uncovers High-Level Chinese Interference in Australian Politics," 9News, May 28, 2018, https://www.9news.com.au/national/chinese-communist-party-interference-australian-politics/a6e8e4e0-28f6-4b7a-a94c-ba4b98ea8aa1.

155   Turnbull spoke before Parliament: "Speech Introducing the National Security Legislation Amendment (Espionage and Foreign Interference) Bill 2017."

155   "poisons the atmosphere of the China-Australia relationship": Christopher Knaus and Tom Phillips, "Turnbull Says Australia Will 'Stand Up' to China as Foreign Influence Row Heats Up," *The Guardian*, December 9, 2017, https://www.theguardian.com/australia-news/2017/dec/09/china-says-turnbulls-remarks-have-poisoned-the-atmosphere-of-relations.

157   "Zhang holds one of the four most important positions": John Garnaut, "China Gets into the Business of Making Friends," *Sydney Morning Herald*, May 25, 2013, https://www.smh.com.au/world/china-gets-into-the-business-of-making-friends-20130524-2k6q3.html.

157 "spider's web on a spider's web on a spider's web": Author interview with Richard Aldrich, June 22, 2021.

158 "Prior to 2016, there were some within the U.S. system": Author interview with John Lee, April 19, 2022.

159 spoken with Tsai in a phone call: Mark Landler and David Sanger, "Trump Speaks with Taiwan's Leader, an Affront to China," *New York Times,* December 2, 2016, https://www.nytimes.com/2016/12/02/us/politics/trump-speaks-with-taiwans-leader-a-possible-affront-to-china.html.

160 Moreover, months of infighting among different factions: Rogin, *Chaos Under Heaven,* 18.

160 The two leaders held their first summit in April 2017: David Nakamura, "At Mar-a-Lago, Trump Welcomes China's Xi in First Summit," *Washington Post,* April 7, 2017, https://www.washingtonpost.com/politics/at-mar-a-lago-trump-to-welcome-chinas-xi-for-high-stakes-inaugural-summit/2017/04/06/0235cdd0-1ac2-11e7-bcc2-7d1a0973e7b2_story.html.

160 a "terrific person": Z. Byron Wolf, "One Reason President Donald Trump Changed His Rhetoric on China? He Really Likes the Chinese President," CNN, April 18, 2017, https://edition.cnn.com/2017/04/18/politics/president-donald-trump-chinese-president-xi-friendly/index.html.

160 "still in search of a strategy": Jeffrey A. Bader, David Dollar, and Ryan Hass, "U.S.-China Relations, 6 Months into the Trump Presidency," Brookings Institution, August 14, 2017, https://www.brookings.edu/blog/order-from-chaos/2017/08/14/u-s-china-relations-6-months-into-the-trump-presidency/.

161 In December 2016, Gen. Michael Flynn, Trump's first national security advisor: Rogin, *Chaos Under Heaven,* 7.

162 The ASIO report's key findings: Stephanie Borys, "China's 'Brazen' and 'Aggressive' Political Interference Outlined in Top-Secret Report," ABC News, May 28, 2018, https://www.abc.net.au/news/2018-05-29/chinas-been-interfering-in-australian-politics-for-past-decade/9810236.

162 "push back against authoritarian interference": "How China Interferes in Australia and How Democracies Can Push Back," U.S. House of Representatives Committee Repository, March 21, 2018, https://docs.house.gov/meetings/AS/AS00/20180321/108048/HHRG-115-AS00-Wstate-GarnautJ-20180321.pdf.

162 U.S. National Security Strategy was released: "National Security Strategy of the United States of America," Trump White House Archives, December 2017, https://trumpwhitehouse.archives.gov/wp-content/uploads/2017/12/NSS-Final-12-18-2017-0905.pdf.

162 "international consensus that China's industrial policies": "U.S. Strategic Framework for the Indo-Pacific."

163 "they were ahead of the curve": Bethany Allen-Ebrahimian and Zach Dorfman, "Newly Declassified Report Lays Out U.S. Strategy in Asia," Axios, January 12, 2021, https://www.axios.com/2021/01/12/indo-pacific-strategy-trump-administration-china.

163 clear campaign of intimidation: Matt Nippert, "Police Fail to Crack Case of Burgled China Scholar Anne-Marie Brady," *New Zealand Herald,* February 12, 2019, https://www.nzherald.co.nz/nz/police-fail-to-crack-case-of-burgled-china-scholar-anne-marie-brady/YPJVXRC3KEIR3Z6TN2RG2VTZ44/.

163 complimenting and lambasting China's leaders: "Trump China Visit: US Leader Strikes Warmer Tone with Xi Jinping," BBC News, November 9, 2017, https://www.bbc.co.uk/news/world-asia-china-41924228.

164 "in almost every field office that the FBI has": "[Open] Hearing on Worldwide Threats," U.S. Senate Select Committee on Intelligence, February 13, 2018, https://www.intelligence.senate.gov/hearings/open-hearing-worldwide-threats-0#.

164 extensive Section 301 investigation into China's trade practices: "Findings of the Investigation into China's Acts, Policies, and Practices Related to Technology Transfer, Intellectual Property, and Innovation Under Section 301 of the Trade Act of 1974," Office of the United States Trade Representative, Executive Office of the President, March 22, 2018, https://ustr.gov/sites/default/files/Section%20301%20FINAL.PDF.

164 "unfair" trade practices: Nandita Bose and Andrea Shalal, "Trump Says China Is 'Killing Us with Unfair Trade Deals,'" Reuters, August 7, 2019, https://www.reuters.com/article/us-usa-trade-china/trump-says-china-is-killing-us-with-unfair-trade-deals-idUSKCN1UX1WO.

164 the United States renamed its Pacific Command: Idrees Ali, "In Symbolic Nod to India, U.S. Pacific Command Changes Name," Reuters, May 30, 2018, https://www.reuters.com/article/us-usa-defense-india/in-symbolic-nod-to-india-u-s-pacific-command-changes-name-idUSKCN1IV2Q2.

164 Trump announced $34 billion in tariffs: Ana Swanson, "Trump's Trade War with China

Is Officially Underway," *New York Times*, July 5, 2018, https://www.nytimes.com/2018/07/05/busi
ness/china-us-trade-war-trump-tariffs.html.

165   what became the Trump administration's China policy: "Vice President Mike Pence's Remarks on the Administration's Policy Towards China."

165   "public indictment" of Beijing: Jane Perlez, "Pence's China Speech Seen as Portent of 'New
Cold War,'" *New York Times*, October 5, 2018, https://www.nytimes.com/2018/10/05/world/asia
/pence-china-speech-cold-war.html.

165   U.S. Department of Justice announced its China Initiative: Office of Public Affairs, "Attorney General Jeff Sessions Announces New Initiative to Combat Chinese Economic Espionage,"
Transcript of speech, U.S. Department of Justice, November 1, 2018, https://www.justice.gov/opa
/speech/attorney-general-jeff-sessions-announces-new-initiative-combat-chinese-economic-esp
ionage.

166   Five Eyes governments also began sharing classified information: Noah Barkin, "Exclusive:
Five Eyes Intelligence Alliance Builds Coalition to Counter China," Reuters, October 12, 2018,
https://www.reuters.com/article/us-china-fiveeyes/exclusive-five-eyes-intelligence-alliance-builds
-coalition-to-counter-china-idUSKCN1MM0GH.

166   "Consultations with our allies": Barkin, "Exclusive: Five Eyes Intelligence Alliance Builds
Coalition to Counter China."

166   "Australia going first meant no one could honestly say": Author interview with Justin Bassi.

166   Australia's ban on Huawei: Cassell Bryan-Low and Colin Packham, "How Australia Led the
US in Its Global War Against Huawei," *Sydney Morning Herald*, May 22, 2019, https://www.smh
.com.au/world/asia/how-australia-led-the-us-in-its-global-war-against-huawei-20190522-p51pv8
.html.

167   boost spending on China spying: Warren P. Strobel and Dustin Volz, "U.S. Boosts China
Spying Budget to Meet Growing Economic, National-Security Threat," *Wall Street Journal*, December 3, 2020, https://www.wsj.com/articles/u-s-boosts-china-spying-budget-to-meet-growing
-economic-national-security-threat-11607037778.

167   "reinstate the Legislative Council members": Reuters, "Five Eyes Allies Call on China to Reverse Ban on Hong Kong Pro-Democracy Legislators," *The Guardian*, November 19, 2020, https://
www.theguardian.com/world/2020/nov/19/five-eyes-allies-call-on-china-to-reverse-ban-on-hong
-kong-pro-democracy-legislators.

167   "beware of their eyes being poked and blinded": Associated Press, "China Says Five Eyes
Alliance Will Be 'Poked and Blinded' over Hong Kong Stance," *The Guardian*, November 20, 2020,
https://www.theguardian.com/world/2020/nov/20/china-says-five-eyes-alliance-will-be-poked-and
-blinded-over-hong-kong-stance.

167   "Australia is always messing around": 胡锡进，"澳大利亚政府近日跟着美国对中国的
指责跳得很高，老胡一直顾不上它，一篇针对澳大利亚的环时社评也没写，我的微博、
视频胡侃还有推特都没有提它。主要是担心写了说了没人看。澳大利亚就那么大分量，
我过去写的澳大利亚的东西，市场效果都很差，很多时候比写新加坡还差，可能是新加
坡离中国更近"("Today the Australian government overreacted and followed the US in its criticism
of China. I don't let it get to me. I didn't write any editorials about Australia for the Global Times,
didn't even mention them on my Weibo, YouTube, or Twitter. Mainly because I was worried no-one
would see it if I did. Australia is apparently such a heavyweight, yet every time I write about them it
doesn't gain much traction at all, often even less so than when I write about Singapore. Maybe it's because Singapore is closer to China."), Weibo, April 27, 2020, https://www.weibo.com/1989660417
/IFjKsiddn?from=page_1035051989660417_profile&wvr=6&mod=weibotime&type=comment.

167   warned Chinese citizens against traveling to Australia: Matthew Doran, "China Issues
Upgraded Travel Warning for Australia," ABC News, July 13, 2020, https://www.abc.net.au/news
/2020-07-13/china-issues-upgraded-travel-warning-for-australia/12451626.

168   it had issued a travel advisory: Daniel Hurst, "China Travel Warning: Australians Told They
May Be at Risk of Arbitrary Detention," *The Guardian*, July 7, 2020, https://www.theguardian.com
/australia-news/2020/jul/07/china-travel-warning-australians-told-they-may-be-at-risk-of-arbitrary
-detention.

168   Chinese investment in Australia also plummeted: Angus Watson, "Chinese Investment in
Australia Plunged Last Year as Tensions Worsened," CNN Business, March 1, 2021, https://edition
.cnn.com/2021/03/01/economy/china-australia-investment-intl-hnk/index.html.

168   Australia tightened rules on foreign investment: Eliza Borrello, "Scott Morrison Tightens
Foreign Investment Rules in Wake of Darwin Port 'Sale,'" ABC News, March 18, 2016, https://
www.abc.net.au/news/2016-03-18/scott-morrison-tightens-foreign-investment-rules/7257624.

168 "the Fourteen Grievances": Jonathan Kearsley, Eryk Bagshaw, and Anthony Galloway, " 'If You Make China the Enemy, China Will Be the Enemy': Beijing's Fresh Threat to Australia," *Sydney Morning Herald*, November 18, 2020, https://www.smh.com.au/world/asia/if-you-make-china-the -enemy-china-will-be-the-enemy-beijing-s-fresh-threat-to-australia-20201118-p56fqs.html?utm _medium=Social&utm_source=Twitter#Echobox=1605683701.

168 "extraordinary attack on the Australian government": Kearsley, Bagshaw, and Galloway, " 'If You Make China the Enemy, China Will Be the Enemy': Beijing's Fresh Threat to Australia,"

168 "helpfully unambiguous ransom note": Kelsey Munro, November 18, 2020, Twitter, https://twitter.com/KelseyMunro/status/1329008912549306368.

168 "a template for illiberal order-building": @RushDoshi, "Beijing sent a list of 14 grievances to Australia supposedly justifying its economic coercion against it. The list is revealing. It shows the PRC holds countries responsible for their free *civil societies* & serves as a template for illiberal order-building. Some thoughts: 1/," Twitter, November 18, 2020, https://twitter.com/RushDoshi /status/1329076203609677826.

169 "shape Australian internal behavior": @RushDoshi, "Beijing sent a list of 14 grievances to Australia."

169 82 percent of Australian iron ore exports went to China: Tracy Hu, "Australia to Continue to Supply Most of China's Iron Ore Despite Trade Tensions," S&P Global Market Intelligence, June 28, 2020, https://www.spglobal.com/marketintelligence/en/news-insights/latest-news-headlines/aust ralia-to-continue-to-supply-most-of-china-8217-s-iron-ore-despite-trade-tensions-59208917.

169 currently developing an ore mine in Simandou, Guinea: Hu, "Australia to Continue to Supply Most of China's Iron Ore Despite Trade Tensions."

169 iron ore prices soared: Elizabeth Knight, "The Only Way Is Up: The Iron Ore Price Boom That Refuses to Die," *Sydney Morning Herald*, April 21, 2021, https://www.smh.com.au/business /markets/the-only-way-is-up-the-iron-ore-price-boom-that-refuses-to-die-20210421-p57l71.html.

169 binding dispute resolution mechanism in the WTO: Colin Packham, "Australian PM Calls for WTO Reform as Tensions with China Mount," Reuters, June 9, 2021, https://www.reuters.com /business/australian-pm-call-wto-reform-tensions-with-china-mount-2021-06-08/.

169 "China will be the enemy": Kearsley, Bagshaw, and Galloway, " 'If You Make China the Enemy, China Will Be the Enemy': Beijing's Fresh Threat to Australia."

9: Hong Kong Outlaws Global Activism

170 Samuel Chu woke up when his cell phone rang: Details from Chu's experience of that day are from author interview with Samuel Chu, January 27, 2022.

170 He'd gone to bed after watching some episodes of *Law & Order*: Samuel Chu, "Why Is China Coming After Americans Like Me in the U.S.?," *New York Times*, August 10, 2020, https:// www.nytimes.com/2020/08/10/opinion/china-hong-kong-arrest.html.

171 the National People's Congress, China's rubber-stamp legislature, convened: Huileng Tan, "China Is Set to Introduce a New Security Law for Hong Kong, Seen Strengthening Hold over City," CNBC, May 21, 2020, https://www.cnbc.com/2020/05/22/china-to-introduce-new-hong -kong-security-law-amid-protests-coronavirus.html.

171 "law-based and forceful measures": "Draft Decision on HK National Security Legisla- tion Submitted to NPC," Xinhua, May 22, 2020, http://www.xinhuanet.com/english/2020-05 /22/c_139078071.htm.

171 "high degree of autonomy, except in foreign and defense affairs": "Joint Declaration of the Government of the United Kingdom of Great Britain and Northern Ireland and the Government of the People's Republic of China on the Question of Hong Kong," https://www.mfa.gov.cn/ce/cohk //eng/syzx/yglz/t25956.htm.

172 Beijing justified its actions: Huileng Tan, "China Is Moving In with National Security Law as Hong Kong Legislature 'Has Failed to Deliver,' Official Says," CNBC, May 26, 2020, https:// www.cnbc.com/2020/05/26/china-proposed-security-law-as-hong-kong-has-failed-to-deliver -official.html.

172 Article 23 of the Basic Law: "Chapter II—Relationship Between the Central Authorities and the Hong Kong Special Administrative Region," Basic Law, https://www.basiclaw.gov.hk/en /basiclaw/chapter2.html.

172 half a million people flooded the streets in protest: Keith Bradsher, "Security Laws Target of Huge Hong Kong Protest," *New York Times*, July 2, 2003, https://www.nytimes.com/2003/07/02 /world/security-laws-target-of-huge-hong-kong-protest.html.

172 canceled plans to introduce a mandatory patriotic education: "Hong Kong Backs Down over Chinese Patriotism Classes," *BBC News*, September 8, 2012, https://www.bbc.com/news/world-asia-china-19529867.

172 called for Hong Kong to enact its own national security law: Jeffie Lam and Gary Cheung, "Hong Kong Should Make Its Own National Security Law Rather than Implement Beijing's, Scholar Says," *South China Morning Post*, January 23, 2015, https://www.scmp.com/news/hong-kong/article/1689353/hong-kong-should-make-its-own-national-security-law-rather-implement.

172 again pressed for the imposition of a national security law: Chris Buckley, "China Vows Tougher Security in Hong Kong. Easier Said than Done," *New York Times*, November 6, 2019, https://www.nytimes.com/2019/11/06/world/asia/hong-kong-protests-china-national-security.html.

173 more than a million people attended a protest against the extradition bill: David Lague, James Pomfret, and Greg Torode, "How Murder, Kidnappings and Miscalculation Set Off Hong Kong's Revolt," Reuters, December 20, 2019, https://www.reuters.com/investigates/special-report/hongkong-protests-extradition-narrative/.

173 "violent criminals" controlled by the United States and other foreign forces: "Demonstrators Betray Hidden US Hand Behind HK Protests," *China Daily*, September 8, 2019, https://www.chinadaily.com.cn/a/201909/08/WS5d75046fa310cf3e3556a5a8.html.

173 a distraction from economic concerns in Hong Kong: Li Yuan, "Why Many in China Oppose Hong Kong's Protests," *New York Times*, July 1, 2019, https://www.nytimes.com/2019/07/01/business/hong-kong-china-protests.html.

173 pro-China students ripped up signs: Naaman Zhou, "Pro-China and Pro-Hong Kong Students Clash at University of Queensland," *The Guardian*, July 24, 2019, https://www.theguardian.com/australia-news/2019/jul/24/china-hong-kong-students-clash-university-queensland.

173 Hong Kong Police Force was using the law to target protesters: Mary Hui, "Hong Kong Police Are Using Coronavirus Restrictions to Clamp Down on Protesters," Quartz, April 1, 2020, https://qz.com/1829892/hong-kong-police-use-coronavirus-rules-to-limit-protests/.

173 the police banned the annual June 4 vigil: Austin Ramzy, "Hong Kong Bans Tiananmen Vigil for 1st Time, in New Challenge to Protests," *New York Times*, June 1, 2020, https://www.nytimes.com/2020/06/01/world/asia/Hong-kong-Tiananmen-vigil-banned.html.

173 conveniently extending the restriction on gatherings: Marc A. Thiessen, "China Is Using Covid-19 to Throttle Hong Kong's Pro-Democracy Movement," *Washington Post*, May 21, 2020, https://www.washingtonpost.com/opinions/2020/05/21/china-is-using-covid-19-throttle-hong-kongs-pro-democracy-movement/.

173 enabling a successful grassroots response to the pandemic: Maya Wang, "Pandemic Strikes New, Authoritarian Hong Kong," Al Jazeera, March 26, 2022, https://www.aljazeera.com/opinions/2022/3/26/pandemic-strikes-new-authoritarian-hong-kong.

173 drove Hong Kong's death rate, by early March, to the highest level: Jack Dutton, "Dead Kept in Body Bags Next to COVID Patients in Harrowing Hospital Photo," *Newsweek*, March 11, 2022, https://www.newsweek.com/dead-kept-body-bags-next-covid-patients-harrowing-hospital-photo-1687137.

174 "While the rest of the world is preoccupied": Chris Patten, "The G7 Must Stand Up for Hong Kong's Freedom," *Financial Times*, May 24, 2020, https://www.ft.com/content/67b03c0a-9da4-11ea-ba68-3d5500196c30.

174 the law fully respected "one country, two systems": "China Fully, Faithfully Implements 'One Country, Two Systems': Premier," Xinhua, May 28, 2020, http://www.xinhuanet.com/english/2020-05/28/c_139096303.htm.

174 the official English translation: "In Full: Official English Translation of the Hong Kong National Security Law," *Hong Kong Free Press*, July 1, 2020, https://hongkongfp.com/2020/07/01/in-full-english-translation-of-the-hong-kong-national-security-law/.

174 The law prohibits secession, "terrorism," and "collusion": "In Full: Official English Translation of the Hong Kong National Security Law."

175 "It literally applies to every single person on the planet": Bethany Allen-Ebrahimian, "With New Security Law, China Outlaws Global Activism," Axios, July 7, 2020, https://www.axios.com/2020/07/07/china-hong-kong-law-global-activism.

175 "quash the international front of the movement": Author interview with Nathan Law, July 3, 2020.

175 "think about what that means for Amnesty International Hong Kong": Author interview with Alvin Cheung, July 6, 2020.

176 "I am not sure how you deal with Xi Jinping's regime": "With Hong Kong Crackdown, Xi

Jinping Signals He'll Pay a High Price for Power," *NewsHour*, PBS, July 2, 2020, https://www.pbs.org /newshour/show/with-hong-kong-crackdown-xi-jinping-signals-hell-pay-a-high-price-for-power.

176 described Hong Kongers as stupid and easily deluded: Yuan, "Why Many in China Oppose Hong Kong's Protests."

176 "returning the favor for Western extraterritoriality": Alex Lo, "China's Long Arm of the Law Falls Far Short of the US," *South China Morning Post*, July 4, 2020, https://www.scmp.com /comment/opinion/article/3091798/chinas-long-arm-law-falls-far-short-us.

176 "I think they wrote it for you": Author interview with Samuel Chu.

177 "naked double standard": David Crawshaw and Shibani Mahtani, "China Slams 'Arrogant and Dangerous' U.S. over Hong Kong Democracy Bill as City's Dysfunction Deepens," *Washington Post*, October 6, 2019, https://www.washingtonpost.com/world/asia_pacific/china-con demns-houses-passage-of-bill-supporting-hong-kong-democracy/2019/10/16/d513a432-efbf -11e9-bb7e-d2026ee0c199_story.html.

177 Chinese government issued retaliatory sanctions on groups based in the United States: Amy Qin, "China Hits Back at U.S. over Hong Kong Bill in a Mostly Symbolic Move," *New York Times*, December 2, 2019, https://www.nytimes.com/2019/12/02/world/asia/china-us-hong-kong-bill-pro tests.html.

177 halted U.S. naval vessels from docking in Hong Kong: "China Bars U.S. Military Ships, Aircraft from Hong Kong, Sanctions U.S.-Based NGOs," Reuters, December 2, 2019, https://www .reuters.com/article/us-hongkong-protests-china-usa/china-suspends-us-military-visits-to-hong -kong-sanctions-us-based-ngos-idUSKBN1Y60IQ.

179 stop the practice of "lunch shaming": Gail Rosenblum, "Lunch-Aid Bill Feeds an Essential Need," *Star Tribune*, February 21, 2013, https://www.startribune.com/rosenblum-lunch-aid-bill -feeds-an-essential-need/191756551/.

180 Trump had called Xi a "good man": Rebecca Klar, "Trump Calls China's Xi 'a Good Man' in a 'Tough Business' amid Hong Kong Unrest," *The Hill*, August 14, 2019, https://thehill.com /homenews/administration/457490-trump-calls-chinas-xi-a-good-man-in-a-tough-business/.

180 White House refused to comment: Michael Crowley and Ana Swanson, "White House Won't Say If Trump Will Sign Hong Kong Bill That Has Angered China," *New York Times*, November 21, 2019, https://www.nytimes.com/2019/11/21/us/politics/trump-hong-kong-china.html.

180 passed a law giving a pro-Beijing committee the power to vet candidates: Dan Glaun, "Chinese Legislature Tightens Control over Hong Kong Elections," *Frontline*, PBS, March 11, 2021, https://www.pbs.org/wgbh/frontline/article/chinese-legislature-tightens-control-over-hong-kong -elections/.

181 117 activists, journalists, and former lawmakers had been arrested: Kari Soo Lindberg, "China Officials Detail Plans to Bolster Hong Kong Security Laws," Bloomberg, July 5, 2021, https://www.bloomberg.com/news/articles/2021-07-05/china-officials-detail-plans-to-bolster -hong-kong-security-laws.

181 Teachers have been fired: Chris Lau, "More Hong Kong Teachers in Firing Line, as Education Minister Reveals 'Relatively Serious' Cases Being Processed After One Is Banned for Life," *South China Morning Post*, October 10, 2021, https://www.scmp.com/news/hong-kong/politics /article/3104990/more-hong-kong-teachers-firing-line-education-minister.

181 educational content considered "subversive" under strict new regulations: James Griffiths, 'No Room for Debate or Compromise' as Hong Kong Introduces Sweeping National Security Rules for Schools," CNN, February 5, 2021, https://edition.cnn.com/2021/02/05/asia/hong-kong -national-security-education-intl-hnk/index.html.

181 Authorities have increasingly restricted press accreditation: Helen Davidson, "Hong Kong Police Tighten Control on Media with New Accreditation Rules," *The Guardian*, September 23, 2020, https://www.theguardian.com/world/2020/sep/23/hong-kong-police-tighten-control-on-media -with-new-accreditation-rules.

181 National Security Law has even impacted the arts: "Hong Kong Artistic Freedoms Caught in Beijing's Tightening Grip," *Financial Times*, May 21, 2021, https://www.ft.com/content/13558cff -a6e2-40b3-9bbe-cbae5007faae.

181 "risk would be in terms of surveillance by Chinese embassies": Louisa Lim, "Hong Kong, My Vanishing City," *Financial Times*, April 28, 2022, https://www.ft.com/content/1878a8f3-fbd4 -4539-b07f-d8ab60df42df.

181 "I would always look at which places are safer to go": Bethany Allen-Ebrahimian, "Interview: Hong Kong Activist Frances Hui on Extradition Fears," Axios, October 26, 2021, https://www .axios.com/2021/10/26/hong-kong-china-activist-extradition-interview.

182 In October 2022, however, the European Court of Human Rights blocked: Christian Shepherd and Emily Rauhala, "Europe Nears a Reckoning in Its Ties to China's Security Operations," *Washington Post*, November 4, 2022, https://www.washingtonpost.com/world/2022/11/04/china-europe-overseas-police-extradition/.

182 effectively outlawing a boycott movement: Kelly Ho, "Urging People to Spoil or Cast Blank Ballots in Elections to Become a Crime in Hong Kong," *Hong Kong Free Press*, April 13, 2021, https://hongkongfp.com/2021/04/13/just-in-urging-people-to-spoil-or-cast-blank-ballots-in-elections-to-become-a-crime-in-hong-kong/.

182 an election ordinance originally implemented in 2000: "An Ordinance to Prohibit Corrupt Conduct and Illegal Conduct at Elections; to Regulate Electoral Advertising; to Impose Requirements with Respect to the Receipt of Donations and the Expenditure of Money at or in Connection with Elections; and to Provide for Related Matters," Cap. 554 Elections (Corrupt and Illegal Conduct Ordinance, Hong Kong e-legislation web archive, March 3, 2000, https://www.elegislation.gov.hk/hk/cap554?p0=1&p1=1.

182 denouncing the move and calling the elections a "sham": "Hong Kong Says Vote—or Else," *Wall Street Journal*, November 29, 2021, https://www.wsj.com/articles/hong-kongs-rigged-election-china-legislative-council-11638224614?mod=article_inline.

182 "We reserve the right to take necessary action": "Hong Kong Issues a Threat to the WSJ," *Wall Street Journal*, December 5, 2021, https://www.wsj.com/articles/hong-kong-china-wsj-threat-election-legco-democracy-freedom-protest-ccp-11638575014.

182 wrote a similarly worded letter, dated December 8, to the *Sunday Times*: @hkfp, "1/ Hong Kong's trade office in London has warned the UK's Sunday Times that its article may be illegal under Hong Kong law which forbids the incitement of an election boycott. The letter says the law is applicable internationally," Twitter, December 10, 2021, https://twitter.com/hkfp/status/1469333399462502400.

182 calling the elections a "mockery" of democracy: "China Shows Its True Colours—and They're Not Pretty," *Sunday Times*, December 5, 2021, https://www.thetimes.co.uk/article/china-shows-its-true-colours-and-theyre-not-pretty-jb90kcmx2.

182 "Overseas Chinese Strongly Support the Hong Kong National Security Law": Xinhua News, May 31, 2020, http://www.xinhuanet.com/gangao/2020-05/31/c_1126055939.htm.

183 more than seventy branches worldwide: Archive of the China Council for the Promotion of Peaceful National Reunification, https://web.archive.org/web/20180429051424/http://www.zhongguotongcuhui.org.cn/hnwtch/.

183 Sun Chunlan, a member of the powerful Politburo: 孙春兰：始终坚持反'独'促统宗旨，促进两岸各领域交流合作" ("Sun Chunlan: Persist in our objectives of opposing 'independence' and promoting unification, and encourage cross-strait exchange and cooperation across various fields"),*China News*, September 6, 2017, https://www.chinanews.com.cn/gn/2017/09-06/8323907.shtml.

184 to freeze the assets of exiled pro-democracy legislator: Helen Davidson, "Exiled Hong Kong Legislator Calls for Action After HSBC Bank Accounts Frozen," *The Guardian*, December 7, 2020, https://www.theguardian.com/world/2020/dec/07/exiled-hong-kong-legislator-calls-for-inquiry-after-hsbc-freezes-bank-account.

184 Hong Kong police froze Lai's assets: Natasha Khan, "Hong Kong's National-Security Police Freeze Media Tycoon's Assets," *Wall Street Journal*, May 14, 2021, https://www.wsj.com/articles/hong-kongs-national-security-police-freeze-media-tycoons-assets-11621009204.

184 sent letters to HSBC and Citibank: Greg Torode, James Pomfret, and Sumeet Chatterjee, "Hong Kong Threatens Lai's Bankers with Jail If They Deal in His Accounts," Reuters, May 27, 2021, https://www.reuters.com/world/china/exclusive-hong-kong-security-chief-threatens-tycoon-lais-bankers-with-jail-if-2021-05-27/.

184 "So much for being a global financial center based on the rule of law": Editorial Board, "Hong Kong Snatches Assets," *Wall Street Journal*, May 17, 2021, https://www.wsj.com/articles/hong-kong-snatches-assets-11621288698.

185 the newspaper had no choice but to shut down: Iain Marlow, "The Assault on *Apple Daily*," Bloomberg, February 3, 2022, https://www.bloomberg.com/features/2022-apple-daily-china-hong-kong-crackdown/?leadSource=uverify%20wall.

185 derives nearly 40 percent of its revenue from mainland China and Hong Kong: Sumeet Chatterjee and Engen Tham, "How Beijing Humbled Britain's Mighty HSBC," Reuters, June 28, 2021, https://www.reuters.com/investigates/special-report/hsbc-china-politics/.

185 Chinese authorities have blackballed HSBC: Chatterjee and Tham, "How Beijing Humbled Britain's Mighty HSBC."

185 United States sanctioned fourteen vice-chairpersons of the Standing Committee: Nick Wadhams, "U.S. Sanctions New Group of Chinese Officials over Hong Kong," December 7, 2020, https://www.bloomberg.com/news/articles/2020-12-07/u-s-sanctions-new-group-of-chinese-of ficials-over-hong-kong?leadSource=uverify%20wall.

185 The bank complied with a Hong Kong police request: Mary Hui, Annabelle Timsit, and Jane Li, "HSBC Is Facing Dueling Loyalty Tests It Can Only Fail," Quartz, February 22, 2021, https://qz.com/1974610/china-and-the-uk-test-hsbcs-divided-loyalties-in-hong-kong/.

185 cut off business with Hong Kong chief executive Carrie Lam: Laura He, "Hong Kong Leader Carrie Lam Is Getting Paid in Cash Because Banks Won't Deal with Her," CNN, December 1, 2020, https://edition.cnn.com/2020/11/30/business/hong-kong-carrie-lam-cash-intl-hnk /index.html.

185 the UK Parliament called HSBC's CEO to testify: Celeste Goh, Nathan Sovall, and Nimayi Dixit, "The Big Picture 2022: Banking Industry Outlook," S&P Global Market Intelligence, November 2, 2021, https://www.spglobal.com/marketintelligence/en/news-insights/blog/the-big -picture-2022-banking-industry-outlook.

186 China's Ministry of Commerce created an "Unreliable Entity List": "MOFCOM Order No. 4 of 2020 on Provisions on the Unreliable Entity List," Ministry of Commerce of the People's Republic of China, September 19, 2020, http://english.mofcom.gov.cn/article/policyrelease /announcement/202009/20200903002580.shtml.

186 analysts have compared it to the Entity List maintained by the United States: Frank Jiang and Scott Yu, "Seven FAQs About China's New Unreliable Entity List Provisions," Zhong Lun, September 23, 2020, https://www.zhonglun.com/Content/2020/09-23/1720132191.html.

186 a private right of action in Chinese courts: Burt Braverman and Edlira Kuka, "China's Newest Anti-Foreign Sanctions Blocking Law: What We Know, What We Don't Know, and What U.S. Companies Can Do," Blog Post, Davis Wright Tremaine LLP, August 30, 2021, https://www.dwt .com/blogs/broadband-advisor/2021/08/anti-foreign-sanctions-law-china.

186 the Anti–Foreign Sanctions Law codifies and expands the previous regulations: Braverman and Kuka, "China's Newest Anti-Foreign Sanctions Blocking Law."

187 Chinese state media explicitly compared the law to the EU blocking statute: "为反制外国歧视性措施提供有力法治支撑和保障——专家解读《中华人民共和国反外国制裁法》" ("To provide strong rule of law backing for the counteracting of foreign discriminatory measures - experts interpret the People's Republic of China Law on Anti-foreign Sanctions"), Xinhua, June 11, 2021, http://www.xinhuanet.com/2021-06/11/c_1127552187.htm.

187 April 2021 explanation of the law: 关于《中华人民共和国反外国制裁法（草案）》的说明 ("Statement on the Draft Law of the People's Republic of China on Anti-foreign Sanctions"), National People's Congress of the People's Republic of China, June 11, 2021, http://www .npc.gov.cn/npc/c30834/202106/99804919249244e593383c9da4e39ddf.shtml.

188 Chinese government temporarily shelved its plans to enact legislation: "北京暂缓表决港澳《反外國制裁法》，為何商界忌憚這部法律?" ("Beijing Suspends Voting on Hong Kong and Macau's 'Anti-Foreign Sanctions Law.' Why Are Business Circles Afraid of This Law?"), BBC News, August 20, 2021, https://www.bbc.com/zhongwen/trad/chinese-news-58279287.

188 the city would allow a yacht owned by sanctioned Russian oligarch: Frances Mao, "Hong Kong Declines to Act on Sanctioned Russian Superyacht in Harbour," BBC News, October 11, 2022, https://www.bbc.co.uk/news/world-asia-63210647.

188 Noel Quinn reaffirmed the bank's commitment to Hong Kong: Goh, Sovall, and Dixit, "The Big Picture 2022: Banking Industry Outlook."

10: China Vaccinates the World

190 Chinese scientists first mapped the complete genome: Jon Cohen, "Chinese Researchers Reveal Draft Genome of Virus Implicated in Wuhan Pneumonia Outbreak," Science, January 11, 2020, https://www.science.org/content/article/chinese-researchers-reveal-draft-genome-virus-implicated -wuhan-pneumonia-outbreak.

190 shortened the amount of time needed to create an effective shot: Rachel Lance, "How COVID-19 Vaccines Were Made So Quickly Without Cutting Corners," Science News, June 29, 2021, https://www.sciencenews.org/article/covid-coronavirus-vaccine-development-speed.

190 Equitable distribution wasn't important merely from a moral standpoint: Michelle Nichols and Stephanie Nebehay, "Global Officials Urge Rich Countries to Donate Excess COVID-19

Vaccines, Money to Help End Pandemic," Reuters, April 15, 2021, https://www.reuters.com/bus
iness/healthcare-pharmaceuticals/shocking-disparity-persists-vaccine-distribution-who-chief
-2021-04-15/.

191   the COVAX initiative was born: Ann Danaiya Usher, "A Beautiful Idea: How COVAX
Has Fallen Short," *The Lancet*, June 19, 2021, https://www.thelancet.com/journals/lancet/article
/PIIS0140-6736(21)01367-2/fulltext.

191   Trump administration refused to join COVAX: Scott Neuman, "U.S. Won't Join WHO-Led
Coronavirus Vaccine Effort, White House Says," NPR, September 2, 2020, https://www.npr.org
/sections/coronavirus-live-updates/2020/09/02/908711419/u-s-wont-join-who-led-coronavirus
-vaccine-effort-white-house-says.

191   in just twenty high-income countries: Jason Beaubien, "What Is This COVAX Program
That the U.S. Is Pouring Millions of Vaccines Into?," NPR, May 19, 2021, https://www.npr.org/sec
tions/goatsandsoda/2021/05/19/998228372/what-is-this-covax-program-that-the-u-s-is-pouring
-millions-of-vaccines-into.

191   "Rich countries behaved worse than anyone's worst nightmares": Usher, "A Beautiful Idea."

191   "morally unconscionable": "Unequal Vaccine Distribution Self-Defeating, World Health
Organization Chief Tells Economic and Social Council's Special Ministerial Meeting," Press Release,
United Nations, April 16, 2021, https://press.un.org/en/2021/ecosoc7039.doc.htm.

191   the number of doses worldwide had risen to 5.5 billion: Hannah Ritchie et al., "Coronavirus
Pandemic (COVID-19)," OurWorldInData.org, 2020, https://ourworldindata.org/coronavirus.

191   In the early months of 2021, the country exported: Seow Ting Lee, "Vaccine Diplomacy:
Nation Branding and China's COVID-19 Soft Power Play," *Place Branding and Public Diplomacy*
19, no. 1 (July 2021): 64–78, https://www.ncbi.nlm.nih.gov/pmc/articles/PMC8259554/.

192   U.S. vaccine hoarding was "strangling" a lifeline: "U.S. Vaccine Hoarding 'No Different'
from Strangling Others' Lifeline: Spokesperson of Chinese FM," Xinhua, July 17, 2021, http://www
.xinhuanet.com/english/2021-07/17/c_1310066685.htm.

193   Russia's Ministry of Health authorized emergency use of Sputnik V: Bianca Nogrady,
"Mounting Evidence Suggests Sputnik COVID Vaccine Is Safe and Effective," *Nature*, July 6, 2021,
https://www.nature.com/articles/d41586-021-01813-2.

193   "potentially the most powerful tool of soft power that Moscow": Kevin Connolly, "Sputnik
V: How Russia's Covid Vaccine Is Dividing Europe," BBC News, April 17, 2021, https://www.bbc
.co.uk/news/world-europe-56735931.

193   WHO declined to approve Sputnik V: "WHO Cites Concerns About Russian Sputnik
V Plant, Which Says Issues Resolved," Reuters, June 23, 2021, https://www.reuters.com/business
/healthcare-pharmaceuticals/who-review-finds-issues-with-one-russian-sputnik-v-manufacturing
-plant-2021-06-23/.

194   Beijing's increasingly robust investment in research and development: Dennis Normile,
"China Again Boosts R&D Spending by More than 10%," *Science*, August 28, 2020, https://www
.science.org/content/article/china-again-boosts-rd-spending-more-10.

194   "a manifestation of my country's scientific and technological progress": "陈薇：争分夺
秒，让疫苗捍卫生命" (Chen Wei: Every Second Counts in the Race to Make Vaccines Save
Lives"), Xinhua, May 14, 2020, http://www.xinhuanet.com/politics/2020-05/14/c_1125981877
.htm.

195   China had promised 500 million doses of lifesaving vaccines: Huizhong Wu and Kristen Ge-
lineau, "Chinese Vaccines Sweep Much of the World, Despite Concerns," Associated Press, March 2,
2021, https://apnews.com/article/china-vaccines-worldwide-0382aefa52c75b834fbaf6d869808f51.

195   WHO approved the Sinopharm vaccine: Stephanie Nebehay, "WHO Approves Sinopharm Vaccine in Potential Boost to COVAX Pipeline," Reuters, May 7, 2021, https://www
.reuters.com/world/middle-east/who-gives-emergency-approval-sinopharm-first-chinese-covid-19
-vaccine-2021-05-07/.

195   Iran was one of the earliest epicenters: Karim Sadjadpour, "Iran's Coronavirus Disaster,"
Carnegie Endowment for International Peace, March 25, 2020, https://carnegieendowment.org
/2020/03/25/iran-s-coronavirus-disaster-pub-81367.

196   Ghaasem, a mechanical engineer living in Tehran: Author interview with Ghaasem, September 2021.

196   "The entire country is red": Reuters Staff, "Whole of Iran on Coronavirus Red Alert Due
to Rise in Deaths, Health Official Says," Reuters, September 18, 2020, https://www.reuters.com
/article/us-health-coronavirus-iran/whole-of-iran-on-coronavirus-red-alert-due-to-rise-in-deaths
-health-official-says-idUSKBN2691PF.

196   out of reach for most Iranians: Jon Gambrell, "In Iran, Slow Vaccinations Fuel Anger in Unending Pandemic," Associated Press, August 11, 2021, https://apnews.com/article/middle-east-health-iran-pandemics-coronavirus-pandemic-33a0bf3247ffdc072f8579c9dd53c71b.

197   just 3.5 million Iranians out of a population of 80 million: Tara Kangarlou, " 'It's a Catastrophe.' Iranians Turn to Black Market for Vaccines as COVID-19 Deaths Hit New Highs," *Time*, August 16, 2021, https://time.com/6090239/iran-covid-vaccine-black-market/.

198   "This approach entails reframing its image": Lee, "Vaccine Diplomacy."

198   "Covid can be a real game changer for China": Lucien O. Chauvin, Anthony Faiola, and Eva Dou, "Squeezed Out of the Race for Western Vaccines, Developing Countries Turn to China," *Washington Post*, February 16, 2020, https://www.washingtonpost.com/world/2021/02/16/coronavirus-peru-china-vaccine-sinopharm-sinovac/.

198   1.4 billion doses of Sinovac and Sinopharm vaccines had been delivered: China COVID-19 Vaccine Tracker, Bridge, https://bridgebeijing.com/our-publications/our-publications-1/china-covid-19-vaccines-tracker/.

199   a desire to present the results "in a more favorable way": Samantha Pearson, Luciana Magalhaes, and Chao Deng, "Chinese Covid-19 Vaccine Far Less Effective than Initially Touted in Brazil," *Wall Street Journal*, January 12, 2021, https://www.wsj.com/articles/chinas-sinovac-covid-19-vaccine-is-50-4-in-late-stage-brazil-trials-11610470581.

199   efficacy rate of 78 percent at preventing infections: Samantha Pearson, Luciana Magalhaes, and Chao Deng, "Sinovac's Covid-19 Vaccine Is 78% Effective in Brazil Late-Stage Trials," *Wall Street Journal*, January 7, 2021, https://www.wsj.com/articles/sinovacs-covid-19-vaccine-is-78-effective-in-brazil-late-stage-trials-11610032825?mod=article_inline.

199   appeared to have only around 50 percent efficacy: Pearson, Magalhaes, and Deng, "Chinese Covid-19 Vaccine Far Less Effective than Initially Touted in Brazil."

199   cherry-picking data: Eyck Freymann and Justin Stebbing, "China Must Stop Hiding Its Vaccine Data," *Foreign Affairs*, February 26, 2021, https://www.foreignaffairs.com/articles/china/2021-02-26/china-must-stop-hiding-its-vaccine-data.

199   Hungary signed a deal with Sinopharm for thirty-six dollars per dose: Sui-Lee Wee and Benjamin Novak, "Hungary Pays Big for a Chinese Vaccine," *New York Times*, March 12, 2021, https://www.nytimes.com/2021/03/12/world/hungary-sinopharm-covid.html.

199   outbreak was viewed as a setback among Seychelles residents: Sui-Lee Wee, "World's Most Vaccinated Nation Is Spooked by Covid Spike," *New York Times*, May 12, 2021, https://www.nytimes.com/2021/05/12/business/economy/covid-seychelles-sinopharm.html.

200   twenty doctors who had received both doses of Sinovac died: Shibani Mahtani, "Ravaged by Delta Outbreak, Southeast Asia Shifts Away from China's Vaccines," *Washington Post*, August 10, 2021, https://www.washingtonpost.com/world/asia_pacific/covid-vaccines-delta-china-asia/2021/08/10/24d0df60-f664-11eb-a636-18cac59a98dc_story.html.

200   five hundred fully vaccinated medical workers contracted Covid-19 disease: Rebecca Ratcliffe, "Indonesian Covid Deaths Add to Questions over Sinovac Vaccine," *The Guardian*, June 28, 2021, https://www.theguardian.com/world/2021/jun/28/indonesian-covid-deaths-add-to-questions-over-sinovac-vaccine.

200   the government of Thailand altered its policy: Mahtani, "Ravaged by Delta Outbreak, Southeast Asia Shifts Away from China's Vaccines."

200   people in Singapore originally inoculated with Sinovac: Dewey Sim, "Covid-19: Singapore Residents Who Took Sinovac Turn to Pfizer to Up Their Antibody Counts, amid Debate on Booster Shots," *South China Morning Post*, August 31, 2021, https://www.scmp.com/week-asia/health-environment/article/3146944/covid-19-singapore-residents-who-took-sinovac-turn.

200   publicly admitted that China's domestic vaccines: Joe McDonald and Huizhong Wu, "Top Chinese Official Admits Vaccines Have Low Effectiveness," Associated Press, April 11, 2021, https://apnews.com/article/china-gao-fu-vaccines-offer-low-protection-coronavirus-675bcb6b5710c7329823148ffbff6ef9.

200   "a stark contrast to the fanfare": Mahtani, "Ravaged by Delta Outbreak, Southeast Asia Shifts Away from China's Vaccines."

200   "China has yet to prove that it can fulfill the role": Yanzhong Huang, "Vaccine Diplomacy Is Paying Off for China," *Foreign Affairs*, March 11, 2021, https://www.foreignaffairs.com/articles/china/2021-03-11/vaccine-diplomacy-paying-china.

201   China would donate one billion doses of its vaccines: "Xi Jinping Pledges a Billion More Vaccines for Africa in the Wake of Omicron," Bloomberg, November 29, 2021, https://time.com/6124584/china-vaccines-africa-omicron/.

201   observers described Taiwan as "vaccine-starved": Huizhong Wu and Mari Yamaguchi, "Taiwan, Feuding with China, Gets Vaccines from Japan," Associated Press, June 4, 2021, https://apnews.com/article/europe-china-taiwan-business-japan-0c31ddf65eaa81ac101f592ec5697c37.

202   Tsai Ing-wen publicly accused the Chinese government: Helen Davidson, "Taiwan Accuses China of Interfering with Covid Vaccine Deals," *The Guardian*, May 27, 2021, https://www.theguardian.com/world/2021/may/27/taiwan-president-accuses-china-interfering-covid-vaccine-deals.

202   "We are firmly against those who exploit the pandemic": "Foreign Ministry Spokesperson Wang Wenbin's Regular Press Conference on May 31, 2021," http://www.fmcoprc.gov.mo/eng/zxxw/fyrth_1/t1880105.htm.

202   "turned a blind eye to the goodwill of the mainland": "Foreign Ministry Spokesperson Wang Wenbin's Regular Press Conference on May 31, 2021."

203   "if the Paraguay government is willing": "Taiwan Says China Uses COVID-19 Vaccines to Press Paraguay to Break Ties," Reuters, April 7, 2021, https://www.reuters.com/world/china/taiwan-says-india-helped-paraguay-get-vaccines-after-china-pressure-2021-04-07/.

203   Taiwan had worked with India and other democracies: Reuters Staff, "Taiwan Says India Helped Paraguay Get Vaccines After China Pressure," Reuters, April 7, 2021, https://www.reuters.com/article/us-health-coronavirus-taiwan/taiwan-says-india-helped-paraguay-get-vaccines-after-china-pressure-idUSKBN2BU0NH.

203   Japan sent 1.24 million doses: Wu and Yamaguchi, "Taiwan, Feuding with China, Gets Vaccines from Japan."

203   again prevented Taiwan from attending the annual World Health Assembly: "Taiwan Blames China for Latest WHO Meeting Snub," Al Jazeera, May 24, 2021, https://www.aljazeera.com/news/2021/5/24/taiwan-blames-china-for-latest-who-meeting-snub.

204   White-collar workers in Shanghai: Shen Lu and Stella Yifan Xie, "China's Covid Lockdowns Drive Middle-Class Citizens to Go Abroad," *Wall Street Journal*, May 13, 2022, https://www.wsj.com/articles/chinas-covid-lockdowns-drive-middle-class-citizens-to-head-abroad-11652460449.

11: Building a Democratic Economic Statecraft

206   "make sure that the rules of the game serve their interests": "A Free Market Manifesto That Changed the World, Reconsidered," *New York Times*, September 11, 2020, https://www.nytimes.com/2020/09/11/business/dealbook/milton-friedman-doctrine-social-responsibility-of-business.html?smtyp=cur&smid=tw-nytimesbusiness.

207   As economist Thomas Piketty pointed out: Thomas Piketty, *Capital in the Twenty-First Century* (Cambridge, MA: Belknap Press of Harvard University Press, 2014).

207   The growing power of large companies also extends: Elizabeth Anderson, *Private Government: How Employers Rule Our Lives (And Why We Don't Talk About It)* (Princeton, NJ: Princeton University Press, 2017),

208   pushing back against legislation that might close off China's markets: Ana Swanson, "Nike and Coca-Cola Lobby Against Xinjiang Forced Labor Bill," *New York Times*, November 29, 2020, https://www.nytimes.com/2020/11/29/business/economy/nike-coca-cola-xinjiang-forced-labor-bill.html.

209   "competition as the defining characteristic of human relations": George Monbiot, "Neoliberalism—the Ideology at the Root of All Our Problems," *The Guardian*, April 15, 2016, https://www.theguardian.com/books/2016/apr/15/neoliberalism-ideology-problem-george-monbiot.

211   "big institutions—big government, big corporations, big labor": Sitaraman, *The Great Democracy*, 2.

211   "reconciled with the values of social community and domestic welfare": Rawi Abdelal and John G. Ruggie, "The Principles of Embedded Liberalism: Social Legitimacy and Global Capitalism," in David Moss and John Cisternino, eds., *New Perspectives on Regulation* (Cambridge, MA: Tobin Project, 2009), 151–62.

211   should not have a "social conscience": Milton Friedman, "The Social Responsibility of Business Is to Increase Its Profits," *New York Times*, September 13, 1970, https://www.nytimes.com/1970/09/13/archives/a-friedman-doctrine-the-social-responsibility-of-business-is-to.html.

212   American corporate governance and of the political zeitgeist that enabled it: "A Free Market Manifesto That Changed the World, Reconsidered."

212   "The acceleration of interest in privatization": Mary M. Shirley, "The What, Why, and How of Privatization: A World Bank Perspective," *Fordham Law Review* 60, no. 6 (1992).

213 "probably the most important economist in the world": Peter Passell, "Dr. Jeffrey Sachs, Shock Therapist," *New York Times Magazine*, June 27, 1993, https://www.nytimes.com/1993/06/27/magazine/dr-jeffrey-sachs-shock-therapist.html.

214 "Late in the afternoon of May 26, 1994, President Clinton stepped to the podium": Davis and Wei, *Superpower Showdown*, 83.

215 brought much-needed change to a dysfunctional system and boosted productivity: John Cassidy, "The Economic Case for and Against Thatcherism," *The New Yorker*, April 9, 2013, https://www.newyorker.com/news/john-cassidy/the-economic-case-for-and-against-thatcherism.

215 Inequality rose, and social mobility fell: Richard Wilkinson and Kate Pickett, "Margaret Thatcher Made Britain a Less, Not More, Desirable Place to Do Business," *The Guardian*, April 10, 2013, https://www.theguardian.com/commentisfree/2013/apr/10/inequality-margaret-thatcher-britain-desirable-business.

215 Some former industrial towns never recovered: Paul Sandle, "In Mining Ruins Left by Thatcher, New Economy Struggles," Reuters, April 12, 2013, https://www.reuters.com/article/uk-britain-thatcher-coal/in-mining-ruins-left-by-thatcher-new-economy-struggles-idUKBRE93B07C20130412.

215 China managed to avoid shock therapy: Isabella Weber, *How China Escaped Shock Therapy: The Market Reform Debate* (New York: Routledge 2021), 7.

215 "systematic elimination of human rights protections": Philip Alston, *Report of the Special Rapporteur on Extreme Poverty and Human Rights*, United Nations Office of the High Commissioner for Human Rights, United Nations General Assembly, September 26, 2018.

216 Thomas Piketty's 2014 book: Piketty, *Capital in the Twenty-First Century*.

216 "market capitalism is not a religion": Tucker Carlson, "Tucker Carlson: Mitt Romney Supports the Status Quo—But for Everyone Else, It's Infuriating," Fox News, January 3, 2019, https://www.foxnews.com/opinion/tucker-carlson-mitt-romney-supports-the-status-quo-but-for-everyone-else-its-infuriating.

217 "the obsession with maximizing profits for shareholders": "Greed Is Good. Except When It's Bad," *New York Times*, September 13, 2020, https://www.nytimes.com/2020/09/13/business/dealbook/milton-friedman-essay-anniversary.html.

217 repeatedly downplayed the severity of the Chinese government's genocide: Jeffrey D. Sachs, "The Xinjiang Genocide Allegations Are Unjustified," website of Jeffrey D. Sachs, April 20, 2021, https://www.jeffsachs.org/newspaper-articles/apfjc5yg352d554k2ar2wwwkk8ryw9.

217 The index measures "personal, civil, and economic" freedom: "Human Freedom Index," Cato Institute, 2020, https://www.cato.org/human-freedom-index/2020.

218 The neoliberal state, writes political economist Isabella Weber, "is neither small nor weak": Weber, *How China Escaped Shock Therapy*, 3.

220 "freedom to seek, receive and impart information": International Covenant on Civil and Political Rights, General Assembly Resolution 2200A (XXI), United Nations Office of the High Commissioner for Human Rights, https://www.ohchr.org/en/instruments-mechanisms/instruments/international-covenant-civil-and-political-rights.

222 The Trump administration briefly imposed such a rule: Veronica Stracqualursi and Kevin Liptak, "Trump Revokes Rule Barring Lobbying by Former Officials as He Leaves Office," CNN, January 20, 2021, https://www.cnn.com/2021/01/20/politics/trump-revokes-lobby-ban/index.html.

222 Preventing Foreign CENSORSHIP: Preventing the Foreign Coercive Export of Non-Consensual Speech and Orwellian Restrictions by Superpowers Hoping to Intimidate People in America Act, HR5830, https://www.congress.gov/bill/116th-congress/house-bill/5830/titles?r=2&s=1.

228 Antony Blinken called for like-minded countries to band together: Sarah Anne Aarup, "Washington Calls on Allies to Band Together Against China's 'Economic Coercion,'" Politico, March 24, 2021, https://www.politico.eu/article/washington-calls-on-allies-to-band-together-against-chinas-economic-coercion/.

228 would raise the reputational costs of such actions: Bonnie S. Glaser, "Time for Collective Pushback Against China's Economic Coercion," Center for Strategic and International Studies, January 13, 2021, https://www.csis.org/analysis/time-collective-pushback-against-chinas-economic-coercion.

228 strong U.S.-EU and global relations would undermine: Hackenbroich, "Chinese Sanctions."

228 German companies began to push Lithuania's leaders: Andrius Sytas and John O'Donnell, "German Big Business Piles Pressure on Lithuania in China Row," Reuters, January 21, 2022, https://www.reuters.com/world/europe/german-big-business-piles-pressure-lithuania-china-row-2022-01-21/.

228 "economic interpenetration can become a liability": Stuart Lau, "How Little Lithuania Dragged the EU into Its Showdown with China," Politico, October 6, 2021, https://www.politico.eu/article/lithuania-china-showdown-eu-impact/.

228 Article 5 that triggers mutual support measures: Michito Tsuruoka, "Is Collective Defense in the Economic Domain Possible? Lessons from the Australia-China Conflict," Sasakawa Peace Foundation, April 8, 2021, https://www.spf.org/iina/en/articles/tsuruoka_01.html.

228 that a broad "alliance of democracies" establish: Jonas Parello-Plesner, "An 'Economic Article 5' to Counter China," *Wall Street Journal*, February 11, 2021, https://www.wsj.com/articles/an-economic-article-5-to-counter-china-11613084046.

229 be more effective at binding a smaller cohort: Hanson, Currey, and Beattie, "The Chinese Communist Party's Coercive Diplomacy."

229 Europe relies on its ability to export to many markets: Hackenbroich, "Chinese Sanctions."

229 unveiled its proposal for an anti-coercion instrument: "Proposal for a Regulation of the European Parliament and of the Council on the Protection of the Union and Its Member States from Economic Coercion by Third Countries," European Trade Commission, December 8, 2021, https://trade.ec.europa.eu/doclib/docs/2021/december/tradoc_159958.pdf.

229 under the auspices of the European Union's common commercial policy: Jonathan Hackenbroich and Pawel Zerka, "Measured Response: How to Design a European Instrument Against Economic Coercion," European Council on Foreign Relations, June 23, 2021, https://ecfr.eu/publication/measured-response-how-to-design-a-european-instrument-against-economic-coercion/.

229 companies ought to be "on the front line": Parello-Plesner, "An 'Economic Article 5' to Counter China."

229 Agreeing not to sell to a foreign market is also potentially complicated: Tsuruoka, "Is Collective Defense in the Economic Domain Possible?"

229 "need to factor in the increasing risk to trade flows": Hanson, Currey, and Beattie, "The Chinese Communist Party's Coercive Diplomacy."

230 proposed strengthening WTO rules: Shin Oya, "Coping with China's Economic Threat," *Japan Times*, July 28, 2020, https://www.japantimes.co.jp/opinion/2020/07/28/commentary/japan-commentary/coping-chinas-economic-threat/.

230 "it would be a 'soft' approach": "US-China Trade Growth Has Australia Asking Whether WTO Can Stop 'Economic Coercion,'" U.S. Coal Exports, September 16, 2021, https://uscoalexports.org/2021/09/16/us-china-trade-growth-has-australia-asking-whether-wto-can-stop-economic-coercion/.

230 would likely not prove a successful forum: Emily Kilcrease, Emily Jin, and Rachel Ziemba, "Containing Crisis: Strategic Concepts for Coercive Economic Statecraft on China," Center for a New American Security, December 7, 2021, https://www.cnas.org/publications/reports/containing-crisis.

230 a plurilateral export control agreement would be an important first step: Kilcrease, Jin, and Ziemba, "Containing Crisis."

231 An interim step toward strengthening resilience: Oya, "Coping with China's Economic Threat."

231 the idea of providing compensation or starting funds: Luke Patey, "The Myths and Realities of China's Economic Coercion," Danish Institute for International Studies, November 24, 2021, https://www.diis.dk/en/research/the-myths-and-realities-of-chinas-economic-coercion.

231 Canadian proposal suggests supporting affected commodity farmers: Duanjie Chen, "How to Counter Chinese Economic Coercion," *Globe and Mail*, September 23, 2019, https://www.theglobeandmail.com/business/commentary/article-how-to-counter-chinese-economic-coercion/.

231 formation of an Agri-Business Expansion Initiative: "Agri-Business Expansion Initiative," Australian Department of Agriculture, Fisheries, and Forestry, https://www.awe.gov.au/biosecurity-trade/market-access-trade/agri-business-expansion#enhanced-market-intelligence-capacity.

232 Japanese opinion writer proposed a "Freedom Alliance Fund": Oya, "Coping with China's Economic Threat."

233 Supply chain security should include a combination: Oya, "Coping with China's Economic Threat."

233 China moved to reduce supply chain vulnerabilities: Tsugami Toshiya, "Three Things to Know About China's 'Economic Security,'" Nippon, March 7, 2022, https://www.nippon.com/en/in-depth/a07902/.

233 "forming the necessary industrial backup system": "Xi Jinping: Certain Major Issues for Our National Medium- to Long-Term Economic and Social Development Strategy," Center for

Security and Emerging Technology, November 11, 2020, https://cset.georgetown.edu/publication/xi-jinping-certain-major-issues-for-our-national-medium-to-long-term-economic-and-social-development-strategy/.

234   Norwegian salmon: "Norway Penetrates China Blockage Through Vietnam," Nordic Page, https://www.tnp.no/norway/economy/3936-salmon-norway-penetrates-china-blockage-through-vietnam/.

234   preserve the market while offering some insulation: Ketian Vivian Zhang, "Chinese Non-Military Coercion—Tactics and Rationale," Brookings Institution, January 22, 2019, https://www.brookings.edu/articles/chinese-non-military-coercion-tactics-and-rationale/.

234   boost consumption of Australian wine: "IPAC Leads Global Campaign to Buy Australian Wine in Stand Against Chinese Government Bullying," Inter-Parliamentary Alliance on China, December 1, 2020, https://ipac.global/ipac-leads-global-campaign-to-buy-australian-wine-in-stand-against-chinese-government-bullying/.

234   "ongoing efforts to negotiate FTAs with major global economies": Benjamin Herscovitch, "Australia's Answer to China's Coercive Challenge," Royal United Services Institute, August 18, 2021, https://rusi.org/explore-our-research/publications/commentary/australias-answer-chinas-coercive-challenge/.

234   launched its "New Southbound Policy": Randy Mulyanto, "Taiwan Makes New Push to Drum Up Southeast Asia Investment," Nikkei Asia, January 18, 2022, https://asia.nikkei.com/Politics/International-relations/Taiwan-makes-new-push-to-drum-up-Southeast-Asia-investment.

234   previous Taiwanese "Go South" policies: Hunter Marston and Richard C. Bush, "Taiwan's Engagement with Southeast Asia Is Making Progress Under the New Southbound Policy," Brookings Institution, July 30, 2018, https://www.brookings.edu/opinions/taiwans-engagement-with-southeast-asia-is-making-progress-under-the-new-southbound-policy/.

234   trade between Taiwan and ASEAN moved from a negative growth rate: Kannan R. Nair, "Taiwan: Renewing a Southbound Vision," Lowy Institute, The Interpreter, April 30, 2021, https://www.lowyinstitute.org/the-interpreter/taiwan-renewing-southbound-vision.

234   hit a historic high in 2021: Liam Gibson, "Taiwan's Exports to New Southbound Countries Hit New High in 2021," *Taiwan News*, February 7, 2022, https://www.taiwannews.com.tw/en/news/4434371.

234   a new incarnation of the Trans-Pacific Partnership: Stephen R. Nagy, "Standing Up to Economic Coercion Requires Middle Power Solidarity," *Japan Times*, May 14, 2020, https://www.japantimes.co.jp/opinion/2020/05/14/commentary/world-commentary/standing-economic-coercion-requires-middle-power-solidarity/.

235   that Japan also needs to find a path to include India: Nagy, "Standing Up to Economic Coercion Requires Middle Power Solidarity."

236   As early as 2012, Eurasia Group founder Ian Bremmer: Ian Bremmer, "Column: Goodbye Department of Commerce, Hello Department of Economic Statecraft," Reuters, August 23, 2012, https://www.reuters.com/article/us-column-goodbye-idUSBRE87L0UW20120822.

236   the 2022 omnibus America COMPETES Act: "America COMPETES Act Includes Casey Provision on Outbound Investment Review, Focus on Women's Economic Empowerment," Bob Casey—U.S. Senator for Pennsylvania, January 25, 2022, https://www.casey.senate.gov/news/releases/casey-applauds-inclusion-of-key-trade-priorities-in-house-competition-bill.

236   the earlier National Critical Capabilities Defense Act: "S.1854—National Critical Capabilities Defense Act of 2021," 117th Congress (2021–2022), Congress.gov, May 26, 2021, https://www.congress.gov/bill/117th-congress/senate-bill/1854/text.

236   The NCCC would consider transactions: "Rules Committee Print 117-31: Text of H.R. 4521, America COMPETES Act of 2022," House of Representatives Committee on Rules, January 25, 2022, https://rules.house.gov/sites/democrats.rules.house.gov/files/BILLS-117HR4521RH-RCP117-31.pdf.

237   first outbound investment screening process: "National Security Update—The House of Representatives Proposes an Outbound Investment Review Regime as Part of the America COMPETES Act," Covington and Burlington LLP, January 27, 2022, https://www.cov.com/en/news-and-insights/insights/2022/01/national-security-update-the-house-of-representatives-proposes-an-outbound-investment-review-regime-as-part-of-the-america-competes-act.

237   Designing a digital currency to compete: Hackenbroich, "Chinese Sanctions."

238   financial and diplomatic sanctions: Oya, "Coping with China's Economic Threat."

238   explicit counter–economic coercion measures: Chen, "How to Counter Chinese Economic Coercion."

238   no longer bound by Annex 2 of the World Trade Organization's Uruguay Round Agreement: Glaser, "Time for Collective Pushback Against China's Economic Coercion."

238   may have some deterrent effect: Zhang, "Chinese Non-Military Coercion—Tactics and Rationale."

238   proposal concerning Australian iron ore: Charlie Moore, "Australia Should Punish China for Banning Barley and Wine by Putting a Levy on Iron Ore Exports to the Communist Superpower, Says Senator," *Daily Mail*, December 14, 2020, https://www.dailymail.co.uk/news/article-9049909/Australia-levy-iron-ore-exports-China.html.

INDEX

Key to abbreviation: CCP = Chinese Communist Party

ABOUT THE AUTHOR

BETHANY ALLEN is the China reporter at Axios. She previously worked as the lead reporter for the International Consortium of Investigative Journalists' China Cables project, as a national security correspondent for the Daily Beast, and as a reporter and editor at *Foreign Policy* magazine. In 2020 she received the Robert D. G. Lewis Watchdog Award and was a finalist for the Batten Medal for Courage in Journalism. A fluent Mandarin speaker, she previously lived in China for four years. She now lives in Taipei.